The Memoirs

Emily Loch

DISCRETION IN WAITING

Published by

Librario Publishing Ltd

ISBN: 1-904440-86-X

Copies can be ordered via the Internet
www.librario.com

or from:

Brough House, Milton Brodie, Kinloss
Moray IV36 2UA
Tel/Fax No 01343 850 178

The Memoirs Of Emily Loch

DISCRETION IN WAITING

TSARINA ALEXANDRA AND THE CHRISTIAN FAMILY

Judith U. Poore

Librario

Tsarina Alexandra, signed "Alix, 1898.

ACKNOWLEDGMENTS

I would like to thank the following for their help. First and foremost Duncan Poore, my husband, who inherited Emily Loch's diaries and albums. He encouraged me in my research and helped enormously in getting the final drafts completed. He also could spell, is skilful with the camera and computer and is responsible for getting 'Emily' into her final form. Thank you Duncan; without you she would still be a jumble of papers and photographs.

The following are listed alphabetically and have helped and encouraged me in many different ways:
Katie Adam, Hélène Alexander, Margaret Allen, Lynn Arnot, Maureen Barrie, Ignatius Bacon, Jean Balfour, John Balfour, Mary Balfour, Francis Bickmore, Jo Boater, Charles Burnett (Ross Herald), Jean Campbell, Monica Clough, Dorothy Davis, Sheila de Bellaigue, Graham Dennis, Olive Duncan, Kathlyn Fforde, George Grey, Viachesla Fedorov, Anne Grimwade, Marguerite Hancock, Simon Havilland, Hubertus Jahn, Amanda Koçur, Mark Lawson, Michael Levey, Davina Loch, John Loch, Meg Luckins, Julie Macpherson, Nicky Macpherson, Steven Main, Jennifer Norman, Maria Osowiecki, Michaela Reid, Jean Rowntree, Alastair Sarre, Sally Spiers, Prudence Sutcliffe, Helen Trilling, Kathleen Wheelan, Marion Wynn, Charlotte Zeepvat (via M.W.).

If I have forgotten any who feel they have helped me, please forgive me. I have talked about 'Emily' to so many people that she has become part of my life and I may well have forgotten them.

VICTORIA = ALBERT
1819-1901 1819-1861

Victoria = Friedrich
1840-1901 1831-1888

Victoria = Adolphus
1866-1929 d.1916

Charlotte
1860-1919

Henry = Irène
1862-1929 1866-1935

Sophie = Constantine
1870-1954 1868-1903

William = Augusta
1859-1941

Margaret = Frederick Carl
1872-1954 1868-1940

Wilhelm
b.1884

Edward = Alexandra
1841-1910 1844-1925

Albert Victor
1864-1892
(Eddy)

George V = May of Teck
1865-1936 1867-1953
Queen Mary

George VI = Elizabeth Bowes Lyon
1895-1953 1900-2002

Elizabeth II = Phillip
b. 1926 b.1921
Duke of Edinburgh

Alice = Louis IV
1843-1878 1837-1892

Victoria = Louis of Battenberg
1863-1950 1854-1921

Alice = Andrew of Greece
b.1885 1819-1861

Louise = Gustav of Sweden
b.1889

George
Marquess of Milford Haven

Louis
Earl Mountbatten
1900-1979

Elizabeth = Serge
1863-1950 1854-1905

Iréne = Henry
1866-1935 1862-1909

Ernest Louis = (1) Victoria
1868-1937 (2) Eleonore

Elizabeth
1895-1903

George Donatus
1906-1937

Louis = Margaret Geddes
b.1908

Alix = Nicholas II
1872-1918 1869-1918

Olga
1895-1918

Tatiana
1897-1918

Marie
1899-1918

Anastasia
1901-1918

Alexei
1904-1918

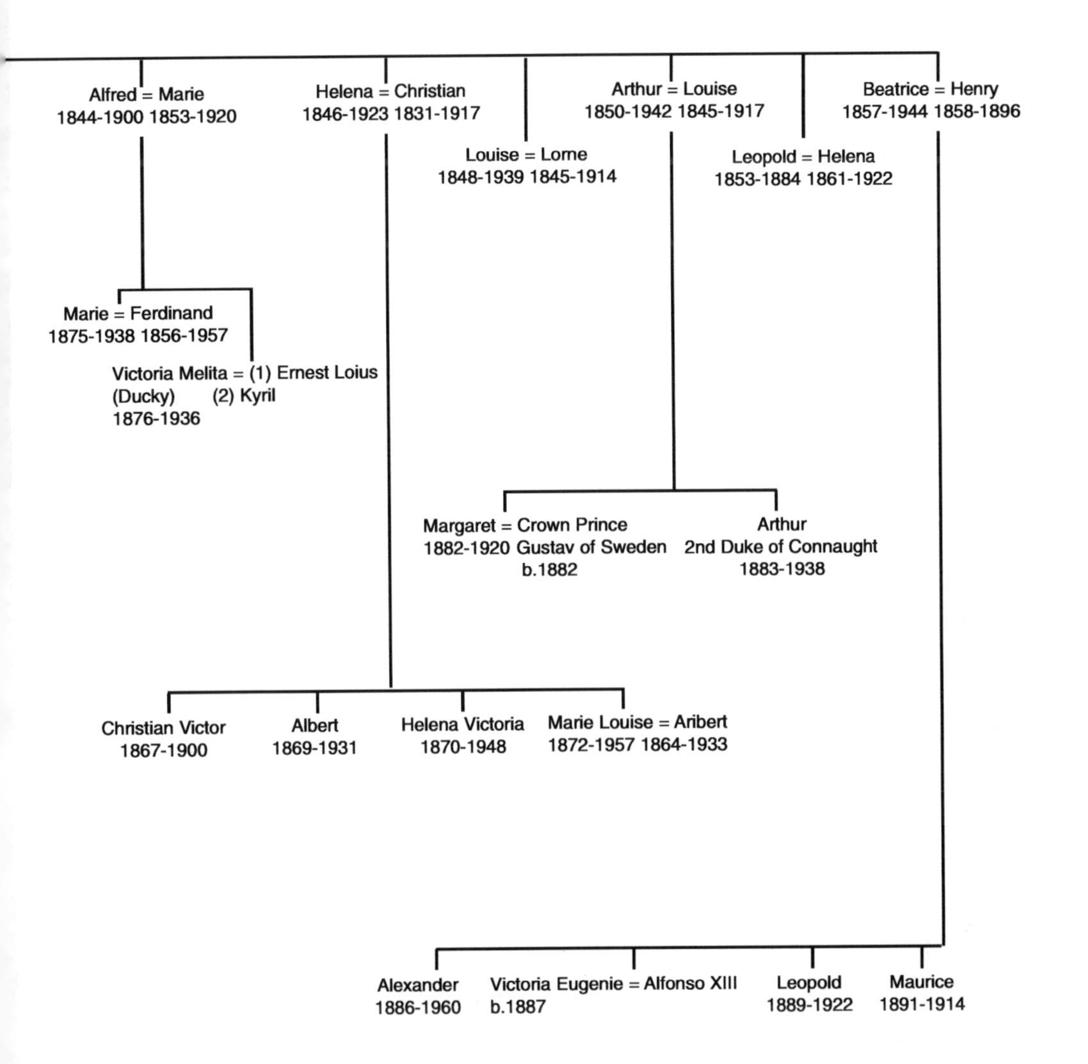

Partial Family Tree of Queen Victoria's descendants

DEDICATION

In memory of Margaret Poore who saved
Emily's memorabilia from dispersal and destruction and
Justin Arundale who encouraged me to revitalise her.

CREDITS

The images of the fan given to Princess Alexandra by Queen Victoria in 1891 (Plate 2) and the quotations from the Royal Archives and Queen Victoria's Journal are used by the permission of Her Majesty Queen Elizabeth II.

The following were kindly sent me by Marion Wynn who has visited most of the places associated with the Romanovs. Portrait of Princess Alice, (Plate 3), and Nicholas and Alexandra's Palace, Livadia, on the wooded slopes above the Black Sea (Plate 7). John Loch lent me Dorothy Seymour's illustrated diary from which the two pictures (Plate 16) showing the Revolution in progress were photographed by Duncan Poore.

All other illustrations and photographs, including those of the painted china are taken from Emily Loch's diaries and memorabilia and reproduced by Duncan Poore.

CONTENTS

Introduction: The Quest

There they were: fifty dark, dingy books in a small bookcase in a little used bedroom; each only distinguishable from its neighbour by the dates of successive years in faded gold leaf. These were Great-great-aunt Emily's diaries. I knew almost nothing about her – one of Great Grandmother's sisters: said to have been a lady-in-waiting to one of Queen Victoria's daughters and reputed to have met the Tsar. Alice her eldest sister always claimed, in later years, to have kept a pickle shop in Windsor. Catherine Grace, the youngest sister, had at the age of twenty-five been allowed to train as a nurse and had had a distinguished career at St Bartholomew's and in the Indian Army Nursing Service. Surely from fifty diaries I could learn something of this enigmatic figure, Emily Loch.

I started by reading the diary of one whole year trying to decipher her handwriting. This was deceptively neat and flowing; but when n's, m's, u's, i's, e's, and r's all tended to be the same, it was fine if I could guess what she was writing about but tricky when I was trying to be sure of a name or when her meaning wasn't instantly clear. But at least she didn't write in code and only occasionally in a foreign language.

At first it was like blundering in a very thick fog. Who was she writing about? Where were they? How were they related? Who were friends and who were relations? What were their real names? But it was as intriguing as a very slow-moving detective story that couldn't be laid down – a vivid glimpse into European court life. It gradually dawned upon me that Emily had witnessed the tumultuous events of the late nineteenth and early twentieth centuries from the privileged viewpoint of one who lived in close contact with Queen Victoria's extended European family – and had recorded her experiences in writing and in pictures.

Tucked into the back of a much cherished book, Le Tragique Destin de Nicholas II, were twenty or so highly coloured and often sentimental postcards and Christmas cards. These were signed Alix, Olga, Tatiana, Maria and Anastasia. The words on the cards were far more than perfunctory greetings; from the angular flourishes real love and affection speak out. How did all this begin? How could such touching messages come to the stiff-lipped and apparently unemotional Miss Loch from the wife and children of the last Tsar of all the Russias? I decided to look more closely.

The earliest of these greetings is dated 1898 to 1899. On stiff card, it is an original watercolour of a rather solid lady in a long gaily coloured dress wearing a matching flat-topped head-dress with a draped scarf and backed by a faint silhouetted Russian roofscape. On the back of the card the message reads: 'For dear Emily, this little lady is to bring many good wishes from Russia where you will be very much missed this Xmas. May the New Year bring you blessings and happiness is also the wish of your affectionate Alix, 1898 – 1899'. (Plate 1A). So, Emily would be missed. The previous Christmas, she had been with the Russian royal family in Tsarskoe Selo.

Emily also left her photograph albums, a portfolio of flower paintings and a slim invaluable notebook – Epitome of the Diary from 1880. Even a few quick glances through the albums give an idea of the amazing number of nineteenth century royalty that Emily had met and of her intimate contact with Princess Christian and her immediate family.

In the most splendid album, red leather with gilt lettering, there are two photographs, both signed 'Nicholas' and dated Tsarskoe Selo, 1897; one of these is a delightful shot of Nicholas with his wife Alexandra (Alix) and their two babies Olga and Tatiana (Plate 1). So Emily had met the Tsar and it must have been through her friendship with Alix that this had come about. But how, where and when had Emily become so intimate with this grand-daughter of Queen Victoria? This became my quest. And whom did she meet on the way?

Inevitably, there were very many. To help you to keep track of them, there are three appendices. Appendix A (Page 370) introduces you to those members of the Royal families whom you will meet, their dates, their marriages and their children. Appendix B (Page 373) lists in alphabetical order all the people mentioned (whether in England, Scotland, Germany or Russia), both by the name with which they first appear and again by their surname. I hope you will find this to be a help, so that the people whom Emily met and knew will also become known to you. Appendix C (Page vi) is a partial family tree of Queen Victoria's descendants.

CHAPTER ONE

The Osborne Wedding

"I will desire my dressmaker, Mrs Metcalfe, 111 New Bond Street, to make 'my body' at once, so that anyone who cares to see it can do so by calling there." The Lord Chamberlain had published this ruling from the Duchess of Buccleuch, Mistress of the Robes to Queen Victoria, to allay the anxiety of ladies invited to the wedding of Princess Beatrice and Prince Henry of Battenberg in Whippingham Parish Church on the Isle of Wight on July 23rd 1885.

A lot lay behind the statement.

Queen Victoria had been on the throne since 1837, forty-eight years, and Prince Albert, her much loved husband and consort, had been dead for over twenty-three. The slim, active and sparkling girl that Lord Melbourne had gently trained in the art of constitutional monarchy had become the stout, reclusive widow, the mother of nine children. Her country, benefiting from its lead in the industrial revolution, had become the richest in the world and her empire had spread so that a map of the globe showed great patches of red on every continent. Her navy reigned supreme; her army, sadly jolted by the war in the Crimea and the mutiny in India, had been modernised. India now came under the Crown and the Queen had become an Empress. Her opinions and concerns affected many of the courts and governments of Europe and the words of her statesmen were heeded in the counsels of the Powers. France, the traditional enemy of Britain for centuries, having endured a cataclysmic revolution, then Napoleon, then monarchies and further revolutions, had been vanquished by the Germans in the short but bitter war of 1870. The Victorian era appeared to be at its zenith but, in the closing decades of the century, its status was being challenged by Germany under the strong and wily leadership of Bismarck and his Emperor William I.

Queen Victoria's children, with their strong German ancestry and connections, were inevitably bound up in, and affected by, these struggles for power and supremacy. Her eldest daughter, Princess Vicky, clever and very much heir to Prince Albert's liberal ideas, had been married in 1858 to Fritz, Prince of

Prussia, and her life was spent in the orbit of the Prussian royal family and the realm of Bismarck. The Queen's heir, Prince Albert Edward, had been a rather wayward child who exasperated his parents as he compared so unfavourably with his clever older sister. He had married Alexandra of Denmark and led his own sociable life among fashionable society in England. Alice, Victoria and Albert's third child, within a year of her father's death, had married Prince Louis of Hesse Darmstadt, a small Duchy close to France in the west of Germany. This became engulfed in the agonies of the Franco–Prussian war in 1870, much to the distress of Princess Alice and her family. Of the six younger children, three married into the princely houses of Germany, and another inherited German titles. Princess Helena, the Queen's fifth child, married Prince Christian of Schleswig-Holstein whose homeland had been acquired from Denmark by Prussia in a war of 1864. This annexation led to fierce divisions between Victoria's children and rendered Prince Christian homeless but he continued to spend much of his time in Germany. Only Princess Louise married a British aristocrat, the Marquess of Lorne.

Now in 1885, Princess Beatrice, Queen Victoria's youngest daughter who had been only four years old when her father died, was about to be married. And to yet another of those German princes. Opinion in the country was very critical. For many years the Queen, herself, had refused even to discuss Beatrice's possible marriage for fear of 'losing' this daughter who had become such an essential companion to her disconsolate and lonely mother. In 1884, however, at the marriage of her cousin Victoria, eldest daughter of Alice of Hesse, to Prince Louis of Battenberg, Beatrice had fallen in love with Henry, one of the bridegroom's handsome brothers. When the Queen realised what was happening she was shocked into oppressive silence and for many weeks never spoke to Princess Beatrice, hardly mentioned her in her journal and only communicated by notes. It is possible that this was done so that the Queen could eventually relent and give her blessing – but with conditions. For, once the Queen saw that it was inevitable, she changed her position and staunchly defended her daughter's decision against all the criticism which was voiced against the match. For a brief moment after the announcement of the engagement all was happiness, but the storm clouds soon began to gather. Objections to the match were loudly voiced in Britain. What was wrong with the young aristocrats of the country? Were none of them suitable to follow in the steps of the Marquess of Lorne? Why should the country continually support young princes from the continent? Russia didn't wish one of the

Engagement photograph of Princess Beatrice and Prince Henry Battenberg.

Queen's daughters to marry the brother of Prince Sandro who was defying the Russians in Bulgaria. Paris questioned Prince Henry's previous life and behaviour, and from Berlin came strong objections from the Queen's old friend, Queen Augusta, wife of Wilhelm I, and her own son-in-law the Crown Prince. It was snobbery on the part of the Prussians – breeding was all important. But the Queen, now that her mind was made up, became her daughter's champion. She won the battles, matters were smoothed out and the marriage went ahead.

What were the conditions that the Queen had exacted? Prince Henry would give up his position in the Prussian Army and in the long term Princess Beatrice and her husband would live in England well within the Royal orbit. In fact the Queen's home would be their home, in fact the Queen would continue to have her daughter's support and the young couple would always be with her. In the short term, Princess Beatrice would be married from Osborne on the Isle of Wight. This Italianate mansion overlooking the Solent had been designed by Victoria and Albert in the idyllic early days of their marriage to accommodate their growing family. In her widowhood it had become the secluded refuge which the Queen loved. The ceremony would take place in the parish church of Whippingham where the Princess regularly

Osborne House on the Isle of Wight c.1885. Designed by Prince Albert and built by Thomas Cubitt to make a family home for the Royal Family.

worshipped. In the summer of 1885 this was all ideal for limiting the number of guests who could be invited to the wedding. It may have been convenient for her Majesty but the decision caused endless headaches for the Household and guests: the correct dress was uncertain and accommodation was a massive problem.

Emily Loch, staying at Buckingham Palace, wrote in her diary for July 21st:

> Very dark foggy and oppressive. Rained a little mid-day. The little Princesses came up from Windsor and we all left by 11.30 train for Osborne. Got there by 3.30. Sir J. McNeil met us. I came up with him and he brought me to Norris castle. Some difficulty in getting in. Found Lady Bidds, Freda and Miss Cochrane. Had lunch and then Freda and I sat in the hay field by the sea ...... The Duke and Dss of Bedford came in from their yacht and came up to the house. We dined at Osborne. I went down with Sir H Ponsonby ...... We were sent for into the royal party after and I was sent for all alone and had to go in by myself! Came back soon after 11 o'C.

This all needs some explanation. Emily had been staying the night at Buckingham Palace as she was to accompany Princess Christian to the wedding. It was to be Emily's first important British royal event – and the occasion when she met Alix for the first time. On the morning of the 21st the 'little princesses', Victoria Helena and Marie Louise, now 15 and 13 years old, came up from their home Cumberland Lodge near Windsor with their governess. They joined their mother ln her journey to Portsmouth, the Isle of Wight and Osborne, for they were to be bridesmaids in their aunt's wedding. Every suitable building on the estate and in the neighbourhood was taken over and many of the guests were accommodated on yachts. Emily, however, so that she could be within walking distance of her Princess, was lodged at Norris Castle near Osborne House and very close to the sea with wide views across the Solent. In her childhood Queen Victoria had often stayed in this mock medieval castle which had been built in 1795 by James Wyatt. 'Lady Bidds' was the widow of Sir Henry Biddulph, who had been Keeper of the Privy Purse until his death in 1878. Lady Biddulph continued to live in Henry III tower in Windsor Castle and Emily frequently visited her and her daughter Freda. Sir Henry Ponsonby was the Queen's private secretary.

The stage was beginning to be set and the cast, principals and supporting characters, were being assembled. Next morning, Emily and her fellow members of the households were again joined by the Duke and Duchess of Bedford at Norris Castle. It was a glorious summer morning, the scent of newly mown hay hung in the still air; the hedges were alive with bees feasting on the bramble flowers and honeysuckle. Occasional late dog roses still flowered. With little to do the guests sat out in the hayfield and 'Miss Cochrane played the banjo'. Later, they walked over to Osborne and went to see the presents. That evening, after dining at Osborne, the guests went out on the terrace. Under deepening blue skies among the flickering light from the oil lamps they enjoyed the warm evening air before returning to Norris, which 'was packed with Lords'.

The morning of July 23rd dawned clear and bright. Excitement was in the air and nowhere more so than in the bedroom where the little Princess Alix of Hesse was sleeping with her sister Irène. They had travelled over from their home in Darmstadt, Germany a few days before. Princess Alix or Alicky as her grandmother always called her, had been allowed off early from her lessons and the strict regime of life at home. She was once more back with her beloved grandmother who had been so kind in the seven long years since Princess Alice and little May had died. The children, Irène, Alix and their brother Ernie, had often stayed at Windsor and so they knew their cousins, Victoria Helena, whom they always called Thora and her younger sister Marie Louis, or Louie, the daughters of their aunt Princess Christian, really well. Now they were all going to be bridesmaids at Auntie Beatrice's wedding and Auntie Beatrice was Alix's godmother.

Imagine Alix running to the window and taking a deep breath of warm slightly salty air. The gardens outside were spacious and green and the trees were in their late summer splendour. On the lawns tents were being erected for the feast after the wedding. Would there be strawberries? Would there be time to play and talk with her cousins, Thora and Louie, and find out how their little dachshunds and the ponies were? Probably not. There was so much to do to be correctly dressed as a bridesmaid. There was one's hair to be brushed and brushed so that it gleamed like gold, which everyone said was so pretty. Then there were all the underclothes, bodices, pantaloons and stockings to be put on before one was even allowed to touch the lovely white satin dress. One had to get the gauze and lace properly draped otherwise the pattern wouldn't show. There was the new pearl necklace to wear and the thin satin shoes; lucky it was so beautifully dry: and last of all, the long white gloves to pull on and each finger to be got in the right place. Auntie had given each bridesmaid a brooch with her initial 'B' and Henry's initial 'H' intertwined. These matched the red of the little bouquets of carnations which had such a lovely scent

At last all the bridesmaids, all ten of them, all nieces of the bride, were ready to be packed off in the carriages, with their older relations, for the ten minute drive to Whippingham church. The route though the country lanes was bright with bunting and flowers and the church was transformed with walls of greenery and bunches and garlands of lilies and roses. The bridesmaids assembled in the vestry of the church to await the arrival of the bride and her mother who would be in the last of the eighteen carriages which bought the Royalty and their attendants from Osborne House. The other guests who had travelled from London in their 'morning dress' had been conveyed to the church and shown their places in good time.

Emily Loch was in the third carriage and, in the '*Ceremonial to be Observed*', is given as lady-in-waiting to Princess Christian. Prince Christian's equerry-in-waiting, Hon A Yorke, shared the carriage. He became a great friend of Emily's and enjoyed life to the full. In later photographs his rather loud check suit and cap gave him the appearance of a cheerful bookie. Their seats were far up in the choir stalls close to the altar and just behind their Prince and Princess who were conveyed in the tenth carriage immediately behind that with Princess Irène and Princess Alix, accompanied by their father and the Grand Duke of Hesse, their great-uncle. During the service the Queen and the swathe of bridesmaids sat or stood just in front of them behind the bridal couple.

The bridegroom, Prince Henry of Battenberg, and his two brothers were due to arrive at the church at '12.55 o'clock', precisely. He was conducted to the right of the altar to a march composed by the organist of St George's chapel Windsor, Mr Parratt. And there he awaited the arrival of his bride. Emily said: 'The Bridegroom had a long wait'. The Queen was due to arrive with Princess Beatrice at 1 o'clock. The Queen graced the occasion by adding a 'white tulle veil surmounted by a diamond tiara' to her usual sombre black dress.[1]

The procession slowly moved from the decorated gateway of the churchyard, passed ranks of guests on the specially built seats, and into the church filled with the scent of lilies and the strains of Wagner's bridal march. The Queen, Princess Beatrice and the Princes of Wales were preceded by the Vice-Chamberlain, the Lord Chamberlain and the Lord Steward and followed by the ten bridesmaids. Far forward in the choir they halted and Prince Henry stepped out to stand by his bride. 'The Queen gave Pss Beatrice away. Both of them spoke most distinctly' was Emily's crisp comment. As the service ended the peals of bells rang out and the new Prince and Princess Henry of Battenberg stepped out into the sunshine and into their carriage back to Osborne House through the cheering crowds which lined the lanes. The procession of carriages followed, Princess Alix and her sister shared the Queen's carriage and before long all the guests were back in the grounds making their way to the wedding breakfast in the tents on the lawn. Perhaps Emily, as she made sure that Princess Christian and the two little princesses had their share of the spread, spoke with Princess Alix; the cousins were almost sure to be in a group. She would have joined in their excitement and descriptions of what went on, the loveliness of the 'Auntie' and the fun of seeing all the Princes of Battenberg together.

The bride and groom left the party about 5 o'clock and the guests began to depart – the day-visitors to catch their boat the *Alberta* at Cowes to begin their journey to London, the others back to change at their lodgings. Emily and her friends 'went back to Norris, had tea, sat out, changed again and went back to dinner at Osborne.' Afterwards they were all out on the terrace to watch the 'fireworks and the ships illuminated. Most beautiful.' So ended this glorious day and the first occasion on which Emily Loch met Princess Alix, the future Tsarina of Russia.

In August the year before it would hardly have been possible to expect such a happy outcome. On the 25th of that month, Emily and Princess Christian had travelled to Berlin ostensibly to celebrate the christening of Prince and Princess William's newly born son. There is a photograph in the album capturing the proud moment, with four generations of the Prussian Royal Family: it was becoming a dynasty to rival Queen Victoria's. In the photo the Emperor of Germany, Wilhelm I, holds the white-robed baby Prince Willy, on his knee. He is watched by the Emperor's son, the Crown Prince Friedrich, and the proud and astonishingly young-looking father of the baby, Prince William, Queen Victoria's eldest grandchild, who was to become Kaiser Wilhelm.

The Prussian dynasty adds another generation with baby Prince Willie, 1894.

It is probable that, at the time, Emily had little idea of the importance of the Princess's journey. It was her first royal visit abroad and she was overwhelmed by the grandeur: the huge palace of Charlottenburg; being met by 'Herr von Pluchrow 7 feet high', being taken in at a different entrance from her good friend Colonel Gordon, who also accompanied Princess Christian – all were somewhat unnerving. But she also met for the first time, and was befriended by, Emma von Cohausen, lady-in-waiting to Princess Charlotte, the eldest daughter of the Crown Prince and the Princess. They rapidly became close friends. On that first night Emily notes:'My rooms were next door to her's'. In the years to come Emma was a person Emily made a point of seeing whenever her travels brought her to Germany.

In the diary, the daily round of helping Princess Christian with her letters, taking walks with Emma, visiting the sights and going to the theatre is interspersed with more notable events. Emily was spoken to by the elderly Emperor in French, and asked by him if she could dance a Scottish reel. She attended the christening with all the splendour and strict protocol of the German court and was driven out to watch the manoeuvres of the Imperial Army. After the christening she wrote:

> All the ladies had been told their places and went and stood before them waiting until the heaps of Princes should come in. I sat next to Prince Ernst of Meinigen who was charming and Prince Ed. of Anhalt who was a nice youth.

She doesn't actually mention Prince Henry of Battenberg, merely noting that on September 5th the Princess went to see the Crown Prince; that Colonel Gordon was very busy on errands for the Princess and that she, Emily, had innumerable letters to write. But, years later when summarising her diary, she wrote in her 'Epitome of the diary':

> Aug.25, 1894, With Pss Ch: to Charlottenburg till Sept. 10 to see Pc. H. of Battenberg with view to his engagement to Pss Beatrice .

When this was finally announced at Osborne later that year Emily was there with Princess Christian. They were staying for a few days between Christmas and New Year and Emily noted that she had many conversations with Princess Beatrice. On the 29th she wrote: 'Princes Beatrice's engagement was formally announced by Lady Ely but we were not meant to know.' One wonders what they spoke about at dinner that evening, when Emily was one of those who dined at the Queen's table, and afterwards when they 'stood about for ages after dinner. The Queen spoke a few words to me and I talked for sometime to Pss Beatrice and Prince Henry'. Next day, however, all was out in the open. Emily was sent for by the Queen and she was most beloved and kind and gave me a big photo of herself and we had a long talk. I dined again at the table and there was drinking of the health of Pss Beatrice and Prince Henry and the pipes were played ... I spoke a little to Pss Beatrice about her marriage.

So, just over six months later, the wedding took place. Emily, among many others, had taken note of the Lord Chamberlain's ruling, had worn her 'demi-toilette body cut down on the back with sleeves to the elbow' and had her hair dressed and bejewelled. Her outfit was suitably in tune with Princess Christian's richly coloured dress. Like many others, Emily was rewarded with a bronze medal commemorating the day: on one side the finely sculpted heads of Beatrice and Henry and on the other the complex coats of arms of the Prince and Princess (Plate 1).

Princess Beatrice and Prince Henry's wedding July 23rd 1885.

In her album Emily has left us two photographs of the bridal party, a newspaper account of the day and an order of the ceremonial to be observed. From the last it is possible to find out the roles of those who were in her carriage in the procession. Major Werner was equerry-in-waiting on His Royal Highness the Grand Duke of Hesse, the uncle of Princess Alix. For this occasion Capt. Bigge, an equerry-in-waiting on the Queen, was in attendance on the Grand Duke. 'Mr Yorke', the Hon. A. Yorke, was acting equerry-in-waiting on Prince Christian and Emily is given as lady-in-waiting on Princess Christian. The Baron Riedesel was part of the Grand Duke's Household and Emily met him on several later occasions when she visited Darmstadt.

The photograph of the bridal party is a glimpse of part of the great tribe of Queen Victoria's descendants. There is Princess Beatrice, slightly plump and well corseted with to her left her handsome husband Liko, Prince Henry of Battenberg, in – at the Queen's command – the dramatic, white uniform of the Gardes du Corps, decorated with various orders, including the newly presented 'Garter'. He has a robust moustache and fine thigh boots. The bride's ornate satin dress is draped with Honiton lace, once part of her mother's wedding dress, and decorated with a swathe of white heather, myrtle and orange blossom. A wealth of diamonds, sapphires and pearls adorn her throat and head. The ten bridesmaids, all nieces of the bride, are dressed in white satin draped with cream-coloured patterned gauze and lace. Each has a brooch with the names Beatrice and Henry intertwined. The four older bridesmaids stand at the back between Prince Henry's brothers, Prince Alexander (Sandro) and Prince Franz Joseph. Princess Irène of Hesse was the oldest at nineteen – Emily was to meet her in Darmstadt that autumn; the other three are the Princesses Louise, Victoria and Maud, all daughters of the Prince of Wales. Princess Thora, Princess Christian's elder daughter now fifteen, already looking slightly forlorn with her long face, stands next to and slightly behind the bride and, between her and her younger sister Marie Louise, is Princess Alix – both at this time aged thirteen. The three youngest princesses – Marie, Victoria and Alexandra – from the family of Alfred, Duke of Edinburgh and Saxe-Coburg-Gotha complete the group.

The newspaper cutting even goes into the details of the dresses of the ladies-in-waiting. Emily's sounds rather garish being 'red and gold satin over cream and green brocade' but with her trim figure and neatly coiled hair perhaps she carried it off successfully. Miss Cochrane's, lady-in-waiting to the bride, sounds more tasteful in sky-blue satin with the same coloured beads looped over the body and the front of the skirt. What to dress in for this wedding had caused much anguish to those invited. The ruling issued by the Lord Chamberlain had settled their queries: those staying on the island came in outfits similar to that chosen by Miss Cochrane and Emily; those who travelled down for the day, bonnets and smart morning dress.

Princess Christian and Emily remained on the island after the wedding. Life became relaxed and leisurely and much time was spent sitting by the sea and chatting. On the 25th, however, there was something more exciting.

> ... Heard I was to go in the yacht with the royalties, Miss Bauer, the germans and Sir J McNeil. Started at 3 o'C. Were to have met the Edinboro' and Connaught children at the Osborne pier but there was a mistake and they had gone to Cowes. Signalled and waited and then went to pick them up at Cowes. Had a most delightful time. Played many games all afternoon. Connaughts, Pss Christian and Pss Leinigen, all the Hesse and Battenbergs and all of us joined. Had tea. We got in soon after 8 o'C. Landed at Cowes and hurried up. Dressed in 10 minutes. Household evening.

So there is no doubt that Emily would have seized the chance to talk with all the children as they played games on the yacht, for she was always a favourite with the Queen's grandchildren. It was in this happy atmosphere of festivity and relaxation, after her Godmother's wedding, that Emily first met the golden haired, pretty Princess Alix who had been allowed to leave Germany early and, for once, miss some of her lessons.

Princess Alix, as Emily first met her, at Princess Beatrice's wedding.

CHAPTER TWO

The Christian Family and Cumberland Lodge

'This Diary was given me by H. R. H. Princess Christian today'. This is the first entry in the diary for 1880: the first of just on fifty Letts 'Offices Diaries and Almanacs' which Emily Loch kept meticulously for forty-nine years recording the minutiae of her everyday life and its interweaving with the royal family, especially that of Princess Christian and her children. Emily then was thirty-two.

Just over two years later Emily wrote on January 14th, a Sunday: 'Lovely bright day. Sat with the Liddells in church. Came home afterwards. Pss sent for me to tell me the Queen had appointed me lady in waiting by her request'. The bald statement gives an idea of Emily's terse style of writing, even this exciting announcement was not greeted, in the diary at least, with any evident pleasure or emotion. Yet Emily had been a friend of the Princess for many years and they had many interests in common. It must have been pleasing that the Princess had chosen her. Now Emily would be able to help and serve her great friend. The official announcement also showed that the Queen herself knew Emily and Emily's family and was satisfied that she was suitable to take up this position. Protocol and the Queen's management of – perhaps interference in – her children's lives, ordained that the appointment was approved and made by

January 1 THURSDAY [1-365] 1st Month 1880

Circumcision. Dog Licenses to be taken out

This Diary has been given me by H. R. H. Princess Christian today –

First entry in Emily's diary.

Princess Helena in 1878. She had been married to Prince Christian for twelve years and had had five children, of whom four survived.

the Queen. Despite Princess Christian being thirty-seven years old and a married woman of seventeen years' standing, her life was ruled by her mother's decisions; she was told off when she stayed at Buckingham Palace without having asked the Queen's permission. The Queen was a very remarkable woman in very many ways; but letting loose the reins of power and allowing her children to run their own lives was not one of her qualities. Outwardly it appeared that Princess Christian accepted the situation rather more stoically than did her brothers and sisters. Possibly she was better at disguising her feelings for the sake of peace but perhaps this repression of her feelings was one of the underlying causes of her ill health so faithfully recorded in Emily's diaries.

Whatever she wrote, it is likely that Emily was delighted with the appointment: not only would it mean that she could be of service to her personal friend, the Princess, but also there is no doubt that Emily rather revelled in the society of royalty. She was punctilious throughout all the years, even in the privacy of her diary, always to give them a title: even Princess Thora and Princess Louie whom she had known from early childhood. More often than not, in the early days, Emily uses the abbreviation 'Pss' for Princess, where the first 's' is the old fashioned, long 's'.

Princess Christian was born in 1846 and christened Helena Augusta Victoria and nicknamed 'Lenchen'. She was only sixteen when her father died in 1861 and she, like her brothers and sisters, became trapped in the sombre routine surrounding the Queen. Until her marriage, she was very much at her mother's beck and call acting for years as an unpaid secretary. The Queen's reluctance, indeed refusal, to take part in public life was, by 1865–1866, beginning to cause much ill feeling in the country and distress to her ministers and family. The necessity to ask Parliament for an allowance for her son, Prince Alfred, who was coming of age, and an annuity for Princess Helena who was about to be married, forced her to open Parliament on February 2nd 1866. The Queen admitted afterwards that she found it a terrible ordeal and only got through 'this exposure by keeping her face utterly expressionless'. Her behaviour was not favourably reported but it did begin her slow and limited re-integration into the life of the country.

Princess Helena's marriage to Prince Christian of Schleswig-Holstein was arranged in that year, 1866, but not before it had caused considerable dissension within the family between the Queen and her two older daughters, Vicky and Alice. The difficulties, however, were resolved. It was stipulated that the couple should live in England and continue to support the Queen. Princess Helena had become an essential part of her mother's life; although never as indispensable as Princess Beatrice, she was to remain within easy reach, where her skills as a secretary could readily be called upon. As things worked out Prince Christian was glad of a home.

The question of Schleswig-Holstein was particularly delicate for the Royal Family. Alexandra, Princess of Wales, who had married Prince Albert Edward Queen Victoria's eldest son in March 1863, was the daughter of the Danish King. In 1864 Prussia and Austria went to war with Denmark and annexed the two Duchies of Schleswig and Holstein. Subsequent diplomatic and military manoeuvrings resulted in Schleswig-Holstein becoming part of the North German Federation under Prussian control – a source of great irritation to Queen Victoria and her family and a triumph for Bismarck's expansionist aims. Prince Christian, a younger son of the ruling family of the Duchies and an unimportant pawn in this game, was almost penniless, unambitious and homeless.

Other members of the Royal family were not impressed by him. They said that he was only interested in smoking, eating and shooting birds. Princess Helena, however, found him acceptable despite his being fifteen years her

Prince Christian, even in later life, enjoyed hunting and other country pursuits.

senior and looking old for his age. Queen Victoria, too, was undeterred. 'His cough would be dealt with' and a good dentist would 'see to his teeth'. Prince Christian, who had been a fellow student of Friedrich or Fritz, Crown Prince of Prussia, the husband of Princess Vicky, Helena's eldest sister, was prepared to accept the Queen's conditions. These provided him with a bride – and a home, first at Frogmore close to Windsor Castle and subsequently at Cumberland Lodge in Windsor Great Park. On his marriage the Queen gave him the Garter and made him Ranger of the Great Park. He was able to keep a fine stable and indulge in hunting and other country pursuits which were what he really enjoyed. A photograph in one of Emily's albums show him, later in life, stout, handsome and bearded, superbly seated on a finely turned-out horse in front of Cumberland Lodge.

The house, which began life in the brief period when England was a Republic, had since been very much a royal house and one in which a sequence of remarkable people had lived at the invitation of the sovereign. These included Sarah, Duchess of Marlborough and the Duke of Cumberland, uncle of George III, and victor of the Battle of Culloden. Many added to the building to suit their aspirations and by the 1860s it had become very large with massive, ivy-covered walls, large plate glass windows and a castellated roof line.

In the first years of their marriage, the Queen ordained that Prince and Princess Christian should live at Frogmore – as had the Prince and Princess of Wales immediately after their marriage – which was within walking distance of the Castle. So, they were not living at Cumberland Lodge on the Sunday morning in November 1868 when Mrs Thurston, a retired housekeeper from Windsor Castle, who had a flat in the house, suddenly had to flee the building, as the roof was on fire. Despite great efforts by the Cumberland Lodge fire engine, the Windsor Fire Brigade and over 100 troopers of the Royal Horse Guards and a Company of Grenadier Guards, the difficulty of getting adequate supplies of water allowed the fire to run its course and much of the building was destroyed. Throngs of spectators came to view the blaze; Princess and Prince Christian and many others from the castle helped to get out some of the furniture and even Queen Victoria arrived, rather late, to survey the devastation.

Rebuilding was essential. Three conflicting views were taken by the different interested parties. The Queen wanted a 'commodious residence' suitable for a member of her family; the Surveyor General 'favoured a new block in gothic style, with the east end of the remaining house altered to harmonise with it; and the Treasury wanted whatever cost least. The Treasury won. The new building was half the size of its predecessor but, at the same time, the kitchens and water

Cumberland Lodge from the garden side as it was when the Christian family lived there.

supply were improved and central heating was installed in the bigger rooms and passages. It was altogether a more comfortable place for living and in 1872 Princess Christian and her family moved in.

By this time Princess Christian's health was giving cause for concern. She had been strong and healthy in her adolescence, preferring outdoor activities and was an accomplished horsewoman. Marriage, pregnancy and childbirth[2], however, had taken their toll, as they did with so many women. The Queen became seriously worried about her daughter's health, and it was thought that the position of Frogmore in a damp hollow was bad for her cough, so the move to Cumberland Lodge was made. The Lodge was not at any great altitude, less than 300 feet above sea level, but on gravelly soil and so considered a healthy location. It lay within the Park, about three and a half miles south of Windsor Castle, close to Park Chapel and rather over half a mile from Bishopsgate which led to the village of Englefield Green.

The Christian family moved to the house in the spring of 1872. The youngest child, at the time, was two-year-old Princess Helena Victoria. Her names were so similar to those of many of her cousins that she was always known as 'Thora', although Emily usually spelled it 'Tora'. There were also two older brothers, Prince Christian Victor and Prince Albert. Like so many of Queen Victoria's family they were given affectionate family names – Christle and Abby. The eldest, Prince Christle had the rather long nose and, as a young man, the long, sad face so common in this family – although Disraeli considered him to be 'the most beautiful child I ever saw'. The chief victim of the long lugubrious face was Princess Thora, and this is said to be the reason for the unkind family nickname of the 'snipe'. Her brother, Prince Christle, had a happy, gregarious nature, was universally liked and a great favourite with his grandmother. Emily was particularly fond of him. In later years she frequently helped him with his photography and they often had long talks together. The second son Prince Abby was destined for Germany and the German army. This, as can be imagined, produced great difficulties and unhappiness in later years. He eventually inherited the family estates from his uncle, and acquired the cumbersome name of Schleswig-Holstein-Augustenburg-Glücksburg.

Very soon after the family had moved to Cumberland Lodge, a fourth baby was born, another little girl. This was Princess Marie Louise, know in the family as Louie. She survived the rest of her family by many years and was still able to take part in the coronation of Queen Elizabeth II in 1953. Emily knew her from her early childhood.

In their new home the family settled down to an unobtrusive, pleasant family life: the Princess deeply concerned in helping the less privileged, the Prince in the life of a well-to-do country gentleman with few responsibilities. But both took an unusual interest in the upbringing of the children. They were

> brought up in the simplest possible manner by their parents. They passed most of the day with their father and mother in that close companionship which is the essence of home-life; and this together with their daily round of school-room life and country pursuits formed the first years of their lives, so that they appreciated whatever came their way with the freshest of minds. Their earliest education was commenced by their father. Every evening he would have the four children down in his own library, and they would sit one on each knee and one on each arm of his chair, and he would teach them reading and German, setting them tasks and having little weekly examinations in what they had learned.

His in-laws may have thought him dull but he was very kind both to his children and animals and could be charming but with limited interests. He may well have been inhibited in English-speaking society by his strong accent and imperfect grasp of the language. Emily, with her fluent German, found him pleasant and, as she got to know him better in later years, became a frequent confidante. He was a keen horseman and the girls as well as the boys were taught to ride at an early age. The whole family were devoted to dogs, and when at home they always had two or three dachshunds with them[3]. The daily life of the two princesses after these very early years was rather different from that of their brothers, who were older and went away to school. Their mother was very much at the beck and call of her mother, the Queen; nevertheless, she ensured that the young girls were brought up in a stable and loving family. In their very early days no doubt there were nurses and nursemaids; these were followed by governesses. By 1880 Fräulein Kirchner had become part of the household looking after the princesses; late in 1884, Baroness von Fabrice, always known as Gretchen, came as a governess. Others, Emily among them, also stepped in if their mother was called away and, from 1880 onwards, even before she was appointed a lady-in-waiting, there are many references to Emily being with the young princesses at Cumberland Lodge or entertaining them at her own home, the Cottage, Englefield Green. Sometimes Fräulein Kirchner came over to the Cottage with them and they all stayed to tea or went exploring the garden with Emily or enjoying the strawberries and peaches when they were ripe. On a June day in 1883, when all the others at Cumberland Lodge had gone off to the Ascot races, Emily stayed with the children and later took them to a corner of the race course where they were able to watch the horses thundering by.

Later that year the two children began to learn to ride tricycles. Emily wrote for October 19th

> Started ¼ to 4 to the Thrings. Pss and I in pony carriage – the two children on the trycicles [sic]. They went splendidly. Sir H Thring was waiting on his at the crossroads. We had tea at Alderhurst [Sir Henry's house] It was quite dark before we got back. The children and I rested in my room. Tea at 7.30. Many amusing stories. Sat in schoolroom after.

This was the first of many days when the princesses were out on their tricycles and in time Emily learned to ride a bicycle. But on other occasions Emily took them out in the pony trap visiting places in Englefield Green, buying sweets from the tall glass jars from one of the shops in Victoria Street. Sometimes they visited the donkey who pulled the little cart that Mrs Loch used on her visits to friends or went to see the more spirited horse Uppat, which belonged to Emily's sister, Catherine Grace, and which she once rode at a gallop through the streets of Windsor. Princess Louie followed in her mother's footsteps and became an excellent horsewoman. A step in this direction was taken in late 1884 when Louie had her first ride on a new cob which her father had selected for her.

Quite often their journeys with Emily were further afield: to Windsor to have their photographs taken or to visit St George's Chapel to hear the organ being played or to attend a carol service, or to London for special lessons and visits to the hairdresser. On June 4th 1884 Emily came up from Cumberland Lodge with

> 'Pss Christian and Pss Victoria [Victoria of Battenberg] … [on the] 10.30 [train]. We took the Pss to Soho hospital and Pss V and I went in a carriage to Liberty and Carlé where we were a long time over 'Tora's fringe'.

For much of the time Emily became part of their life, being there to sit with them when their mother was busy, singing to them on many occasions or telling them stories. She appears to have been equally popular with their cousins from Germany. When in 1880, they visited their grandmother Queen Victoria, they embroidered a cushion for Emily and begged her to come and visit them in Berlin.

In these early years, although the two Princes were away at school, Emily saw something of them, particularly during the summer holidays when cricket matches were played on the ground between Cumberland Lodge and Royal Lodge. On hot summer afternoons, the young men in whites would be watched by friends and members of the household seated on comfortable

A page from Emily's album introducing the Christian family in 1884.

basket chairs beneath the trees: the ladies in magnificent wide-brimmed hats and the men sporting striped blazers and caps. Prince Christle was a keen and proficient cricketer, He captained the Wellington First XI. When at home in 1883 and 1884, he got up a Cumberland Lodge team who took on various opponents including a Guards team whom they beat. The two brothers were at different schools and matches between Wellington College and Charterhouse would be played and watched with intra-family rivalry.

As the princesses grew older their interests naturally changed but Emily continued to see much of them and continued to be involved in their lives especially when Princess Christian was staying at spas in Germany.

While in England, Emily's life at the Cottage was frequently interrupted by calls for help from the Princess. As well as keeping an eye on the little princesses she was always at hand to help with correspondence or run errands in Windsor. Both the family from Cumberland Lodge and Emily regularly attended Sunday services at the Park Chapel only a short distance from Cumberland Lodge and within easy walking distance of the Cottage. Even when living at home Emily frequently walked back to the Lodge afterwards, chatting with the family before returning to her own house. Emily's church-going appears to have been fairly conventional; her visits to St George's Chapel at the Castle were mainly for the music. There is no great emphasis on her religion throughout the diaries and she seems to have accepted her sister's conversion to the Roman Catholic church without comment. Going to church was as much a social as a religious activity.

At regular intervals, when she was in-waiting, Emily moved into Cumberland Lodge and one of Emily's most regular occupations was to accompany the Princess on the train to London – noting precisely the train times – taking her to wherever she wanted to go and fetching her later. Reading the accounts of their days in London makes one quite breathless with their constant hansom cabs here or carriages there, visiting this person and that, until they finally reached Paddington and got back in the train for the short journey to Windsor. They always travelled first class and this sometimes caused problems if Alice Loch or one of their friends was also travelling – more economically. Visits to London were frequent, often to the dressmaker or doctor; sometimes for the Princess to attend business meetings in connection with one of her many charities, such as the Soho Hospital, the Nurses or, one of the most frequent, the School of Art Needlework which the Princess had founded.

Both the Princess and Emily attended dress makers, usually different ones. They both went regularly but, if they were about to go abroad or there were special court occasions, there would be a rush of visits. It could be frustrating when the garment didn't fit or when it wasn't ready in time. It was the 'body' that required the most careful fitting and caused the most trouble. Emily never became heavy or fat and always in her photographs appeared neat and elegant, so the tedious fittings were worthwhile. The Princess's dresses were more elaborate and required expert adjustment as her figure became more mature.

Emily quite frequently unpicked dresses when at home and had them re-made – for economy and to keep them in fashion. Material for new dresses was bought at shops in London such as Marshalls, Harveys and Libertys. Often, especially when she first took up her appointment, the Princess was most generous in giving Emily new dresses or 'stuff' for them to be made up. The Princess did this even before Emily became her lady-in-waiting, giving her a new dress, so she was suitably attired, for a very grand bazaar at Bagshot in 1881. No doubt, too, a special effort was made on April 14th 1883 when Emily attended her first 'official' dinner at Cumberland Lodge, given in honour of Princess Beatrice's birthday.

Wearing a hat or a bonnet was obligatory. They were elaborate affairs with much decoration such as whole birds or bird wings, ribbons and artificial flowers. Emily frequently noted that she trimmed a hat in the evening and, once or twice, she trimmed them for Princess Victoria when she was staying at Cumberland Lodge. Like many ladies of her time, she was good with the needle although, between them, Alice and Emily Loch had a lady's maid, Jeanne, who no doubt dealt with the more intimate pieces of clothing. Some years later, Emily became a regular knitter and made socks for various relations and there was a period when she became very enthusiastic about making fancy waistcoats. She never mentions doing embroidery or canvas work as such, but often ends the day by saying 'worked in the evening'. This may have covered embroidery; for it seems strange that she did not do any, especially when Princess Christian was an embroidery expert and did such beautiful work [4].

Princess Christian was noted for being very good at putting new members of the household at their ease and no doubt she helped Emily when they visited the courts of her relations. Emily was distinctly nervous, though, at her first luncheon with the royal household: 'very formidable at first sitting at table and I knew none of them'. On this occasion, away from the helping hand of the Princess, it was Lady Ely and Lady Roxburghe who were 'most kind'.

The Princess was always interested in finding about how ordinary people lived and worked and, where possible and necessary, improving things, such as setting up a crêche for working mothers. Emily certainly benefited from her thoughtfulness until she had found her feet. The Princess also took special efforts to help those in times of trouble especially through illness. When Mrs Liddell died, she visited the family regularly to comfort them and both she and the Prince attended the funeral. Later, in cheerful contrast, when the Liddell family had become comfortably established at South Lawn down near the

Thames at Eton, Emily records a number of happy summer days when the Princess was able to join in expeditions with the Liddells or other friends on the river.

The weather in June and July of 1884 seems to have been particularly summery. On the Whit Bank Holiday, Emily wrote:

> Lovely Day. Princess and I started at ¼ to 12 in victoria and drove to the Jenne's near Twyford. Lovely drive. Got there before 1.30. Mr and Mrs Huxley, Mr Greenwood and Mrs Malloch there. Had lunch. The others went in a boat up to Sonning. I drove Mrs Huxley in the pony carriage to meet them. We got the key of the church, ordered tea and then waited for them. Had tea in the garden, very amusing. I went back in the boat and Mrs Jenne and Mr Greenwood drove. We dined at 7.30 and started to drive home at 9.15. Lovely drive. Got back at ¼ to 11. Had some supper.

And on the 1st July, Emily and Fred Liddell

> joined Gerry and Jock at the raft and they rowed us up to Maidenhead where we had tea and strawberries and on to Cliveden where we found the Pss and Marcia. It was heavenly. We had dinner there which Marcia brought and started back at ¼ to 9. Fred, Jock and Gerry rowed down in 2 hours. Marcia sent Pss and me back in her Victoria. Got back at 11.30.

It is good to think of the Princess enjoying such a relaxing time with friends. On both these occasions it seems that the Princess was in good health and not worrying about herself. There is no doubt that she did suffer a considerable amount of discomfort and ill health, but it also seems that she gave in quite easily, which her mother deplored. Many times Emily writes that the Princess was 'overdone', 'very tired', 'voiceless' or 'suffering'. Usually on such days she retired to bed early or remained in bed till noon and, from Emily's concern, it appeared that she was really ill … but she would be up and about within 24 hours and no more was said.

From the earliest days of the diary, whenever they went to London, the Princess often went to the doctor. From the early 80s this was Dr MacLaggan.

His wife was also a friend of Princess Christian and she frequently lunched at the MacLaggans's house. He attended the Princess when she was unwell in London. One such visit occurred after a particularly tiring day, in which the Princess and Emily had shopped in the morning, including the Princess buying a ring for Emily, followed by choosing furniture for the Queen to give the Duke of Edinburgh: then going back to Buckingham Palace to get suitably dressed for Lady Holland's garden party and back again to the Palace to prepare for an evening party. By this time the Princess decided that she could take no more. Emily, one feels thankfully, settled down to read quietly and Dr MacLaggan came to the Princess. But she was up and about again next morning.

Such was Emily's life with the Princess and her family at Cumberland Lodge, a gentle rhythm of activity which was interrupted at irregular intervals by special royal occasions and visits abroad to Germany.

This was the family which the Emily, her mother and sisters, had known for many years, their near neighbours in the park, and the family which became as familiar and dear to Emily during the next fifty years as her own. She devoted her life to them and so met people in all walks of life, not only in England and Scotland but in Germany and, for a brief period, Russia. It was through her friendship with the Christian family that she came to know the children of Princess Alice of Hesse and eventually to visit the court of the Tsar of Russia.

CHAPTER THREE

The Lochs at the Cottage

Emily Loch and her family lived in the Cottage on the edge of the village of Englefield Green just outside the boundary of Windsor Great Park. A private gate gave the family quick and easy access to Cumberland Lodge. In the early days of the diaries there was a constant to-ing and fro-ing between the two houses.

In Queen Victoria's journal it is recorded for May 20th 1886, after noting what was happening in Bulgaria – of considerable interest as Prince Sandro, recently King of Bulgaria, was Princess Beatrice's brother-in-law,[5]– that the Queen went: 'Out driving with Beatrice & Ethel C, taking tea first in the cottage at Frogmore. Visited the Miss Lochs, in their pretty little Cottage near Parkside. They have just lost their mother, & live now alone together.[6] It was there, I went to see their dying Father.'

The Queen over many years had taken an interest in the Loch family. Earlier in the month, on May 3rd, she had sent a telegram of condolence on the death of Catharine Loch, Emily's mother, to which Emily had replied in the most fulsome language. It must have been nine years before, in 1877, that the Queen had visited George Loch.

George Loch, who had been a QC and for a while an MP, had before his retirement been Commissioner for the huge estates of the Duke and Duchess of Sutherland in Scotland and Staffordshire. He had followed in the footsteps of his father James Loch and between them they had been Commissioners for over half of the 19th century. After George retired in about 1870 he had settled down with his wife Catharine and their four talented daughters to a comfortable and interesting life at the Cottage. It remained their home after their parents died – for Mamy until she married, for Cathy until she became a nurse, and for Emily and Alice until their old age.

To understand what their life was like in the late 1870s and early 1880s let us imagine that we can peep in on a sunny morning in the summer of 1879 when three of the sisters were still living at the Cottage with their mother.

The sun was streaming in at the high windows of the new 'painting room' at the Cottage. Emily was busy packing a set of cups and saucers which she had just finished painting with a design of violets. (Plate 2). The sketches of the flowers that she had used as a guide were still lying on the table. The china was now off to the kiln to be fired and its return awaited with some trepidation to see that the colours were right and that none of the delicate Wedgwood china had cracked in the final firing.

Her younger sister, Cathy, now approaching her twenty-fifth year, was putting the finishing touches to the album she had been making over the years; recording, in a mixture of photographs set in lively and amusing sepia wash drawings, the life of the Loch family, their relations and friends. This vivid collection gives us, over a hundred years later, a glimpse of their life in the 1860s and 70s. There are scenes of shooting and fishing on the Sutherland estates near Dunrobin; there is a page with the Duke and his steam plough and a vivid sketch of the fire engines tackling a fire in a London street; attending fires was a 'hobby' which the Duke shared with his friend the Prince of Wales. There is a young lady, Lady Florence Leveson Gower, the Duke's daughter, surrounded by the ubiquitous pigeons in Saint Mark's square, Venice; there are members of the Smart Social Set viewing the summer

George Loch's enlarged Cottage at Bishopsgate, Englefield Green where the Lochs lived from the 1870s until 1930. This is the group of workmen who carried out George's plans.

A page from Cathy's album. The Duke of Sutherland surrounded by scenes from his life: a steam train, a fire engine and a steam plough.

exhibition at the Royal Academy; and in another, a lady, having hooked an enormous salmon, anxiously awaits the arrival of the gillie with a net. There are also straightforward portraits, beautifully captioned, of members of the family. Altogether a humorous and lively account of their family life before their father died. Cathy was soon to leave her mother and sisters to realize her long-held wish to become a nurse.

Alice Loch, the oldest sister, had a magnificent spray of globe artichokes in a huge jar on the floor and, with great skill and immense patience, was making a brilliantly life-like painting in gouache.

There was a knock and a maid's head, with a starched cap perched on her hair, looked round the door and said, 'Miss Geraldine Liddell' and opened the door wide to let in Gerry, a great friend of the family who lived not far off at Holly Grove with her mother and her father, who had been the Deputy Ranger of the Park since 1870. Gerry came in clutching a sheaf of music and, after greeting Alice and Cathy, said to Emily: 'Do come and try out this new piece of Mr Sullivan's with me'. Temporarily the china and wrapping paper were abandoned and Emily and Gerry went off to try the piece on the piano in the hall. But there were more visitors at the door. Fräulein Kirchner had come with Princess Christian and the two little princesses, Thora and Louie.

They had walked over from Cumberland Lodge to visit Mrs Loch. Alice and Cathy were called down to come and see the Princesses and, as it was so fine and warm, the bath chair was brought from the back hall and the whole party moved out into the garden with Cathy pushing her mother. They sat on the seats under the great elm trees and the maids brought out cordials and wine for the party.

Alice had brought a ball and began to play a game with the two children and, when they were tired, drew pictures for them with a pencil and paper from her pocket. Cathy was telling Princess Christian of her excitement at going off shortly to begin her nurse's training at the Royal County Hospital, Winchester.[7]

The visit ended with them all making arrangements to go over to Cumberland Lodge in the next few days to see a new hunter that Prince Christian was trying out. Soon the Princess got up to leave. Emily let them out through the wicket gate into the Park and she and Gerry walked with the party back to Cumberland Lodge.

The youngest sister, Catherine Grace, had already left home by the time Emily began to keep her diary for when she was twenty-five Cathy was allowed to start training as a nurse, her desire for several years. She went as a probationer to Winchester Royal County Hospital but came home whenever she was granted leave. So, from 1880, it was the two older sisters, Emily and Alice, who were running the Cottage for their mother, she being something of an invalid. There are daily accounts in Emily's diary of Mama's health; she tired easily and suffered from spasms when stressed. She still went out for little drives round Englefield Green and the neighbourhood and occasionally to London to stay with her married daughter, Mamy Deverell. Once a year, with ample support from daughters and maids, she travelled to rented houses near Bournemouth for a month by the sea. Many neighbours from Englefield Green, Windsor, and nearby villages and friends from the houses in the Great Park came to call and among these was Princess Christian her long-standing friend. She came most often when the Prince was away. Then the Princess would stay to tea or dine in the evening.

The life of Alice and Emily by this time had become that of devoted daughters caring for their widowed mother – similar to that of many spinster ladies of the period. They had a wide circle of friends, both men and women, but all thought of marriage and establishments of their own had gone with the years. By 1880 Alice was forty and Emily in her thirties. Just once, while in

Germany with the Princess, it appears that Emily slipped out on her own and met someone which when she came to write up her diary later that day, she considered 'most improper'. Shaken by her temerity, she only records the incident in a series of exclamation marks – thirty-five in all. Such straying from the straight and narrow path of propriety was never recorded again and any romantic occasions were in future enjoyed vicariously through the lives and loves of her friends, cousins and nieces and the grandchildren of Queen Victoria.

Alice Loch, the eldest of the family and remembered long after as great fun. The need to keep still for a photograph tended to induce a severe expression.

Alice was the eldest of the family. Earlier in her life, in the 1860s, she had trained in Paris as an artist and showed considerable talent.[8] By the 1880s she was specialising in flower painting but occasionally she went to paint at the National Gallery and did a lot of sketching when on holiday ... 'Alice was out sketching the sand dunes till it was almost dark.'

Her main painting, though, was indoors. She developed beautiful and realistic designs of flowers and leaves for decorating fans. (Plate 2). She did several commissions for Queen Victoria and other members of the Royal Family producing these delightful accessories for the well-dressed lady – a reproduction of one, with mistletoe and Christmas roses, was used by the Royal

Household for their 1990 Christmas card and in the Fan Museum in Greenwich there is another example, a spray of orange blossom and myrtle, made for Princess Louise of Prussia: perhaps for her wedding to Prince Arthur Duke of Connaught on March 2nd 1879. (Plate 2)

Violets and eucalyptus leaves came by post from the south of France, rhododendrons and chrysanthemums from the nearby gardens of Baron Schröder and the Ballantynes. The Schröders also grew exotic orchids and Alice would disappear for days at a time to paint these in the hothouses. She made very careful studies, some of which remain in the portfolios. These could then be copied on to fans and mounted. They were sent for finishing to Duvelleroy[9] of Regent Street, London. For very special presents Alice painted screens – she finished one with apple blossom for the Queen in July 1880, another was entered for an exhibition. She did a few friezes, one for her sister Mamy's house in London where 'Clemmie came to dinner. She helped A and me to put up a big piece of A's frieze on the scaffolding she had brought'. There was a celebratory dinner for another frieze, done in their Aunt Louisa's house.

As the sister who was more interested in outdoor activities, Alice kept bees, with Sharratt the coachman's help; it was he who collected the swarms but Alice did much of the other work. Early one summer, while helping Sharratt rearrange the hives, she was badly stung, with nearly disastrous results. Emily had to rush back from visiting friends and found Alice with her face very swollen and 'her eye bunged up'. Emily was instructed to paint her with 'Iodoform in Colodian' and gradually, as the days passed, the swelling subsided and poor Alice was able to take a little chicken broth but she had become sensitised and suffered badly from a sting later in the year.

Apart from her interests and commitments at home, Alice was much involved in charitable works and other activities. She gave knitting classes for local girls in the village, painting classes in Windsor, and she had some private pupils. She became deeply involved in the affairs of the Union Workhouse. She was also interested in history and current affairs. In the early 80s she regularly went to lectures organised by Lady Ponsonby at which some of the Eton masters taught; notably Oscar Browning – 'Alice to Browning' was a frequent entry.

Increasingly, as the years went by, she became more and more involved with Beaumont College, a Roman Catholic boys' school founded in 1861, which was within walking distance of the Cottage. Alice often spent the whole day there, perhaps teaching art and certainly befriending some of the boys, often bringing them back to a good homely lunch on Sundays. A number of the teachers, Jesuit priests, became friends of the sisters and came for meals. On a cold February night in 1897, Father Raphael dined and told ghost stories late into the night.

Alice entered the Roman Catholic Church in 1891 and for a while this dominated her life; it always remained very important to her. Later she became much involved in the affairs of the District Council and, in November 1903 and again in 1907, was elected to the Egham Urban District Council.[10] She often used her tricycle to attend the meetings and for getting around the neighbourhood. She was still riding one in 1922, in what would have been her eighty-second year. In October, that year, she had a bad fall from her machine at the bottom of Egham hill but 'got on again and tricycled home'. Despite extensive bruising she made a very good recovery and was 'delighted with herself' according to Emily.

Although the family tradition was that Alice was somewhat aloof from, if not dismissive of, her sister for being a lady-in-waiting, Alice in her turn was often called upon by the Christian family to help out: writing difficult speeches for Princess Christian and attending her on occasion. In 1884 the Princess was asked to contribute a Memoir to the new and popular edition of the letters of her sister, the late Princess Alice, wife of Louis of Hesse-Darmstadt. Alice Loch was asked to help with this and, several times towards the end of that year, Emily noted that the Princess came over 'to do her book' and that it was finished on December 22nd.

Whether Alice was aware of all the copyright problems that Princess Christian ran into is not mentioned in Emily's diary. In 1883 a German publisher had brought out a book of Princess Alice's letters, made available by Queen Victoria to a Dr Carl Sell who translated them and added a biographical sketch. Princess Christian was anxious that there should be an English edition. Eventually, after considerable difficulties, John Murray, the publisher, silenced the demands for copyright payment by replacing Dr Sell's biographical sketch with a 'Memoir' contributed by Princess Christian. It was this that Alice Loch helped her with.

Alice quite often accompanied the young princesses to drawing lessons, notably with a Mr Rischgity who came to give lessons in Windsor. Much later on, when the young Princesses were grown up, she had a memorable time with Princess Marie Louise on a visit to North Africa and Italy in 1898. Alice – 'the greatest fun imaginable' according Marie Louise accompanied her on a visit to

Tunis. They took part in the excavations in Carthage and journeyed into the interior, to the town of Kairouan at a time when it was visited by few Europeans. They returned through Italy where the Princess had an audience with the Pope. Alice, who by this time was a Roman Catholic, to her great delight, was one of the party.

Alice lived until 1932. She was fondly remembered by her young relatives who survived into the 21st century. She was wonderful with children; for a forgotten reason they called her 'Edgy Annie' and she always found something to entertain them.

Emily Loch.

Emily was the business woman of the family – doing the accounts, engaging the servants and seeing to repairs and improvements to the house and, rather surprisingly, running a laundry. The Cottage had on its land a number of useful, smaller buildings such as stables, small cottages and a laundry. In the early days the latter was just for the family and their close friends. It was run by Mrs Sharratt, wife of the coachman, both of whom had come with the family from Tittensor, the house on Lord Stafford's estates where they had lived before George Loch's retirement. Later, the laundry became Emily's small business, bringing in some income but also causing much anxiety.

In the 1930s long after our period, and after Alice's death in 1932, all the buildings except one were demolished. Only Shelley's Cottage[11], named after the poet who had briefly lived there, remains, at the beginning of the 21st century: a very desirable and securely protected residence. The black and white gables of the Cottage itself apparently still survive, incorporated into a large house in Englefield Green built in the 1930s. The Cottage of Emily's diaries has gone but fine tall trees and waving grass remain in the field where the Loch sisters once had their home, and where their private, locked gate gave them easy access to the wide expanses of Windsor Great Park.

Back in the 1880s Emily was as much engaged in painting as her sister Alice. She was never quite as talented or versatile as Alice or as good at catching the character of people and animals as Cathy, but she developed considerable skills as a painter of china. She produced many tea sets and dessert services for her friends, undertook commissions and was occasionally paid.

She made careful sketches of her subjects; these were often fresh flowers. There are records of sets with violets, gentians, roses, pine twigs, blackberries and many more (Plate 2). But she sometimes resorted to books when doing birds – Gould's Birds were consulted for a dessert service. When trying animals, such as the tortoise and hare plate or the rabbits on the children's mugs, she sought the assistance of Cathy – although she once painted a dead rabbit herself! She used white china, usually Wedgwood (the family were friends) and, having made the initial studies, traced her design on to the blanks. Painting was the next stage; this was done meticulously and she spent hours on end, occasionally remarking rather crossly in her diary that so and so had interrupted. The time spent was sometimes noted down, often two or three hours and, once, nine hours in one day. When the pieces were finished they were carefully wrapped and sent off for firing. Then there was the anxious wait to see if all had survived. Sometimes there were disappointments, such as when 'the flowers disappeared off the hawthorn plate' or the china cracked. One cracked cup decorated with gentians, gilding and Queen Victoria's monogram is still with us as a reminder of a sad day in 1898 when all was not well – but the diary records that the Queen was pleased with the rest of the set. (Plate 2)

For brief periods Emily ventured into decorating other objects such as tiles and plaques. There was a busy period in 1883 when tiles, perhaps influenced by the work of William de Morgan, were in demand. The year before it had been plaques. The designs for two of these remain in the portfolio. Done on heavy paper and using paint almost neat from the tube a most pleasing design has been created and an incredibly realistic picture of a mass of wallflowers;

their petals velvet soft and the warm, red flowers so densely packed that one can almost catch their unmistakable scent of late spring. On the other, gleaming yellow corn marigolds burst out from a background of glaucous leaves. One such plaque took 63 hours to complete and Princess Christian, once, gave her £4 for such a plaque. Emily continued her china painting for many years, often carrying the pieces and paints with her when she was staying away from home. She finished a wild rose plaque while staying with her Uncle Henry Loch's family on the Isle of Man,[12] and noted that she had spent 30 hours on the painting. She was a great enthusiast and persuaded many to have a try, both among her immediate circle and among members of the royal family. Princess Calma, Prince Christian's sister, became a considerable enthusiast; and another entry reads 'ordered paints for Pss William', the wife of Queen Victoria's eldest grandson in Prussia.

Apart from their own artistic efforts the sisters were always interested in other artists' work, visiting their studios and going to exhibitions. Alice and Emily went to the private view days at the Royal Academy and Emily, in 1884, made a special journey to London to see Sir Frederick Leighton's frescoes. He had been President of the Royal Academy since 1878 and was one of the most successful artists and sculptors of his day. That same year Sir Frederick, later Lord Leighton, was called in to help in obtaining better examples of painting on china for the National Gallery of Victoria, Australia by Lady Loch, Emily's dear aunt Lizzie. She had seen and admired Emily's china painting and was now in Victoria with her husband Lord Henry Loch, who had become the Governor of the State. She was shocked with the standard of wares displayed for students to study in the gallery. At her suggestion letters began to flow between the Trustees of the Museum, who had allocated £100 for the purpose and the Agent-General for Australia in London. A selection was made, pieces were purchased. The bill exceeded the allocated £100 but as it was at the request of Sir Frederick Leighton the Agent-General felt obliged to pay. Although the request was made to Lord Leighton, it appears that the selection was actually made by Emily Loch. She was thanked for her efforts by the President of the Trustees who said 'we think your choice most happy ... and we do not doubt that the work done in this Colony will be largely influenced and improved by the exhibition of the works which we owe in so large a measure to your generous assistance.' Among the pieces is a magnificent, ruby-red glazed earthenware bowl decorated with white birds, leaves and berries made by William de Morgan.[13]

While on holiday in the Lake District in 1881 Emily was thrilled to visit Ruskin, the art critic who was so influential throughout the Victorian period; she and Alice would undoubtedly have read his *Modern Painters* and probably the *Stones of Venice.*

It was a great privilege for Emily and her cousin Clemmie Nicolson to call on this famous man, now sadly suffering from mental illness. He was living quietly at his home Brantwood overlooking Coniston Water, being cared for by Mr and Mrs Arthur Severn. On the afternoon when they arrived he was out in the 'wood chopping trees with the elder Webberlin girl.' Emily makes no comment about his, perhaps unusual, companion but says that 'he was most kind and nice to Clemmie and me and made much conversation and shewed us some most beautiful old missals and mss. of Sir Walter Scott'. How much Emily and her circle at the time would have known about the intimate details of Ruskin's life is uncertain but, as the leading art critic of the century, she would have been most impressed and perhaps even more delighted when on a second visit, a year or two later, he showed her some of his own drawings and books.

Although it was her sister Cathy who took up a career in nursing, Emily showed great concern with anyone who was unwell and was very interested in medical matters. Perhaps this was one of the characteristics that made her so congenial and useful to Princess Christian and in later years to the Tsarina. From the very beginning of the diaries there are regular entries of 'mixed meds'. Unfortunately she never gives the ingredients of her 'meds' and only occasionally what they were for. The majority were given to the 'poor people' whom she visited regularly and who were probably grateful for any relief from their symptoms and pain; but Princess Calma was convinced that it was Emily's medication that cured her on more than one occasion. In the 1880s and 90s there are frequent references to 'mattei'– it was Miss Melly, whom they stayed with in the Lake District, who introduced her to this form of 'alternative medicine'.[14] Ingredients for this were bought, ground in a pestle and mortar, mixed, and the resulting medicine dispensed to number of friends including Gerry's mother, Mrs Liddell.

Music played an enormous part in Emily's life and was certainly the occupation that she shared most enthusiastically with Princess Christian. Both were proficient performers: Emily had a fine contralto voice and the Princess was a talented pianist. Being able to perform in some way or another was very much a necessity for every Victorian lady; an aspiring maid-of-honour for

Princess Beatrice was required to 'play the piano and read music on sight'. In general, all young ladies were expected to be able to perform something – perhaps not always to everyone's delight. Emily records one evening when staying with friends near Cambridge, 'two couples dined here. Music all evening ... everyone trotted out in turn' – not the most appreciative comment.

From 1880 onwards, Tuesday evenings for much of the year were devoted to journeys to London to sing in the Bach Choir which held its practices at the South Kensington Museum. The choir, an association of amateurs, was founded in 1875 by Otto Goldschmidt. Princess Christian, a founder member, often sang and was also involved in the management of the choir. Many of their friends from Windsor were members and, at one time, there was quite a group of them who went up and down in the train together – the 'Windsor troop'.

The ladies of the choir also benefited from the enthusiastic teaching of Mr Goldschmidt's wife, the great Jenny Lind, a very fine bravura soprano. She had made her debut on the London scene in 1847 and was known as 'the Swedish nightingale'. Emily first heard her at a concert in Windsor Castle in 1880: 'It all went very well and Mrs Goldschmidt sang splendidly. It was indeed a thing to have heard her. She had a great reception. The Princess played very well and the room was crammed'.

In addition to her wonderful singing, Mrs Goldschmidt's extensive philanthropy, creating scholarships in the Arts in her native Sweden and endowing an entire hospital in Liverpool – among many other acts of amazing generosity – endeared her to Princess Christian. On April 20th 1894, the Princess unveiled a medallion to Jenny Lind in Westminster Abbey.

A musical highlight of the early 1880s were the 'Richter' concerts which were 'splendid': Emily and Gerry were always delighted when they were able to attend. Hans Richter was born in Hungary in 1843 and had worked as an assistant to Wagner – he was the man who made the fair copy of the *Niebelung Ring* for the engraver. He was first introduced to English audiences in 1877 at the famous Wagner concerts, sharing the conducting with Wagner himself. In 1879, Richter initiated the 'Orchestral Festival Concerts', and these became known as the 'Richter' concerts.

There was also much music when she was at home in Englefield Green. Besides that in private houses, there were organ recitals in St George's Chapel given by Mr Parratt (later Sir Walter) who had been appointed organist in 1882; there were the regular meetings of the Madrigal Singers, which he also conducted and which gave concerts at Christmas and Easter; and there were the 'Pop' and People's concerts, and charity concerts for a variety of good causes. The Princess was much involved with these, the more prestigious of which took place in London – at the Court Theatre in aid of the Kilburn Home or the even grander ones at Grosvenor House in Aid of the Soho Hospital. In June 1884, at a concert in Berkeley Square organised by Lady Ponsonby, Emily sang, 'in the first two part songs'. But, more often, she took part in modest events such as that at St Mark's School, Windsor, in December 1883. 'A very good concert Pss and Miss Skinner played Handel and Schumann, Mr Parratt and Miss S, Beethoven in C. I sang Caller Herrin. Good Glees.'

This was in the early days when Emily first met Miss Skinner. Her violin playing was always much admired and she rapidly became the very dear friend, Shem, who married Gerry Liddell's brother, Fred. Her career as a concert violinist was then just taking off: by the end of the following year in December 1884, Clemmie Nicolson and Emily went to 'the Prince's Hall for 'Shem's concert ... Shem played a Schubert and a Schumann with Miss Agnes Zimmermann. Very successful and she looked quite charming in the new black gown Lou [her sister] had given her'. Later that evening Shem came back to where they were staying, 'just as we had gone to bed very radiant and pleased'.

Shem sometimes stayed at Cumberland Lodge and helped the young princesses with their music – 'Pss Louise practised diligently'. One evening the Princess and Shem dined at the Cottage 'and made music for Mama and Alice'. Pieces by Corelli, Tartini and Max Bruch were played. After another dinner, on a rather grander occasion, it was Emily who entertained, when she and Princess Christian attended a small dinner given for Prince Henry of the Netherlands at Bagshot. This time, Emily sang and the Princess accompanied her on the piano. Many years after this, in 1895, Emily and Gerry sang in the chorus at a concert in Buckingham Palace. Comment: 'it was very amusing, very bad supper after.'

So, music permeated their lives; but going to the theatre was also enjoyed, and Emily was quite prepared to dash up to London for a theatre visit, staying overnight with her sister Mamy or with the Nicolsons. Clemmie and Emily went to see Henry Irving and Ellen Terry in *The Cup* and *The Belle's Stratagem*; they were in the dress circle and it was very hot but they greatly enjoyed it. Lady Ponsonby took dinner guests to see *The Ironmaster* – 'Kendals acting. Quite excellent and very chokey'. The Princess took a large party to see *Much Ado* at the Lyceum – 'quite heavenly' and so it went on. Towards Christmas, for many years, an amateur group, the Strollers, got up by the Liddells and others including Alick Yorke put on a show in Windsor and there was always a flurry of activity. In many country houses there were amateur theatricals but it appears that Emily didn't like acting much. She was, however, persuaded to take part in a Strollers' production in 1907.

Many of Emily's friends were, in one way or another, associated with one of the Royal households. There were the Gordons – Constance and her father, Colonel George Grant Gordon – who lived at Royal Lodge; he was Prince Christian's equerry. The Liddell family were very close friends; Colonel Liddell had been appointed Deputy Ranger in 1870, so he had worked closely with Prince Christian – they lived at Holly Grove and later at South Lawn. Mrs Wellesley, widow of a former Dean of Windsor, lived in the town. She was a member of the Bach Choir and, for a while, part of the Windsor troop.

Emily's and Gerry's closest friends were the Davidsons; he was the Queen's personal chaplain. From 1882 to 1891 he was Dean of Windsor and later moved on to become a Bishop in various dioceses – to Rochester in 1891, Winchester in 1895 and finally, after the death of Archbishop Tait, his wife's father, to Canterbury. Emily became firm friends with both the Davidsons; in the diaries, they mutated from the Dean and Mrs Davidson – or Mrs Deaness – to Edie and Roffen. Emily and Gerry had several memorable holidays with them on the continent; one in particular when Davidson was completing his biography of St Catherine of Sienna. During this the Davidsons, Emily and Gerry followed in the footsteps of St Catherine and saw relics of the Saint and many of the places where she had lived. Emily continued to visit the Davidsons for many years, often staying with them, first in Farnham Castle and then at Lambeth.

There were many others who lived around Windsor and Englefield Green. All were kept in touch by regular 'calling'. Sometimes they were in, sometimes out; but a card was left and contact maintained. Whether Emily adhered to the strict rules laid down in an article in the *Lady* magazine in the 1870s is not spelled out[15], but there is no doubt that she was punctilious in calling when she was abroad and she frequently went the rounds when at home in Englefield Green. Cards were always handed in personally, never sent by post; and calling was done on foot if close enough, but more often in the donkey cart, especially in the early 80s when Mama also took part.

Then there was the close family who kept up a constant stream of visits. The Deverells, William – who had married Mamy, one of the Loch sisters – and their children Molly, Margie and Harry, had a town house in Onslow Square. The children were motherless after the birth in 1885 of Helena, Princess Christian's goddaughter. They frequently saw the Henry Lochs; Henry, Emily's uncle, was her father's youngest brother and was married to much loved Aunt Lizzie. Then there were the Brandreths, Aunt Louisa and Uncle Ed . He was Mama's brother, and she was a close friend of Princess Christian; the two young princesses spent the night before their Grandmother's Golden Jubilee celebrations at Aunt Louisa's house in Elvaston Place. Finally, the Nicolsons – who lived in William Street, London. Clemmie Nicolson was Emily's first cousin and almost the same age; Clemmie's well-known nephew, Harold, only made a fleeting appearance. In 1885, Clemmie married Baron Bemelmanns and went to live in Germany; and their very close ties were broken,

Gerry Liddell, Emily's life-long friend, from Cathy Loch's album of cut-out sepia photos inserted in pen and ink drawings. Here Gerry drives her pony pulling a calash along the coast road near Scourie in Sutherland.

This was not the case with Gerry Liddell. Both Emily and Gerry remained unmarried and devoted friends throughout their long lives. Even from reading the factual lines of the diary, one gets the feeling that everything in life took on a different complexion and was more amusing for Emily when they were together. When apart, one can almost see Emily's eyes light up when a letter arrived from Gerry. She became a lady-in-waiting to the Queen and, even before that, was a constant friend of Princess Christian having known the Princess since childhood. Gerry was a very talented musician but perhaps it was her sense of humour which made her such a favourite. There is a story, attributed to Gerry Liddell, in which Lady Errol – a rather humourless lady-in-waiting – trying to comfort Queen Victoria on the death of some relative, said: 'We will all meet in Abraham's bosom'. To which the Queen retorted: 'I shall *not* meet Abraham'.

After the death of Gerry's mother, she and her father came to live at the Cottage until a house, South Lawn, could be found for them in Eton. After Mrs Liddell's death it was always Gerry, with the assistance of Emily and her brother Fred, who were engaged in the business matters – Col. Liddell played no part. It appears that he suffered from some mental disability or perhaps it was just old age for he required constant care; he was affectionately known by the family and Emily as 'Pupsey'. After his death in December 1888, Gerry was again homeless and spent much of her time at the Cottage. The Liddells were the first of many who found refuge at the Cottage in times of trouble and benefited from the kindness and generosity of the Loch sisters.

CHAPTER FOUR

Princess Christian's Health and Spa Life

August 27th 1885, just a month after the wedding in Osborne, dawned dull and stormy with a high wind. Emily did her last-minute packing, saw that Jeanne had strapped up her trunk, put her overnight clothes in a small case and ensured that her dressing case with her brushes and combs, hairpins and creams had everything she would need. She wrote her final notes and letters, said goodbye to her sister Alice, the first time since their mother's death, paid farewell visits to the old ladies in the cottages and joined the Princess at Cumberland Lodge. After a 'mealtea' (high tea) at 5 they caught the 6.11 train to London where they were met by their friends Colonel Gordon and Marcia. They were seen off on the 8.30 boat train from Victoria station amid the steam and smoke from the engines and the bustle of porters with trunks. Soon they were at the port of Queenboro' on the Isle of Sheppey. There was a branch line to the pier where the ferry boat was tied up and so they had only a short walk up to the deck and their cabins. 'I had my usual cabin' wrote Emily. She had used this crossing two years before and was always happy to find familiar places. That night she only slept a little as it was very rough and the poor Princess, who was not such a good sailor, had a wretched time and felt 'very ill'.

Next day they were both tired out and found the journey on the train from Flushing to Frankfurt long and tedious. They dozed most of the day but stopped at Cologne for lunch in the 'Emperor's rooms'. There were no restaurant cars on trains in those days, and so provision had to be made either for a meal at a restaurant in the station or for a basket to be taken on board. Unusually after this, their train crossed the Rhine to the west bank making them late for their arrival in Frankfurt which caused Emily much anxiety. But Vice-Consul Goldbech was there to meet them, gave them a meal in a hotel and saw them on their way to Homburg where they were greeted by Mr Jocelyn, the Anglican minister, Mr Bourke and Hugh Frazer. Then they were taken to their lodgings in Kisseleffstrasse where they found the Princess's old friend from London, Mrs Alice Frazer. Tired but relieved that all had gone well, Emily and the Princess settled into their rooms and began the first of many visits to a German Spa.

A constant in Emily's diaries is noting the weather for the day. Each entry begins with a line on this subject. Not quite so regular but appearing time after time – there must be hundreds of entries over the years – is the state of people's health and predominant among these is that of Princess Christian. There is no doubt that the Princess suffered some ill health – the move to Cumberland Lodge from the damp low-lying Frogmore in the early years of her marriage bears this out. But as the years went on, she became convinced that she was really unwell. Perhaps it was reassurance that she wanted. There is a letter from Emily to Dr Reid in 1885, asking him to call in and see the Princess when he is on one of his walks in Windsor Park[16], adding that the Queen would be glad for him to see her. Dr Reid, on the other hand, certainly by the '90s, when he had been seeing her regularly, considered her to be 'kindly, if indiscreet and on occasions suffered from imaginary complaints. She was also given to taking drugs such as opium and laudanum'.

Exactly what she suffered from has been a matter of speculation and unfortunately Emily in her devoted discretion does not enlighten us: probably she didn't know. Dr Reid, after all, was never able to examine, physically, his most august patient – he had to treat the Queen purely from conversation – and so missed her prolapse and hernia. Some think that Princess Christian succumbed to post-natal depression after the death of a fifth baby. In her case the causes were almost certainly a mixture of physical and psychological and the cures attempted appear at times to have exacerbated the situation. The Princess had her doctors in Windsor and London – Dr MacLaggan of London, was Physician to her Household. When he attended the Princess one day in July 1884 at Cumberland Lodge, his visit was sandwiched between Mr Fairbank's in the morning and Dr Reid's in the evening! In further efforts to improve her health the Princess followed the habit, fashionable in the late nineteenth century, of visiting European health spas. This gave a regular rhythm to her – and Emily's – lives for several years. The visits were, however, not only for health. They enjoyed a holiday away from the cares at home, rather like a modern cruise, but usually in the company of many of their 'circle' from home. Centred on the health regime laid down by their spa doctors, they were able to relax, enjoy the company of their friends, listen to music in the Kurhaus, eat, drink and, perhaps, experience the thrills of gambling – if they so wished.

The visit which Princess Christian and Emily made to Bad Homburg in 1885 was the first time that they were together in one of these remarkable towns devoted to this combination of health cures and pleasure. From Roman times, certain places had been found where the waters were – or were thought to be – beneficial to health. The water in these springs was highly charged with various minerals. Some of them were extremely rich in sulphur and consequently produced characteristic and unpleasant smells. This may have added to the mystique of the cures. Celia Fiennes made a tour of the English spas in the late 17th century; some she found quite disgusting! In the 18th and 19th centuries the popularity and number of spas grew phenomenally as entrepreneurs saw opportunities to exploit the possible medicinal benefits and attract more and more people. Doctors, honest and quack, flocked to them and additional attractions were provided: meeting places or assembly rooms, entertainments and concerts by well-known performers and, most notably, casinos. One such spa which became a favourite resort with the British and European royalty in the 19th century was Bad Homburg.

The casino there was opened in 1841 by the brothers Blanc. It became notorious as a 'gambling hell' and was observed by Dostoevsky during his tour of Germany in 1862 who used it as material for his notorious character 'the gambler'. Prussia annexed Homburg to the greater Germany in 1866 and ordered the closure of the Blancs' casino. The Blanc brothers went on to found the much more famous establishment in Monte Carlo, but the slightly risqué atmosphere remained, interspersed with drinking the 'waters', taking medicinal baths and following often austere diets. One such, at Wiesbaden, was said to consist solely of grapes, just the flesh, neither the skin nor the pips. But this was recommended only for those with a strong constitution.

Having successfully made the journey to Homburg, Emily, immediately on the morning after their arrival, set about making their rather austere – and probably modestly priced lodging – into 'home'. The day started wet, chilly and uncomfortable. Emily wrote:

> Unpacked and arranged rooms morning and wrote. Saw Mrs Frazer and she is better. M. Goldbech, yesterday's vice consul came to say Pss could have box at Frankfurt Opera whenever she wished. Lord Kenmare came to write down his name and I found him hovering on the stairs. Hugh Frazer and I went out

in the rain after lunch and bought crockery and books. Pss gave tea in Mrs Frazer's room.

She had bought the essentials to make the lodgings fairly comfortable. 'Arranging the rooms' was something Emily did in many different places and palaces, and over many years. She made a familiar, comfortable base from which to launch out. Their lodgings had a piano, an essential. If there wasn't one, as happened in some of their rooms in other places, one was immediately hired. She had bought books but cooking arrangements were minimal. Serious meals had to be taken at hotels and restaurants. In their first week they patronised Herr Ritter's – advertised as the best in Homburg – just across the road; but, as they found their feet, they took their custom elsewhere. Emily notes their meals with great regularity: she disliked missing meals herself, but it was a matter of importance to find somewhere that the Princess liked for two substantial meals each day.

The lodgings in Kisseleffstrasse were near the Park with its lawns and walks, shady trees, brooks and ponds. The buildings were substantial and fairly new with cast iron balconies and fine plate glass windows. Recently planted trees lined the road. Emily was responsible for the running of their temporary

The substantial houses in Kisseleffstrasse, Homburg, with newly planted trees.

household: she did the accounts and paid the bills. Jeanne, her personal maid, was a great standby and help. It was Jeanne who came to the rescue in minor crises and she probably helped Emily in carrying out the health regime prescribed for the Princess: taking her to the medicinal baths, collecting the 'waters' each day from the *stahl brunnen* or chalybeate spring – numerous pots were bought for this purpose. Sometimes the Princess herself walked to the spring where the Kurkarte was displayed with instructions to the clients. 'One drinks with small swallows, walking slowly up and down to the exact instructions of your Doctor.' Little is mentioned about a diet. Both Emily and the Princess, as well as their two meals a day, liked their drinks at Brahe's, usually chocolate, which can have done little for the Princess's health or waistline. Certainly she had put on a lot of weight in the last few years; Emily on the other hand remained slight and elegant Throughout her life Emily suffered from 'sick headaches'; yet, although staying in a spa, she rarely took any of the treatments. Ironically, however, it was she who was smitten with an attack of rheumatism soon after they arrived and, despite treating herself with a 'good dose of salicine' which temporarily helped, had eventually to call in the doctor who 'ordered me a pine bath: ' ... I liked it immensely but it made me feel worse and I was so cold ... I went to bed in flannels and hot drinks'.

Perhaps Kisseleffstrasse was chosen as it was so close to the Park, for exercise was an important part of the cure. Emily usually went with the Princess. They would discuss the events of the previous day and think about what they were going to do in the afternoon, such as going to 'Prof Corroli's atelier, Miss Coles came too'. On other days the Princess and Emily were joined by one of their friends such as Miss Hennicker, Mrs Wardrew, Colonel Antrobus or General du Plat. The last was a member of one of the royal households. When the Crown Prince of Germany came to pay a visit to his sister-in-law, his 'gentleman' accompanied Emily, while Prince Friedrich walked with the Princess. On this occasion, when all the flags were flying in honour of the Crown Prince, Herr von Wittingof, the 'gentleman', arranged a truly splendid spread at their favourite restaurant, the Kursaal. They dined there many times with several different hosts and hostesses. The Kursaal had the advantage that they could listen to music, which they did frequently in the evening, sometimes coming on from another restaurant. Depending on the weather, they might sit inside on the tightly upholstered gilded chairs or sometimes out on the terrace; but outside there might be dangers – wasps during lunch or getting chilled in the evening. Music was one of their abiding interests. They both played the piano

The Kurhaus in Homburg or as Emily calls it the Kursaal where she and the Princess took some meals and were able to listen to music.

in their apartment and sometimes Miss Cooper came to play with Princess Christian. Emily practised her singing. She often sang with the Princess and also at Miss Cooper's. Throughout their visit, music was their most frequent relaxation, a change from the endless little visits for chats and, possibly, gossip.

There is little evidence of the latter but once, on a fine hot day, there was a distinct frisson when it was reported excitedly by Miss Henniker and Colonel Greville that 'Mrs Williams' maid, Jane Smith, had been put in prison'. Unfortunately the diary never vouchsafes for what crime, but there was a bustle of worthy men such as General du Plat, Colonel Greville, and Sir S Mallet, (from the Embassy in Berlin). It continued to be discussed and, a few days later, Colonel Greville came to report that the trial had been postponed. The affair is mentioned on the day of the trial but, sadly, Emily does not enlighten us about the outcome. If anything could be done to help, the Princess would have done her best. She was a great one for practical solutions and got things done in her own quiet way.

The Princess had no transport of her own, but her many friends and acquaintances came to her rescue, especially those who lived in Homburg. Lord Kenmare, found 'hovering' on the stairs the first morning, was assiduous in his attentions and often one of their escorts. On their second day he took them to visit the Schloss. On this occasion they walked up through the town, in through the magnificent old gateway with its elaborate coat of arms and into the two courtyards formed of elegant 18th-century buildings with shuttered windows under steeply pitched roofs. Beyond, a 60-foot tower, standing in the second courtyard at the top of a cliff, dominated the town. From the ramparts they could get distant views of some of the places they would visit when a carriage was available. One acquaintance, Mrs Round, was very attentive and lent them her carriage. On two afternoons she took Emily and the Princess to Saalberg where the Roman ruins were being excavated and reconstructed on the orders of Prince Wilhelm. These were on a hill top about five miles north of the town. There were fine views from the road up to it and it was so quiet that they got out and walked part of the way down.

Herr Goldbech, who had greeted them on their arrival in Frankfurt, lent them his carriage for a visit with Mrs Wardew to the castle of Königstein, the home of the Duke and Duchess of Nassau, six or so miles from Homburg through the beech woods. The visit drew one of Emily's rare comments: 'A most beautiful drive, only an hour and a quarter'. While the Princess was with the owners, Emily and Mrs Wardew carried on a conversation in French with 'the Romanian lady in a small hot room'.

Herr Goldbech's offer of a box at the opera in Frankfurt was taken up on several evenings. A short train journey took them into the city where the carriage met them. After a little shopping including visiting 'the cushion shop', they dined at the Casino and then moved on to the Opera. On the first visit they heard Wagner's '*the Walküre*' which was 'very wonderful but the box was too near just over the orchestra.' No further complaints, however, when they went to hear *Der Freischutz, Herodias* and Gasparini's *Ambleto.*

Emily was very concerned about Alice Frazer. She was very unwell, according to Emily, and often in a bath chair. As her rooms were on the ground floor of their lodgings, Emily and the Princess frequently called to have a word with her as they went in and out. She was well enough, however, to go out to the cake shop with Emily and the two young princesses, Thora and Louie, when they spent a day in Homburg on the way to Darmstadt with their father. A couple of days later, again, she was well enough to join the Princess and Emily when they went to listen to the band in the Kurgarten, even if she did have to sit in her bath chair. But Emily continues 'Mrs Frazer very bad when she came in from her bath chair and sent straight to bed'. The Doctor, however, thought she would be well enough to travel to Vienna a week later – and she was – despite Emily's worries! There is no doubt, in these early years of the diary, that Emily had a tendency to exaggerate the gravity of ailments. According to Emily, as they said goodbye, 'She looked very ill and low' but when Emily and the Princess returned from the opera that night, they 'found an enormous basket of flowers for the Pss from Alice [Frazer] at the station'. Despite Emily's gloomy forebodings, Alice Frazer lived for many years and they frequently saw her in her London house.

Interspersed with all this activity – running errands for the Princess, buying and arranging the flowers, finding places to eat – there was Emily's ceaseless 'writing'. She was in fact the Princess's secretary without any modern facilities; she wrote little notes to make arrangements for this engagement and that, kept up with her own family, and still had the energy to enter a few lines in her diary each night when she came to bed, often ending 'very tired'. Only by the end of the 80s is there any indication of more modern methods. In November 1889 Emily noted that 'The Pss printed a letter to Prince Christian with her new machine'.

As their time in Homburg drew to a close, they began to say farewell to their friends. Some they had only seen once or twice; some they met almost daily, such as the Misses Cole, Miss Cooper, Colonel Antrobus and Lord Kenmare. Just before they left, the Misses Cole accompanied them to Schichs,

A studio photograph of the Misses Cole with Princess Christian and Emily in 1884.

the photographers, and had a photograph taken with Princess Christian and Emily. Now, in the album, is Emily's copy of the four rather starched ladies, with excellent deportment and elaborate hats.

Before Emily could leave, she had to run around 'unceasingly paying the bills and doing other last things'. There was the large bill from the Kurhaus, some from the hat shop and the photographer – and many more. The most mysterious is the one at the 'stick shop' for the 'smash'. Cards were left and farewell calls made including one to Frau Hoecher, the doctor's wife. After a final dinner with the Coles and Mrs Round, they were packed and ready to leave on the 29th September. Colonel Antrobus, gallant to the end, presented both Emily and Princess Christian with bouquets. They were received by Consul Oppenheimer and Vice-Consul Goldbech in Frankfurt, and the carriage took them to catch the 'saloon' for Darmstadt.

This first visit set the pattern for visits in the following years, each a mixture of medical treatment and a holiday with friends. In later years the spa changed to Wiesbaden, the young princesses spent more and more time with their mother and found their own friends. And, as the 80s wore on, Princess Christian's health became more and more precarious. The great advantages of Bad Homburg and Wiesbaden were their closeness to Darmstadt and the family of the Grand Duke of Hesse, widower of the late Princess Alice. Princess Christian could visit her sister's family and Emily became friends with some of her children, Princesses Victoria, Elizabeth (Ella), Irène, Prince Ernie and, most important, Princess Alix.

The timing of the Princess's visits to the Spa, late August to late September, and the pattern followed was much the same but the details varied. In 1887 Princess Christian's oldest brother, the Prince of Wales, visited Homburg. He was able to enjoy the rather risqué atmosphere with his pleasure loving friends but, as his sister was there, he gave luncheons and dinners in her honour. She reciprocated with tea parties. Emily records that there was much changing of clothes to fit in with this smart set. The Prince was a stickler for the correct dress. Once, he was reputed to have left a button undone on his waistcoat. This was observed by the tailors of Europe and became 'de rigueur'. On the whole, the brother and sister got on well but Emily wrote of one hot August day when 'there was a fracas. We had ices at Brahe after'. There was a happier occasion when both were given a 'gorgeous luncheon at the Palmengarten in Frankfurt by the Consul and Vice Consul' and, on another evening, there were fireworks in Homburg which were 'very beautiful and there were many Oh's'. Tennis tournaments, photography – particularly when Mr Jocelyn became more expert with his camera and took groups of friends – and mesmerism all brought added interest and entertainment.

Mesmerism was a new craze. There were a number of séances led by two brothers, the Lloyds, which gave rise to much discussion. During one séance Emily was mesmerised and had 'to do what Mr Lloyd told me to do'. Perhaps Emily felt that these experiments were somewhat dangerous and might bring retribution: they were not repeated. She noted rather curtly on the day after the séance that 'Mr Lloyd went down with ague' – probably an attack of malaria following a period in India.

It was also from the Lloyds that both the Princess and Emily began to take lessons in Hindustani or, as Emily wrote, 'Hindoostani'. This new venture was probably at the wish of the Queen, to keep up with her new found enthusiasm for India. 1887 was Jubilee year. A few days after her Golden Jubilee, on June 21st, she had appointed two Indian servants to her household; one of them Abdul Karim, the Munshi,[17] later became a considerable embarrassment and irritation to her family and senior members of her household. The lessons in Hindustani begun in Homburg and Darmstadt were continued in Britain that year, both in London and Balmoral.

During her later visits, Emily saw more of the surrounding countryside.

Queen Victoria on the arm of the Munshi, Abdul Karim.

They visited the von Dieshaus at one of their estates, Retterhof, near Kronberg. To get to Retterhof the carriage went round by Königstein through the beech woods. Once they drove past Königstein – on their way back by moonlight: it was very beautiful.

But the most memorable expedition was to Jugenheim, the home of the Battenberg family. On September 14th, 1886, a fearfully hot day,

> Started at 9. Pss and I, Gen du Plat. Got to Frankfurt at 9.46. Began hurrying and then found ourselves an hour too soon. Mr Oppenheimer came in his carriage, we saw him pass as we waited under the trees. Went to Brickenbach by 10.50 train. Prince and Pss Louis [Princess Victoria of Hesse] came to meet the Pss. They went on first and we followed to Jugenheim. A most lovely place perched up on the hills. The whole of the Battenberg family there and they all came to meet us and were most kind. Pss of B [mother of Louis] took me to a little drawing room after a few minutes and then came back and sat with me a little and told me all about her son ... We had dinner at 1.30. I sat between the Prince of Bulgaria [Prince Alexander, Sandro] and Pce Franz Joseph [Sandro's brother]. We sat out after. A French gentleman was there who had helped Prince Alexander with the finances in Bulgaria. He had come all the way from Lausanne to see the Prince for a few hours .We left at 4.15. The train was very late and we nearly got boiled. Got back to Homburg by 7.10. Had a little food at the Kursaal and went to bed very early.

An eventful day, and one that Emily would remember when she and Princess Christian made a special visit to Jugenheim two years later at the request of the Queen, who wanted to know how her grandson was faring in the years after the traumatic end to his reign as King of Bulgaria.

Perhaps the most memorable, certainly the most extraordinary, character that Emily and her princesses met at the spas was Elizabeth, Queen of Romania.[18] Their autumn visit to Wiesbaden in 1889 was much enlivened by the presence of this flamboyant lady – the most unusual character to appear in any of Emily's diaries or albums. In the red-leather 'Book of Snobs', three photos, in dramatic poses, are pasted above her signature, Elizabeth Carmen Sylva, Oct '89. This fills the entire space below, a good 12 inches by 3.

A page from 'The Book of Snobs' with the flamboyant signature of Queen of Romania.

Emily first met this Queen, wife of King Carol I of Romania, on November 2nd 1889. The diary entry reads

> Went to the station to meet Pss Victoria, Pss Irène and Pss Alix and Graf. Rangau. We had dinner in the dining room downstairs and then the Psses all went for a drive. I went to the station to see them off at [the] 4.50 train. The Queen of Roumania came also and took Pss Ch. and Pss Louie back to tea. I drove the Vacarescos a little and then home and wrote hard for the messenger.

The family from Darmstadt had come over to see their aunt, something they did fairly often as the cousins grew older. This time they also met Queen Elizabeth who was in Germany because her husband had banished her. She had been sent back to Wied, her family home near Wiesbaden, having committed a misdemeanour in Romania. She had befriended Crown Prince Ferdinand, a nephew of Carol I and his heir to the Romanian crown. She had encouraged him to fall in love with one of her ladies-in-waiting, Helène Vacaresco, and he wished to marry this brilliantly witty, temptingly plump and talented lady. But to marry a commoner was against the rules for a Hohenzollern and an heir to the throne. King Carol said 'No' and banished his wife.

Now Queen Elizabeth had set up her 'court' in Wiesbaden and, for the first half of November, the Princesses and Emily saw it in action, Two days after their first meeting, there was a 'reading' for the various Royals in the town. The Princess was one of the guests. The Queen considered herself to be very artistic and gathered around her a group of similar-minded ladies who admired the poems she composed and recited; her painting and piano playing. Missy, a first cousin of Thora and Louie, who eventually married Ferdinand and who went on to be a very remarkable Queen herself, considered Elizabeth quite absurd. She thought that Elizabeth and her sycophants were indulging in the 'glorification of mediocrity'.

The Queen of Romania visited Princess Christian several times and Emily saw much of the two Vacarescos, her ladies-in-waiting, and thought them charming. On November 10th:

> The Queen of Roumania came see the Pss at 4.30. The two Vacarescos had tea with me and talked 19 to the dozen ... Pss Louie took the Queen down in the lift and I took my ladies down the stairs.

The following day, there was much 'disappointment and grief' from the young princesses because, although Emily 'had bought cakes and prepared a lovely tea' for the Vacarescos, they never came – the Queen had fallen asleep! But Emily's friend Emma Cohausen, whose home was in Wiesbaden, came and helped eat the neglected cakes. However, Emily did hear one performance of the 'court'. On the 17th:

> Then at 4.30 we went to the Queen of Roumania. All the Royalties and people in waiting there. There was singing and the Queen read.

The Queen liked to have her admirers – her acolytes dressed in white – gathered round, in suitable attitudes of adoration. Their attention assured, she read to their adoring gaze: everything had to be spontaneous, unmarred by criticism. One wonders if her 'Royal audience' accepted her in the same way, or sat and chatted as they did so frequently during many performances. The next day the Queen took herself and entourage off elsewhere, and the Princess and her family returned to their own quiet ways. Like a flaming comet, Elizabeth Carmen Sylva had sped past for a few brilliant days and then disappeared into space.

During the years from 1885 to 1890 the Princess's health gradually deteriorated. She changed her doctors and the spa she attended in the hope of finding a cure and usually each visit was followed by a period with her Hesse relations but 1886 was an exception. There was no visit to Darmstadt; instead, Prince Christian, who was not often with her at the Spas, and Prince Christle joined the ladies at the end of their stay at Homburg and they all went north through Hamburg to visit Prince Christian's ancestral home in the flat lands of Schleswig and Holstein. Before they left Homburg, the Prince gave Emily 'a charming brooch of horse chestnut leaves and fruit, as there were so many of them at Gravenstein', one of his family's most beautiful palaces.

The party came from Hamburg by train to Flensburg. The diary goes on:

> Got out there and got into the steamer. Several officials and an old man of 90 met the Prince and came with us in the boat. We got to Gravenstein about 2 o'C. Canons [sic] and decorations and officials in white ties, evening coats and white kid gloves. Speeches and bouquets and little girls in white dresses. There was a considerable amount of people. We had lunch soon after arriving and 3 gentlemen sat with us The Pss rested after as she was badly The Prince and Prince Christle went for a walk. I wrote and read. We dined at 7 o'C. Fireworks and singing after. The Princess went early to bed ... The Prince told me about early family history.

The Princess continued to be in a poor state of health and spent much time in bed. Two days after their arrival, she retired to bed immediately after dinner. This time she really did seem to have been ill. The intermittent pain was diagnosed as neuralgia, a fashionable and non-specific complaint of the time – nevertheless very painful. On October 3rd, five days after they arrived, Emily wrote:

> The Princess seemed better before dinner but was dreadfully bad all evening with neuralgia and everyone was in despair. The Prince sent for Lenscher and it was arranged to telegraph for the

> Dr at Flensburg. The Princess got a little relief from mustard leaf on the temple and behind the ear.

She gradually got better and so was able to visit the old Schloss at Sonderburg and some of the other castles before they made their way home. It was sad that this one occasion, recorded by Emily in the early years, when she could have enjoyed herself and enjoyed meeting the people in the Prince's homeland was marred by a vicious attack of pain and real illness

The following year, 1887, Princess Christian and Emily were again in Bad Homburg for a little over three weeks during August. By this time it wasn't only her general health that was causing the Princess concern but her eyes were giving her a lot of trouble. Remembering her love of fine needlework and embroidery this was a serious matter. Her eyes were causing much discomfort, so she and Emily made five visits to get treatment from a reputed eye specialist, Dr Pagenstecher, in Wiesbaden.

The Princess had such faith in the doctor that she and Emily moved to Wiesbaden the following year. This may also have been a precaution as there was an outbreak of typhoid in Homburg. At first, in 1888, the Princess and Mr Lloyd were examined by Pagenstecker's assistant and the report on Mr Lloyd's eyes was good. Not so for the Princess and she 'was very low'. A week later Emily was back and looking for suitable rooms in Wiesbaden. These were found in the 'Villa Schmidt' and soon she and the Princess were established there with their books and piano.

The internationally renowned Wiesbaden Eye Clinic was the reason for the move. The clinic was founded in the 1850s and, in 1870, Dr Alexander Pagenstecher took over as director; but he died in 1879 from a shotgun accident. The doctor who treated Princess Christian was his younger brother, Herman. He was born in 1844 at Bad Schwalbach in the Taunus Hills and died at Wiesbaden in 1932. He studied medicine in Berlin, Prague and Marburg and did a considerable amount of research into the detailed anatomy of the eye. In 1873 he published the 'Atlas of pathological anatomy of the eyeball' with exquisitely detailed drawings of sections of the eyeball showing a variety of ulcers, wounds, occlusions and cataracts.

From Easter 1870 until the autumn of 1871 he assisted his older brother and then went to study in Britain with Lord Lister, professor of clinical surgery at Edinburgh University and discoverer of the importance of antiseptic treatment, which revolutionised modern surgery. He had also found that the size of the pupil of the eye was regulated by the plain muscles of the iris. Both these discoveries were immensely important in eye operations and so were vital to Pagenstecher's work. In 1872 he returned to Germany and became his brother's partner until Alexander's death in 1879. Herman then took over as the head of the clinic. Both the brothers had gained a high reputation, especially among the Royal families of Europe. The Crown Princess Vicky (later Empress Vicky) spent a considerable time as a patient in 1873 and in 1877. After her second visit, her suggestion – that a Ladies' Committee should be formed to raise money for the Clinic – was taken up, with Frau von Knoop as its head. Frau von Knoop was a friend of Princess Christian and the young princesses got to know her family well in the late 1880s. Her committee held a most successful bazaar in 1878 in the Wiesbaden Assembly Rooms, which raised 10,000 marks for the clinic.

Later in the century, in 1896, Dr Herman Pagenstecher visited Osborne to examine Queen Victoria. The Queen's sight had been failing, and the two English ophthalmologists who examined her diagnosed that she had nuclear cataracts in both eyes. They prescribed eye-drops and improved glasses, but she was not satisfied, having heard from her daughters of Dr Pagenstecher's 'miraculous cures'. Despite ruffling the feathers of the English doctors, she insisted on a visit from Pagenstecher, and his friendly, confident manner reassured her although his written diagnosis concurred with that of the English doctors. Dr Reid, her own physician, in discussion with Pagenstecher, found that the latter considered it a part of his medical treatment to tell his patients nothing that would disturb them. So, if they complained of poor vision and no mature cataract was present, he told them that their condition was due to turbidity and could be cured without an operation. Princess Christian was convinced by these statements and reported that he could cure cataract by 'absorption'. The sceptical Dr Reid questioned the doctor directly about this and Pagenstecher admitted that it was 'absurd and should be contradicted'. When, however, Pagenstecher was consulted in desperation by the Queen on January 15th 1901, his opinion coincided with that of Dr Reid that her inability to see clearly was due to 'cerebral degeneration' rather than her cataract.

His treatments, however, must have been reasonably successful and not dependent solely on an excellent 'bedside manner'; but whether the Princess's eyesight really improved is never explicit in the diaries. The doctor had become very experienced in the removal of cataract and operations on glaucoma. It is thought by some that Princess Christian may have suffered from one or both of these conditions; possibly something quite different. From Emily's accounts, however, the treatments sounded very painful: for example, having 'caustic put in her eye' and 'the eyelid being turned inside out and burned'[19]. Again, in his discussions with Dr Reid, Pagenstecher was somewhat scornful of Princess Christian's conviction that he had cured her from blindness, saying that 'there was absolutely nothing wrong with her eyes, that her symptoms were simply the result of her nerves being for the time shattered by stimulants and narcotics, and ceased when these were for the time being cut off from her'. These remarks echo so much of Dr Reid's own opinion of Princess Christian that they should be considered in that light. Even from Emily's remarks, however, it does seem that the Princess was much better when not attending a clinic too assiduously and had other occupations to fill her time.

Cocaine was certainly used both as a local anaesthetic and for expanding the pupil during operations. Relief from pain was usually achieved with laudanum, a tincture of opium. The overuse of these analgesics may well have been the cause of many of Princess Christian's troubles, especially before the dangers of drug addiction had been recognised. Yet, much of the time, the Princess continued to carry on a busy and active life, pursuing her own particular interests – nursing and the welfare of nurses, and the School of Art Needlework, as well as opening bazaars and laying foundation stones.

Back to 1888: the day after the Princess and her party settled in at the Villa Schmidt, she went to Dr Cohn. Thereafter there were frequent treatments by Dr Pagenstecher and Dr Cohn was visited or came to the Princess almost every day. The Princess's health had definitely taken a turn for the worse; for instance on September 28th Emily wrote:

> Pss very bad with neuralgia and staid in bed all day and was very unwell. I never left her all day except for meals and an hour before supper … Dr Cohn came twice and Dr Pagenstecher 3 times to the Pss. I staid with her all night until she slept. I wrote letters and was startled by the doorbell which rang three or four times. I was afraid it would disturb the Pss and asked out of the window and it was a man with a telegram. I went down and took it in. Found the Pss up and rather alarmed. It was from the Queen about the old nurse's death. Pss rather badly and so staid with her a little and then went to bed.

Her health, mental and physical, continued to be very poor. In October, she spent nearly all the time from the 11th onwards in bed or confined to her room. Emily had to call on her friends to come and sit with the Princess when she had to go out. The Princess was never left on her own. By mid-November Emily was writing:

> Pss very badly morning but got better towards evening. Dr Cohn came 3 times. I was with her a good part of the morning ... The 2 Pses and I ran out at 12.30 down to Emma's to say I could not come and to Dr Cohn with a message ... Canon Wilberforce came to enquire after the Pss and I came down to see him. Emma came at 5-o'C and came up to my rooms to have tea. Dr Cohn came at 5. I sat with the Pss from 6 to 7 and we had food. The Pses, Julia and the Burgoynes went to the music at the Kurhaus. I sat with the Pss. Dr Cohn came at quarter to ten. I wrote a little upstairs and then came down ready for the night in the drawing room. Dr Cohn talked with me when he left the Pss. I slept on the sofa and went in to the Pss whenever she wanted me.

The next night Emily again slept in the drawing room. The following day a night nurse was found, but the Princess took a dislike to her. The day after that, the Princess was worse and had to have 'poultices all day which I did for her'. The next day the Prince returned (he had been away for some time); he sat with the Princess much of the following day and a Sister Clara was engaged to help. The Princess liked her, she was a good nurse and at last the patient began to get better. A week later she was sufficiently well for them all to be able to leave Wiesbaden by train and return to England.

In 1889 the Princess and her daughters made two visits to Wiesbaden. On March 5th, the party had a perfect crossing in the *The Empress*, a long train journey through a snowy landscape and arrived at the Park Hotel in Wiesbaden about 6 o'clock in the evening. Dr Cohn was there almost at once to see the Princess. He continued to visit very regularly throughout the next two months. Dr Pagenstecher was visited almost every day. Princess Louie also became a patient and Princess Thora went to him once. On the whole though, this spring, the Princess's health was somewhat better. The two young princesses were with her all the time and Prince Christian made a short visit in April. Her younger son Prince Abby was studying in Germany. Rooms had been found for him in Darmstadt and he came over to see his mother several times. So the Princess had more of her family around her.

During this period the Princess still became tired very easily and retired to bed early, but on the whole she was fitter and busily engaged in a number of activities, such as the Easter bazaar got up by Frau Schmeling and Mrs Schneider in the Kurhaus. On the Tuesday after Easter, Emily and the Princess went in the morning to the Casino to see how the preparations were getting on. Then

> the Princess kept quiet till lunch. We dressed and went at 2.30 to the bazaar. It was beautifully arranged and a great many people came. The Princesses sold flowers. We had tea after 4 o'clock and supper at 7.30. Frau von Knoop did the buffet and a great many people dined. The Princess was terribly tired but stopped till 9 o'clock. We staid on till 10 o'clock- very exhausted. A great deal of money was made 6,075 marks.

And that was not all. The following day poor Princess Christian 'was laid up in bed all day' but after a busy, bustling morning, including seeing a Herr von Below about furniture for Prince Abby's room, Emily and the young princesses dressed hastily and went back to the Bazaar.

> We had a very successful time and took 980 marks. It finished up with a dance of about half an hour with the band that came to play. We got home by a quarter to eleven.

Soon after the Easter bazaar, the party returned to England.

There is only one mention of Prince Christian during this period and he did not join his family at all during the four months, later in the year, when Emily and Princess Christian were in Germany. That autumn, life at the spa resumed its routine of doctors' appointments in the morning, shopping, paying calls and visits to friends in the afternoons or drives into the countryside.

The Princess and Princess Louie were regular visitors to the clinic throughout these four months. Princess Louie was also undergoing the painful treatment of having her 'eyes burned each day like the Princess.' Dr Cohn was frequently called to the hotel and, as Princess Christian's health deteriorated, sometimes came several times a day and at all hours. He, again, prescribed poultices which Emily made up with linseed. Each month there are records that the Princess 'stayed in bed'; sometimes just with a cold, often neuralgia; sometimes it seems to have been with something worse. There were four days in September, five in October and November and, during December, she was in bed for eleven of the nineteen days that Emily was with her. The Princesses remained in Wiesbaden for the rest of the year, while Emily returned to England to be with her family over Christmas and the New Year.

1890 opened with Emily being 'commanded' to visit Queen Victoria at Osborne. She travelled down by train to Southampton and crossed to Cowes by 3 o'clock.

> A carriage met me and a fly for Jeanne [her maid]. Drove up. Sir John McNeil met me at the door. Went up to my room and Harriet Phipps came to me. Went out driving with her and Miss Drummond and then sat with her till teatime. There were rehearsals for the tableaux after tea. The Queen and all the Princesses came to it. They all spoke to me. The children were there. Ponsonbys etc. I dined with the Queen and sat between Major Bigge and Col. Collins. The Queen talked to me for a long while after and then the Duchess of Albany and Princess Louise. I talked a little to the gentlemen when they left and then went upstairs to the household. Found them playing 'How?, When? and Where?' Soon went to bed.

The next day, after church in the morning, lunch with the Biddulphs, a walk in the wild, windy weather, she was sent for by Princess Beatrice who also had the Duchess of Albany in her room. The three had a long talk together until 8 o'clock and Emily had to dress very quickly to be in time for dinner with the Household. She sat next to Major Bigge and Dr Reid. Afterwards they

> 'all went to the Queen's drawing room. The Queen talked to me and then I stood a long time and talked to Princess Louise'.

Emily left the next afternoon having had another short talk with the Duchess of Albany and visiting Sir Henry Ponsonby for a discussion.

As ever, her discretion prevents Emily from mentioning what was talked about, but the topics were almost certainly Princess Christian's health and behaviour. Emily had left her very unwell with long spells in bed – one day in November she had shut herself away from everyone and would not come out of her room. As not only the Queen, but also Princess Christian's sisters, Princess Louise and Princess Beatrice, and the Duchess of Albany, her sister-in-law, widow of Prince Leopold, all had long talks with Emily it seems that whole family were very worried about the Princess' health. During her dinner with the Household, Emily sat next to Dr Reid and surely he asked her about the Princess. As mentioned earlier, he was very doubtful about the physical basis of the Princess's illness and, over the next few years, came to the conclusion that she compounded her hypochondria with overdoses of drugs. Frequently the diaries record that Princess Christian suffered from neuralgia and there were all those visits to Dr Pagenstecher and his remarkably rigorous and painful treatments.

Life went on much the same when Emily returned to Wiesbaden towards the end of January 1890. The Princess was still keeping to her bed. A night nurse had been engaged. While Emily was in England the young princesses had stayed with friends, the Dieshaus in their nearby estate of Epstein. The morning they returned, their mother had a 'suffering night' but three or four days later she began to show signs of improvement. She was given a setback when they received a very disturbing letter from the Prince on February 1st. This, however, was made better by a much more friendly telegram received the same evening. Each successive day after this Emily noted that Princess was getting a bit better; she managed tea with Frau Knoop, accompanied by her daughters on the 6th and, by the 13th, she decided to discontinue the night nurse. That evening she also managed to come down to dinner and two days later tried a 'tiny walk'. This signalled a return to a more active life and she was definitely up and about by the time Prince Christian arrived late on February 23rd. He had come to be with the family for Prince Albert's birthday on the 26th; the young prince came over for the day from Darmstadt, so the Princess had most of her family around her. Emily left in April and the Christian family returned to England for the summer months.

They were back in Wiesbaden at the beginning of September 1890 and were already installed in their lodgings by the time Emily joined them. She found a much more cheerful household with the Princess's health much improved. Although a doctor was in regular attendance, there were far fewer visits to Dr Pagenstecher. She was back into the regime of regular medicinal baths. Emily never mentioned her taking the 'waters' of Wiesbaden which were reputed to taste of chicken soup! Altogether, the Princess seemed far more able to cope with life. And there were more exciting things to do: there were all the preparations to be made for going to the wedding in Berlin of her niece. In the flurry and excitement there were far fewer references to the Princess being tired; ill health was pushed into the background.

The Princess's drug addiction which coloured so much of their lives in 1890 was not tackled seriously until some years later. Dr Reid noted in his diary on November 20th 1894 that he had driven to Cumberland Lodge to see Prince Christian about his eye which had been badly damaged in a shooting accident and, afterwards, that he had talked about the Princess. He also discussed matters to do with the Princess with the Bishop of Rochester (Emily's friend Randall Davidson) soon after this. But it was not until Princess Christian was on a visit to Cimiez with the Queen, in the spring of 1896, that Dr Reid at last took steps to end her addiction. By this time Prince Christian was no longer able to ignore the situation and he had pleaded with Dr Reid to do something about it. Reid noted on April 20th that the Princess was complaining of facial neuralgia but he doubted its 'reality'. Two days later, however, he was convinced that she was 'still pretending neuralgia. Stopped all narcotics and stimulants'. There are no details in either diary as to how the Princess survived this drastic withdrawal but Emily's diary suggests that all went smoothly. Perhaps the Princess found other interests and certainly some of the tensions disappeared after her mother's death.

CHAPTER FIVE

Princess Alix in Hesse-Darmstadt

In the early years of the nineteenth century Darmstadt remained a medieval German city. The market place had been built in the 14th century as a trading centre and the Schloss and the old City Hall dated from the 16th century. The narrow cobblestone streets threaded their way between steeply roofed houses ornamented with carvings. The palace of the Grand Duke stood in the middle of the town surrounded by a park filled with linden and chestnut trees. By the time of Princess Alice's marriage in 1862, the town had grown: the streets widened and a new palace built – a wedding gift from Queen Victoria to her daughter. There was an Opera house, a museum and a newly built railway station. This was the Darmstadt that Emily came to on a cold cloudy evening late in September 1885. The photographs in her album show the palace where they stayed as a very substantial, three-storied building behind stone balustrades

The palace in Darmstadt built for Princess Alice and her growing family.

with large plate glass windows and gently sloping roofs. Gardens, walks and drives all sheltered by trees, some quite young, surrounded the new buildings.

The day may have been cloudy and cold but the welcome which she and the Princess received was quite the reverse. Their host, Grand Duke Louis, was away from home. In his stead they were greeted by his eldest daughter Princess Victoria and her husband Prince Louis of Battenberg. They were delighted to see Victoria's aunt again and hear how she had been getting on in Homburg. Victoria and Louis had been married for little over a year and now had baby Alice – another great-niece for Princess Christian.

Also in the party at the station were Fräulein von Grancy and Baron Westerweller, two longstanding members of the Grand Duke's household. Both became well known to Emily in the years to come. On this first visit the Baron took Emily, a few days later, to show her the heirlooms of the Hesse family and the treasures of the palace. Emily saw a lot of Fräulein von Grancy; it was she who introduced Emily to the many new faces who made up the household. Together, Fräulein von Grancy and Emily visited the theatre and beauty spots in the country in addition to more mundane occupations such as little walks in the park and visits to the post office. They met in each other's rooms for chats, meanwhile doing odd jobs such as 'bobs for caps', catching up on the mild excitements of life or making arrangements for the next day's activities. One evening as they were on their way to bed, Fräulein von Grancy guided Emily through the intricacies of a 'german letter'. Fräulein von Grancy became very important to Emily and they continued to meet and enjoy each other's company for many years, whenever Emily visited one of the Grand Duke's residences. On the day of her arrival, Emily after a brief visit to chat with the Royalty during tea, retired to her room and got everything 'arranged' and shipshape before supper at 8.00 with 'word games' afterwards.

Emily's two young princesses, Thora and Louie, were both already staying with their cousins by the time she and their mother arrived at Darmstadt. Emily frequently referred to the 'children' in her diary. These, in 1885, were Princess Thora, Princess Louie and Princess Alix, all much the same age; they had all been bridesmaids at Princess Beatrice's wedding two months earlier and were enjoying being together again. Princess Alix's father, the Grand Duke had also been at the wedding. By July 1885 he had been allowed back into the fold: the previous year, 1884, this had seemed most unlikely.

By July 1885 his mother-in-law, the Queen, had forgiven what she considered his appalling behaviour at the time of Victoria's marriage to Prince

One of Cathy Loch's drawings of the hired ponies in the Pyrenees
from her book *The Adventures of Miss Brown, Miss Jones and Miss Robinson.*

Louis of Battenberg in 1884. The Grand Duke had been a widower since Princess Alice's death in 1878. Seven years later, on the morning of his eldest daughter's wedding, April 30th 1884, he himself married his recently divorced mistress, Madame de Kolemine. Nearly everyone among the royalty gathered in Darmstadt for the wedding knew what was in the air – except Queen Victoria. Once the event had taken place it was decided that she must be told; and this unenviable task fell to Lady Ely, her Lady of the Bed Chamber. Consternation and then action was the Queen's response. The marriage must be annulled and annulled it was. Grand Duke Louis really had no choice: a small state like his only prospered by its alliances with the great powers. For it to survive, he had to repair this appalling breach of protocol and by the summer of 1885 he had done so. All was forgiven.

While staying with the Hesse family in Darmstadt, Emily, apart from being at the beck and call of Princess Christian, spent much of her time with the young princesses. She was a favourite with the 'children', often going for walks with them, taking them shopping and accompanying them on drives or playing the piano and singing to them. Quite often she remarked that the children 'came to sit with me'. She probably drew and painted with them as she did

The difficulties of taking their hired ponies through the snow in the Pyrenees.

with Thora and Louie at home in England.

She certainly read to them and possibly she entertained them with the enchanting book which her sister Cathy had written and illustrated a few years previously, called *The Foreign Tour of the Misses Brown, Jones and Robinson being the History of what they saw and did at Biarritz and in the Pyrenees*. The children would have enjoyed Cathy's delightful drawings and the crisp comments of the participants as they, Miss Brown (Miss C G Loch), Miss Jones (The Lady Florence Leveson Gower) and Miss Robinson (Miss Bragge, the chaperone) battled with the problems of travel and foreign hotels; getting porters to carry their mountains of luggage and hiring ponies. They stayed in Bordeaux, Biarritz, Fuentarrabia, and Pau: they 'did' the chateaux, and Lourdes where they bought a few small remembrances. The children would have laughed at the amusing series of drawings as they made a four hour climb, encumbered with long skirts and unnecessary waterproofs, up a Pyrenean peak at Argelès. Miss Robinson gave up in the heat but the two young ladies pushed on to the summit, flopped down, exhausted, to survey the view. There, they were accosted 'by a little wild herd girl' who begged 'imperiously in unintelligible Basque'.

In the story, the journey back to England was made no easier by the acquisition of a fluffy white puppy, small at purchase but obviously destined to become a large Pyrenean hound. Patou became his name. They bought him a large basket and hoped to smuggle him on the train but his piercing shrieks gave him away and he was put in the guard's van. A kindly railway official finally brought him back to their carriage and, after this, Miss Brown and Miss Jones took it in turns to carry him and he got heavier and heavier. Back in Paris, all four, the three ladies and the pup, took refreshing drinks of milk in a splendid cow house round the back of a café in the Bois de Boulogne. Poor Patou was very seasick crossing the Channel – there is a picture of him looking very miserable on the deck of the ferry – but finally they all reached England safely. A tale to delight the children and special, as Emily's sister had written it.[20]

During her visits to Darmstadt, Emily got to know most of the Hesse family very well. In 1885 Princess Irène, the Grand Duke's third daughter, was still living at Darmstadt. Later she married into the Prussian Royal family. Emily mentions her quite frequently in 1885. Princess Victoria was living at the Battenberg family home, Jugenheim, a few miles away, whereas Princess Elizabeth, Ella, married in the same year, was away in far-off Russia with her husband, Grand Duke Serge, brother of Tsar Alexander II. Emily met her on later visits to Darmstadt and there is a photograph of her, a great beauty, in one

Princess Alix and her sister Irène in Darmstadt before Irène's marriage into the Prussian royal family.

of the albums. (see P297). It was with Princess Alix, however, that she spent most time. Alix and Louie were the two youngest and often did rather different things from their older sisters. Sometimes when the older princesses were visiting relations Emily and Miss Jackson took the younger ones shopping in the town.

Emily was often in the company of Miss Jackson, the governess who had been with the Hesse children for many years, having joined the family before Princess Alice's death. Her influence on the development and tastes of Princess Alix, the youngest and the one she was with the longest, was considerable. Miss Jackson was a serious and devout person, a very staunch Protestant – she had left her previous employer because she became a Roman Catholic. She was interested in politics and had a horror of any form of gossip. These tastes found a ready pupil in Princess Alix who, perhaps because of the sudden deaths of her little sister and her mother, was unusually prone to religious thinking and introspection. As a result, as she got older she found distasteful the light-hearted whirl in which many of her relations lived and even more the society which she eventually entered in St Petersburg after her marriage. Yet, as a young woman she enjoyed riding, dancing, games and lively conversation. When she first met the man who later became her father-in-law, Tsar Alexander, she enjoyed his teasing and jokes. It is only later when ill health – her own and her son's – came to dominate her life that the characteristics acquired from Miss Jackson became so evident. Miss Jackson, herself, became very difficult in her old age and Queen Victoria, who had relied on her so much in the years after Princess Alice's death, was caused to remark that Miss Jackson was not a fit person to be with Alix.

Another visitor to Darmstadt during that first year was Princess Christian's sister, Louise of Lorne. She had wanted to join the Christian family for the return journey to England but Princess Christian would not alter her plans. The few days she was in Darmstadt, however, gave Emily the opportunity to meet her. Princess Louise had married the Marquess of Lorne in 1871. She was the most artistic of Queen Victoria's children, but was very temperamental with great swings of mood. Her marriage followed suit. The Queen regarded her as 'her difficult daughter'. By 1885 she lived apart from Lord Lorne although they had a flat in Kensington Palace. She spent many months each year on the continent visiting relatives and attending clinics in attempts to repair the damage done by two serious accidents she had sustained in Canada and the United States.[21]

Princess Louise was a sculptress of considerable talent. In the 1860s she had designed the font for the church at Whippingham on the Isle of Wight. She loved the world of the Arts and enjoyed to the full the company of many artists of the period. She was a person with an insatiable interest in everything, great and small, and she entertained – or shocked – people with her racy conversation. The Lornes never had any children: this may have fuelled her jealousy of Princess Christian, for she much enjoyed having them around. In later life she remarked that her house needed the voices of young people to bring it alive. No doubt, on this visit to Darmstadt, she enjoyed the company of her nephew and nieces and they delighted in her high spirits and spicy stories told in her deep guttural voice with its rolling rrrr's. Emily had several conversations with her and was particularly intrigued to watch the Princess 'drawing on wood' one evening as they all listened to Princess Christian playing the piano.[22]

Among all this crowd of females, the arrival of Prince Ernie with his tutor Herr Mütter from England brought a welcome change. Prince Ernie was the only surviving son of Princess Alice and Grand Duke Louis. His brother Fritty, had been afflicted with the dreaded haemophilia – so it was known to be in the family – and had died as a result of a fall from Princess Alice's window when he was three. Prince Ernie escaped the disease and was now, in 1885, seventeen years old. Emily may have seen him earlier on one of his visits to England but this was the first time she had the chance to know him better. Two days after he arrived, Fräulein von Grancy took the older of the young people, Princesses Irène, Thora and Prince Ernie to visit the Battenbergs at Jugenheim for lunch and, that evening, Fräulein von Grancy and Emily took the youngest princesses and Prince Ernie to the Opera. Afterwards he joined Fräulein von Grancy, Irène and Thora in 'a jolly little supper party' followed by the older ladies singing.

Two years later, in 1887, after the visit to Homburg, Princess Christian, her two daughters and Emily found Prince Christian and Prince Albert staying with the Hesse family. Princess Alix was at home and Emily recorded being with the princesses on many occasions. She was frequently with Miss Jackson and learned a lot about this attractive young Princess. The whole party stayed (always written staid) in the old Schloss, as the Palais 'was being fitted up with electric lighting.'

Emily made herself and Princess Christian at home in this new setting. She had large bare rooms near those of the young princesses, on the floor above Princess Christian. Emily was always 'running down to the Pss'. With so many young people about there was much activity: tennis, drives and walks into the country and through the beech woods. Prince Ernie was out of action for much of the time, having sprained his ankle very badly and Emily often visited him. She went for drives with Miss Jackson and the two youngest Louie and Alix. They went shopping, played games, sang and played the piano together. Emily had been provided with her own piano. She noted a day or so after arriving at the Schloss that 'Herr von Westerweller came to see about the piano and made a fuss'. A week later she took Louie, Alix and Thora, to the photographers and was there nearly an hour. During this visit to the Darmstadt Schloss the whole party frequently ate together, although she occasionally noted that 'Miss Jackson and I dined alone.' One of her other tasks was seeing to the maids Jeanne and Jessie. They usually were busy, unobtrusive and unmentioned but occasionally they broke the surface, for instance when they went to the opera, *Trovatore*, or out on a picnic on the Saalberg. One wonders what happened to them when Emily had to rush round to get Princess Thora's hot water bottle and did they do the washing-up after the homely evening during which 'the Princesses sat in my room when we came in. I sang and practised a little and we baked ginger bread nuts'?

Among their many activities the young people got up a *tableau vivant* with scenery and costumes from the theatre. The show was 'Quite excellent'. Unfortunately the albums have no photograph of this particular tableau but it was no doubt similar to the one that was put on in Berlin in March earlier that year when vast numbers of the royal families assembled to celebrate the 90th birthday of the Emperor of Germany. In this tableau another of Queen Victoria's grand-daughters, another Princess Victoria, daughter of the Crown Prince and Princess of Germany, was the central figure, Yum-Yum. The photo of the Berlin spectacle appears in Emily's album as '*Mrs. Tarley's Waxworks*' and each player is identified in elaborate lettering.[23]

Whilst staying in Darmstadt, they frequently went to the theatre – nine times in little over a fortnight on their first visit – '*Carmen* was most enjoyable'. There were also concerts; once the celebrated violinist Pablo de Sarasate played.[24] They usually went with a party of the young people; they heard Weber's *Silvana*, which was 'very well given and lasted from 6 till 9.30' and on another evening they all went to the *Meistersinger*. Only the youngest, however, were taken to Weber's '*Der Freischütz*'. Perhaps this piece based on a German folk story was considered particularly suitable for the young ones. In all, there was plenty of entertainment.

On the evenings when there was no visit to the theatre, the household and the royalty joined in games of cards such as whist and word games which were a favourite with Princess Christian. Quite often there was singing. Emily really enjoyed singing and, having a good voice, was often called upon to perform. One evening they all played 'caroline billiards'[25] and 'had great fun'. This bears out the general feeling about life in Darmstadt: that it was fun and light-hearted. Protocol was far less rigid than in other German courts. This was probably the reason why so many of Queen Victoria's children and grandchildren were drawn to the place.

As we have seen, Prince Christian took an active interest in the early education of his children. It was not the fashion, however, to train young ladies – after they had left governesses, tutors and the schoolroom – for any particular job or profession. In the case of Princess Thora and Princess Louie, they continued to perfect their languages, particularly German and its literature, and were given the chance to continue with music and general appreciation of the arts. This they were able to do, whether at home or when they were away, staying with their mother on her visits to various places such as Wiesbaden. From 1888 onwards, they spent several months of the year in Germany and, as Emily was generally with the Princess during her 'cures', much of her time was spent with the young princesses. Great efforts were made to ensure that there was plenty for them to do, engaging tutors in singing and music and, briefly, even in logic and leather work. Emily accompanied them to plays and operas, often having vetted them first

There was a spring visit to Wiesbaden in 1889 during which they stayed at the Park Hotel. Princess Thora was in her nineteenth year and Princess Louie two years younger. The weather was kind that spring and there were several expeditions to friends and relations in the neighbourhood. A particular favourite was Königstein, just to the north-west of Frankfurt. They went by train, with a change at Höchst, and were met by a carriage – sometimes closed, sometimes open – for the last part of the journey to where the Duke and Duchess of Nassau were waiting to greet them. Emily described the hosts as 'nice and hearty'. 'Hearty' is a word she used frequently to describe people, meaning cordial or genial and not carrying the vigorous overtones of the 20th century.

Life at the Spa went on in the same tenor with a widening circle of friends – the von Dieshaus, the Knoops, the Cohausens and others – for the young princesses. Princess Christian had Else Blücher, a native of Wiesbaden who was very musical, as a companion. The Princess was well enough to help in the Easter bazaar got up by Frau Schmeling and Mrs Schneider. There were many visits to the theatre and, on quiet evenings at home, writing letters, playing Patience or Piquet and winding silk for pen wipers. The last was a frequent occupation. It was certainly necessary, judging by the amount of writing that Emily did. These particular pen-wipers took the form of fluffy balls of floss silk which she bought by the skein from Walter Head and Sons of Sloane Street in London. There are frequent references throughout these years to 'winding silk for pen-wipers'. They were decorative and made useful gifts, being much in demand at bazaars, other charitable sales and as small presents.

Among the concerts they attended in the autumn of that year was one of particular interest to Princess Christian given in aid of the Red Cross Sisters. This was on 18th November at the Casino in Frankfurt when only music composed by Frederick the Great, a talented flautist, and his nephew Prince Louis Ferdinand, was played. The Princess had taken a special interest in the Red Cross since its inauguration over twenty years before on the initiative of M Jean Henri Dunant. After the publication of his book *Souvenir de Solferino* describing the horrors of the Austro-Italian war, it was felt that something had to be done for the victims of conflicts. The Red Cross Convention was signed by many countries and its work of impartial help to the injured and wounded was becoming well recognised. The concert combined two of the Princess's great interests: help for the sick and injured, and music.

There were expeditions to places of interest round about. One, undertaken by a large party, consisting of Emily, the young princesses, Else and others was to the Rochers Kappell at Bingen. Bingen was on the site of a Roman settlement, at the junction of the river Nahe and the Rhine: it had been an important place at the meeting of two trade routes for centuries. As a result, the town and the castle, Burg Klopp, which dominated the town, had had a stormy history and much had been destroyed. In the years after 1875, Burg Klopp was rebuilt in the style of a 15th-century Rhine castle; and, just before this visit, the town council had bought the castle and was using it as a town hall and museum. To reach Bingen, the party had to take a train to Rüdesheim and cross the Rhine. After lunch, they walked up to the Chapel from where they had wonderful views of the great bend in the Rhine; the steep slopes down to the river covered with vineyards, tinged green with new leaf; and the river itself busy with the traffic of barges. On their way back they explored the lower town, its shops and booths, while they waited for the steamer for their return journey. They were not back in Wiesbaden until 8.00 in the evening and they found Princess Christian exhausted. It had been a long day for Emily too, for she had started it with a morning ride with the princesses; but she still had the energy to discuss the events of the day with Else until late that night.

Riding became an important activity on this visit: it was one they all enjoyed, particularly Princess Louie, who was becoming a very proficient horsewoman. They hired horses from a riding school owned by the Knoop family. Their first ride was on April 8th. Emily writes:

> Princess Louie and I went out riding. We went to the riding school and mounted there and then rode towards Biebrich, a short way up the river, but had to come back as the horse Princess Louie rode pulled so. We got the bit changed and then started away again and went all the way to Biebrich. Got back at 12.30 and found all Wiesbaden collected to see us. Got off, changed and had lunch.

The next day they were out again and went to the Nerothal, on the northern outskirts of the town. Sometimes Thora joined them – before they had left England, Emily had taken her to a London tailor to have a new habit made. Once Emily 'had a dreadfully ugly roan animal' but she and Louie continued to go out regularly. Thora joined them for a really good expedition on the first of May.

> I and the two princesses rode after lunch with Herr Hans von Loew to the Platte. It was very hot. We got off there and had coffee and went to the top of the Schloss and then mounted again. Princess Louie and I rode each other's horses. We came down a new way through the woods, very steep and tree-y and got home at 5.30.[26]

Just before they left for England, all three had another 'good long ride with Herr von Loew, going to the Cramers' place where they had tea and were lent a groom to see them home'.

When the party returned in the autumn, there was a little riding until the weather got too cold. Emily mentions the names of some of the horses they rode; the princesses on Dolly and Lucie, and she on 'the young chestnut,

A snapshot of Emily, Princess Thora and Princess Louie accompanied by Herr von Loew returning to Wiesbaden from a ride with a number of interested onlookers among the trees.

Gretchen'. One ambitious outing was undertaken which might have ended in disaster. They set off from the riding school to Rettersdorf at 9.00 in the morning. The diary goes on:

> Princess Louie was taken badly with breathlessness after the horse ran away with her so I changed and was more or less run away with the whole way to Rettersdorf. Arrived exhausted. The whole family there. We had some food on arriving and then made ourselves tidy and then sat and talked till lunch at 1.30. Sat and talked after. Started back at 4 o'C. I rode another horse home as I was too tired to undertake the pulling animal.

Nothing so exhausting and alarming occurred on the last ride. Princess Louie and Emily settled for Dolly and Faust, a new grey. It was a good ride. They went to Neroberg and, as it was so late in the year, November 6th, it was nearly dark by the time they got in.

In addition to the friends that they made in Wiesbaden, it was easy for the princesses to meet their young relations in Darmstadt. One day in April 1889,

The Kurhaus in Wiesbaden where the party from Darmstadt and Emily listened to 'rousing music'.

Gretchen who had been with the Hesse family since the previous May, brought Prince Ernie and Princess Alix over to spend the day in Wiesbaden with their cousins. It sounds as if they all had a good time with lots of chat and laughter. After lunch, leaving Gretchen to keep Princess Christian company, the rest – Emily, the three young Princesses Thora, Louie, Alix and Prince Ernie – walked in the Colonnades and looked at the shops. They went into the jewellers and Prince Ernie bought one or two pieces, including some 'little rings'. Emily was left to pay the bill at the end of the month. There was a short stop at the Kurhaus to listen to the rousing music of the band, and then a visit to one of their favourite places during this period in Wiesbaden – tea at Lehmann's. One can imagine them in the elegant shop: the small round tables with beautiful white linen, fine china cups of delicately scented tea or rich chocolate with foaming snowy heads of cream and the delicious cakes, mouth-wateringly tempting. The happy day ended with Emily seeing them off at the station, just in time to catch the train to Mainz, then across the Rhine, and so back to Darmstadt.

A few days later, Princess Christian, Thora, Louie and Emily went over to Darmstadt for the day. On this occasion, they were met at the station by Fräulein von Grancy and Princess Alix and all went up to the Palace. The two older ladies went for a walk, and Emily ordered gloves at Zorns, a favourite shop, which she had patronised in previous years. On their return they sat with Gretchen and, later, all the princesses came in and talked. A pleasant family lunch followed with Princess Victoria, Prince Louis and Prince Abby.

The 1889 spring visit ended on a happy note, with most of the Christian family together in Wiesbaden. Princess Thora celebrated her 19th birthday on May 3rd. Her father came to join them towards the end of April, and the Princess and her daughters had some good days with him. The day before Princess Thora's birthday, the Prince took the young princesses into Frankfurt where they lunched with the Landgräfin, but were back in time to be with the Empress Vicky and her three daughters, who were making a quick visit to Princess Christian in Wiesbaden. They had come from Schlangenbad where the Empress was living while her new palace, Friedrichshof, near Homburg, was being built. After the visitors left, Emily dashed out to order the flowers for Princess Thora's birthday and, next morning, a table laden with flowers and presents greeted the nineteen-year-old.[27] Prince Abby came over from Darmstadt for a family luncheon and, in the evening, there was a party at the Knoops', where there was dancing until midnight. The Knoops had a family with children of the same ages as the young princesses and they played an increasingly important role in the lives of the princesses in Wiesbaden. They were also the owners of the riding school.

In the autumn of 1889, Princess Victoria, Princess Irène and Princess Alix came over to Wiesbaden once. They all lunched in the hotel and then went driving: Emily saw them off on their train. Princess Louie saw them once or twice more, later in the autumn, by which time Princess Thora had left the party in Wiesbaden. Emily was left very much as the companion for the younger princess, as her mother's health was so poor. Prince Albert sometimes came over from Darmstadt. He was there one day when they went over to the Knoops' and had 'great fun with a racing game and a slide' followed by a formal dinner. In their lodgings Princess Louie did not want always to meet the many people who came seeking an audience with her mother – it was one of Emily's jobs to arrange these – and so would keep 'popping in and out of my room' to avoid the importunate!

Later that year, Prince Christle and his brother discovered an unusual entertainment when 'Buffalo Bill' came to Frankfurt. Their reports of it were so enthusiastic that the whole family was encouraged to go. Everyone was talking about it. Here was something completely different. Emily made a short note: 'We all went to Frankfurt to join the Dicshaus and went to Buffalo Bill'. This was certainly a change from the endless operas and classical plays. William Cody, Buffalo Bill, had begun his theatrical extravaganza of the Wild West in 1883. By 1887, it was being performed in Madison Square Garden in New York and then went on tour in Europe. Queen Victoria saw it three times; and so it had been given the seal of Royal approval. Away in Germany, the Christian family joined their friends to see this show with Indians, amazing trick riders and skilful ropers. The thunder of the horses' hooves, the swishing of their tails and manes, the parades of wild animals such as buffalo, moose and deer and the precision of Annie Oakley's sharp-shooting, all compounded to make a thrilling evening. One can imagine the excitement of the younger members of the party and the lively chatter on the train back to Wiesbaden.

This was the princesses' life while abroad: a mixture of entertainments, music, concerts, dances, parties and riding; instruction in some subjects – but none too intensive – attending their mother and bearing with her ill health; friendships with a few families and frequent meetings with their relations, particularly Princess Alix. During these years, important events for both the Princess and Emily were going on elsewhere. Princess Vicky and Prince Sandro of Battenberg were passing through very difficult times: Princess Christian and Emily became slightly involved with both. And Emily's sister, Catherine Grace, was following her chosen career in nursing – one dear to the heart of Princess Christian – and one which she and Emily followed with interest

CHAPTER SIX

Two Tragedies: Potsdam and Bulgaria

The year 1888 saw the tragedy of the brief reign of Friedrich III, husband of Vicky, Queen Victoria's eldest daughter, as Kaiser of Germany. This clever and liberal-minded man, who had been waiting for many years to succeed to the throne of Germany, was desperately ill with cancer of the throat when his father finally died at over 90. His reign lasted just 98 days and Wilhelm II his son could hardly wait to get into the saddle and push his mother firmly and brutally into the background, ably abetted by Bismarck. All the liberal ideas which Vicky and Friedrich had waited so long to implement were overturned. Bismarck, who for years had mistrusted Vicky with what he considered her

Crown Prince Friedrich and Princess Vicky in 1885. Three more years were to pass until he succeeded his father by which time cancer gave him only 98 days to reign.

undue English influence over her husband, was able with Wilhelm to set Germany on the aggressively nationalistic and expansionist course, which eventually led to the First World War.

A little over a month after Friedrich III's death, on June 15th 1888, Emily found herself accompanying Princess Christian on a journey to Berlin and Potsdam to try and console and help her sister and her three daughters. The Dowager Empress was still being allowed to live in Friedrichskron, the palace at Potsdam where her husband had died, but she can barely have recovered from the ruthless way in which she had been treated by her son immediately after his father's death. Both Wilhelm and Bismarck had become obsessed with the idea that Friedrich and Vicky had been hatching plots and had sent German state papers to England. They were convinced that incriminating evidence would be found in the Palace; so, almost the minute his father died, Wilhelm had ordered that the Palace should be surrounded by troops and a thorough search made of all the rooms and bureaux. Nothing incriminating was found, but that didn't stop Bismarck and others, who had once apparently been loyal to Friedrich, from spreading the word that Vicky had purloined state papers and had sent them abroad with a view to their publication. It is true that Friedrich and Vicky, suspecting the worst, had sent boxes of private papers back to

Emily in her mourning dress at Friedrichskron, the palace in Potsdam where the Dowager Empress Vicky was still living in 1888.

Dowager Empress Vicky and her three daughters in mourning.

England. At first, Vicky was adamant that her mother should not return any papers but later was persuaded that some should be sent back to Germany in order that the Minister of Justice, who appears to have been one of the few people that Vicky trusted, could look through them and vouch that there were no state papers. Vicky urged her mother to keep the correspondence between them, as this was the only record she had of her life with Friedrich: for, unlike her mother, she had never kept a journal.

These moves were all part of what appears to have been a concerted plan by his son to eliminate the record and memory of Friedrich III from the history of Germany. The funeral had been ordered within 72 hours of his death; there was barely time for viewing the body; no lying in state in the capital and no great funeral cortège, as there had been for the 90-year-old Kaiser who had died just three months before; no heads of state were invited to pay their last respects. But the Prince and Princess of Wales had managed to be there. The poor widow was so upset that neither she nor her daughters attended the ceremony in the little Church of Peace in the Park but held a private service in their farmstead in the village of Bornstedt.

Taking no time off to mourn his father, the new Kaiser, a month after his accession, sailed off to Russia to visit Tsar Alexander III. This certainly did not please Queen Victoria who considered that his first visit abroad 'to show himself off' – as she put it – should have been made to her. It was at this time and against this background that Princess Christian made her visit to Potsdam. She and Emily arrived on July 19th, suitably dressed in deep mourning, and were met by Princess Victoria and several ladies. Emily was shown to her room 'where I put on my cap' and there is a photo of her suitably and sombrely attired. Later that first evening

> The Empress came in through my rooms and was most kind. We had supper at 8 with the Empress and the Psses. Went out on the terrace a little with Pss Victoria.

During the visit Emily had many chats with Princess Victoria who was going through a very difficult time. She had fallen in love with Prince Alexander (Sandro) of Battenberg, during the time when he was the Prince of Bulgaria and had become the hero of the battle of Slivnitza. Her love was reciprocated and they became engaged. Her parents and Queen Victoria were pleased. Not so Bismarck, Wilhelm or the Russians. Circumstances changed, Prince Alexander abdicated and Wilhelm forbad the marriage. Princess Victoria became just another pawn, cast aside in the intrigues of the great powers. So, disappointment in love was added to the sadness of her father's death. As with Princess Louie in the '90s, one gets the impression that Emily was a willing and sympathetic listener, just the person for the young to confide in.

The next evening after dinner, the Princess and a Mlle Bujard were able to give Emily her first sight of fireflies. These had appeared in the very hot weather during which many of the party suffered from headaches and the Empress had a bad attack of neuralgia. These ailments could well have been caused by the emotional strain as well as the very sultry weather. Hanging over the Empress was the uncertainty as to where she could live in the future. Her son had declared that he did not wish her to remain in Friedrichskron and had made little effort to put another suitable palace at her disposal despite at least two firm letters from his grandmother, Queen Victoria.

They visited the late Emperor's coffin in the nearby Friedrichkirche several times during the first few days – one evening driving over with the Empress and walking back in the dusk among the fireflies. They viewed the thousands of wreaths which had been sent from all over the world on display in the orangery. But it wasn't always something to do with the funeral: the Empress and her children did much to show her sister and Emily the delights of the country round about. They went driving with them to visit other houses and palaces. On the 24th, five days after they had arrived, they went on quite an expedition:

> I drove out with the Empress, Princess Christian and Princess Sophie. Princess Victoria and Princess Mossy followed in a little cart. We drove past the Wild Park to the Hafel. Got out and walked along the heavy sandy road. Crossed over in a ferry punt, carriage and all and came round the other side of the water and back through Potsdam. Stopped at the Friederichkirche and then walked home from there. Sat out evening.

The mornings were fresher and cooler and on many of them Emily enjoyed a couple of hours' riding, usually with Princess Victoria, once with Prince Leopold, and with other members of the household and grooms. Emily was allowed to ride the late Emperor's favourite horse, Härte, on two occasions and really enjoyed it. On another morning she was given Count Sechendorff's Irish horse and was delighted with the more comfortable saddle and fine mount.

It wasn't all pleasure and relaxation: there was work to be done. Emily spent even more time than usual writing letters; and Princess Christian was very busy too and needed much help 'arranging' papers. She doesn't say what papers but, interestingly, this is the only time she mentions 'papers' as such – not letters or accounts but 'papers', and the word occurs twice in a few days. Saturdays were especially busy. This was the day the 'messenger' (diplomatic) bag went and Emily was always hurrying to get as many letters done as possible.

On the day when Princess Christian and Emily were about to leave the Empress, there was a very touching ceremony when the late Emperor's old charger, Wörth, was brought round at the Empress's command. This day, August 6th, was the anniversary of the battle of Wörth in 1870.

> He came in his rug with oak leaves on his head and she fed him with sugar. He looked very thin and old but in good health – the poor Empress broke down quite.

Memories of her husband in his prime when he rode this fine horse into battle were very poignant. In a letter written to her mother the same day, Vicky wrote 'How proudly it carried him all day (his day 18 years ago) and at Sedan'. By this time, she, Vicky, was one of the few people left in Berlin who dared to speak or write about her husband's role in the Franco-Prussian War or its aftermath, the unification of Germany. The propaganda machine had ensured that all the credit for this had become Bismarck's.

Princess Christian and Emily travelled directly from Berlin to Homburg Spa for their yearly visit, arriving on August 7th, and they remained in Germany until nearly the end of November. Emily saw little of the family from Darmstadt that year, but she did meet the Battenbergs when she and Princess Helena visited Jugenheim towards the end of September at the request of Queen Victoria. Prince Alexander and his wife were there to greet them. She had formerly been the Countess Julie Hauke and this morganatic marriage many years before had caused great disapproval, especially in Russia, where the Prince, brother of Marie the then Tsarina, had been serving in the Russian Army. But the years had softened opinions and all was now calm. Also at home were their daughter-in-law Princess Victoria, wife of Louis Battenberg, and their second son Prince Alexander (Sandro), lately Sovereign Prince of Bulgaria. It was he that Princess Christian had come, especially, to see.

This was only a few weeks after Princess Christian and Emily had been staying in Potsdam; so no doubt both were anxious to talk to the young man

Sovereign Prince Alexander of Bulgaria, Sandro Battenberg.

Valentine Chirol: an impeccably dressed English gentleman. He spent much of his career as a newspaper correspondent travelling in the Middle and Far East.

who had meant so much to Princess Victoria, whom they had just been visiting, and to hear of his amazing adventures. Prince Sandro by now had abdicated finally from his unhappy position in Bulgaria, had retreated from the political stage and was recuperating at home.

Perhaps he told them a little of how he had come to play this part in history. He had been serving with the Russian Army in the Turkish War of 1877 when the great powers were jockeying for position and influence over the various emerging states of the Balkans at the break-up of the moribund Turkish Empire. As a result of his achievements and general bearing Prince Sandro was held in high esteem by Tsar Alexander II. When the small state of Bulgaria, autonomous but still subject to the formal suzerainty of Turkey, was created under the Treaty of Berlin (1878), the great Powers – but in reality he, Tsar Alexander, with Bismarck – persuaded Prince Sandro in 1879 to become the Sovereign Prince. It had been an impossible job from the beginning in this impoverished and corrupt country; the 'palace' he was expected to live in was a decayed two-storey building with the roof falling in. For a while he had the backing of the Tsar of Russia and it was just possible that he might have been able to make a civilised country of Bulgaria. But, after Tsar Alexander II's assassination in 1881,[28] and after a Russian-engineered coup d'état in Bulgaria which Sandro in the beginning appeared to support, he was put in the position of choosing between standing up for his own people, as the Bulgarians had become, or slavishly following the selfish policies of Russia and condoning the corruption of the Russian officials sent from St Petersburg to carry them out. The Powers had thought they would have a compliant puppet. They discovered a man of integrity.

Valentine Chirol, a reputed newspaper correspondent who had in 1881 reported on the position in Bulgaria after the Russian-inspired coup, returned in 1885. By this time Sandro had become the idol of the Bulgarians. He had united parts of the country without bloodshed, but also without the approval of the Russians, and had defeated their protégé, Serbia, decisively at the battle of Slivnitza. He had also become engaged to Princess Victoria of Prussia. Within a year, however, his position became untenable. A small band of soldiers mutinied, abducted him at pistol point from his own palace and conveyed him as a state prisoner in his own yacht down the Danube into Russian territory. Although he was released and allowed to return briefly, much to the enthusiasm of a large part of the population, it was only to abdicate. He had become convinced that this would be best for his adopted people to save the country from the hatred of Tsar Alexander III and Bismarck.

Chirol accompanied Prince Sandro on this last sad journey from Bulgaria and was able to get the Prince's own explanation as to why he had made this decision – a decision questioned for its wisdom by many of Sandro's friends and admirers and found utterly bewildering by most ordinary Bulgarians. Chirol gives a moving and graphic description of the journey.

> No railway had then reached Sofia and ... the most convenient alternative was the carriage road over the north-eastern spurs of the Balkans to Lom Palanka on the Danube.
>
> Outside the Palace, then the only modern building of any importance in a capital which had hardly outgrown the squalor of a small provincial Turkish town, was drawn up a procession of some fifteen or twenty ramshackle travelling carriages each with its team of three wiry little horses harnessed, Russian fashion, abreast. Into these were packed the Prince's suite, a few personal friends, some Bulgarian officials and officers. Two State carriages drove out of the Palace courtyard, in the first was the Prince himself with his devoted brother, Prince Franz Joseph of

Battenberg. A great roar of cheering, which had something in it of the deep wail of mourning, arose from the dense mass of people collected in the square and the adjoining streets to catch a last glimpse of the Prince who had transformed Bulgaria from a geographical expression into a Balkan power with which not only the older Balkan states but the Great Powers of Europe had already to reckon. Never perhaps was his popularity greater but bewilderment was almost equally apparent amongst the crowds that only gradually thinned down as the cortege began to climb the foothills of the Balkans on a hot early autumn afternoon. The peasants whom we passed on the road doffed their caps and stopped to watch the long procession of carriages in obvious amazement. Wherever we halted for a few minutes' rest or to change horses we were plied with anxious and wondering enquiries. The road was bad, the dust was almost suffocating and the drive over steep and sinuous hills was long and wearisome up to the Petro Han Pass, nearly 6,000 feet above the sea and down again into the valley of the Danube.

The second day was already well advanced when at last we reached Lom Palanka and the steamer waiting to convey the Prince up the Danube to a Rumanian railway station at Turn-Severin. Another large gathering of Bulgarians had hurried from all the adjoining districts and again at Widdin, where the Prince landed for a couple of hours, the last he ever spent on Bulgarian soil, to appeal once more to the patience and self restraint of his army and people whose national interests he could no longer serve except by leaving them, there were signs as there had been in Sofia, not only of passionate grief but utter incomprehension. Why? Oh why, was the Prince deserting them?

Prince Alexander may have seen some such thoughts lingering in my mind also, when he sent for me to join him as we steamed up the river and soon left the Bulgarian shore far behind us. He asked me whether I approved of his decision, but without waiting for an answer he went on to say with the utmost emphasis that it was the only decision at which it had been possible for him conscientiously to arrive. He referred at once to a telegram from the Tsar handed to him at Rustchuk, at

> the moment when his own people were welcoming him back to Bulgaria, after he had been shamefully kidnapped at Russian instigation. The telegram he could only regard as a definite ultimatum, since it told him that Bulgaria would have to take the consequences if he elected to cling to his throne in defiance of the Tsar's wishes. Was it not merely the culminating expression of hostility which Alexander III had displayed towards him almost from the moment he had succeeded to the Russian throne?

Prince Sandro had been caught in the complex web of intrigue which was endemic to the Balkans and his skills as a military man were no match for wily political manipulators such as the Tsar and Bismarck. When Emily met him at Jugenheim, these momentous events were in the past, but the soreness and sadness remained. He appeared to be a broken man who had relinquished all his princely titles and was now content with the newly-granted Hessian title of Count Hartenau. Sandro no doubt found sympathetic listeners in Princess Helena and Emily who had come at Queen Victoria's wish and they no doubt reported back to her the gist of their conversations.

More happily, his future personal life took a turn for the better. He fell in love with a beautiful opera singer, Johanna Loisinger, and married her in 1889. They had four happy years together before his death from appendicitis in 1893. The future of Princess Victoria, perhaps, appeared to take a turn for the better. In 1891 she married another minor German royal, Prince Adolf of Schaumberg-Lippe; and Princess Christian, Princess Thora and Emily attended the wedding in Berlin.

CHAPTER SEVEN

Nursing at Home and Abroad

The change in nursing during the nineteenth century from the 'Nursing Record'.

The development of nursing gathered momentum throughout the 19th century. Mrs Gamp and her bottle of gin were replaced by increasingly well-educated and respectable women, even 'ladies'. Germany led the way: the foundation of an institute in 1836 at Kaiserwerth on the Rhine, provided systematic training – Florence Nightingale attended this institute in 1851. As a result, when the terrible sufferings of soldiers in the Crimean war, caused by inefficient nursing and the dreadful state of the hospitals, became known, she was ready and able to volunteer her services. She sailed to the conflict in 1854 accompanied by thirty-four nurses; the difference they made is well known. They gained a great reputation, sometimes perhaps too sentimentally expressed; for she was in fact a formidable organiser.

Miss Nightingale's fame spread and influenced many women who had a desire to help their fellow beings; Princess Christian was one. She was really interested in nursing but her position made it impossible for her to have practical experience. Perhaps this is why she took such an interest in the career of Catherine Grace Loch. Early in her life Cathy had expressed a desire to nurse but her father, like so many other parents of the time, was reluctant to see her take up this work. It is said that Princess Christian was the one who persuaded him at last to change his mind. When Cathy reached the age of twenty-five in 1879, two years after her father's death, she was allowed to begin her training. She started as a probationer at Winchester; then, in 1882, she was appointed sister-in-charge of the men's surgical ward, Darker Ward, at St Bartholomew's, London.

Catherine Grace Loch, Cathy, in her nurses uniform c.1882.

At this time, Miss Manson – a forceful, efficient twenty-four-year-old – had recently been appointed Matron. She had very definite ideas about the training of nurses. She set out to raise standards, extend the training period to three years and improve their food, off-duty hours and holidays. How much this affected Cathy is not known; but she must have done a good job as the sister of Darker Ward, for she remained in the post until late 1887. In this year Miss Manson resigned, married a well-known physician, and started the campaign for the registration of nurses.

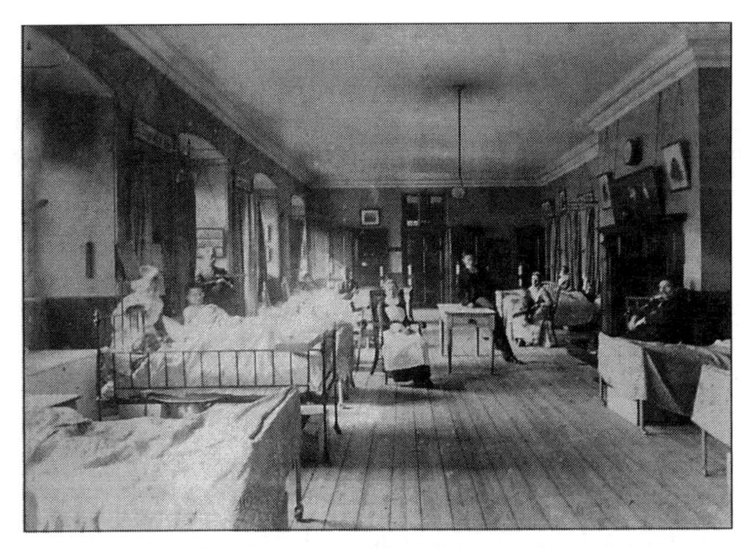

Darker Ward in St Bartholomew's Hospital, London in the early 1880s.

An Operating Theatre in St Bartholomew's Hospital, London in the early 1880s.

Princess Christian would have had close contact with Mrs Bedford Fenwick as Miss Manson now became. It was Mrs Fenwick who called a meeting of matrons in 1887 to discuss the future organisation of the nursing profession. It was decided to form an association of nurses and later in the year this was given the name of the British Nurses' Association. The Association was formally launched at a public meeting in February 1888 and Princess Christian accepted the presidency. Four years later in 1892, with the Princess's help, the Association – now with the prefix Royal, after scrutiny by a Privy Council enquiry – was granted a Royal Charter of Incorporation (Plate 3). Emily in her diary noted that the Princess was immensely pleased. The evolution of the nursing profession was not all plain sailing, however. The Princess must have had many anxious moments over the years, as the different factions argued about how the nursing profession could best be organised. Although the registration of professionally qualified nurses was the underlying aim of all involved, it took a quarter of a century before the Nurses' Registration Act 1919 was on the statute books. By this time, Princess Christian was 77 but, even at this age, she still retained an active interest in nursing and hospitals – attending, in just one week in March of that year, a meeting on 'Midwives at Mrs McKinnon's house', paying a visit to the Royal Free Hospital and giving a paper at a meeting on 'First Aid against tropical diseases'.

In 1887, the year that Mrs Bedford Fenwick resigned from practical nursing and took up campaigning, Cathy heard that the India Office had decided to send out Nursing Sisters to work in the British Military Hospitals in India. She had wished to go to India all her life; here was her opportunity, many of her relations had served in India and Burma. She felt that now she was competent to undertake this new challenge, sad though she would be to leave her colleagues at Barts. In February 1888 she sailed on the troopship *Malabar* and arrived in Bombay in March. Cathy had been appointed one of the two Lady Superintendents and there were eight nursing sisters. She was posted, with five of these, to the garrison town of Rawalpindi, not far from the North-West Frontier of British jurisdiction in India. Her early letters[29] to her sisters were full of her impressions: what the place was like; the weather with the great heat and the appalling sandstorms, and her work in the hospital. But, on October 10th while Emily was in Germany, she 'heard from Cathy that she and some of the sisters were to go with the troops up to the Black Mountain expedition'. This was one of many expeditions made by the army at intervals to assert British domination over the various tribes of the North-West frontier.

On September 29th 1888, Cathy and Sister Latch set off on horseback from Murree – the hill station at 7,500 feet about forty miles from Rawalpindi, to join the expeditionary force at Oghi. At first, they rode through magnificent forests of coniferous trees above deep valleys with, in the distance, range upon range of blue mountains. Later, they were among bare hills, with occasional huts and small patches of cornfields, which reminded Cathy of parts of

The Nursing Sisters outside their quarters at Rawalpindi, India c.1888.

Sutherland. It took them four days to reach the small military station of Abbottabad, where they were joined by three sisters who had travelled directly from Rawalpindi. They set off with an armed guard and, a couple of days later, reached Manserah and Kakhi where they dined

> camp fashion with the officers of the 15th Bengal Cavalry and heard distant firing, a smart engagement having taken place that day with the enemy tribesmen at Oghi.

Her letter to her sisters written on October 6th continues:

> We got up at five o'clock, and sat in a row shivering, for it was bitterly cold before sunrise, while the tents and things were being packed on the mules and camels. I do think camels are horrid animals, so ugly, and they snarl and roar all the time they are being loaded and make a terrible noise; there is no romance about them at all! We went on our way with our armed 'sowar' (cavalry man) either following or leading, and climbed up and up the fearfully steep zigzagging narrow path of the Sussel pass,

Camels, which Cathy thought had 'no romance' waiting to be loaded in the camp at Haripur.

all covered with water-worn boulders in confusion, and Scots firs and brown fir needles. It was very beautiful and wild, especially as we got higher. For a long time, at every turn in the road, we looked back at Kakhi and the river and corn fields beyond. Then all at once, one gets over the top and suddenly finds oneself in the entrance of the Oghi valley, bounded by the Black Mountain all down one side of it and one could plainly see all the spurs where they fought yesterday and the Base camp, like little specks, about seven miles off. By the time we got there, Oghi, it was intensely hot … I have been round the tents this afternoon. There are three or four men from yesterday's fight wounded severely but not dangerously … Our troops have gone over the crest of the mountain and we could not see any of them, but we heard the shots and saw smoke of burning villages. Oghi is not a pretty place; it is in the Agror valley, very wild and bleak, and too much down in a hollow. There is a little peep of a Kashmir snow peak straight in front of our tents, and this is a great joy to me. We and the servants are all under martial law of course and our tents are pitched in straight camp lines with all

> the others. Every one has to be up and every tent has to be opened wide and tidy before eight in the morning so they can see through the camp from end to end. On our left is the Fort; and about forty prisoners were marched down the hill this afternoon firmly bound, and taken into it. The gate is about fifty yards from our tents, and if they tried to rush this camp as was done at Darband, I don't think my dear little revolver would protect me for long! Some of the Seaforth Highlanders are here and we have bagpipes going all day. At night a double guard of Seaforths marches up and down and constantly challenges.

The next letter, written only four days later started off by saying that, now they were settled in at Oghi and had been there for a day or so, it no longer felt exciting and seemed 'quite ordinary and natural'. They got on well with Dr Welch who was in charge and, once he had seen that each of them could do a dressing, he left them to get on with it. About four to ten wounded were brought in each day and all seemed to be well under control. A few days later, however, two sisters were ordered to Darband about fourteen miles away and the headquarters of the Hasara field force. There was no direct road and a much

A studio portrait of Sister Welchman in riding dress.
She accompanied Cathy on their epic ride from Oghi to Darband.

more roundabout route had to be taken. It was decided that Cathy and Sister Welchman should go and, because of administrative muddles, they had a very exciting time getting to Darband.

They set off from Oghi and went via Abbottabad and on to Haripur where they were unable to obtain an escort of 'sowars'. Their own ponies were not available, so they hired bazaar animals with their drivers and hoped to reach Darband before nightfall 'by pressing hard'. But, after a hot and quite strenuous ride through cultivated lands with several river crossings, night overtook them. The pony men talked nervously of robbers. In the darkness they came to a campfire and the pony men would go no further. There was no choice; they were obliged to remain there for the night. Supping off a tin of soup, biscuits and cocoa, they slept at the road side. The next morning they set off for a very hot ride of eleven miles through arid country. There was

> nothing but hills which were merely big mounds of shingle dotted over with little green bushes, which made the hills look as if they had broken out in a rash.

Their route climbed all the time, and eventually they came to a pass and saw the Indus far below them. They reached a rather unprepossessing village and managed to obtain some food – 'tea and eggs nearly raw and eventually some chupatties spread with stinking butter and curried fowl'. They were stuck for hours, in their thick clothing, in great heat until three minute donkeys were brought from a nearby village. They were 'no bigger than the goats to be seen drawing carriages at an English seaside place.' They did the job, however, and eventually the party set out on the seven miles to Darband. It was 4.30 in the afternoon. Cathy's letter went on:

> The road is very good, and after a bit the mountains close in altogether and the Indus runs through a narrow gorge; and the road rising higher and higher we seemed to be hemmed in by precipices all round. The sun set about 6.30 and our pony drivers got more and more frightened and expected to find robbers behind every rock; one stayed behind altogether and the other bemoaned himself all the time. The road then became frightful and if it had not been for the moon we must have sat down under a rock and waited for day ... it seemed for ever to wind

round and round ravines and precipices and often was nothing but a water course. Once we mistook a real watercourse for the road and wandered up it and had some difficulty in getting back again when it turned out to be impassable. I never saw such huge boulders, some of them as big as a large house ... it is most weird altogether. The native with us was perfectly terrified and I can't tell you how glad Sister Welchman and I were that we both carried revolvers. I don't think either of us was frightened ... only excited.

Darband Camp 1892, Surgeon Captain Murray in camp in the Indus valley.

They found that the camp was another two or three miles beyond the village, without a real road – only a track over a shingly plain with boulders and deep sand, but at last they heard a bugle, were found by a kindly soldier who put them on their way to the hospital which was, of course, at the furthest end of the camp. At last, weary and hungry, they found the medical officer, Dr Fawcett, who was astonished to see them, as it was long after dark and all at the camp had gone to bed. He found them their tent, doolies, brown hospital blankets and even 'provided us with a tin of his own cocoa and raked up a piece of bread and cold mutton-bone from somebody's rations'. After all their effort there wasn't much to do in the way of nursing wounded from the battles:

Darband Camp, 1892 A patient shaded, from the bright sun, in hospital tent.

several Tommies had bayonet wounds 'given to each other during a night scare', and a few cases of enteric and fever. The white ants and the fine white dust, like flour, were very tiresome. The Commander-in-Chief Sir Frederick Roberts and Lady Roberts paid the camp a visit just before the close of the campaign and both were very pleased with the difference they found that the nursing sisters had made.

The ride which Cathy and Sister Welchman had undertaken became 'quite historical' and they heard of it from all directions. They found that the Indus valley was much more unhealthy than Oghi and there was a 'good deal of fever and dysentery among the men in spite of the gravelly soil.' Enteric fever cases were their most common patients, and many died from this cause despite the nursing. They took great care of the sick men, frequently sitting up with them all night, and were grieved and saddened when death intervened. Nursing care was often all that could be offered. Neither the cause nor the cure of many complaints were known at the time, and so the care of the Nursing Sisters was of paramount importance to the patients. Cathy did distinguish enteric from typhoid, but the term enteric was used to cover typhus and dysentery. Both probably occurred, and both may well have been made worse by the patients also suffering from malaria which, on its own, she referred to as intermittent

Bridge over the Jhelum river in Kashmir looking peaceful and clean.

fever. In 1888 Donald Ross had not even begun his studies on malaria: the cause of the disease and the life cycle of the parasite, which involved anopheles mosquitoes and humans, were not discovered until 1897 – 98.

The most dreaded disease was cholera; Cathy noted, on several occasions, outbreaks in various military stations, including the hill station Murree. She did not make the distinction that it is a waterborne disease and spread through poor sanitation, but hinted at it when she wrote on June 3rd 1892 that:

> Cholera in Kashmir seems to be frightfully bad and I greatly fear the epidemic will ultimately come down here; it is sure to come down the Jhelum river … it always does.

Later that same year, she was again in Haripur. This was at the time that Prince Christle was with his regiment on a Black Mountain expedition which made Princess Christian very anxious. The two did meet briefly, Prince Christle mentions meeting Emily's sister in his diary. Cathy noted that all the nursing staff are very well and she took a photograph, with her newly acquired camera, of the 'Queen's Own (Cholera) Dodgers'. There had been some cases of cholera in the camp and the staff were not allowed to return to Rawalpindi

Haripur Quarantine Camp where the nurses were all well despite cholera. Cathy and Sister Murray with Sam. Wherever she was in India Cathy always had a dog with her.

until a period of quarantine was finished. But, in a letter written a few days later, she went on to say that she didn't believe that cholera was transmitted by direct infection.

> If it were infectious in anything like proportion to its virulence as an epidemic, doctors and nurses would have no chance at all, whereas as a matter of fact they rarely take it … I should say less often, certainly not more, than any other individuals who happen to be in the District. In the recent epidemic at Murree the three doctors who died got it as ordinary individuals, because they were living in the houses which were chiefly attacked; they did not get it in the course of their work.

Emily would often have told the Princess much of what was in Cathy's letters. On several occasions, especially when they were at Wiesbaden, she read them aloud to the Princess and her daughters. There was particular interest when Prince Christle was out there. The Princess would have been interested in the descriptions of the nursing and the young princesses would have been

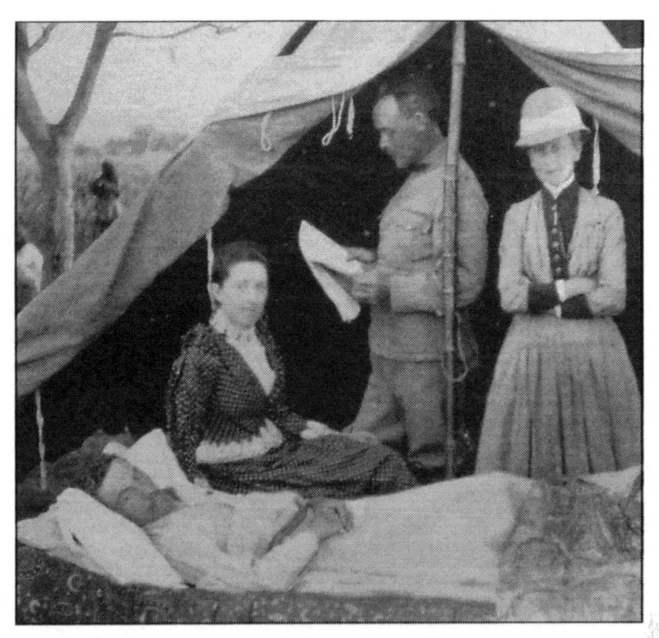

Cathy's camera records the 'Queen's Own (Cholera) Dodgers' in Haripur. Lieutenant Moore, the patient, is accompanied by his wife, Cathy and an orderly in the Haripur Quarantine Camp.

fascinated by Cathy's adventures with her dogs and on horseback. Later, Cathy's comments on cholera would have been of use to the Princess, for, in 1892, there was a very bad epidemic in Europe and the Princess was one of the members of the cholera committee set up in London.

Cathy was a person with strong views about the organisation of the nursing and the treatment of her staff. She frequently crossed swords with the military authorities in Simla. She used her letters to her sisters to let off steam, and I am sure that, though her protests to the senior medical people would have been strongly worded, they would have been reasonable, her spleen having been vented in her private correspondence. There is no doubt that it was not an easy assignment. There were only ten nursing sisters in the first group and these, immediately on disembarking at Bombay, were split up. Cathy with five sisters being sent to Rawalpindi; the other Lady Superintendent and three nurses sent to Bangalore. The Medical Officers received them respectfully and they were introduced to the other officers of the cantonment as 'ladies'. This was important and defined their status in the strict hierarchy, but also brought its problems; there was the danger of too many invitations to dances and dinners coming to them. As they were so thinly spread, if they accepted them all, they would be quite unfit to work. When she decreed that she would not give leave for dances as this would keep them out so late, 'they took it very well'.

The medical authorities had a tendency to direct the nursing sisters to other camps and cantonments without consulting Cathy and this infuriated her. Late in November, after her return from the Black Mountain expedition, orders came to send two nursing sisters from Rawalpindi to Peshawar and three to Sialkot. She considered that three sisters were not enough and that two sisters could not possibly work a station hospital satisfactorily. 'They would either kill themselves or they could not be responsible for the patients, perhaps both!' The difficulties of inadequate numbers recur time and time again in her letters, but also the great importance of having nurses of the right calibre. The conditions under which they lived and worked were distinctly trying. The clothing they wore, the intense heat, the dust storms and the flies, not to mention the armies of 'beasties' which came to share night duty with them, all taxed the good humour and resilience of the sisters.

Their work in the wards, directed by the medical officers, was backed up by the army orderlies. They took their orders from the nursing sisters and, if they were the same group of men for a considerable period, things went smoothly, but the secondment of men to this job was of secondary importance to the regimental officers. Men were taken from whichever regiment happened to be in the station at the time, and so the arrangement was far from satisfactory. As Cathy wrote at the end of December 1888:

> Dec. 22 ... We are frightfully busy just now. I do not think we have ever had so many cases or so many bad ones before, chiefly enterics and pneumonias and one or two liver cases and it makes it very difficult to manage extra things, being only three of us. There is so much to do now that we have to go on two together in the mornings and so get a few hours off by turn in the afternoon.
>
> Dec 28 ... The work in the wards seems easier now; I do not know why, for we have just as many patients, in fact more. But it is very odd, how at times when one is nursing a large number of cases there seems to be a perfect rush for a few days and then somehow things get in a groove and there seems less to do although the patients may really be just the same. For one thing

> we have been going through much tribulation with the orderlies. We had some very good men in our original ward, but in the new ward and for the extra cases in the verandah we had a wretched lot belonging to a regiment which was only passing through Pindi. They did not care a fig, and were quite stupid and not civil and frequently drunk. Several times I had to put the night orderly to bed and do his work myself. They drank the patients' brandy too, so we had to give every drop ourselves. Our own special orderlies took their Christmas festivities in much more methodical fashion. They each went on the booze of course – no soldier would think he had spent Christmas properly without – but they did it in turns.

Most of the time that she was in India Cathy continued to do battle with the administration, but always with tact and firmness. Gradually, the sterling work that the Nursing Sisters achieved was recognised. Early in 1889 she noted that she had just been writing to Miss Nightingale in answer to one of her's in which it is obvious that news of what was happening in India was reaching her and many of the reports were very favourable. Cathy also mentions that 'we shall have medals for the Black Mountain, which will be very jolly'. She acknowledges that she got a lot of support from Lady Roberts, the wife of the Commander-in-Chief. On November 19th 1891 she wrote:

> I have got a very friendly and hearty telegram of congratulation from Lady Roberts about the Royal Red Cross (medal) ... if you (Emily) are writing to the Queen or through the Princess (Christian) could you say something for me as to how pleased and proud I am at the honour being given to the three of us. (The Sisters who nursed on the Black Mountain expedition of 1888).

Cathy, with periods of leave back in England and some fascinating travels, either on tours of inspection or on local leave to parts of India, Kashmir, Ladakh, Nepal, Tibet and Burma – recorded in several photograph albums – remained working in India until her career was cut short by a stroke in 1901. She was sent back to England and kept hoping that she would be able to return. But her health had been undermined and she never fully recovered. She

Sister R A Betty, Cathy's great friend who succeeded her as Senior Lady Superintendent of Nursing.

was appointed a member of the Ladies' Board at the India Office in February 1903. Writing in a letter to her great friend Miss R. A. Betty (always referred to as Betty) in 1903 [30], Cathy expanded on this:

> I am formally offered to sit on a Board consisting of two ladies only, at the India Office four times a year, for choosing candidates for India ... This is an offer without prejudice to my return to India at the end of my present leave should the Medical Board then report me fit for duty ... I accept the nomination, as it does not require me to give up all thoughts of India.

Emily felt that Cathy was immensely gratified at being asked to fill this post She wrote, after Cathy's death:

> I think it prolonged her life; for it quite broke her heart when she had to resign her work in the service and this gave her a little hold on the former life and interest, and was really the only interest she had in the last year of her life.

The Tsarina's Hospital train in Russia during the 1914-18 War.

When the final decision was made by the Medical Board of the India Office, Cathy wrote to Miss Betty again, saying:

> They were all very nice and kind; however, it is all over and done nothing makes any difference. It has come so suddenly at the last that I sit most of the time in a blank … Oh! It is very sad, and I have nothing to do except remember and think over the past delights and glories. I cannot imagine any kind of nursing work that would appeal to me after our life in India and our work there.

Behind the scenes Princess Christian remained in contact with Cathy. She had followed her career in India, perhaps helped with the appointment to the 'Ladies' Board' and visited her at the Cottage. It was sad for her to see this young protégée, through whom she had learned so much about nursing abroad and who was loved a respected by so many – from the Surgeon-General to the nurses and orderlies – fade slowly away, so comparatively young, in 1904.

Princess Christian had an active interest in nursing all her life. She undertook some practical training in the early 1880s and continued her involvement on committees until the 1920s. Inevitably changes took place. Queen Alexandra took over the Army Nursing Service, including the Princess Christian Army Nursing Reserve. The Queen Alexandra's Royal Army Nursing Corps, the QAs, were brought into being. But, as mentioned earlier in the chapter, the Princess was able in 1919, at last, to see the passing of the Nurses' Registration Act. She had also taken a great interest in the establishment of hospitals and the care of the wounded. During the Boer War and the 1914 – 18 War this took the practical form of endowing hospital trains. In 1904, Emily was with the Princess during her visit to South Africa when she visited many of the hospitals and her hospital train which had been so valuable in helping the sick and wounded during that war.

So far, Princess Alix has appeared as a young girl but as her life progressed she too became very interested in nursing and helping the injured. When war between Russian and Germany broke out in 1914 she and her older daughters all took some nursing training. One of the last postcards which Emily received from the Tsarina early in 1917 was of one of her hospital trains (Plate 16).

CHAPTER EIGHT

Berlin 1890: a Wedding and a Betrothal

Now let us return to some of Queen Victoria's extensive family as they appear in Emily's diaries. Princess Thora and Princess Louie were two of the Queen's brood of granddaughters, over twenty of them, of whom fourteen were of marriageable age at the beginning of the nineties, the majority still unmarried. The Queen, having said that she renounced matchmaking in 1885 after Princess Beatrice's wedding, 'was inexorably drawn into a fresh round on behalf of her grandchildren'. The young Kaiser also liked to have his finger in the pie. In the late 19th century marriage was still the main aim of the majority of women; and, although the economic imperative was perhaps not so pressing among royalty as with poor ladies in Jane Austen's novels, they were vulnerable to diplomatic manoeuvrings, frequently being pawns in dynastic affairs.

Unter den Linden in Berlin packed with crowds in 1890 for some royal occasion when Emily was in the city for the wedding of Princess Victoria.

At the end of their visit to Wiesbaden in 1890, Princess Christian and the young princesses spent a good month in Berlin with their cousins before the wedding of Princess Victoria to Prince Adolphus of Schaumburg-Lippe. This time Victoria had chosen, or had been persuaded, to marry an uncontroversial figure. The match suited the Kaiser; he gave his blessing. On a bright warm morning in mid-October the Empress Friedrich and her daughters were at the door of the Palais in Berlin to greet Princess Christian, Thora and Marie Louise when they arrived off the night train from Frankfurt. They settled into rooms in the Palace with Emily at first on the same corridor as the Empress, and the Princesses on the floor above. As more relations arrived for the celebrations, Emily and even Princess Christian had to move, Emily eventually being found a room at the Hôtel de Rome. There were compensations: a carriage being at her disposal most of the time. On one occasion, when she had gone to a musical evening and then back with people from the British Embassy, she forgot that a carriage had been arranged for her and was much embarrassed when she found it had waited in vain. Emily, as usual, was busy dashing about from one person to another and, as her great friend Gerry Liddell was studying music at the Conservatory, her life was a lively mixture of very royal events, contrasting with quick visits to the pension where Gerry lodged and meeting the teachers and other music students for cheap meals in restaurants. She managed it all: carriage journeys alternating with droshky rides and short journeys on the trams and suburban trains; listening to concerts in the royal palaces and calling in to hear rehearsals at the Conservatory.

The young princesses were much engaged with their cousins, but Emily usually saw them in the mornings. Princess Christian is mentioned infrequently, as her time was spent chiefly with her sister and her health was not giving trouble.

It was Princess Louie who had to take to her bed for few days, and thereby missed one of the hunts in the Grünewald staged for the Emperor's guests. A Dr Krause attended her and, as she got better, she visited him at his clinic. Emily took her there on November 15th, and they found him 'very excited about the Koch cure for consumption which has begun to be tried with great success'. Unfortunately, this cure for the dreaded disease of tuberculosis didn't live up to its initial promise; but tuberculin, which Professor Robert Koch of Berlin University was preparing at that very time, proved to be a useful diagnostic tool. His work in bacteriology led to a better understanding of the causes and possible cures for many diseases. Emily, in her weekly letter, told her sister Cathy in India about the exciting developments.

Princess Thora and Princess Victoria, the bride to be, found plenty of time for music together, and very much enjoyed having Gerry in Berlin with them. One evening, Gerry and Conga, another music student who also lived at the pension, came to play two-piano music with the princesses.[31] Singing lessons were arranged for Princess Thora. Gerry was asked to play for the Empress at musical evenings in the Palais. She also played at the Mendelssohns where she dined several times. On the first of these, Emily joined the party after dinner, when she

> found all the men smoking. Joachim was there. We soon went upstairs to the music room and then had a quartet of Mendelssohn's and Mozart C minor quintet. It was quite lovely. We had supper after in the Kneiperoom [32].

The next time was a smaller affair, when only Franz Mendelssohn and Gerry played music of Handel, Schumann and Spohr to an audience of four or five. It was the sort of evening Emily particularly enjoyed and Gerry 'played quite splendidly'.

There were many grand entertainments which came to a climax just before the wedding. At the end of October, Emily got ready for one of these which was held in Potsdam, reached by a short train journey. She was ready, in the Palais in Berlin, rather earlier than the rest of the party, so, while she waited in the reception room, she 'listened to the Meistersingers thro' the telephone'. A day or so before this, the Emperor gave a very special evening for his aunt, when Emily dined with her 'Herrschaften' – that is the Christian family – and went with them to the Schauspielhaus (playhouse) to see the Quitzows. She goes on:

> the Emperor had ordered it specially for my Princesses and he came to take Princess Christian there himself. Most of the other royalties went too.

There is little doubt that the Kaiser was very fond of his aunt and could be very kind and thoughtful – when it suited him. There were dinners at the Schloss with Emperor Wilhelm and the Empress. There were dances. The first, when Emily – dressed in her 'low white dress' – was able to remark that she saw '*scarcely anybody but princesses there*' and she was 'very pleased: I danced like anything quite contrary to my intentions. Got home at 2 o'clock very tired.' Only a day or so later, she was at it again, staying at Duke Ernst Günther's ball until the 'bitter end', and not getting home again until 2 o'clock. This was after having already dined at the British Embassy and having attended a gala performance of *Das Nachtlager in Granada* and *Copelia.* No wonder she was very tired.

Two days before the marriage there was a

> tremendous big gala dinner at the Schloss with the Royalties. Cercle was made after and presentations, and then there was a gala performance of Oberon a beautiful sight ... very dull opera. Relevage in between with the company in the Foyer.

'Relevage' and 'releve' – perhaps 'relevé' when she is not in a hurry – were two words that Emily began to use frequently in her diary around this time. Sometimes it seems to mean discussion and going over some event which she and others had just attended, sometimes there was a suspicion of gossip.

The day after the gala performance of *Oberon* there was another grand dinner at the Marschall's Tafel at the Schloss. These events were announced in the detailed orders issued by the Master of Ceremonies, Count A Gulenberg, so that all ranks should know where and when they would be dining. When, after the Marschall's Tafel, Gerry and Emily got back to Emily's room, they found that the maids were having a party in her room with one playing the piano; so the two of them sat down and, in the much more relaxed atmosphere, joined in the chat and laughter. Emily ended the day with 'a bread and butter and milk supper'.

At last the day of the wedding dawned. All the plans and discussions about the clothes and jewellery to be worn came to fruition. The choosing of materials, the visits to dressmakers, the tedious fittings and the excitement of seeing the finished garments were over. Emily's and the Princesses' clothes had been prepared well in advance in Wiesbaden and possibly London. Emily's bonnet, however, was obtained from Frau Basty after she arrived in Berlin and she was still fussing with the trimmings shortly before the wedding. Gerry had taken Emily up to her room in the pension, as soon as they met in Berlin, to show her the clothes she intended to wear. A week later they had gone together to Gersons and had chosen 'a lovely grey train for Gerry for the wedding'. The feathers to complete her outfit and the bonnet from Frau Basty were delivered at the very last moment, on the morning of the wedding.

Emily wrote for November 19th:

> Went to the Schloss early and waited for ages, as they were decorating the Chapel and got back to Rome [the Hotel] about 12 in time to tell them that we were to lunch again with the Emp. The girls came bringing the feathers for Gerry. Her bonnet also came from Basty and looked quite beautiful and suitable. Nice homely luncheon. We flew back and began to dress about 2.30. Consequently were ready without any fuss to receive Frl. v. Floton and Frl. Hanne. We went to the Schloss by 4.15 and joined our Hoheiten [Royalty] who looked beautiful and so well dressed. The marriage was very interesting but very hot and tiring. We fed after the ceremony in the Marinen Saal. We stood about after and then defilierte [filed past] and hugged Princess Vicky who was beloved.

A cousinly account by Princess Louie, written many years later, saw the ceremony from a different perspective.

> Curiously enough there are not many solemn vows taken in the German Lutheran Service. [This was something that shocked Nicholas II]. The bridegroom is asked whether he wishes to take the bride as his wife, and he answers at the top of his voice, 'Yes'. Then the bride is asked the same question, and she also, perhaps not quite so loudly, answers in the affirmative. Then comes the endless sermon, telling the happy pair of all the duties of husband and wife and everything to do with married life.

Princess Louie goes on:

> After that we proceeded into *Der Weisser Saal* – the White Room. Here there were congratulations and a few tears. After the wedding feast 'there was a torch-light procession when the bridegroom, preceded by pages, holding in their hands can-

delabra, had to lead each Princess right round the room, bowing to the Emperor and Empress. The best man then led the bride round in the same manner, and all the princes and princesses did likewise. You can imagine how long this took and how very bored we became. About ten or eleven at night the bridal pair left for their honeymoon. Instead of distributing favours, as we know them, the bride distributed her 'garter'. This consisted of pieces of white satin ribbon, rather like a bookmarker, with initials, crown and date inscribed on them

Emily kept the huge piece of paper detailing the order of the bridal procession. So we can see who were in the first twenty rows, as the galaxy of Royals moved in their elaborate dress to positions in the Chapel of the Schloss. Princess Victoria, attended by her Chamberlain, and five ladies and two pages, walked beside her bridegroom, Prince Adolf. Her brother, the Emperor – 'Seine Majestät der Kaiser und König' – and her mother – 'Ihre Majestät die Kaiserin und Königin Friedrich' – were just behind, with the young Empress behind her mother-in-law. Emily's great friend at the Palace, Gräfin Margarethe

Prince Eddy, Albert Victor, eldest son of King Edward VII and Queen Alexandra. Queen Victoria hoped that he and Princess Alix would marry but she turned him down. He died before his marriage to his later fiancée May of Teck could take place.

von Perponcher, referred to in the diary as 'Deta Perponcher', attended the Dowager Empress, Vicky. Behind them were Princes and Princesses, Highnesses and Serene Highnesses, Dukes and Duchesses from all over Europe. From England had come the Connaughts. He was Prince Arthur, Queen Victoria's third son and his wife, Louischen, a Princess of Prussia; also the Duke of Clarence, Prince Eddy, eldest son of the Prince of Wales[33]. There was the Duchess of Edinburgh, born Marie of Russia, sister of Tsar Alexander III. Princess Christian's family was well represented: the Princess herself was attended by Miss Loch; Prince Christian of Schleswig-Holstein by Captain the Honourable North Dalrymple, whom Emily had met off the train a few days before; Princess Victoria, Thora, by Miss Liddell; and Princess Louise by two pages. Prince Albert was there, placed beside His Highness, Prince Albert of Schleswig-Holstein-Sønderburg-Glücksburg, whose successor to this portmanteau title he became. The Queen of Romania, wife of King Carol, who had enlivened their time in Wiesbaden so much, was also there.

Some very official photographs are pasted in Emily's album as a remembrance of this day. Princess Victoria stands in her wedding dress – a buxom young lady with a sweet unsmiling expression and a painfully well-defined waist. Her dress, of richly embroidered material with garlands of

Memento of the wedding of Princess Victoria and Adolf Prince of Schaumburg Lippe with her garter.

flowers around the low neckline, has short sleeves, falls in a cascade from her waist and along the gracefully placed train. Around her neck she has a magnificent necklace of diamonds and in her hands a small bouquet of flowers. On the opposite page, a rather sterner young lady looks out, with her hair curled closely to her head, giving her an almost boyish appearance despite her sleeveless, lacy black dress. A firm signature confirms her to be Victoria, Princess of Prussia. A silk marker – the bride's 'garter' mentioned in Princess Louie's account, with a gilt crown and date, 19 Nov 1890 – lies between this photo and one of the newly married couple. In this, she is wearing a dress with a tight-fitting bodice and long sleeves, the close-fitting skirt with a swirl of material falling from the bustle. He appears as rather gentle-looking with fine eyes, a central parting in his dark hair and a luxurious dark beard. He stands in a military uniform with five rows of ornate braiding across his chest, decorated with large jewels of various orders. He wears tight trousers and high boots, and has his hand on his sword. His signature is neat – Adolf Prinz zu Schaumburg Lippe. Did any recollection of Sandro flit through Victoria's mind? Was this was a love match with a happy life for the two – not just another marriage engineered by those in power? It was planned by the Kaiser, her brother. Celebations continued after the wedding; the British Ambassador held a particularly splendid evening the following night. Princess Christian and her family remained in Germany for another month. Life for the princesses and Emily went on in the same way; grand dinners, many theatres, some with gala performances. For Emily there was the added delight of having Gerry with her. When they were together, just the two of them, it was music and more music. They listened to the Joachim and Kruse quartets; they went to student concerts and visited their friends at the Conservatory.

During the autumn of the previous year Gerry had been with the Princess and Emily when they returned to Wiesbaden early in September, 1890. A second piano had immediately been hired and, that very evening, 'Gerry and the Princess played Bach 2 piano things after'. The next day, Emily arranged with a Professor Mannstadt to come and play; and she was able to record that, on September 19th, '8 hands played for an hour' obviously something which was very exciting. For nearly a month that autumn, the apartment hummed with music.

Gerry had left Wiesbaden at the end of September and moved to Berlin. She had auditioned before Joachim, the great violinist, and Rudorff, a professor at the Conservatory, and had been accepted as a student at the Conservatory.

It is not actually said, but it is pretty clear, that the Dowager Empress, Empress Vicky, was instrumental in getting Gerry auditioned. She had discovered what an excellent pianist Gerry was – probably first from Princess Christian – and had heard her play several times at Windsor in late 1888. Gerry threw herself into the student life with enthusiasm. As a result, when Emily came to Berlin in 1890 for Princess Victoria's wedding, Gerry was already there, deep in her studies. Emily made herself useful translating for her, as her German was much more proficient. Now they were in Berlin together, they were able to mix their duties to Royalty with their other great love, music, and they became close friends with Joachim and Kruse. They had already heard Joachim and his quartet in London.

Princess Christian and Prince Christian left Berlin for about a fortnight soon after the wedding and returned with Else in early December. Emily stayed with the young princesses and moved into the Schloss. Princess Thora went riding, indoors, with the Empress. Then there was further family excitement.

Emily writes for December 8th:

> Dull cold day. Very late in the morning as no one called us. Else and I had breakfast at quarter to ten up in my room. The Princesses came up. I went with the Princess to the Palais ... Went back to the Schloss and changed and went down to Potsdam by 12.20 train. Prince Aribert of Anhalt got out at Potsdam too! Else and I dined with the Hofhaltung [royal household]. We were summoned after and the engagement of Princess Louie to Prince Aribert was announced and everybody congratulated everybody. It had all been settled before lunch quite quickly. We came up again on the 3.2 train ... Came back by 5.30. Stood about, while telegrams were being written. Dressed and dined with Else upstairs at 7 o'clock. I went with Princess Thora to the v Kotge's ball. The Princess and Princess Louie went to the Palais to meet Prince Aribert. Princess Thora and I got home at 1.30.

No comment, as usual; and Emily was probably as happy as everyone else. Luckily no one had a crystal ball: no one could foresee that the marriage would decline into unhappiness and end in annulment. In December 1890 all was sweetness and light. Shortly after the announcement, the whole family left for Dessau[34] to spend a couple of days with the future bridegroom's parents. They, too, appear in the album, looking plump and prosperous. Princess Louie says that she became very fond of her mother-in-law. Prince Aribert's father and Prince Christian had been students together and had been extremely lively young men; but now protocol was very strict in Anhalt circles, as Princess Louie was to find out when she lived there after her marriage. On this occasion, however, all went well – with presentations, a state dinner and a special operatic performance in the picturesque setting of the ancient castle at Dessau. When the Christians returned to Berlin, the young couple went to Hofferts for their engagement photographs. These, too, are in the album – the young couple looking pensive. He wears a knee-length double-breasted coat and sports immaculately parted hair and splendidly curled moustaches.

Prince Aribert and Princess Marie Louise at the time of their wedding on July 6th 1891.

CHAPTER NINE

1891: A Momentous Year

The year 1891 started quietly enough but something was in the air. The diary, for the first weeks of the year, is full of concern about clothes: buying material – 'yellow silk' and 'two selling-off pieces from Marshalls' – and visits to dress makers. New ladies were tried; Princess Christian tried Miss Brown; and Emily, Mrs Keswell and Mrs Washbourne. Emily had a lot of trouble with Mrs Keswell. Despite going to several fittings in the early months of the year; as the day of the wedding approached, things were not ready: some outfits were only finished just in time and still the fit wasn't entirely satisfactory.

As well as ordering new clothes, wedding presents had to be chosen and obtained; personal ones from the Loch sisters and also a suitable gift from

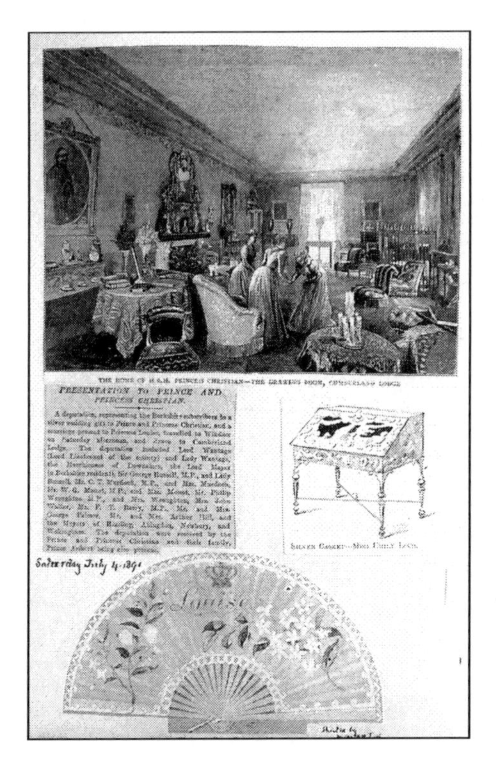

A page from Emily's album with a view of the drawing room at Cumberland Lodge, the fan Alice painted for Princess Louie on the occasion of her marriage to Prince Aribert and Emily's gift to Princess Christian on the anniversary of her Silver Wedding in July 1891.

Prince and Princess Christian July 1891, on their Silver Wedding anniversary.

members of the Household. Alice's artistic talents were turned to making a screen for Princess Louie with a design of peacock's feathers. She took it over to Cumberland Lodge on July 1st. Fans were also prepared for the special occasion. One afternoon in London, Emily 'drove to Duvelroy with Aunt Louisa and ordered the fan to be mounted'. A picture of this appears in the album; it was a gift to Princess Christian, painted by Alice, for use at Princess Louie's wedding.

The wedding took place on July 6th, Old Midsummer Day, according to Emily's Lett's Diary. It was arranged as near as possible to the Silver Wedding Anniversary of Prince and Princess Christian, but the date had also to fit in with the engagements of Emperor William of Germany. He, her cousin, felt that the betrothal had been very much his doing and he was determined to attend. It was a time of much celebration. The German Emperor made a State visit to his grandmother. July 4th was a great day, Emily writes:

> Fine day. Went over to Cumberland Lodge soon after breakfast and found lots to do. Two presentations: one from Englefield Green Ladies of a lovely flower bowl and then Berkshire presentation of silver plates to the Pc and Pss … a diamond and

pearl necklace to Pss Louie and a pen to Prince Aribert. 25 people came. Hurried home and found the dressmaker come from Mrs Keswell to alter my gowns. I tried on. Changed dress, had lunch and then Miss Learmonth and I were called for and fetched the ladies from the Dell[35] and went down to the Castle for the Emperor's reception. It was a beautiful sight. Every imaginable Royalty and the people in waiting and the whole of Berlin besides. Got home by 6 o'C. Had tea. Dressed and we dined at C. Lodge. I had a very pleasant evening. I sat next to Prince Aribert. Pss Christian sent for me before dinner. I talked chiefly to the two Pss after dinner.

There was a Ball at Buckingham Palace, a Garden Party at Cumberland Lodge and many dinners. Emily went up and down to London. There was a state concert at Buckingham Palace on June 25th. Emily attended Princess Christian and, just before the concert, the Princess gave Emily a beautiful bracelet as a memento of her silver wedding. No doubt Emily wore this for the great day when Princess Louie was married at St George's Chapel, Windsor. Emily writes a detailed account of that day when her young Princess, whom she had known since early childhood and had seen so much of in recent years, prepared to leave the simple life and close-knit home of Cumberland Lodge.

On July 6th there were heavy showers but it was fine after 4 p.m. Emily goes on:

Gerry and I went over to C. Lodge at 9.30 and sat a long time with Princess Louie and Princess Thora and the brothers came in and out. I went for a bit to Princess Christian. We came away at 11 o'clock. Alice went to very early mass [Alice had become converted to Roman Catholicism in February of this year]. We had lunch at 1-oC and dressed before. Sat waiting 1/2 hour for the carriage and started at 2.15. All our servants went down in a fly to various places with tickets. We fetched people at the Dell and then divided into two carriages at Royal Lodge. I went to the Castle and waited at the State door and Sir Fleetwood came and took me round to the Queen's door. Met all the royalties on my way, and was given the bridesmaids' lockets which I put in my pocket. Waited a long time with Miss McNeil, Duchess of

> Buccleuch and Lady Ampthill and at last was sent in a carriage alone after the other ladies and Princess Victoria. The Queen and Princess Christian followed at once and we processed up the church from the South door. The Bridegroom came immediately after and then the Bride looking lovely and dear. It was a lovely service. Got back to the castle and stood about for ages and then formed a lane through which the Bride and Bridegroom and all the royalties passed to their food. We went to ours. I went to Princess Louie, where she was dressing in Princess Beatrice's room, and took her the lockets. The bridesmaids all came up and she gave them to them. We went down to the door and saw her off, the Emperor [the Kaiser] throwing shoes and rice.

For the ceremony, Princess Louie, as she writes in her memoirs:

> had a wedding dress made from out of my mother's wedding lace which, as was the fashion of the day, she wore over a crinoline and half the lace had therefore to be sewn underneath my train. I also used her wedding veil.

The six bridesmaids, who later received their lockets, were dressed in off-white silk and wore wreaths of Marshall Ney roses in their hair and carried shower bouquets, just coming into fashion. There was genuine anguish in the Princess's parting from her parents and sister, before she and her husband drove off through the crowds, including the boys from Eton College, to begin their honeymoon at Cliveden.

So she wasn't there the next day when Emily went over to Cumberland Lodge and found Princess Christian and Princess Thora 'deep in telegrams'. Cumberland Lodge was awash with presents for the two important events. Even as Emily discovered them reading the telegrams, two ladies came down from London to present gifts from the School of Art Needlework, of which the Princess was patron. These would be added to those which had appeared over the previous days: silver candle sticks from the staff of Windsor Park; a silver salver from the Egham tradesmen; the Life Guards' magnificent silver bowl; a pair of square silver salvers from the ladies and gentlemen of the Household; and an entire silver dinner service from the County of Berkshire. A deputation

The public showed much interest in the life of the princesses at the time of Marie Louise's wedding as illustrated by newspaper articles and pictures.

of nurses gave Princess Christian a magnificent diamond star. All the presents were displayed at Cumberland Lodge, and Gerry and Emily with many others saw them; but soon the time came when all had to be packed or put away. Emily helped Princess Christian start making lists just three days after the wedding, but the packing was not completed until late in the month. There was much discussion about sending Princess Louie's boxes to Germany. At last it was decided to register them right through for £2 10s for every £100 up to £1000. Princess Louie and Prince Aribert returned from Cliveden for a few days and finally left Cumberland Lodge for Germany on July 20th.

After the excitement of Princess Louie's wedding and the celebrations for the Princess's silver wedding there was a week's pause and then it was time to pack again. Prince Christian, Princess Christian, Princess Thora and Emily set out to visit the beloved relations in Darmstadt. This was going to be a real holiday for all of them. When they arrived at the Palais in Darmstadt late at night after the usual sea crossing and long train journey, they found not only the Grand Duke and Prince Abby there to greet them but also the newly married couple, Prince Aribert and Princess Louie. These two, however, left for Bayreuth a few days later. On the very first morning, all the younger ones including Princess Alix came to talk to Emily and Princess Thora. There was so much to remember about the recent events, so much to discuss about the holiday to come.

They stayed in Darmstadt just one night and then were off to the Grand Duke's summer residence of Wolfsgarten, a few miles away. This friendly and substantial group of warm brown buildings lay in gently rolling country of beech woods, meadows and orchards. The ducal family and their friends stayed in the main building with a central tower. In this building, as well as reception rooms such as the dining and drawing rooms, there was a piano room. Other buildings surrounded a large open courtyard; gentlemen of the household had their rooms in one, the ladies in another. Immediately on arrival, Emily recounts:

> Gretchen and I went round to see all the animals and places and then I came in and wrote diary etc. We dined at 2o'clock. Came back to our house. Sat and talked and then I came to my room and unpacked and got straight.

Gretchen had heard that Princess Christian, Thora and Emily would be coming to Wolfsgarten in August in a birthday letter from Alix written to her earlier in the summer. In it Alix had remarked that Gretchen could have Emily Loch to herself a good deal of the time while she, Alix, tried to cheer up Thora. By this time Emily and Gretchen had become very good friends and, as this was Emily's first visit to Wolfsgarten, she particularly enjoyed being shown round this entrancing estate by Gretchen. There were animals: horses and ponies, tame deer and fawns. They walked in the beautiful gardens and orchards set among the magnificent beech woods.

The family settled into a routine of morning occupations: riding before breakfast for Princess Thora and Princess Alix, followed by reading, playing the piano and singing. There was lots of singing; sometimes Emily alone, sometimes with Gretchen and sometimes with the young princesses. One evening, soon after they arrived spirits were so high that, after singing in the music room, they 'sang round the house when we went to bed'. Sometimes there was tennis. Emily played once or twice and the younger members of the family more frequently, while their elders sat by the tennis ground and watched. There were drives out into the surrounding country in the late afternoon to some beauty spot, usually taking tea. One day, after a morning visit to the Battenbergs at Jugenheim:

> We all drove together in the break with five horses to Mönchsbruch where we had tea. Walked about after for a little and then drove back – it was a lovely drive through the woods.

And two days later:

> We went out driving, all of us except Frl.v Grancy, at 5.15. It threatened a fearful storm and rained a little but it passed over or rather round. We went on some terribly bad roads and got nearly upset, and once, the three front horses had to be unhooked and the carriage lifted round, we all having got out. We got to a small sort of mushroom summerhouse and had tea. Came back another way round and got home by 7.30.

They also visited Kranichstein, a hunting lodge deep in the forests, which Emily had been to the first time she stayed with the Hesse family. The countryside was ideal for shooting, both deer and game birds such as woodcock and capercailzie. Prince Christian and Prince Abby went out several times. Emily records that the Grand Duke shot two buck and, one evening when the party returned from their drive, there he was with his trophies laid out on the grass, waiting for them.

Emily took many walks though the nearby woods and meadows with Gretchen or Fräulein von Grancy. She also tells us that two of the maids went out one day and got lost. Poor Jeanne was nearly hysterical when she returned late, because she wasn't there to help Princess Christian dress for dinner. Emily was especially happy in being able to stroll out with Fräulein von Grancy one evening and pick a bunch of gentians to send to Gerry, well wrapped in damp moss. They walked along a cool grassy ride through the forest, the Kelb Schneise, and out into a meadow bathed in the warm evening sun. At this time of year, in late summer, the damp meadow would have been a patchwork of colour. The brilliant blue of the tall gentians, the pale, dusky pink of valerian; purple-red betony; and the creamy white of meadowsweet set in a background of the silvery-purple moor grass shimmering in the evening breeze. Not all outings were quite so pleasant. The weather was very variable, with some deliciously fresh days but others were thundery, heavy and sultry, and Emily was bothered with flies. As she rather crudely puts it, 'the flies were something awful'. She was also bitten by gnats. One bite made her ankle swell very badly and, on another day, her dress got burnt with the 'touch-wood' which they lit to ward off the gnats. She put up 'the mosquito curtains and arranged her books', when moved into a room in the main house. She was, however, more fortunate than Herr von Riedesel who was stung on the tongue by a wasp in his wine. On another occasion, his leg became entangled in the wheel of the pony carriage, but fortunately did not get broken.

The manoeuvres, an important part of life in this small Duchy, were a highlight of this visit. There were serious military reasons for them, and the Grand Duke and the young Princes were all deeply committed to the army. Prince Abby's regiment was stationed nearby and Prince Christle on leave from the British Army in India was also there. Emily records that, on August 25th, Prince Christle rode principally with General Such, the Inspector General of Cavalry in India. The social side had not entirely disappeared. The older ladies were driven out in carriages to watch – faint echoes of those ladies who watched the British army making their heroic charges in the Crimean War. There is a photograph in Emily's album of two ladies, wearing exotic hats and holding parasols, in an open carriage driven by a top-hatted coachman: in the background are ranks of helmeted cavalrymen.

The younger princesses were particularly excited when Prince Abby's

The older ladies off to the manoeuvres in a carriage.

regiment came through the grounds of Wolfsgarten, on their march from Darmstadt to Frankfurt. They were up and ready to see the soldiers and officers soon after 8 o'clock – it reminds one of the excitement of the younger Bennet sisters when the militia were stationed at Meryton. But they had to wait an hour or more before the cavalry arrived, their horses steaming, their uniforms bright in the early sun and the harness gleaming with polish. The officers all dismounted near the house and had a meal before moving on. Three days later, the whole party set out from Wolfsgarten at 7 o'clock in the morning and drove to Nieder Roden. Herr von Riedesel had taken their riding horses much earlier and, by 8.15, joined by the Princesses of Prussia, they all set off to follow the manoeuvres for the next two and a half hours. This was thrilling but exhausting for Emily: on later occasions, she stayed with the older members of the household, Fräulein von Grancy and Herr von Westerweller, or drove in a carriage. Princess Alix and Princess Thora however, were out several times. As Emily wrote for August 28th:

> Everyone but Frl v Grancy and I went early to the manoeuvres. Ps Thora and Ps Alix rode and Fr. v Riedesel rode with them. They had a charge with the cavalry. They all got home by 1 o'clock.

The manoeuvres continued when the whole party with their horses, carriages and all boarded the Grand Duke's special train at Langen station and travelled north to another of the Hesse palaces. Emily writes:

> We went straight through Frankfurt without stopping – and Gliesen to Romrod getting there just before 6 o'clock. Drove to the Schloss where a lot more gentlemen were waiting. A wonderful and delightful old place. The Grand Duke took us to our rooms. Unpacked by degrees and dressed for 8 o'clock supper. There was a large dinner with all the gentlemen. The dining and drawing rooms were all in one, a sort of long old German Hall with a curtain to divide it into two, raised sort of dais place in a deep window at the end and at the side of the room. There was a little game playing after dinner until very late. The Grand Duke joined our *poch*.[36]

A studio photograph of the two cousins Princess Alix and Princess Thora in 1891.

There was no piano in this old castle and no theatres within reach, so in the evenings various people read aloud to the small group or there were games of various sorts; sometimes poker, sometimes old-fashioned card games such as Pope Joan[37]; and sometimes Schwarze Dame, Whist, Alma, Loo and Chess took their turn. Once, there was Dumb Crambo and once 'Blots and Drawings'. Princess Victoria played Backgammon with Princess Christian and Emily became deeply involved in Bezique with Princess Alix which they played several nights running, sometimes going on until 10.30 or later. During this time Emily got to know Princess Alix very well and it is clear that Princess Thora had become a very special friend. There is a charming photograph of the two princesses in Emily's album – Alix with her delicate, fine-cut features and Thora with her long, heavy face. They had known each other for years but, in the less formal atmosphere at Romrod, they had plenty of opportunity to become more intimate. Emily noted that she, Princess Thora and Gretchen accompanied Princess Alix to her German Lutheran church on several Sunday mornings: it was the difficulty of leaving the Lutheran Church and converting to Russian Orthodoxy which delayed for several months Princess Alix's acceptance of Nicholas's proposal of marriage.

That was all some time into the future and far from this relaxed family holiday; but it seems quite possible that Princess Alix and Emily discussed Russia. Emily was reading Tolstoy's *Anna Karenina* on this holiday and Princess Alix had already been to Russia on three occasions. When she was still a child, she had attended her sister Ella's wedding in 1884 to Grand Duke Serge, the brother of Tsar Alexander III. Sometime during that visit the sixteen-year-old Nicholas, already an admirer, had given her a brooch. She subsequently returned it but a seed had been sown. When Alix was just over sixteen, her father took her to St Petersburg for her first ball in the winter of 1888. She had a wonderful time at Peterhof, the palace near the Baltic west of St Petersburg: tobogganing and skating to music in the moonlight, balls and carnivals. Great efforts were made on the part of the Russians, ably assisted by Ella, to provide many opportunities for Nicholas and Alix to be together. In higher diplomatic spheres a struggle was going on between the Russians and Germans on one hand and Queen Victoria on the other to find a suitable husband for the last of the Hesse daughters. Queen Victoria's invitation arrived late; her candidate, her grandson Eddy, Duke of Clarence, came a very poor second to Nicholas. Also, Balmoral was cold and damp: it couldn't compete with the glamour of a St Petersburg season. Princess Alix was not expecting a proposal from Eddy, didn't find him attractive and turned him down. Queen Victoria was not pleased but was philosophical – Princess Alix was still very young. When her father took her to Russia again in 1890, a year before this visit to Romrod, Queen Victoria was still hoping that 'Alicky would not go to the Russians'.

Emily did not have the status or the knowledge to discuss the scheming of politicians and royalty. Probably Princess Alix herself was unaware of all that was going on. It seems likely, however, that they did talk about Russia: Alix telling Emily about her exciting experiences and Emily discussing some of the gripping Tolstoy story that she was reading.

This was just one of the many books read during this holiday. One morning, after Emily had finished her stint of writing, she notes in her diary: 'Princess Thora came at 12 and we read the first chapter of the "Life"'. This can only have been the book on the life of St Catherine of Sienna[38] which Dean Davidson had completed earlier in the year during the visit that the Davidsons, Gerry and Emily made to Italy in April. They had visited Florence and then Sienna, where they had seen many relics of St Catherine. The Dean had questioned the old sacristan at the church of San Domenico about her. They had visited various rooms where the saint had lived and the church where she was buried. So this book, 'hot from the press', was of particular interest to Emily and Princess Thora as they both knew the author so well. The religious theme continued when Fräulein von Grancy read *La neuvaine de Colette* to them all. This was a series of prayers and devotions for a span of nine days, based on the life of the minor saint, Colette, who set out to make the Society of the Poor Clares return to their strict vows of poverty.

While Fräulein von Grancy read to them, as the weather was warm, they all sat out on a wooden balcony – there is a photograph of this in Emily's album – or on the walls of the old castle. It appears that not all the party appreciated these religious topics too much. On the first occasion, Emily wrote that during the reading 'Prince Abby shot sparrows and disturbed us'. Perhaps it was just as well that he left Romrod to return to his regiment and so missed the later readings.

On the whole though the holiday was a time of light-heartedness. One Sunday, while they were still at Wolfsgarten, the Prince of Wales, the Empress Friedrich and her two daughters, Princess Vicky and Princess Mossy (Margaret), came over from Homburg. Such an enjoyable time was had that the visitors were very late going to catch the train back and it had to be kept waiting for them. The young cousins who remained at Wolfsgarten that evening were then in such high spirits that, after a walk in the woods, they sat with Emily and Gretchen and 'made much noise until dressing time'.

At Romrod, there were at least two dinners when the officers came to dine at the old Schloss and all the ladies put on their best clothes. As the dinner took place in the old hall, the ladies, when they left the officers to their after dinner drinks and gentlemen's conversation, had to go and sit in the Grand Duke's room. Certainly, in this small castle, the Herrschaften and the household lived much closer together; their meals were taken together in one room and when 'Jeanne sprained her foot (she) was looked after by everyone'. After dinner that night:

> the two young princesses, Gretchen and I danced to the band in the servant's dining room. Herr v Riedesel joined us. Late going to bed.

A couple of days later she continued:

> I wrote for the messenger morning and rubbed out my drawings. The two young princesses rode. They insisted on our

> dancing after dinner to the barrel organ. Frl.v Riedesel came at 3.15. We all went driving at 4 o'clock and took our tea with us. We went to see the stables when we got back and then went to watch Princess Alix' horse being shod. I titivated up drawing until dressing time ... we danced after dinner to the barrel organ. The whole party played games until 11o'clock. It was very amusing.

The whole party would have included Princess Christian and Princess Victoria, who was there to look after her aunt; she had sent her small daughters to stay with their grandmother at Jugenheim. There is no mention of Princess Christian's poor health in the whole of this visit and one feels that she was enjoying herself during this busy but relaxed time – and so was Emily.

The following account gives some idea of the pleasant richness of their days.

> September 3. Very hot, bright day. Thunder early and a few drops of rain. Fl.v Grancy and I went out at 10 to the Ober Rod chapel to sketch. Missed our way and took nearly an hour instead of 20 minutes. Got there tired and heated and made a pencil sketch. Went right up to the chapel after and saw troops collecting at Niederbach. Came home the right way very quickly and fell right in among the Alsfeld troops who were bivouacking near the big beech and we had to walk straight through them. Got back at 1.20. Hastily changed for dinner at 1.30. The Gd Duke and his gentlemen were not back. Directly after, at quarter to three we all started out to the fishing place and F v Grancy and I took our sketching things and worked until I got a sick headache and had to leave off. Pss Ch. Pses Thora and Alix & Pc Abby went home sooner and went on to the bivouac at Niederbach to see Pc Abby's camp. Ps Victoria staid longer to fish and so we did not get back in time to go with them to the camp. Dressed sat out a little and felt better. Dinner at quarter to nine. Douratsthly [a game] after till 10.30. Wrote to Alice when I came to bed.

The drawing of the chapel has not survived, but Emily has pasted a sketch

Emily's sketch of the old castle at Romrod where she and the family from Darmstadt stayed in late summer 1891.

she did of the old castle of Romrod in her album and so we can get some idea of the delightful jumble of buildings which surrounded the old Schloss.

Fräulein von Grancy is a person who appears many times in the diary. She came of a family who had been with the Grand Duke's family for many years. Princess Alix's mother, Princess Alice, in a letter to her mother Queen Victoria, written in the 1870s, mentions a Marie Grancy several times. She was Princess Alice's lady-in-waiting for nine years and was sorely missed when she married General von Hesse in 1871. Emily continued to meet 'her' Fräulein von Grancy for many years. When Emily was with Princess Christian at another of the Grand Duke's castles in 1910, she was still there; a photograph shows her as an old lady and, in her diary at the time, Emily voices her concern about the old lady being able to walk up a hill. During this visit she and Emily had many walks together but on one occasion, when the party made an expedition to Feldberg and walked up from the foot of the hill, Emily was already anxious that it would be too much for Fräulein von Grancy: but she managed it.

Mrs Orchard was another member of the Grand Duke's household whom Emily met on this visit and who had been with the Hesse family for many years. While Emily was at Wolfsgarten, Mrs Orchard celebrated her twenty-fifth year in the service of the family; and, on August 15th, there was an anniversary presentation of many gifts. She had come first to help with the children and was referred to by Princess Alice as Orchie, later graduating to Orchard, and by 1891, to Mrs Orchard. She continued in Princess Alix's service and moved to Russia with her. She was there when, on January 5th 1898 – Christmas Eve of the Orthodox calendar – Alix, now the Tsarina, had a tree for Emily in Princess Thora's room. 'Quite lovely' wrote Emily, who was left on her own that evening; but 'the servants came in at supper to see my tree and have things. Mrs Orchard came too.' By then Mrs Orchard would have been in the service of the family for thirty-two years.

After ten carefree days at Romrod the party returned to Wolfsgarten, and were soon back into the round of visiting friends by day and going to the theatre in the evening. There were days in Wiesbaden to see the Cohausens, the Laux family and the Knoops, and to Rettersdorff to the von Dieshaus. The Grand Duke's birthday was celebrated in style and Prince Christle photographed the assembled party. At this time, there were several references to Prince Christle taking photos. Emily helped him 'mix his photographic fluids' on August 19th. Two days later he 'photoed us all by the well'; and, the next day, 'Prince Christle made some more photographs – little Alice[39] with Emma,

Family group taken on the Grand Duke's birthday in late summer 1891 by Prince Christle.

the roe fawn and a group of everyone on the steps'. In the album there is a copy of the family group on the steps. At the back stands Princess Christian flanked by two 'gentlemen'; one, the accident-prone 'Herr von Riedesel.'[40] In front of Princess Christian sits the Grand Duke, stout and bearded; to his left is Gretchen von Fabrice and, on her left, Princess Alix. To the Duke's right sits Princess Thora in a boater and, slightly behind her, Fräulein von Grancy[41] with Emily in front of her. Lastly, to the right of Princess Alix, sits her eldest sister Victoria also in a hat with two-year-old Louise on her lap and, beside her, 'little Alice', who would have been about five. There are also two of his photographs of Wolfsgarten showing the substantial but fairly plain buildings standing in spacious lawns with fruit trees between the buildings. Emily liked Prince Christle very much and frequently had long talks with him; and one can imagine her delight at being able to assist him in mixing his 'photographic chemicals'. It was particularly sad for her that she missed his departure from Darmstadt; because no one told her the exact time he was leaving. He left for England to return to his regiment in India. It was during this coming tour of duty that his regiment saw active service on one of the Black Mountain expeditions.

Perhaps the climax of the last fortnight of this holiday were the *tableaux vivants*. There is no mention of them in the planning stages and the tableaux appear fully fledged three days before the party broke up. Emily notes for Sunday 20th September:

> The two young Pses and we four ladies went to the German church. Directly after we went down to the dress rehearsal of the tableaux and all the gentlemen came to join. It lasted until nearly 1o'clock.

The next day's entry goes on:

> Fine quite early, rain from 8 to 2 o'C. Fair afternoon. Ps Thora and Ps Alix went out riding before breakfast. I wrote after breakfast. There was a dress rehearsal at 11-oC. Only one scene was rehearsed as a lamp was upset and the stage caught fire. It was rather bad for a few minutes but plenty of help put it out. Great excitement and the rehearsal had to be put an end to.

After a full afternoon of farewell calls, she continues:

> Dinner at quarter to 7 for the performances. I dressed after. It began punctually at 8 and lasted an hour. Very successful.

The charade was based on the name of 'Romrod'. Emily noted who played the various characters in the scenes. They were:

> R   Romeo and Juliet Herr v Riedesel and Ps Alix
> O   Othello and Desd: & Father Pc Henry and Ps Thora, Gen Werkser
> M   Marie Ant. Ps Chris: H v Grancy, H.v Roder
> R   Rebecca. Gretchen, Eleager, H v Westerweller
> O   Oedipus & Antigone. H v Grancy and Miss E Loch
> D   Dornröschen. Frl. v Plänchner & Herr v Schwarzkoff

> Romrod; Everybody who was at Romrod seen in various occupations of the place.
>
> We danced after and had nice tea first and supper after. Various ladies came and Fr v Riedesel and the Ps played the dance music. Lasted till 10-30. Packed when we came to bed.

Quite a day – and what a lot of fun and excitement they had, losing themselves in make-believe and dressing up. They were able to indulge in a lively 'relevage', to use Emily's term, of their delightful visit to the old castle of Romrod. It was a wonderful end to this happy interlude. This holiday had been more relaxed and natural than almost any other occasion in which Emily was with members of the Royalty. Princess Christian was well and joined in magnificently, which so rarely happened; and her musical talents contributed to the gaiety of the party. During this holiday not only did the cousins and aunt have time to enjoy each others company but Emily and the other members of the household were able to join in wholeheartedly. And this was remembered, when the visit to Russia was mooted three years later. Circumstances would have changed dramatically: but the deep friendships engendered would have been remembered by Princess Alix.

This fascinating year was not yet over for Emily. She, the Princess, and Thora returned to England towards the end of September, spent a couple of nights at Buckingham Palace and then took the night train to Aberdeen to join Queen Victoria and her party at Balmoral. It was a small gathering which included Princess Beatrice, her husband, Prince Henry of Battenberg, and their three children – the family which brought such delight to Queen Victoria in her old age. The children were Prince Alexander, now aged 5, and Princess Ena who was very special to Balmoral having been born there: hers was the first royal birth in Scotland since the early 17th century. Prince Leopold, now 2, was soon to be displaced as the youngest by the imminent arrival of a new baby. He, Prince Maurice, duly made his appearance on October 3rd and was christened in the castle drawing room at the end of the month. Princess Thora was consulted about the hymns for the service and Emily helped to do the flowers. Emily writes for October 31st:

> Everyone assembled in the Drawing room which was very prettily arranged. A very nice service by Dr. Lees, the Dean of the Thistle, and a choir which sang very well. Lunch for everyone at 1.30.

The occasion no doubt was very similar to Princess Ena's christening in 1887 captured in Robert T Precept's painting. In this, Queen Victoria holding the baby beside the font is surrounded by her family and Household. In 1891, the artist was a Mr Reid. Princess Christian, Princess Thora and Emily all sat in turn for their likenesses to be sketched by him before they left the Castle early in November.

After the lunch following the christening, Emily wrote:

> I went out walking with Pss Tora and Pc Ernie up Craig Gowan. Sat down a good deal. Had tea with them and then the children came and I sang to them.

Indoor occupations and letter writing were the usual morning routine at Balmoral followed in the afternoon by walks or drives in the countryside. The Queen always drove taking various companions – Princess Christian or Princess Thora, or one of her ladies. Emily went with her once when they drove into the hills on a very stormy afternoon. In the early evening, Emily often sang to Princess Beatrice's older children.

Prince Ernie had arrived at the Castle on October 9th and his coming certainly added gaiety and spice to life. That evening the whole party 'played the Spoof band after dinner and made the most fearful noise and the Queen nearly died of laughter.' On most evenings there was some form of entertainment, usually of a musical nature. On the day of the christening, Minnie Cochrane played. A rather special lady, 'Jacontha', was engaged for one evening and Emily was the one who had to write the letter of invitation. The lady duly came and played but Emily and the others were much mystified and astonished by the peculiar vows which Jacontha had taken and which she had no hesitation in telling Emily about; but Emily in turn does not tell us!

Queen Victoria had loved the theatre and dancing as a young person and now, in the seclusion of Balmoral, and with so many of the younger generations around her, she was able again to enjoy them fully. After a very stormy day, both for the weather and temperamentally, Emily:

> dined with the Queen and dressed very hurriedly. Very stormy day with agitation's [sic] and running around. Prince Henry's birthday. Curtis' band played and we danced for an hour after dinner in the drawing room with the furniture pushed back. The Queen danced one quadrille quite beautifully. Came to bed at quarter to 12 rather exhausted.

The agitations of the day sorted out and forgotten in the fun! The Quadrille, a square dance with five movements, had been popular throughout the century and could be danced to music based on any tune, often one that was currently the rage. This was only the first of several dances while Emily was at Balmoral. There was a servants' ball on October 10th to which they all went and, the next evening:

> The girls from Invercauld and young Mr Borthwick dined here and came for the Cotillon. It began at 10.15 and lasted nearly an hour and was a great success and amused the Queen very much.

In the cotillion – a series of dances, quick waltzes, polkas, and gallops – the leading couple set the style and all the others follow. Partners could be exchanged, so that each man had a chance to dance with each woman. This made an excellent entertainment for the variety of people at the castle. It is no wonder that the Queen was so much amused and delighted to see her grandchildren and neighbours enjoying themselves. In fact, it was such success that a few nights later, when 'The Borthwick boy and girl came, we had to get up an impromptu cotillion by order of the Queen which turned out very successful. Got to bed very late'.

For the last week of their visit, the dance was the Bolero. On October 20th, after Emily, who had had quite a busy day, was settling down quietly in her room in the early evening, she 'was fetched by the young people to learn the Bolero. Very hot and exhausted.' The next day soon after breakfast, she:

> was fetched by Pss Thora. We went to the drawing room with Miss Hughes and she played and we practised 'Bolero' and then tried songs.

After that, there was a practice some time almost every day for the next week, except on the 24th when the 'Russian Mazurka' was danced. Emily writes:

> At 6 o'C we [Pss Tora, Pc Ernie and Emily], Pc Henry, Harriet, Miss Hughes, Herr Müther and Sir Fleetwood all met in the ballroom to practise the Russian Mazurka which we did hard for an hour.

After dining with the Household, they all joined the Queen to show her the dance. 'She liked it so much that we had to do it twice in spite of nearly dying of exhaustion and it went very well on the whole'. Prince Ernie had thrown himself whole-heartedly into the entertainment and it was he who organised the head-dresses and scarves. Perhaps his high-spirited enthusiasm was a bit much for Princess Thora for, between the practice and the performance, Emily 'brought Princess Thora to my room and made her lie on my bed and Mrs Anglier came to massage her leg'. Finally, on the last day of the month, the Bolero was considered ready for performance. After dinner with the Household,

Prince Ernie acting a 'romantic' scene with Princess Thora
and Emily while at Balmoral in the autumn of 1891.

> The Bolero was danced for the Queen just before we went to bed. The ladies staid but not the gentlemen. Prince Ernie dressed in Herr Müther's clothes and was very well got up as a Spaniard.

There are three spirited photos in Emily's album of Prince Ernie, kilted and bonneted in the Scots manner. He is engaged in some flirtatious acting – proffering a rose – to Princess Thora and Emily. He was particularly interested in the arts generally and was probably behind the acting, dressing up and dancing that went on during this visit. Emily records on October 23rd that 'Pss Tora went to Pss Beatrice and Pc Ernie did his ballet "Scene" while Mrs Hughes played' and the following day:

> I sat with Pss Tora and Prince Ernie afternoon – we went in to see the children – it was Pss Ina's 4th birthday. We 3 had tea together and Prince Ernie nearly made us die of [laughing at] the " Automaton tea drinker".

During this visit Emily spent many hours with Princess Thora and Prince Ernie chaperoning them as they walked, talked and sang together. Towards the end of their time Emily writes:

> I rode afternoon with Pss Tora and Pc Ernie. We went to Bowmonts Moss and round by the hill. Came back along the footpath through crowds of deer and roaring and fighting stags.

Despite the romantic ride back down the glen in the evening light and the wonderful sight of so many deer this possible romance did not flourish and Princess Thora remained a spinster all her life. Nevertheless, when Princess Christian's party left Balmoral, Prince Ernie was up early in the morning to see them off. Two days later the party broke up. Princess Christian, Princess Thora and Emily paid a brief visit to the Duchess of Roxburgh near Dunbar, and then returned to Buckingham Palace. Here Prince Ernie again met them but they soon left London to return to Cumberland Lodge and the Cottage. There is no doubt that Emily spent a lot of this visit as a chaperone for Princess Thora – she obviously enjoyed the company of the two young people and the light-hearted fun of Prince Ernie. It appeared that Queen Victoria was not averse to the two young people being together and had probably invited them both to Balmoral with the hopes of an engagement. But it was not to be.

By the following year, however, the Queen had begun to look elsewhere for a suitable bride for Prince Ernie, who early in 1892 had become the Grand Duke of Hesse-Darmstadt.[42] Prince Ernie was reluctant to make up his mind about marriage; but streams of advice from his Grandmother and sisterly letters from Princess Victoria finally made him decide in 1894 to marry another cousin, Ducky, Princess Victoria Melita, daughter of Queen Victoria's son, Affie, Duke of Edinburgh and Grand Duchess Marie. This marriage which seemed to some of the relations so auspicious and to others rather doubtful began as a great success. The two young people were merry, and given to many amusing pranks, but they were also wayward and irresponsible. And, sin of sins, did not answer letters; to the extent of not thanking for wedding presents, even eleven months after the event!

1891 had been a momentous year in the lives of Emily's Royalty. So much had happened and she had got to know Princess Thora – now left on her own at home – so much better, and had begun to accompany her on many of her engagements. Princess Christian's health, with many interesting events to fill her days and no treatment at a spa to sap her energy, seemed much better; and her illnesses did not dominate Emily's life, or not, at least, her diary. Above all Emily had laid the foundations of lasting friendship with Princess Alix.

CHAPTER TEN

The Early Nineties: Changes Great and Small

After the excitements of 1891, the years 1892 and 1893 settled into a gentle rhythm for Emily and her princesses. Princess Christian, having got her younger daughter married to what appeared to be a suitable German princeling, settled down to her usual quiet but busy life at home, interspersed with visits to her relations in Germany. It was a time of weddings, when many of her nephews and nieces were taking this important step. These were always a great opportunity to meet the crowds of relations who were scattered around Europe and, for Emily, they were a chance to keep up with her particular favourites, Prince Ernie and Princess Alix in Hesse, and Princess Louie now settled in Germany. The family at Cumberland Lodge was reduced to Princess Thora, although Prince Christle visited fairly frequently when his regiment was stationed at nearby Aldershot.

From Emily's diary there is some evidence that Thora missed her sister very much in the early years after her marriage. Emily records that Princess Thora, usually accompanied by Else Blücher, came over to the Cottage frequently in '92 and '93, especially when her mother was away. There are entries saying that her father often took her out riding with him and, on a few days, Emily noted that 'Pss Tora went hunting', something that she had not mentioned in earlier years. The Princess had become very much the companion of both her parents. Like her father, she loved dogs and horses, and was usually accompanied by some small canine friend. She interested herself in the domestic life of Cumberland Lodge, for example being discovered by Emily decorating a Christmas tree just after New Year.[43] She played the piano and frequently sang, sometimes with her mother. She continued to practise her painting, sometimes with Alice's help. Most princesses and ladies of the aristocracy undertook charitable works, and Thora was no exception. Quite often she was away from home on some work for charity; sometimes she was away visiting friends. She

Princess Thora standing by her Grandmother seated in a light pony carriage.

spent much time with her young nephews and nieces, especially the Battenbergs and the Connaughts. She also became a useful companion for her grandmother. Emily has a photo of the Princess standing by the ageing Queen, sitting in her low-slung pony carriage and, as the years went by, Princess Thora became a trusted confidant of 'Dearest Grandmama'.

Princess Thora became one of the family who took part in the Queen's round of engagements. In 1892, just before going to Germany, Princess Christian and Princess Thora were at Osborne for Cowes week; Emily was with them, and did not waste the opportunity to have 'tremendous discussions with Dr Reid on Mattei and Homeopathy'. What Dr Reid thought is not recorded! The Emperor of Germany was taking part in the regatta and was proudly showing off his yacht which, to his chagrin, was beaten in the races. Many of Queen Victoria's huge family were there to enjoy the gala occasion. One afternoon Princess Thora and the Connaughts – Prince Arthur and Princess Louise of Prussia, and their children were among the many guests entertained by the German Emperor aboard his yacht. He paid particular attention to his aunt, Princess Christian, and perhaps astonished his guests by handing round the teacakes and bread and butter. The Emperor was exerting all his considerable charm. But signs that the future might not be so peaceful were becoming apparent; competitive re-arming was getting into its stride. A few days later Princess Thora and Emily visited Portsmouth and were shown over the naval destroyer, the *Resistance*, which 'had been riddled with shot as an experiment'.

Princess Christian was also deeply involved in charitable works; these reflected her various interests and talents and it does not appear that the troubles with medication and drugs affected her adversely. Medical matters, particularly nursing, had been a keen interest from early days; this was shown in the help she gave to Catherine Loch in her chosen career and her enthusiastic following of all Catherine's achievements, especially in India. The Princess regularly spent much time on the subject of nurses and nursing services, and she attended endless meetings in London in her capacity as President of the Royal British Nursing Association. She worked hard at this from the 80s and her efforts were rewarded in March 1893 with the granting of the Royal Charter to the Association. Emily writes: 'The Bishop of Ripon was there and made a charming address and the Pss gave a very nice little answer'. Nearer at home she established a Nurses' Home in Windsor in 1892 and took a keen interest in its running. A Miss Simpson[44] was appointed Matron in November that year and the Princess made regular visits to ensure that all was well (Plate 3).

In 1892, while Princess Christian was in Homburg with her sister, Empress Vicky, Emily records that, one evening, the Empress and others spent much of the evening discussing the cholera epidemic which was sweeping Germany and that this made many of the guests 'very uncomfortable'. This was listened to with interest by Princess Christian for, as soon as she returned to England, she was attending meetings at the Mansion House in connection with 'the cholera committee'.

During the 19th century a number of cholera epidemics had swept around the world. There had been three in Europe in the last sixty years: each epidemic lasted months if not years before it faded out. This 1892 epidemic, which appeared to have started in Paris, spread rapidly through Germany to Russia. In Hamburg alone there were nearly 17,000 cases and over eight and a half thousand dead. Even if the exact figures had not been known to the Empress and her friends, the virulence and rapid spread of the disease would have been enough cause for alarm. It was the enormous contrast between the number of cases in Hamburg where the inhabitants used untreated river water, and the few cases in nearby Altona where the water was filtered, that indicated that clean water was all important. This pointed the way to prevention. Princess Christian would have heard something about the spread of the disease and its treatment from the accounts which Emily read to her in Cathy Loch's letters from India: Cathy had many cases through her wards. It was in this very year that she remarked that cholera, being prevalent in Kashmir, would come to them down the Jhelum river; 'it always does'.

The Princess's other continuing interest was 'The School of Art Needlework' of which she was a founder member. The diary repeats again and again 'took the Pss the Sch. of Art'. The Princess's connection with this lasted for many years and she was herself a skilled needlewoman. There were regular exhibitions and bazaars each autumn and the Princess was a regular attender. Business at the 'School' was often the first appointment of the day when the Princess and Emily travelled up from Windsor. The headquarters was in Kensington and, after the meeting, she often visited one or other of her friends who lived in that part of London. Emily's aunt, Louisa Brandreth, lived in Elvaston Place and the Princess frequently lunched with her. Refreshed, she would then go on to further meetings for the nurses or to some function such as laying a foundation stone or, on a more personal level, visit her doctor Dr Maclaggan who, although appointed to her Household, lived in London. Often the day ended with a visit to the theatre. For these visits, the Princess and Emily stayed at Buckingham Palace but, except for breakfast, they rarely ate there. If there was no invitation to dine with friends, they went to the Buckingham Palace Hotel.

Music remained a great interest. The Bach choir rehearsals were attended whenever possible, but these were more of an 'indulgence', the Princess and Emily doing something they both enjoyed. There were many charity concerts to attend and, for a number of years on Boxing Day, the Princess played the piano in charity concerts in Hackney Wick.

Emily's picture of her is of a hard-working lady who liked to get things done, not much given to being in the public eye; very kind, often giving presents, enjoying a regular routine and loyal to her friends and husband. The two led separate lives in many ways and yet, if Prince Christian was late returning from a walk or suddenly wanted to change plans, the Princess got very upset. This may well have been caused by the medication she was taking, but Emily is not one to tell us such confidential details. As mentioned earlier, Dr Reid eventually in 1896 withdrew 'all narcotics and stimulants'. It does not appear that he was a very sympathetic doctor as regards Princess Christian but

The front entrance to Friedrichshof with its amazing mixture of styles.
Emily watched the building grow during the early 1890s.

probably his action did, in the end, help her.

Princess Christian was very fond of some of her extended family and, certainly, the visits to German spas were often used as ways of seeing both the family of her deceased sister Alice and her eldest sister Empress Vicky. During the annual visits to Homburg or Wiesbaden she and Emily were able to watch the emergence of Friedrichshof, as it was being built for Empress Vicky in its amazing mixture of styles and, eventually in 1896, to stay there (Plate 6). These visits abroad gave the Princess a chance to escape a little from her mother's immediate influence; for it seems that she was in considerable awe of her mother, especially as it is likely that she had heard some of her mother's unkind remarks. When at Cumberland Lodge she spent much time dealing with the Queen's correspondence and daily affairs, as did Princess Beatrice. In turn, Emily spent an enormous amount of time writing for Princess Christian. Almost every day, if they were together, Emily was writing and, if not writing, making arrangements either for people to see her or for the numerous journeys near and far.

For the three Loch sisters, the highlight of the first half of the 90s was Cathy Loch's return in 1893 for a year's leave from service in India. Cathy disembarked from her ship in Italy just before Easter and joined Emily in Florence, where she and Gerry had just arrived to be with the Davidsons. The Bishop was there as part of the Queen Victoria's entourage at the Villa Palmeri. The visit became a mixture of intensive sightseeing with their friends and attendance upon the Queen, when commanded. The two sisters were part of the choir which sang in a Good Friday service for the Queen; they dined with the Queen, chose hymns for the Easter service and listened to excellent sermons. Princess Louie came to join the galaxy of relations around the Queen, and Emily had many long talks with her before the gathering dispersed, and the sisters and the Davidsons moved on to Venice. Back in England during the summer, Cathy was honoured for her work with the Army Nursing Service in India by dinners at Windsor Castle, Chester and the City of London. Then all three – Alice, Emily and Cathy – went for a family holiday at Alice's chalet close beside the sea in Brittany. Here they were able to have a very relaxed and informal time swimming and paddling, being entertained by the locals; all was spiced with Cathy's wit and humour.

The year before, early in September 1892, Emily and Princess Thora spent a couple of days at Wolfsgarten while Princess Christian continued her spa treatment in Homburg. Princess Louie was there and they all joined Prince Ernie, now the Grand Duke, and the family. It was back among friends and, if anything, the atmosphere was even more relaxed, one might almost say, childish – not that Emily uses such language!

Alix and Victoria greeted them. After lunch they all went to the 'tennis ground and did *pas de géant*'.[45] Emily and Fräulein von Grancy had time for a walk to pick bunches of heather and look at each other's sketches before dinner; then whist and music. The Grand Duke, as Emily now usually refers to Ernie, played duets with a Frl. v. Schenk. This was only a prelude to the next day, Sunday, when Emily writes:

> Fine morning cold. All went to Eglesbach church ... back by 11.15 ... Changed and went out to Pas de Géant and tennis. Came in at 1.30, changed again for lunch. Played a wild game after lunch, Guten morgen Wie Geht es Ihnen?' Fell down heavily in running. Wrote to Freda [Biddulph] when we came in. Sat with Frls. v Grancy and Schenk. Sang a little with her and then went to the tennis ground. They all did Pas de Géant. I did not. We had tea and then I changed dress for the 4th time and

> played tennis until it was quite dark. Music evening. I sang. Frl.v Schenk played a long time very well. We came to bed late.

The visitors left Wolfsgarten the next morning and returned to Homburg, where Princess Christian was staying with her sister, the dowager Empress, in the old Schloss. The Princess had retired to bed and remained there for the next few days, so it seems that, yet again, she was in a poor state of health, but the two young princesses played tennis and visited the shops and friends. Emily took them to 'be photoed'. It was a great joy for Louie and Thora to be together. Princess Louie had arrived from Berlin on August 19th, not looking very well. Every day for the next three weeks, Emily was with the young princesses and there were many long talks and 'many conflabs'.

Naturally, in 1892 – just a year after her marriage – there must have been much to tell; a husband; a new way of life and routine; the very strict protocol of the small German court and having to make new friends. All common experiences for young princesses but it sounds as if she wasn't too happy. She had to leave a luncheon given by the Prince of Wales soon after she arrived and, the next day, couldn't be found when Dr Detz came to see her. At last she was found in her sister's room, and Emily

> sat with them some time trying to calm Pss Louie. Sat with her again later. Detz came to Ps Louie later in the evening and prescribed Marienbad waters for a fortnight.

Next day,

> Sat with the Pss all the morning and there was much talk. In the evening, Ps Louie told me the whole history of Parsival.

The following day Emily was with her most of the time and they went off to buy a new hat. She became much more cheerful again a day later, when Emily brought an old friend, Madame Millie Moineaux, to see her. Soon after this, there was another happy occasion when Ernie and Alix came over and they all discussed plans. Princess Louie had one visit to Dr Pagenstecher not long before she left and, later, Emily went with her to choose a present to take to Prince Aribert. It sounds as if she was much refreshed by her holiday and more able to cope with the future. Emily had been a comfort and a confidant.

The sisters were together early the next year, 1893, when Prince and Princess Christian, and Princess Thora travelled to Berlin in the depth of winter for yet another royal wedding, that of Princess Mossy, Empress Vicky's youngest daughter, and Prince Friedrich Karl von Hessen. On this occasion their train from Flushing to Berlin travelled across snowy covered landscapes in Holland and Germany. They had a 'large saloon carriage with an iron stove that alternated between too hot and freezing'. The train was delayed by heavy snow, but Princess Louie and Prince Aribert were on the station in Berlin, at 10.30 in the evening, to greet them. So were the Mallets, the British ambassador, and all the corps diplomatique. 'Came to the Embassy, had supper and then came up to bed all most heavenly comfortable'. Emily always found the beds in the British Embassy particularly comfortable.

It was clear that the two princesses were delighted to be together again, and there were many long talks with much to-ing and fro-ing between the Embassy, where Princess Christian's party were staying, and Princess Louie's house. Emily and Thora went to watch Louie rehearsing for the mounted quadrille which she was to perform as part of the wedding celebrations. There were several rehearsals in the covered riding school: 'Very amusing but bitterly cold' remarked Emily. They went to watch the Military ride at the Dragoon barracks on a foggy and freezing cold afternoon two days before the wedding ceremony, and were joined by Ernie and Alix, who was suffering from earache. 'It all went off beautifully and Pss Louie did very well' wrote Emily: Louie hadn't let down her husband, who was a major in the 1st Dragoon Guards.

As usual the visit was a series of grand occasions and spectacles, but arrangements didn't always go smoothly; this upset both Princess Christian and Princess Louie and irritated Emily who was used to careful planning so that everything ran on oiled wheels. January 19th was a bad day. In the morning Emily found Princess Louie 'much disturbed in mind because of arrangements'; and perhaps rightly so, for, in the evening after a splendid reception when trains were worn, there 'was a grand confusion about meeting the princesses at their door and they had no one and no pages at first' – a real problem when the royal ladies emerged into the bitterly cold night with snow on the ground and no one was there to carry their long and elaborate trains. And this was not the only time when arrangements went awry.

The wedding day came just as the weather changed – rain and a 'thorough thaw and the streets were a fearful mess'. They dressed in their smart clothes at 3 o'clock in the afternoon and

> went to join the Princesses in their rooms and went up with them. We stood from more or less 4.30 till 10.15. First there was the procession into the Chapel. Pss Christian walked with Gd Duke of Weimar and Ps Henry. The music in the Chapel very good. Processed back to the Weisse Saal for the Cour which lasted one and half hours. Then procession back and the royalties had dinner while we had a few sandwiches and tried to find some place to sit down. Then the procession and the Fackeltzug (sic) [torchlight procession] which was a very pretty sight. I was rather occupied with one of the Empress' ladies whose nose bled. It was all over at 10.15 and we accompanied our Psses back to their rooms and came home dead tired. Had some milk and sardines.

and as an afterthought:

> Pss Mossy did it all beautifully and looked very nice. Prince Fischy looked very ill.

Nicholas, the Tsarevich, also made notes of this wedding in his diary and they are not so glowing. Perhaps he was irritated because, although he had been given permission by his mother and father to 'start finding out about Alix' while in Berlin, he never had an opportunity to speak to her seriously. Also, the Kaiser, whom he was not fond of, had presented him with the Order of the Black Eagle and he, Nicholas, had had to put on a particularly uncomfortable red cloak: 'I nearly died of heat in it'. He thought the church service gave no indication that marriage was a sacrament; and the ceremony, when the newly weds were congratulated by each lady and each man, was very tedious and took two hours. It was just another wedding of another German cousin.

For Emily and the Christian family, however, Princess Mossy was rather special. Princess Christian always made a particular effort to keep in close contact with her eldest sister and the younger members of the Empress's family. She frequently saw them either in England or Germany. Princess Mossy, nicknamed after the mossy look of her hair at her christening, was more correctly Princess Margaret Beatrice Feodora. She had been sixteen at the time of her father's death, and was one of the princesses that Emily had got to know in the sad days when she had gone with Princess Christian to be with the Empress Vicky in her bereavement during the hot summer of 1888.

The formal marriage ceremony was not quite the end of the festivities. There were more elaborate meals, two operas – one newly composed by a Dane which Emily thought very dull and 'we didn't stay till the end'; and 'a big dinner at the Mallets to the newly married pair and to the Empress'. She also found time to visit her friends from previous visits to Berlin. The highlight was an evening with the Mendelssohn family. The playing of her greatly admired Joachim was 'heavenly' and the familiar music of Mozart, Beethoven and Schumann exceedingly enjoyable. Louie and Thora met every day until the time came for the family to return to England.

Their separation wasn't for too long. By late August 1893, Thora and Emily were back in Wolfsgarten, and Princess Alix was again there to greet them on their arrival. Louie was also there. In her memoirs Princess Marie Louise said she was particularly fond of her Hessian cousin who was almost the same age, and she no doubt felt very much at ease in this happy household. Again it was a very musical time. Herr Wolff was staying when Emily arrived, and he and Princess Alix played for two hours that afternoon and again the next day for most of the morning. Emily and Alix sang after he had left, and so it continued

Princess Thora accompanying Herr Wolff on the violin.

with all taking turns to play, including the Grand Duke Ernie. He had been laid low with a dislocated knee when Emily arrived and, at the first luncheon, appeared in a wheelchair or, as Emily writes, *rollstuhl*; but he recovered quickly and they were back to 'wild games'. A new venture mentioned was cooking. The diary for August 30th reads:

> Grey most of the day. Close. A little sunshine. Did music with Ps Tora after breakfast Then walked with Princess Louie. Then wrote till lunch. We cooked all afternoon, and Prince Ernie and I made the most excellent shortbread. Prince Henry of Hesse came and we all had tea together. Tennis after tea and much out of tune part songs evening.

There was a lot of tennis during this visit and riding in the mornings; once the three princesses, Alix, Thora and Louie, took out six horses and had a great time. After a very relaxed fortnight the party broke up. Louie returned to Berlin, Emily and Thora to Princess Christian in Homburg and Alix was left at home.

1894 dawned. Changes were in the air, but the magnitude of the changes for Emily, her family and the young royalty she loved could hardly be envisaged. Cathy who had been on leave from India for nine months was beginning to think of her return. At the end of January she paid a visit to Florence Nightingale, no doubt to give a first-hand account of her experiences in India and possibly to receive instructions and advice about how to improve the nursing service for the troops out there. Cathy's letters to her sisters were full of the problems in India, not just the physical ones of climate, pests and diseases but friction with the officers and some of the doctors.

On February 11th, Emily noted that she 'packed Cathy's dresses for India' and, on the 16th, the whole day was spent seeing Cathy off at Portsmouth. The sisters travelled down by train from London in the afternoon and eventually found Gerry who had come separately.

> We went on board the 'Serapis' and found Cathy's berth etc. … We unpacked and settled Cathy's things a little … we stayed some time on board and then went back to tea at the Hotel. Gerry then rested as she had a headache and C and I went in a tram into the town to buy her a belt. We walked back. Sat in our

> room and went down to dinner at 7.30. Very good and it was very cheerful. Went up to our room after and C smoked and we talked till 10 o'C when we took her on board again and left her and went back to the hotel to bed.

Three days later Emily was back on duty at Cumberland Lodge. Princess Christian's health was again rather poor and she spent a good deal of time in bed. Princess Thora was hunting and riding with her father; one day she and the Prince took Emily to look at the horses in the stables. On February 21st there was 'much upsetment in the evening by a letter from Pss Louie begging Pss Tora to go out to her'. She could not go at once as there were visitors at the Castle. The Empress Vicky, Grand Duke Ernie and Princess Alix were staying with the Queen and Thora and Emily were needed to help entertain them either at the Castle or Cumberland Lodge. A few days later Emily wrote:

> The Gd. Duke, Pss Alix and Mr Wemyss came to lunch. I sat with them a little after ... We all went down to Windsor. The Pss [Christian] to the Castle and we all to St George's.

The young Grand Duke was paying a visit to his Grandmother, just as the family had done almost every spring since the death of Princess Alice, but this time it was rather special. In a couple of months he was going to marry his cousin Ducky, having at last been persuaded to overcome his indecision. This was his last visit as an unmarried man. Princess Alix was with him, and her life was going to change too. After his marriage, her position as his boon companion was bound to alter[46], and she was also under considerable pressure to make up her mind to marry Nicholas of Russia. He was passionately in love with her; and the uncertainty as to whether she would be able to overcome her reluctance to give up Lutheranism for the Orthodox faith was making him ... and her ... quite ill. But, by April, when the marriage of Ernie and Ducky took place in Coburg amongst a galaxy of relations including Queen Victoria, Princess Alix had made up her mind.

So, in May, the youngest of the beautiful sisters from Hesse-Darmstadt was again visiting her beloved grandmother in England. This was to be her last visit before her marriage[47]. Emily wrote a short note in her diary for May 9th 1894: 'Went to the Green Pk. Club and had a successful lunch there – and then went to the New Gallery and got caught in the rain'. In the years to come this short entry brought back memories of this happy day and in her imagination she saw it all again.

Walking along one of the passages in Buckingham Palace, Emily said to the footman,

"Richard, would you send a message to Gretchen, that I shall wait for their Highnesses just outside in the garden."

She stepped out through the door pulling on her gloves as she went. The day was rather grey and chilly and she was glad that she had worn her new mauve cape, just come from Opitz, her favourite dress shop in Wiesbaden. She looked across the garden. The branches of the horse chestnuts and planes were tossing in the wind but the rain kept off, and there were moments of sunshine. Not a very auspicious start for her outing with Princess Thora and Princess Alix, but she had arranged this luncheon so that the three of them would have a chance to reminisce before Princess Alix returned to Germany. Emily was glad that she had arranged for a cab to pick them up when the three of them had had their short walk across the gardens.

A few minutes later she heard laughter and the door opened again. Two smartly dressed young ladies stepped out. Princess Thora was wearing her green, well-cut skirt and jacket, with its leg-of-mutton sleeves and matching waistcoat, which had just come from the tailors. Emily was glad to see that she had her fashionable boater well secured against the wind. Princess Alix had chosen a lovely russet skirt trimmed with bronze-coloured braid and had a short velvet jacket with huge puffed sleeves. The russet ribbons and bows danced in the wind on her broad-brimmed hat. The whole outfit set off the princess to perfection and was a warming picture on such an un-spring-like day.

As the three went, down the steps and across the gravel Emily asked, "Did you have a good journey, your Highness?" Princess Alix had come up from Windsor, where she was staying at the Castle as guest of her Grandmother. Emily and Princess Thora had come up earlier in the morning from Cumberland Lodge, with Else and Princess Christian.

"Yes, thank you Miss Loch, Gretchen came with me and we took a cab from Paddington station".

"Well, I thought we would walk across the garden and I have ordered a cab to meet us in about half an hour and then we will drive along to the Club for luncheon."

"That will be lovely," both princesses replied together and then broke out laughing.

"So let us start walking," continued Princess Thora. "And we can show Alix some of the garden".

All three ladies set off, each with her umbrella, in case of rain. Emily was proudly using her 'en tout cas' which Princess Thora had given her for her birthday the month before. She had hoped to use it against the sun but, today, its use as an umbrella seemed more likely. They walked along the edge of the lake, the wind whipping the surface so that the reflections of the shrubs and trees were all blurred. The ranks of stiff tulips bent in unison before the wind. Princess Thora pointed out the summerhouse, which their grandfather had built for the Queen, but which was rarely used now. As they neared the wall of the garden, the noise of the traffic outside became more insistent – the clip-clop of the horses' hooves, the grinding of the iron-shod wheels, the shouts of the drivers and the occasional neighing of startled animals. The gate in the wall was opened for them by a porter and they stepped out on to the pavement. In the road, the whirl of vehicles, cabs, carriages, wagons and tradesmen's vans was almost bewildering. Their cab was waiting for them and all three got in. Emily gave instructions for them to be taken to the Green Park Club.[48] *They joined the stream of traffic round the Arch of Hyde Park Corner and passed the famous Duke of Wellington's mansion. Princess Thora pointed out a troop of Lifeguards splendid in their scarlet uniforms and gleaming helmets trotting in the Park, as they joined the flow of vehicles in Piccadilly. Soon their cab turned off into the comparative calm of the side streets and brought them to the door of the Green Park Club in Grafton Street.*

Emily had been to this club several times, sometimes with Princess Christian; so she had discovered that it was a suitable place to take the young princesses. They were welcomed by the staff with bows and curtseys and taken through into a private dining room. A table was laid ready, complete with starched white cloths and napkins – gleaming silver and cut glasses reflecting occasional gleams of sunshine; bunches of violets added their scent to the room. Emily and the princesses sat down, but the meal was almost forgotten in the flow of conversation.

"Do tell Emily about the wedding in Coburg," Thora prompted her cousin.

"Oh! It was all so exciting," said Alix. "Of course we had all gone there to see Ernie and Ducky on their great day. And it was a great day. All the aunts and uncles and Grandmama. Everyone in their best clothes. Ducky looked lovely, sparkling and laughy, and Ernie was very handsome in his uniform. They seemed to be having such fun, always sharing some private joke. No one seemed to remember all those horrid things which were said about cousins marrying – look, half our cousins have married each other – who else is there to marry? But the disease which poor Fritty had is so very frightening … But no one spoke of these things and Grandmama really seemed to think that it was a marriage made in heaven. We all had a glorious time."

"Yes," said Thora, "but do tell Emily about you know who".

Princess Alix's lovely face took on a radiant look and her pale complexion became delicately flushed.

"Yes, please tell me about his Royal Highness," said Emily.

"Well, you know I have liked dear Nicky for ages ... really since we were children, that time we first met in Russia when Ella was married and he gave me the brooch ... but I did give it back! The more I liked him, the more difficult it became because, as you know, since dear Mamma died I have got much help from my pastor and I find his teaching such a help. But you see Nicky and all those Russians have quite a different faith and teaching and I really was not sure I could change. But Nicky was so kind, so patient, and so understanding at Coburg, and Grandmama and Nicky's aunt Michem[49] *were so persuasive and pointing out how awful it was for Nicky ... that in the end I couldn't resist any longer and ... Oh! Now I am so happy and every one is being so kind ... and I think it will be all right. I am not sure what Miss Jackson would think, oh dear! But I couldn't be without Nicky. Already he has become so very dear. But I do find the lessons in Russian very difficult and I shall never be able to pronounce the sounds correctly."*

"Oh, I am sure you will, your Highness," said Emily, "but it will take some hard work. You have got Fräulein Schneider to teach you."

"Yes, she is here with us now and she will be coming to Harrogate with me when I go there at the end of the month. And, do you know, Victoria is going to come too and be with me for my birthday. I am so glad, because I am not really looking forward to all those peat baths and sulphur baths. Drinking that horrid, sulphur-smelling water sounds terrible ... but, do you know, I have heard that there is a delicious toffee that I can suck afterwards and so the awful taste goes away[50] *... And I do hope people won't stare at me too much. I don't like it but they do it so often, now they know I am engaged to Nicky. Oh well! I must try to do something about this sciatica and my wretched legs; they are so painful."*

After a pause while the plates were removed Thora changed the subject a little.

"It is funny, though, isn't it, Emily. You first came to know Alix when Mama went to Homburg and Wiesbaden to try and get help with the waters there, and now Alix is going to Harrogate in this country for the same sort of reason."

"Yes, it is a coincidence. I do hope you get some relief, your Highness. It has been wonderful for me get to know your family. I think the happiest time was when we went with your father such a short while before he so sadly died, on that wonderful holiday in Romrod. Do you remember the fun we had there?"

"Oh yes! and the amusing charade we did on the name 'Romrod' when we got back to Wolfsgarten", said Alix.

"And do you remember the morning the stage went on fire? It was lucky that it

wasn't worse", Thora joined in.

"And you, Alix, were Juliet. Was von Riedesel a romantic Romeo?" Thora laughed and Alix retaliated with "And what about Henry being your Othello?"

"Come on your Highnesses, I think that is enough of that. Let's go on now and look at some of the pictures at the New Gallery before we have to go back to the Palace. I hope we don't get caught in the rain. It is getting very dark."

So, Emily and her two young charges set off for the short walk to the New Gallery,[51] *unaware of the bustle of the London street in their recollections of the happy carefree days of holidays in Germany; and they hardly noticed the rain.*

A few mornings later when all three were staying at Buckingham Palace Emily sat and talked with Princess Thora and Princess Alix and, just before Princess Alix left for her cure at Harrogate, she and Princess Thora came to have tea at the Cottage. This was quite usual for Princess Thora but is the only time Alix came to the Cottage. This was, even then, a rather special day for Emily. Later, looking back, it must have seemed even more special.

Next morning, Gretchen, Fräulein Schneider and Princess Alix left for Harrogate. Her sister, Princess Victoria, joined her there, and they had great amusement going about, trying to be incognito in tricycle bath chairs pedalled by a man at the rear and racing in the sloping gardens of the Spa; a relief from the strict regime of douches, peat baths and glasses full of the sulphurous waters – and instruction in Russian and the Orthodox faith. After this, Emily records no more about Princess Alix until the crisp statement on November 1st, 1894: 'The Czar died today at 2-oC.'; and in her Epitome adds 'Pss Alix became Czarina'.

PLATE I

For dear Emily.
this little lady
is to bring you many
good wishes from Russia,
where you will be very
much missed this Xmas.
May the new Year bring
you blessings & happiness
is always the wish of your
affectionate
Alix
1898-1899.

Top: Emily's first card from Alix. *Centre:* The Russian Imperial Family in 1897.
Bottom: Bronze medal struck for the wedding of Princess Beatrice and Henry Battenberg, July 23rd 1895.

PLATE 2

The fan given to Princes Alexandra, Princess of Wales, by Queen Victoria in 1891 as a Christmas gift. Painted by Alice Loch. *(by the permission of Her Majesty Queen Elizabeth II)*

Original gouache painting by Alice Loch in preparation for the 1891 fan.
Cup and saucer from a set decorated with violets painted by Emily Loch.

A reject from the set painted for Queen Victoriain 1898.

PLATE 3

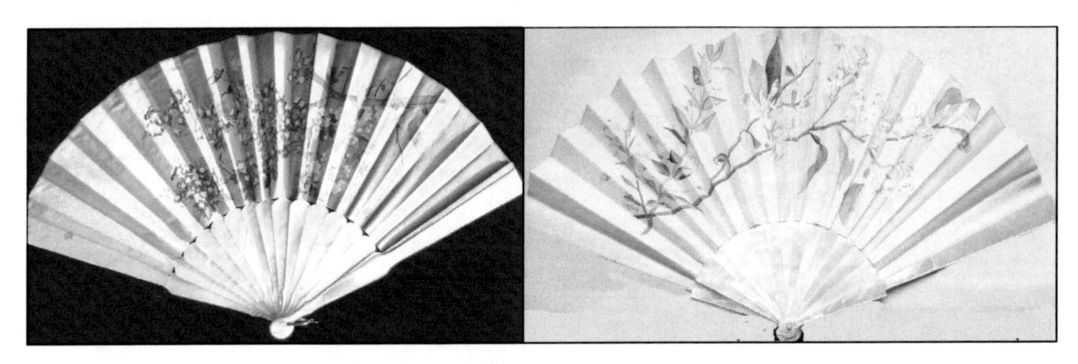

I painted a great many
for Queen Victoria, ordered
through Princess Christian, about
1896 & later. They were all for
wedding presents of orange flowers
Later the Queen ordered this
one for herself. Princess Christian
gave it to me after the Q
death. Alice Helen Loch

Top left: Alice Loch's fan painted by Alice Loch for Queen Victoria in the late 1890s. *(courtesy of Lady Loch).*
Top right: One of many fans commissioned by Queen Victoria from Alice Loch for a wedding; orange blossom and myrtle. *(courtesy Greenwich Fan Museum).*
Centre: Note written by Alice Loch about the fans she painted for Queen Victoria.

Left: Portrait of Princess Alice. (courtesy of Marion Wynn)
Right: Programme for a concert in aid of the Royal British Nursing Association.

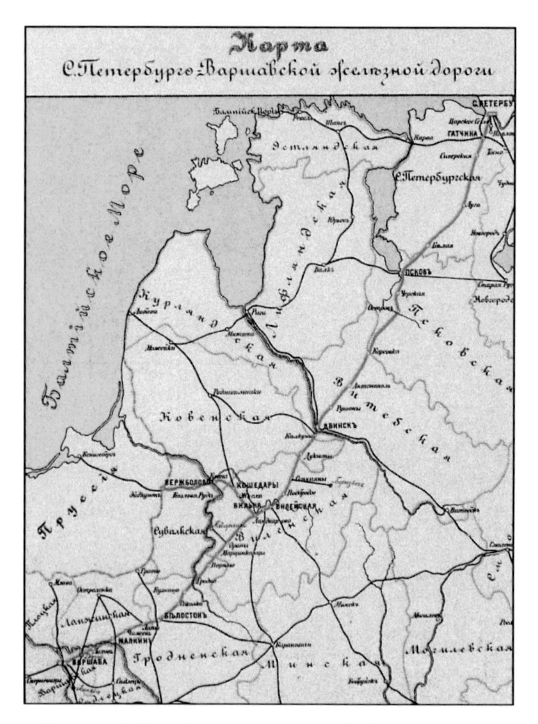

Above left: The Russian version of the itinerary of the journey which Princess Thora and Emily made with the Russian Royal Family from Darmstadt to Tsarskoe Selo in late October 1897.
Above right: St. Petersburg. The spire of the Cathedral church in the Peter and Paul fortress.

Right: The front of the Winter Palace facing the River Neva. The state rooms are on the first floor.
Below left: The side entrance of the Winter Palace.
Below right: 'The Bronze Horseman'. Falconet's magnificent statue of Peter the Great.

The menu for the dinner on the Feast of the order of St George Martyr and Victorious.

PLATE 6

Emily's sketch from Princess Thora's room in the Winter Palace. Electric train on the frozen Neva.

Above left: The Exchange and the Rostral towers in November in the late twentieth century. The river has not yet frozen and factory chimneys smoke in the background. *Above right:* The garden front of Friedrichshof in 1997 very similar to is appearance to the black and white photograph in Emily's album. *Below:* The Statue of Prince Christle at the foot of the hundred steps in Windsor.

PLATE 7

Above left: The gate house at the entrance from the town to the Castle at Friedberg.
Above right: The 'Schloss' of Emily's diary in early 1997, under snow and re-construction.

Above left: Nicholas' and Alexandra's Palace, Livadia, on the wooded slopes above the Black Sea. (courtesy Marion Wynn). *Above right:* One of the timetables presented to Princess Christian for her journey from Pretoria to Johannesburg in 1904.

PLATE 8

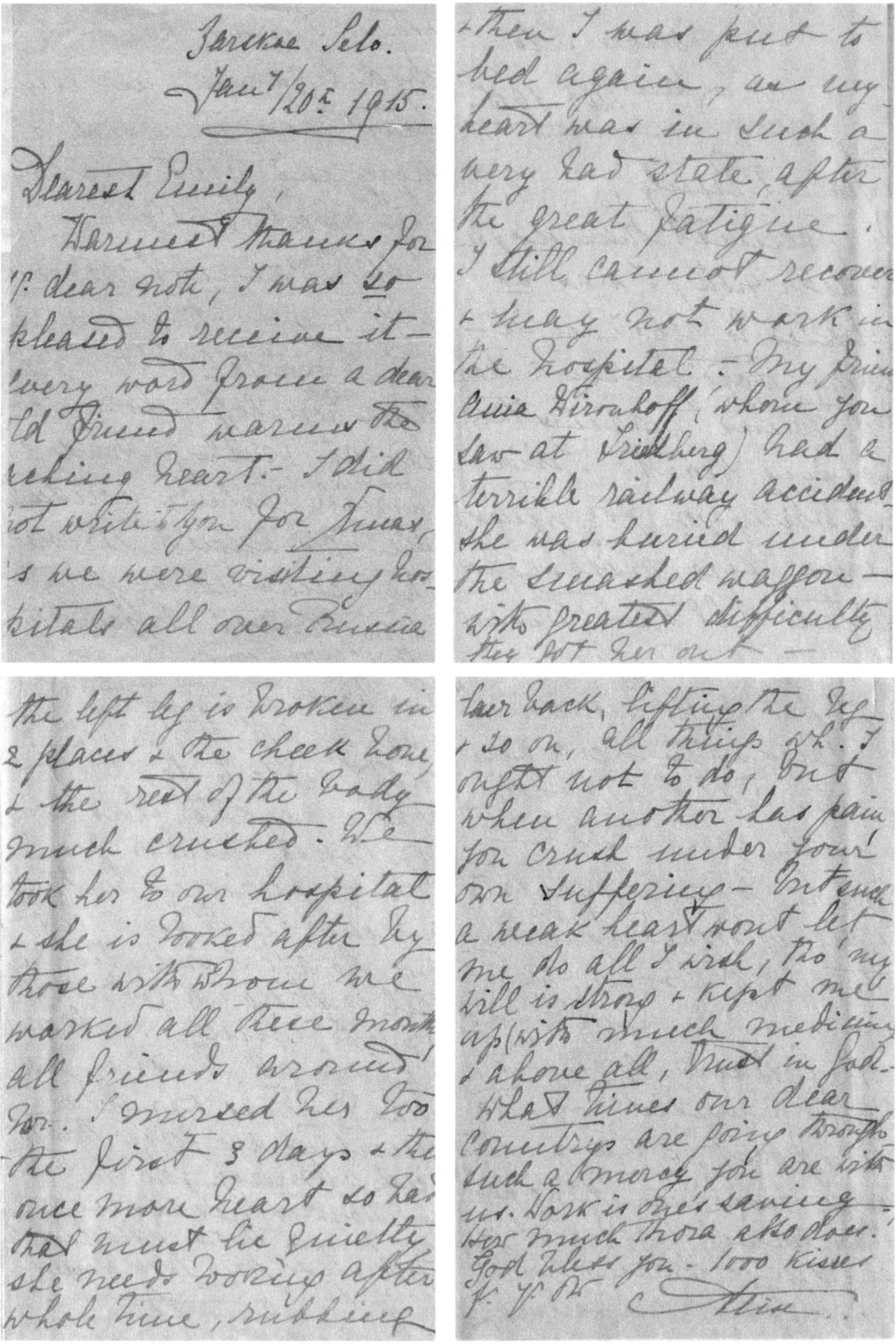

Zarskoe Selo.
Jany 12/20th 1915.

Dearest Emily,

Warmest thanks for yr dear note, I was so pleased to receive it – every word from a dear old friend warms the aching heart. – I did not write to you for Xmas, as we were visiting hospitals all over Russia & then I was put to bed again, as my heart was in such a very bad state after the great fatigue. I still cannot recover & may not work in the hospital. – My friend Ania Viroubоff (whom you saw at Friedberg) had a terrible railway accident, she was buried under the smashed waggon – with greatest difficulty they got her out – the left leg is broken in 2 places & the cheek bone, & the rest of the body much crushed. – We took her to our hospital & she is looked after by those with whom we worked all these months, all friends around her. I nursed her too the first 3 days & then once more heart so bad that must lie quietly – she needs looking after whole time, rubbing her back, lifting the leg & so on, all things wh. I ought not to do, but when another has pain you crush under your own suffering – but such a weak heart wont let me do all I wish, tho' my will is strong & kept me up (with much medicine & above all, trust in God. – What times our dear countrys are going through. Such a mercy you are with us. Work is one's saving. How much Nora also does! God bless you – 1000 kisses fr. yr old

Alix.

Letter from Alix to Emily written in January 1915, characteristically on pinky mauve paper.

Christmas and New Year wishes for Emily from Alix 1901-1902

Card from Alix to Emily bringing Christmas wishes for 1906,
showing the Russian Royal Family with Alexei still in long clothes.

PLATE 10

Tsarskoe-Selo
1910
December 26

With best love
from Olga
to
you dearest Miss Loch, &
many loving thanks for
your nice Xmas-card.—

Card from Olga to Emily thanking her for her good wishes, 1910.

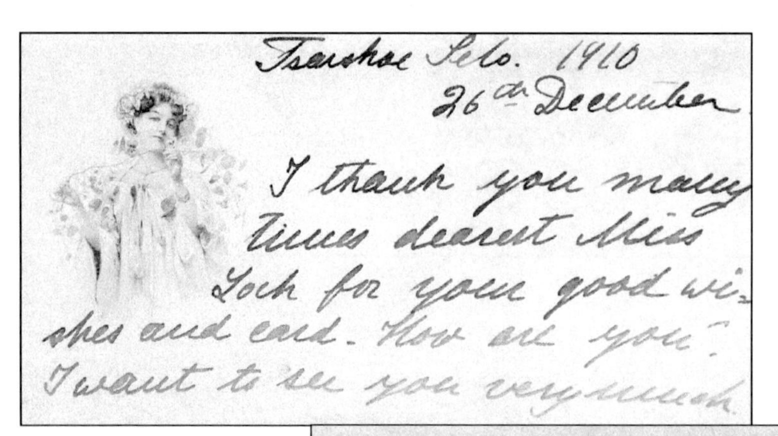

Tsarskoe Selo. 1910
26th December

I thank you many
times dearest Miss
Loch for your good wi-
shes and card. How are you?
I want to see you very much.

We got so many presents
from Papa and Mama.
Much love & kisses from your
affectionate friend

Tatiana.

Card from Tatiana thanking Emily for her Christmas card, 1910.

Card from all the Grand Duchesses with their names in order of age, the capitals forming their cypher OTMA.

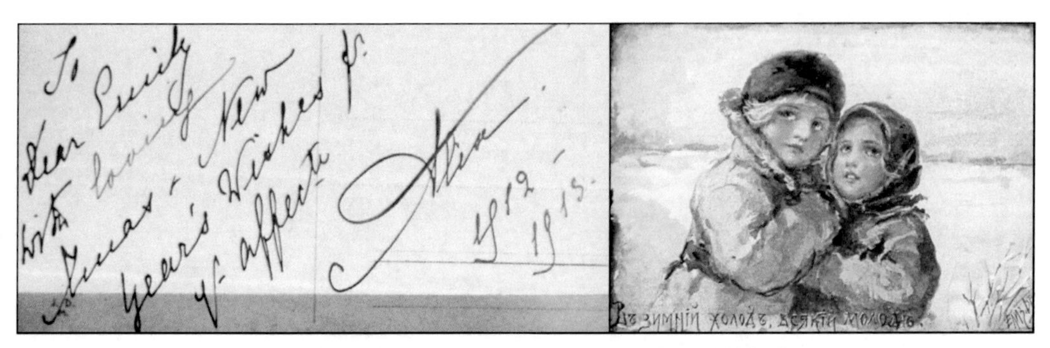

Card from Alix with Christmas wishes to Emily 1912-13.

PLATE 12

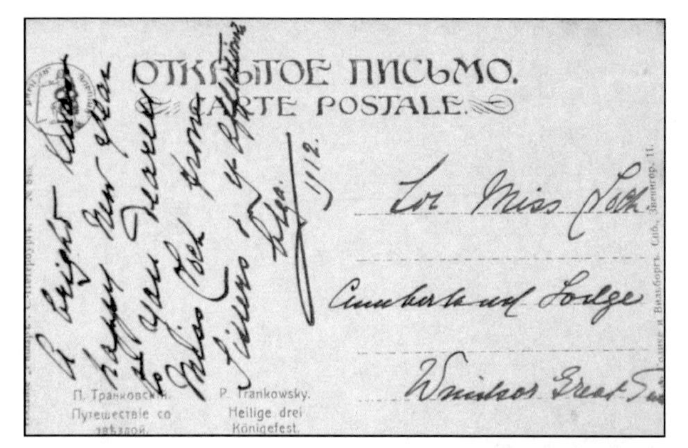

Card from Olga and her sisters wishing Emily a bright and happy New Year 1912.

A thank-you card from Olga and Tatiana thanking Emily for some gift.

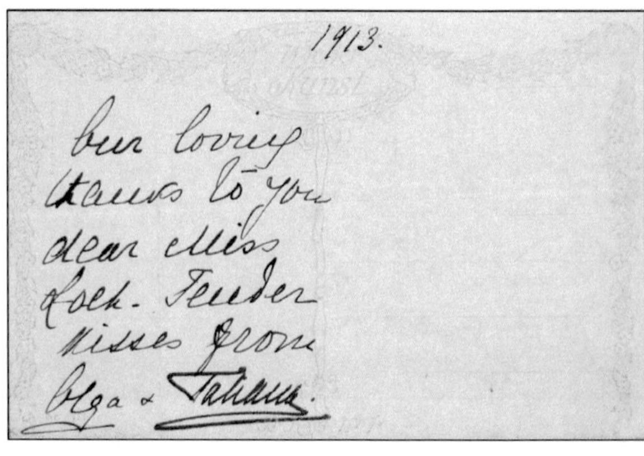

PLATE 13

Easter wishes to Emily from Olga, 1913.

Card of Christmas greetings from the four Grand Duchesses, 1914.

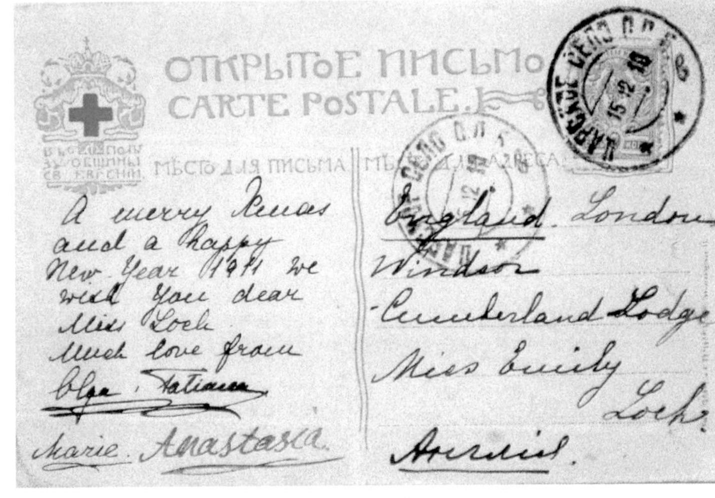

PLATE 14

The Tsarevich and the four Grand Duchesses, signed above their heads and with signatures below forming their cipher OTMA.

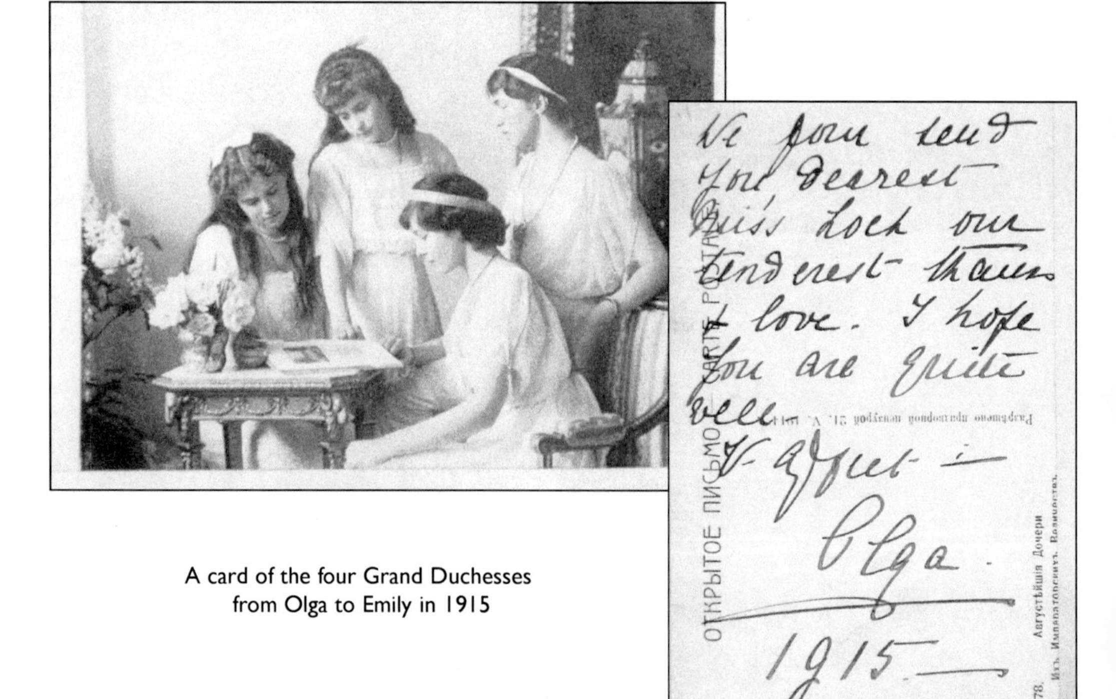
We now send
You dearest
Miss Lock our
tenderest thanks
& love. I hope
you are quite
well.
V. affect —
Olga.
1915

ОТКРЫТОЕ ПИСЬМО CARTE POSTALE

Августѣйшія Дочери

A card of the four Grand Duchesses from Olga to Emily in 1915

Alexandra sends her blessings and thoughts to Emily for Christmas 1916. Her message reads: 'Dearest Emily, I send you my warmest Xmas wishes and every blessing for 1916. God grant the New Year may bring this terrible war to a glorious end for the allies. Have terrible much to do, the heart gets again worse and cannot work in the hospital. The Emp and Alexei come off and on for a week from headquarters front and fr. inspecting the troops. Ernie and Irene are well, our R sister saw them. An affectionate kiss fr. Yr. loving Alix.'

ОТКРЫТОЕ ПИСЬМО.
CARTE POSTALE.

Tsarskoe Selo. Nov. 24. Dec. 7. 1915.

Dearest Emily,
I send you my warmest Xmas wishes & every blessing for 1916. God grant the New Year may bring this terrible war to a glorious end for the allies. – have terribly much to do, the heart gets again worse & cannot work in the hospital. The Emp. & Alexei come off & on for a week fr. headquarters, front & fr. inspecting the troops. – Ernie & Irene are well, our R. sister saw them. An affecte kiss fr. yr. loving Alexandra.

И. Ф. Шультце Зимний вечеръ
I. F. Schultze Winter Abend.

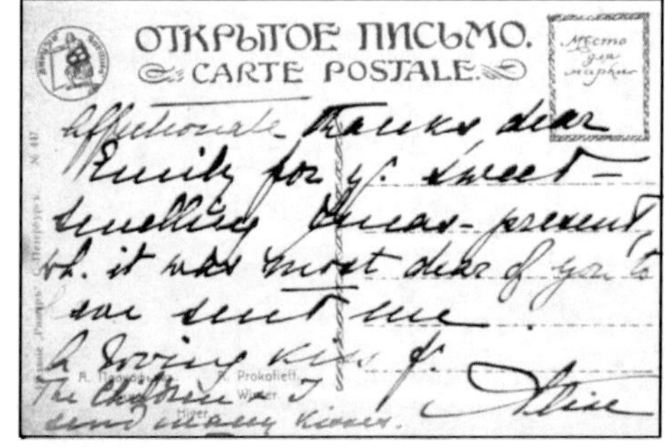

ОТКРЫТОЕ ПИСЬМО.
CARTE POSTALE.

Affectionate thanks dear Emily for yr. sweet-smelling Xmas-present, wh. it was most dear of you to have sent me.
A loving kiss fr. Alix.
The Children send many kisses.

R. Prokofieff Winter

Alix send her thanks to Emily for her sweet smelling present, probably 1916

PLATE 16

Left: A page from Dorothy Seymour's diary. Petrograd March 1917. Bread queues, the officer's sword being thrown in the Fontanka and Cossacks riding down the crowds. (*courtesy John Loch*)

Right: A page from Dorothy Seymour's diary in March 1917 with scenes from the early days of the revolution in Petrograd (*courtesy John Loch*)

Below: The reverse of the card of the hospital train. 'Dear Emily, I send you my best love and wishes for Xmas and the New Year 1917 – Think so much of you all and all dear old friends. One's heart is so full of sorrow but faith in God's mercy keeps one up. A kiss fr. Alix

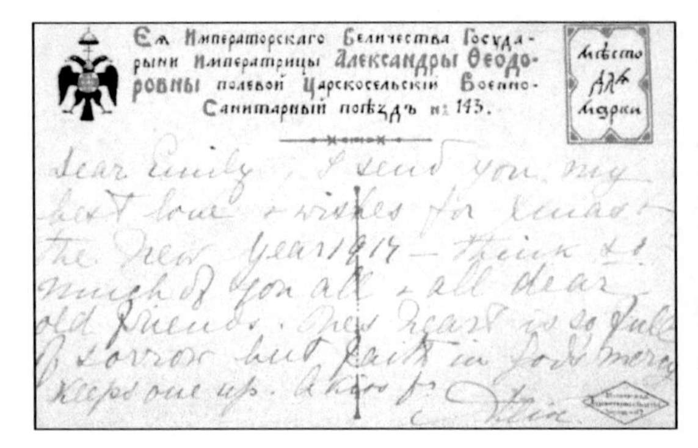
Ея Императорскаго Величества Государыни Императрицы Александры Феодоровны полевой Царскосельскiй Военно-Санитарный поѣздъ № 143.

Мѣсто для марки

Dear Emily, I send you my best love & wishes for Xmas & the New Year 1917 – Think so much of you all & all dear old friends. One's heart is so full of sorrow but faith in God's mercy keeps one up. A kiss fr. Alix

CHAPTER ELEVEN

Animals, Ashanti and Bicycles

In great contrast to these changes, Princess Christian's annual visits to the spas continued in the same even tenor with minor variations. Perhaps it had been suggested to Prince Christian that in 1895 he should accompany his wife when she went to the Spa at Nauheim. Only once before had he spent more than a day or two with the Princess while she was undertaking a cure: this time he stayed with her off and on, for nearly three weeks. Was it due to his anxiety over her drugs? After all, he had sought Sir James Reid's help in November the year before. Now on August 3rd 1895, the Prince announced that he was coming with Emily and the Princess, at the last moment just as they were about to leave England. The Princess was considerably put out, but come he did, and so did his dog Hans. They all stayed at the Villa Anna but, while the Prince was elsewhere for a couple of days a little over a week after they had arrived, Hans fell ill and the vet was called. Then Hans got lost. Emily 'Tore round to find him and after supper the Pss came out to look and call but all in vain'. He was found next day 'very exhausted but not worse'. The next evening, however, Emily 'found Hans still very bad. The Prince came home about 9.30 and was very fussed about him. He was put in my sitting room for the night'. It was no good: the following afternoon the Prince, Princess and Emily drove up to 'Winterstein Forsterhaus to ask about Hans'. Later in the evening the forester came and took Hans away: a few days later the dog was dead. Their dogs were very precious to them all and many anxious moments are recorded when a dog had run off or was ill and to Prince Christian horses and dogs appeared to be more important than his family.

Apart from visits from several doctors and many 'baths' and 'little drives' around the countryside, Emily and the Princess made one short visit to Kronberg, staying in the Schloss but spending much time inspecting the house and gardens, the dairy, laundry and stables of Friedrichshof, all of which had nearly reached completion. There was also a day visit to Wolfsgarten where the Grand Duke and Duchess, Ernie and Ducky, and Ella and Irène were there to meet them. By this time Princess Alix was in Russia, a married woman, and Tsarina. Princess Christian had two glimpses of her son Abby before they returned to England in mid-September and, almost immediately, set off to join the Queen at Balmoral. They found Princess Thora already there, as were the Duchess of York with her new baby and the Battenberg children. After a few days in the castle, Emily was somewhat embarrassed, when returning from an afternoon outing, to find that

> The smell was dreadful in my rooms when I got back. Sir J Reid and all ran round and Dr. Profit[52] and a man were fetched. They think it is a dead mouse. I am to sleep in the next room in consequence. I dined with the Queen.

A few days later, she moved to stay with Lady Biddulph and her children, Freda and Victor, at Birkhall. During this period she frequently went up to the castle and one evening dined with the Queen when she was entertaining the Kaiser's brother, Prince Henry of Prussia – always referred to by Emily as the naval one – and Prince Christle. On the last day of September; a little over a month later, Prince Christle announced that he was off to the Ashanti war in the Gold Coast. The local King was threatening the stability of the region, which was rich in resources: gold and agricultural products. This was the period when Britain was exerting her power to maintain stability and further her interests in many parts of the world – her 'gunboat' diplomacy. Field Marshall Lord Wolseley was about to take an expeditionary force out to settle the disturbance and Prince Christle had been invited to accompany the Field Marshall.

Princess Christian must have accepted that there was an element of danger to Prince Christle as he moved from one area of active service to another – she had been very anxious when his regiment had taken part in the Black Mountain expedition on the north-west frontier of India – but he had returned safely. Again now in 1895, although distressed, she accepted that he should go. She was upset but the consequences for her sister Princess Beatrice were far greater.

Early in 1896 Emily and Gerry Liddell were on holiday in Cannes with the Davidsons. He was by now the Bishop of Rochester and they were generally known as the Roffens. They were in the south of France probably for the sake of his health, which had been very poor for several years. Once established in the house the Roffens had rented, their lives became a round of quiet occupations: walking and driving in the neighbourhood, writing letters, sketching, visiting the numerous friends who were also wintering in the south of France, and reading together in the evenings. This calm was shattered on January 22nd. After detailing the events of the day Emily wrote: 'A telegram came late in the evening to say Prince Henry had died on 20(th) and a telegram had been rec.d this morning from Sierra Leone'.

No wonder her entry next day, after the inevitable weather report, goes on

> An agitating day with heaps of Royal telegrams about Roffen going back to the Queen. We all wrote letters all morning more or less about Prince Henry.

Later in the day they went down into Cannes and Emily bought a black dress.

> Gerry went with Roffen to the Post Office and Cook's Office to take places home [on the train] on Friday ... All wrote again after tea.

Gerry and Emily saw them off the next day. They went with them to the station and saw them into their sleeping compartments on the 3.45 train and then, disconsolate, were at a loose end.

> Gerry and I then glue nosed at the shops— bought handkerchiefs and collars etc. Had tea at Rohrs and walked home.

How had this tragedy for the Royal Family come about? In the decade since Prince Henry Battenberg had married Princess Beatrice he appeared to have accepted the life which the Queen ordained for him. The Princess and he brought up their growing young family in the Queen's orbit bringing joy to the ageing monarch – even if Nicholas of Russia thought they behaved very badly. But as the years went by Prince Henry who was in the British Army became increasingly frustrated that he had never been on active service and, when it became known that Prince Christle was to join the Ashanti expedition, Prince Henry saw his chance or perhaps there was some collusion between the Battenbergs and the Christians. David Duff continues the story

> Six days later, as they were finishing breakfast, Prince Henry suddenly told his mother-in-law that he also wanted to go to Ashanti. Astonished and concerned, the Queen said that such a course would never do – and that was that. But that was not that, for she reckoned without Princess Beatrice. The Princess was firmly behind her husband in his decision. She told her mother that he had set his heart on going, that he was smarting under his enforced inactivity, and that all his brothers had been on active service ... she stressed that the Ashanti force presented a unique opportunity for Henry, as he could volunteer without stepping into anyone else's shoes.
>
> The Queen, dwelling upon the dangers of fever, called upon the medical evidence of Sir James Reid to support her case, but the Princess answered that, while she appreciated the dangers, the campaign would be short and that Henry could take care of himself.
>
> Still the Queen protested ... Then Prince Henry wrote to the Queen. "I hope, by volunteering in a national cause, to prove my devotion to my adopted country." The Queen gave in.

Sadly, the Queen was right. It wasn't the fighting which killed Prince Henry; it was fever. The telegram, which had disturbed the tranquillity of the Davidsons and their two friends in Cannes, was part of the train of events which began with an evening stroll in Africa and ended with a funeral service in Whippingham – in the little church where, ten years before, Emily had watched the marriage of Princess Beatrice and Prince Henry of Battenberg.

The Prince landed in Africa but, as the expeditionary force was marching towards Kumasi, he fell ill with fever. The doctors ordered him back to the ship despite his protests that he wished to remain on African soil until Kumasi was taken. But it was too late: a virulent form of malaria had taken hold. The doctors got him back to the ship, which immediately set sail for England. Worrying about disparaging remarks in the newspapers and sensing that all was not well, Prince Henry sent a message for Princess Beatrice: 'In case I die, tell the Princess from me that I came here not to win glory but from a sense of duty'. And so he died at sea. The loss to Princess Beatrice was overwhelming but she remained firm in her belief that her husband had been right to go.

After these dramatic and disturbing events at the beginning of the year, 1896 became for Emily the Year of the Bicycle. She had been introduced to riding a bicycle by her cousin, Edie Loch, while staying with her Uncle Henry Loch's family at Uppat, Emily's old family home, during October of the previous year. By the end of that month, she and Princess Thora were out having bicycling practice with Furness, probably a groom, around Cumberland Lodge. They were wobbly at first but three days later she reported that they had both got on much better 'but needed a starter'. On this occasion Alice 'strode about but would not ride.' Alice being older probably followed the general opinion of a few years before that bicycling was considered 'quite unsuitable for ladies', although later she took to a tricycle. Thora and Emily were soon proficient enough to go for a long ride round with Furness a few days later. Then Princess Thora ordered a special costume from Richards in Windsor. The Countess of Malmesbury's article in the 1897 *Encyclopaedia of Sport* is firm on the subject of dress.

> Nothing light. Wool next to the skin essential. The wearing of a skirt is still a much debated question. England has never encouraged the unbecoming attire of French cycling women and I hope it never will. The skirt if properly cut helps to conceal the ugly action of the knees and legs and never need be a cause of danger if fastened down with elastic straps and not made too wide and too long. A complete change of clothing after a ride is essential.

Emily certainly needed to follow the last instruction, often coming back very hot and exhausted from her rides.

In '96, bicycling graduates from being a pastime to becoming a useful means of getting around the neighbourhood – making it possible to visit friends without having to ask Sharratt to get the pony out or putting it up at the White Hart in Windsor. It is only late in the year that this state is reached, bearing out Henry James' dictum to Emily's niece Margie, 'Young lady, emancipate yourself from the thrall of man. Ride a bicycle!'

As the year progressed, the problems inherent in keeping and riding a bicycle were tackled. While bicycling from her Aunt Mary's house, Broad Green near Liverpool, a 'nice round was spoiled by getting a thorn in my tyre and it was punctured'. The next day her cousin 'Henry went off to Liverpool to get the stuff to mend my tire (sic) but we couldn't find the puncture so it was no good'. So next day:

> Went into Liverpool with Henry by the 9.38 train. Took my punctured tyre to be mended and left it at Stades in Bold St. We went on the overhead Elect. Railway and then walked a long way back by the sea and inside warehouses and among the docks. Fetched the wheel and came out again by the 1.15 train.

Two days later she achieved an eight-mile ride and the next day packed her bicycle to take back to London with her on the train.

By November Emily was using her bicycle for errands. In mid-November, the 'roads were horrid' when she and Gerry cycled over to Clewer,[53] where previously they had always had to go in a cart or trap; but it was exhausting and quite a struggle to get back to the Cottage in time to greet the Princesses Christian, Thora and Louie for tea. Care and maintenance are mentioned at the end of the year when she had to take the bicycle to Brahe 'to have the valves seen to' and just before Christmas 'the boy came to clean the bicycle for the first time'.

Their life at home was a mixture of interesting engagements and domestic trivia. Emily relates them all in the same clipped sentences. So, discovering the kitchen alive with black beetles in the middle of a sleepless night seems to receive the same emphasis as the yearly visits to Friedrichshof; and the knitting of 'knee caps' – presumably for the cold knees of small boys – is given the same weight as having her 'head galvanised'[54] at Mrs Rumballs, in an effort to rid her of headaches. The diary was a series of notes to remind her of what had happened and most particularly whom she had met but throughout the entries there are the constants: Alice's devotion to Beaumont and Roman Catholicism (a highlight for her was witnessing the laying of the Foundation Stone of the Cathedral in Westminster on June 29th 1895) and also her continuing skills with the paintbrush – fans were still in demand and Alice painted them year after year[55] (Plate 3). Emily remained the china painter and, as Christmas approached each year, another set was produced: an Alice-in-Wonderland set for Cathy; a sweet pea set; a set with violets for a Majoribanks wedding present; and, late in the decade, a set decorated with brilliant blue gentians and gilding for the Queen herself (Plate 2).

There were changes in technology too: not only the rise of the bicycle but the beginning of the demanding intrusion of the telephone. This was first remarked on at Balmoral in 1895, when Emily was staying at Birkhall with Lady Biddulph. One afternoon there was great agitation, as the Queen had telephoned wanting to come to tea and they weren't in. And, on another day, their quiet reading was 'constantly interrupted by the telephone'. Throughout, though, there is Emily's devotion to the Princess and her family and her complete discretion. Allied to this was her awe of the Queen and, like the rest of the Household, she felt bound by her Majesty's every command. But even Emily, in the seclusion of her diary, hints at the absurdity of playing with the Battenberg children at Birkhall and giving them tea outside on a cold foggy afternoon in late October 'at the Queen's desire'.

CHAPTER TWELVE

Jubilee Year

Queen Victoria had been on the throne for the whole of Emily's life and also for that of most of her friends and relations. The way of life which we know as 'Victorian' had become thoroughly established and was the accepted way that society at all levels behaved. During the sixty years since Victoria had come to the throne Britain had seen the Queen weather many storms. Her popularity rose and fell, and rose again, as she became the mother figure of the Empire and Empress of India and the Dominions. Her popularity reached its peak in the year of the Diamond Jubilee, 1897, and Princess Christian and Emily like so many of their friends and families took part in the celebrations which marked the Queen's sixty years on the throne.

At the beginning of the year life went on much as before: with Emily visiting the Davidsons at Farnham with Gerry; seeing to the running of the house and cottages; and Alice busy painting fans, doing good works around the neighbourhood and spending much time at Beaumont College. It is possible that the financial situation of the sisters was causing some concern: there was very little earned income coming into the household and there are mentions of shares and share certificates late in the previous year. Considerable time and money was spent during 1897 improving 'Shelley Cottage', probably to let it at a higher rent. By September it was ready for letting and found 'to be charming'. For several years the Cottage itself had been let during August and September; this year they had to find a new tenant as Mr Potter, who had rented it for several years, had died. A Mr Waley came in June to view the house and Emily 'showed him all over'. Emily always noted 'netting the books' before letting the house, presumably to make sure that none of their books, many of them inherited from James Loch, would disappear.

Throughout the early months of the year, both Princess Christian and Emily paid an unusual number of visits to dressmakers, preparing for the many events to come. They patronised various dressmakers in London: Mrs Washbourne whom they had used before, but Mrs Murray for Emily and Mrs

Fairbank for the Princess were new. In later years Mrs Fairbank and her husband became close friends of the Princess and were called upon in times of stress and unhappiness. Mrs Washbourne had numerous outfits to make for Emily: on May 14th, just before the festivities got into full swing, 'Mrs Washbourne tried on for two hours'; quite an exhausting performance with the lady titivating the fit here and there, her mouth full of pins. Evidently Miss Tatwell in Windsor worked to a satisfactory standard, as she was the source of hats and bonnets for many years. 1897 was no exception: Emily ordered two hats and a bonnet early in May.

In February, March and April music and musicians were again much in the air. During the previous year, Gerry Liddell had gone on a long tour through Italy with the Joachim family and, in February, Ellie, Joachim's wife, came to stay at the Cottage. She and Gerry played together and they all went to hear the music at the Sunday evening service in St George's Chapel before Ellie returned to London. Emily saw her again towards the end of the month when she was the hostess at a private dinner and concert in Airlie Gardens in London at which the Joachim Quartet played. Emily wrote: 'Lovely playing, Schumann D minor, Max Bruch Romance and a Romance of Joachim's own'. Emily sat next to Joachim, now referred to as Uncle Jo, during dinner and 'Borwick and Tadema' were also there. Leonard Borwick became a great friend of the family. He was a very accomplished pianist who had trained with Mme Clara Schumann and in his earlier years became one of the finest exponents of her style. He had had his London debut at a Philharmonic concert in 1890 with the Schumann concerto. Tadema, usually known as Alma Tadema, was an artist of Dutch origin who was very popular with the Victorians although, by this time when he was in his 58th year, tastes were beginning to change.

This private concert was an appetiser for the season to come. Two days later, Joachim gave a concert at the Sheldonian in Oxford which Emily and Gerry travelled down to hear. They had to leave early, as this was the season of the Buckingham Palace Drawing Rooms, when young ladies attired in evening dress and ostrich plumes were presented. For many years the Princess of Wales stood in for her mother-in-law but, in this important year, the Queen herself was sometimes present. On February 24th, Emily wrote: 'The Drawing Room was a very long one. Quite two hours and the Queen staid (sic) an hour'. Other members of the Royal family were also present to see the well-rehearsed curtseys of the debutantes.

Princess Thora left England in March, accompanying Queen Victoria on her holiday to Cimiez, and was away until the beginning of May. At this time, a row about how the 'Munshi' should be treated caused much friction between the Queen, her Household and Ministers. Poor Harriet Phipps with whom Emily often chatted was delegated to give the ultimatum to Her Majesty that the Household would not tolerate the 'Munshi's' presence in Cimiez. Things had come a long way from the time when Princess Christian and Emily were having lessons in 'Hindoostani' from Mr Lloyd in Homburg.

Emily was in-waiting in March but by early April she was back at the Cottage. On the first Sunday there was great excitement. The Joachim quartet and Ellie Joachim came to stay. Gerry and her brother Fred were there with Emily to meet the visitors at Windsor station. They had hoped to take the Quartet to hear the anthem at St George's, but the train had been so late that they missed it, although they heard some singing. After a walk round the Castle, however, the quartet played for a while in the Chapel, and then in several flys[56] drove to the Cottage for lunch. One can imagine all the fine silver and glass, the old furniture gleaming with polish, and the Loch sisters bustling round to see that their guests were happy. The Quartet at this stage was composed of Joachim himself, Johann Kruse who was in his final year as second violin, Emanuel Wirth who played the viola and the cellist Robert Haussmann. Both

Joseph Joachim in the garden of the Cottage.

the last two had been part of the Quartet since the late 1870s. After lunch, they walked to Cumberland Lodge to sign the book,[57] and then round through the Park past the Obelisk Pond and back through the little gate into the garden of the Cottage. Refreshed, they immediately began to rehearse in the large open hall of the Cottage. They continued until 10 o'clock, entrancing their audience; Emily and Alice listened from their beds and the others sat at the top of the stairs. At last a halt was called and supper served. Finally, they retired to bed around midnight, their heads still humming with the tunes they had heard and the brilliance of the playing and the excitement of having Uncle Jo and his music in the house. Next morning:

> they dawdled around and then practised a Brahms. Gerry, Alice and I packed for them in a great scurry. Sent the three off at 11 o'C for the 11.35 train. Uncle Jo and Ellie staid a little and then we drove down to Lady Bidds. Freda took us to the Memorial Chapel and then up to the Library and saw miniatures and books. Had luncheon with Lady Bidd and came up by the 2 o'C train.

All travelled together to London and then went their separate ways – Emily and Gerry to get tickets from Chappels for the forthcoming season of concerts. From April 5th till the 12th, except Palm Sunday, there was a concert every night – during March Princess Christian had purchased two season tickets for these concerts for the sum of £4. At the beginning of the week there was the 'Monday Popular Concert', to which Emily went from Buckingham Palace with Princess Christian. It was the 'second appearance of the Joachim Quartet', according to the programme left in Emily's diary. One of the items played that night was Brahms' quartet in A minor; perhaps the one they had been practising that morning at the Cottage.

On Tuesday the Princess, Emily and Gerry, sitting together in a row on chairs at the front in the Queens Hall, listened to the St Matthew Passion which, according to Emily, went better than expected – 'in fact was good'. This was the first of the Festival concerts and Mr Robert Kauffman, one of the soloists, had come over to England 'expressly for the Festival'. The Conductor, Mr C Villiers Stanford,[58] was presented to the Princess in the interval. The Bach Choir gave a performance of Bach's Mass in B minor on the third day. There was a Quartet concert on the Friday and a matinée performance of the

Mass on the Saturday. A break from music at Cumberland Lodge on the Sunday brought them back refreshed for a final Quartet concert in London on Monday, when Beethoven's A major Opus 18, Brahms G major quintet and the Schumann piano quintet were played. Emily and Gerry joined 'the fearful crush in the artists' room to say good bye to their dear friend Joachim after this great feast of music.

Over Easter Princess Christian became very enthusiastic about photography. Perhaps this had been suggested to her by Prince Christle, as an interesting diversion when she was having a bout of depression. He had been busy taking photographs while they were all staying at Wolfsgarten back in 1891: Emily had helped him 'mix his photographic fluids'. Now in 1897, the Princess was helped by a Miss Taylor, who guided her through all aspects – 'taking the shots, developing the films and making the prints'. On the Saturday before Easter, Emily was despatched 'to Eton to fetch photographing things for the Pss'. The next day the Princess and Miss Taylor got down to printing and, on Easter Monday: 'The Princess and the Taylors did photographs most of the morning both inside and outside the house'. And there they are in Emily's Album: views of Cumberland Lodge; a view of the Lime Avenue with a Dalmatian dog; the Chapel in the Park where they went to church; a well-

One of Princess Christian's photos. A view of the lime avenue at Cumberland Lodge.

groomed horse held by a rather overdressed Emily, and an indoor shot of the corner of a sitting room complete with a stag's head. More supplies were required; so, while they were in London the following day, the Princess and Emily went 'to Harrods to get photographic liquids'.

Now began the run up to the Diamond Jubilee celebrations. Emily's entry for May 21st reads:

> Bright hot sun, tearing cold wind. Jeanne and I were fetched by the C. Lodge cab 10-oC. We went down with Princess Christian to the Castle and went with the ladies down to the train. 11.35 started. Ly Southampton, Minnie Mallet and Ethel. Had luncheon basket at 1.30. Got to Sheffield at 5. The Queen had the most wonderful reception. Thousands of people along 6 miles of splendidly decorated streets. 50,000 school children on the slopes of a park who all sang together. I was in a carriage with Ethel, Sir M White Ridley and Sir Fleetwood. The Life Guards had come up for escort. The Queen, Pss Christian and the Duke of Connaught. Tremendous enthusiasm and perfect order. We went last to the Camel Foundry and saw an enormous red-hot sheet of iron put under the roller for an iron clad.[59] Got onto the train again at 7.20 and went straight on to Scotland. A hot dinner served on the train. Minnie and I share a sleeping compartment.

While Emily was in Scotland, we learn that she pasted the cuttings and photographs of this memorable day into her album. Emily was in the second carriage with, as she says in her diary, the Hon. Ethel Cadogan, the Right Hon. Sir Mathew White Ridley (Secretary of State for the Home Department) and Lieutenant Colonel the Right Honourable Sir Fleetwood Edwards (Keeper of the Privy Purse). The Queen was in the fourth carriage. The details come from the Court Circular she kept. The report goes on for two and half columns of fulsome description. One gets a better idea of the excitement and the boisterous welcome of the crowds from the photographs and drawings, despite them being black and white. A fine drawing shows the Queen a small dumpy figure in black, sitting in her carriage. To her left sits Princess Christian and, with his back to the horses her son Arthur, the Duke of Connaught – in full ceremonial dress, complete with waving plumes on his helmet. The vanguard of the royal procession, formed by officers and men of the 17th Lancers, and the Sheffield Squadron of the Yorkshire Dragoons Yeomanry Cavalry in ceremonial dress, led the way through the elaborately decorated streets of Sheffield to the New Town Hall. The Recorder read the address of welcome which was presented to the Queen in a golden casket. Her Majesty replied and then opened, with a golden key, the entrance gates of the new Town Hall. From this important but not unusual ceremony the procession moved on, first through Norfolk Park which is shown in another photograph in the album, and then to the Cyclops works.

The picture of Norfolk Park, almost an aerial view, shows an enormous crowd which is truly impressive. A huge flag blows gently over the mass of humanity. The figures, which are large in the foreground, with a fine display of elegantly trimmed hats, boaters, top hats and umbrellas, diminish in size towards the centre. Here an open lane, down which the Queen's carriage drove, separates them from the thousands and thousands of children on the further slope, distinguishable only as a mass of black and white dots. Near the carriageway is a three-tiered stand from which Dr Coward conducts the massed choirs of the elementary and Sunday school children singing the National Anthem, an especially composed hymn and Rule Britannia. When the Queen came near, she paused and the gallant conductor was presented.

Finally to the Cyclops works which, according to the coloured leaflet commemorating the occasion began life in the year of the Queen's accession. It now employed 10,000 men and had received orders from the Lords of the Admiralty for 122 ships for her Majesty's Navy. The Queen's carriage was driven right into the foundry so that she could witness the making of a piece of armour plate. There is a simple but dramatic sketch. In the foreground is a huge piece of red hot steel coming from the hydraulic presses guided by unusually well-dressed workmen who labour in the searing glow of the metal. In the background, seated in the carriage, the Queen and Princess Christian face the drama. The Duke of Connaught has to twist round in his seat to see, and the members of the Household stand around the carriage. It made a great impression; showed the immense power of British industry and the might of the British Navy with its steel-hulled Dreadnoughts.[60]

The Queen's train was able to leave from the siding at Messrs Cammell's Cyclops works and continue smoothly on to Scotland. In the album there is a beautifully produced

Queen Victoria viewing the rolling of a sheet of armour plate from the safety of her carriage

> Time Table showing the stations at which Her Majesty's train stopped on the Journey from Windsor to Sheffield (via Leamington, Nuneaton, Market Bosworth, Burton and Derby) and Sheffield to Ballater (via Manchester, Wigan, Carlisle and Aberdeen).

They arrived at 8.20 in the morning on the 22nd May. The different Railway companies on the route, the precise timing of the arrival at the stations on the way, and the stops for refreshments are all given. So, in addition to her hot supper, Emily was also able to get cups of tea, always an important part of her life. On another sheet, the carriages and exact disposition of all the passengers is displayed. The return journey is shown on another page, which is even more delightful, as it has a drawing of all the carriages including the large Royal Saloon, the double saloons for all the Household – No. 71 is for Munshi Abdul Karim and his fellow Indian attendants. The penultimate truck is the Queen's *fourgon* or luggage van.

Queen Victoria and her two daughters, Princess Christian and Princess Beatrice, settled down to a month of homely Balmoral life. Princess Beatrice, who had travelled separately to Balmoral, was joined by her two sons, Prince Leopold who was 8 and Prince Maurice, now 6. They had both accompanied their grandmother in the train and enjoyed the excitements of Sheffield. The Royalty and the Household visited old friends and servants. Princess Christian and Emily bicycled one day to enquire after the Queen's maid, Annie MacDonald, who had gone home as she was ill; they visited the Clark's at Tillypronie, whom Emily had frequently visited when she had stayed before; but poor Lady Clark, who had been such a friend, had become helpless with a stroke. There were picnics in favourite places. The one to the Glasallt, when Emily and others followed the Queen and Princesses in a separate vehicle, did not go well.

> Our horse broke a blood vessel going up the steep hill and we could not go on. Willy Brown[61] ran like a lamplighter to the farm and sent a horse and man to tell the Queen what had happened.

There were painting days, when Emily was able to get outside and do some watercolours – on several occasions various people came to see her forget-me-nots – but, on other days, work intervened. As usual, she wrote sheaves of letters. On the morning on which Princess Beatrice left the party to go to Fontainebleau, Emily 'took business letters to Sir Fleetwood' before sitting

The Household at Balmoral during a respite in the Diamond Jubilee celebrations 1897.

View of Balmoral from across the river. The trees are still young but the view is less open than when the Queen and Prince Albert began building over fifty years earlier.

down to chat and knit until lunch. Most evenings, all the ladies dined with the Queen, and Emily had several conversations with her. In the drawing room after the meal, they sat around while the Queen did her silk crochet. Games such as Halma were played, or they listened to visiting singers or musicians.

Just before the visit ended, the Household was photographed. There is a good shot of them in Emily's album, as well as the signed photograph, which the Queen gave her, and a view of Balmoral from across the river. After this restful time, they all left Balmoral on a day of pouring rain and a

> hurricane of wind. River in flood ... We left at ¼ to 2. Stopped at the photographers on the way. Settled into the Queen's train and started at 3-oC. A beautiful comfortable journey with sumptuous meals, sent in. Marie and I had the same sleeping compartment. Tea in the middle of the night at Carlisle at 12-oC given us by Ethel.

They arrived back in Windsor the next morning and, after seeing a number of her friends, Emily drove back to the Cottage 'in a tumble down old fly'.

The next week was one of celebration, thanksgiving and grandeur. For the inaugural event, on June 19th, Emily got a good window with her red ticket giving admission to St George's Hall, and 'saw it beautifully'. This was the Military Tattoo, staged in the grand quadrangle of the Castle. Unfortunately it poured with rain. Her album has an artist's impression of the troops holding flaming torches, pipers in their kilts and Guards in bearskins and greatcoats. Civilians stand beside the Castle walls sheltering under umbrellas. The rain is slashing down, but there is the wonderful backcloth of the Castle and the great central window from which the Queen and Royal family watched.

The next day was something special for the Queen, her family and their friends and Households. Emily writes:

> Sunday 20th June: Cold grey day. High wind and no rain. All went to St George's for the service for the Queen in the morning at 11. Lady Biddulph and I in the choir to the stalls. Gerry, Freda and Victor to the Organ loft. It was a beautiful little service. Read by the Dean. 'Now thank we all our God' from the *Lobgesang* [Song of praise], special prayers, lesson and psalm. A Te Deum by the Prince Consort and a second hymn by Sullivan. The Queen called all her daughters, sons and sons-in-law and grandchildren and kissed them after the service – a most touching and moving sight ... At ¼ to 3 we were again in the Chapel for the Hymn of Praise which was sung by our Madrigal Society, Windsor and Eton Choral and the Orchestra and Queen's Band. The whole Church was absolutely full: a beautiful performance. Albani and Ed. Lloyd[62] sang, both rather out of tune.

And that wasn't all; after tea at the Biddulph's, she and Gerry caught the 6.15 train to London and she was with her Aunt Louisa at Elvaston Place in time for dinner. The next day, last-minute arrangements for all the family for the great day were made and Emily's regular dressmaker, Mrs Washbourne, visited to try on her mauve dress. They all went to see the encampment of troops in Hyde Park and then called in at Buckingham Palace to write their names in the 'book'.

Jubilee Day June 22nd dawned grey and sunless. An early breakfast at Aunt Louisa's and then they were off to the Palace by 8. With their tickets, they got in

> perfectly easily at the riding school entrance. Left At. L and Alice in tent with Miss Taylor and Miss Martin, and we three [Gerry, Geoffrey and Emily] walked round the garden to our 'H' stand. It was a glorious sight from beginning to end and we enjoyed it immensely. After the Queen passed, we had our food in the stand and then Gerry and I went into the Palace to join At. L. and Alice. We had a splendid second view of the return procession and then went back into the garden and sat till the carriage came at 2.30. Saw all the Colonial troops come by again and drove back to Elvaston Place. Had delicious tea and changed.

The minutiae of life were always important to Emily but fortunately she has also pasted in a long account from *The Times* and several photographs.

Months and months of meticulous planning came to fruition that day, when the people of London and the country were able to see their venerable Queen and the splendour of her great Empire. Even the weather played its part. As *The Times* puts it:

> The early morning was cloudy and still, and those of doubting tendency trembled. But there was something touching in the confidence of a sturdy constable who announced that it would surely be fine "because she was such a good Queen".

And fine it was. As the Queen's carriage emerged from the Palace, the sun came out. 'The rest of the morning and afternoon were permeated with the spirit of happy sunshine'. The account continues in the same vein, congratulating everyone and everything for the trouble-free day. Only once is an untoward incident mentioned, when two men who had climbed a tree in the Mall nearly fell on the Queen's carriage on its return to Buckingham Palace. She was concerned and 'directed an officer to enquire and report as to the nature of the accident'. One man was rather badly hurt and ended up in St George's Hospital.

The Times report begins by describing the crowds who stood just outside Buckingham Palace near where Emily in her Stand 'H' saw the great procession. It reads:

> Shortly after 9 in the morning the ground was already resplendent with soldiery, and every place where the general public was admitted was densely thronged. The public from the outlying districts, indeed, had been travelling up to London and murdering the sleep of the inhabitants on their lines of march all night.

Outside the Palace the crowd was densely packed 'but the most striking feature was the gathering of spectators on the roof of the Palace itself'. The procession was headed by the Royal Horseguards and their band. Next the colourful contingents from every part of the Empire: Canadian Hussars, Dragoons and Mounted Police, New South Wales Lancers and Mounted Rifles with their graceful felt hats and brown boots, and so on through all the states of Australia: on to Africa, with the Natal Mounted Troops and the Umvoti, Natal and Border Mounted Rifles; then the mounted troops of the Crown Colonies, Zaptiehs (Turkish Policemen)[63] from Cyprus and the Trinidad Mounted Rifles. All these were rapturously received and applauded 'by virtue of their picturesque and soldier-like appearance, their good seats and their general excellence of horsemanship.' More bands followed and then the foot soldiers. Of these 'the Borneo men, the same who gave the savage dances at the Tournament, attracted the most attention'. The writer goes on to say that, despite their present law-abiding appearance, one of their number is said to have taken 13 heads in the days when he was a head-hunter. Detachments of Royal Niger Hauzas and Gold Coast Hauzas were followed by detachments from Hong Kong and the Straits Settlements. The coloured troops received a very warm welcome, for there was no question that they had become very popular in the neighbourhood of Chelsea where they were quartered.

So the account goes on, column after column of closely printed words: bewildering confusion, perhaps, in the mind of the observer, with so many detachments from so many countries, so many bands and so many wonderful groups of horsemen; but the organisation was impeccable. There were getting on for fifty thousand troops either in the procession or lining the route; they all had been assembled and looked after satisfactorily. There were the troops from India with their colourful dress, troops from foreign powers – especially mentioned are the 1st Prussian Dragoon Guards – military and naval attachés, London dignitaries and many more. Lastly, and by no means least, as a further account by an observer stationed just outside the Palace relates:

> The People were expecting the Queen but, before her Majesty was to begin her great progress, the procession of 40 princes had to pass and a truly magnificent spectacle did they present. Every uniform that is worn under the sun seemed to be represented, some comparatively austere, and some like that worn by the Crown Prince of Montenegro, pretty enough to please the most exacting ladies' taste.

At last, the carriages came. The first were dress landaus with the foreign envoys; and it was noted 'with amusement that the Papal Nuncio and the representative of the Emperor of China, who carried a fan, occupied the same vehicle.' All the Royal family were there. Unusually, Princess Beatrice was not travelling with her Mother, for precedence ordained that the Princess of Wales and Princess Christian should be with her Majesty. Poor Princess Christian; she wasn't even honoured with a description of her gown, after all those fittings at the dressmakers! The Queen, a dignified little figure in black silk trimmed with white lace and a bonnet to match, sat beneath a white parasol and opposite the Princess of Wales, 'whose dress was of an exquisite heliotrope shade'.

The Queen touches the button to transmit her message to all parts of her Empire.

Before the Queen set off on this most heart-warming and moving drive through the crowds, she had 'touched a button which gave a signal to be transmitted to all parts of her Dominions' on a telegraphic instrument placed at the Grand Entrance of Buckingham Palace. The message ran: 'From my heart I thank my beloved people. May God bless them'.

The immense cavalcade moved slowly and majestically through the streets of London. A panorama is pasted in the album showing the route up Constitution Hill, through the great Arch at Hyde Park Corner, along Piccadilly, and down St James' Street to Trafalgar Square. All along the way, the buildings and streets were decorated. The roars of the crowds travelled like a great wave of sound through the capital. As the newspaper cutting records:

> Nor was there room for doubt that her Majesty accepted with no ordinary pleasure, but with demonstrative delight, the tributes of eager loyalty which were showered upon her from every side. In St James' Street, now far and away the most profusely and tastefully adorned street in all London, the demonstrations of loyalty were the same, and the roars of cheering were heard at great distances.

Apparently, in the stands near Trafalgar Square, some amusement was caused by 'short women' becoming hysterical in their efforts to jump sufficiently high to see the Queen.

The procession continued along the Strand where the Lord Mayor presented the Sword at the entrance of the City; and the Queen's carriage moved on to St Paul's. There is a fine photograph of the Royal carriage beside the steps of St Paul's with all the pageantry of the cavalry. The huge crowd fills every available space. Here a short service of thanksgiving took place at the steps of the Cathedral. Emily has included a newspaper picture of the moment when the Archbishop of Canterbury is giving the benediction, and the Queen and the two Princesses sit in the stationary carriage, the beautiful cream-coloured horses, with their gorgeous crimson and gold lace caparisons, held quietly by the postillions.

After St Paul's, the procession moved eastwards along Cheapside, Poultry and King William Street, across the Thames on London Bridge and then through residential areas south of the river and back over Westminster Bridge, past Big Ben and the Houses of Parliament, up Whitehall, through the Horseguards and home up the Mall. A final quotation from the contemporary account:

> Before 1 o'clock the troops returned to their former positions in front of the Palace and the guards of honour were reformed. The Royal procession, in which it may be mentioned that neither the Turkish Special Envoy nor the Turkish Ambassador took part,[64] came straight up the centre avenue of the Mall, and the troops composing it turned off to the right on reaching the roadway in front of the Palace and passed up Constitution Hill for the second time. This route was followed by all the procession except the mounted foreign representatives, the escorts of Royal Princes, and the Indian Escort, who formed into semi-circles on either side of the outer gates and there awaited, a glittering throng, the arrival of the Queen. This was probably as fine a scene as had been witnessed throughout the whole length of the route.

Emily had watched this final scene. It is not surprising that her closing remarks for the day, after seeing the illuminations, was 'A real Jubilee Day'.

This was the high point of the celebrations but not the end. Later there was a State Ball, a Garden Party at Buckingham Palace and a State Concert in London. However, the day after her triumphant progress through the capital, the Queen returned to Windsor. She was greeted at Windsor Bridge with an Address by the Thames Conservancy and then was driven slowly up Thames Street amid 'much enthusiastic cheering and waving of handkerchiefs from the thousands of spectators assembled in the streets' and in every available space. At her statue in the High Street she was received by Prince Christian, the Lord High Steward of Windsor. Yet again, God Save the Queen was sung; and this time Emily was one of the singers.

The Eton College Torchlight procession took place a couple of days later and Emily, despite having her pink ticket, had the greatest difficulty in finding a space in St George's Hall. She

> found every window full. Rather despair and difficulty but got settled at last and all squeezed in to see what we could. It was a lovely sight and the Eton boys did their torch drill and songs beautifully. It was not over till past 11o'C.

In the middle of the celebrations in London and Windsor, Princess Christian went to Birmingham to represent her mother on the occasion of the opening of the new General Hospital. Emily's terse personal account sets the scene:

> July 7th. Fine bright day with wind. Breakfast 8.30. Carriage fetched me at 9, Picked up Colonel Eliot. We went to Euston and arrived at 9.30. Waited in the Royal Special until Prince and Pss Christian and Ps Thora came – got to Birmingham at 12.25. Long and varied function. Crowded streets and enthusiastic reception. Decorations from St James' street on Jubilee Day had been got by the Ld Mayor from Harrods Stores. Addresses and replies and a big lunch and speeches in the Town Hall – and opening of the hospital and going all over. Started back at quarter to 5 and got back to London at 7oC. I had a long and interesting talk with Pss Thora coming back in the train.

It was appropriate that Princess Christian was the daughter delegated to do this for her mother. Her interest in hospitals and nurses was sincere and knowledgeable. In her response to the Address presented to her at the hospital she was able to reply, after acknowledging their loyal wishes to the Queen, that she thanked them for their ' kind recognition of the sincere interest that she herself had taken concerning the sick and suffering'. One can imagine that her questions and remarks when 'going all over' – as Emily puts it – were pertinent and thoughtful.

It is good to know that the Lord Mayor of the bustling and thriving industrial city, Mr Councillor James Smith, was thrifty and made use of the much praised Jubilee decorations from St James' Street London, which presumably had been available second hand from Harrods store. On this occasion the account does take notice of the Princess's outfits.

> Princess Christian wore a handsome dress of silver grey moiré trimmed with passementerie [trimming of gold and silver lace], and a toque ornamented with damask roses, lace and osprey, Princess Victoria wore a fawn-coloured dress with pale blue trimmings.

Princess Christian had a tendency to have outfits rich in decoration; and it seems that the precursors of bird protection societies had not yet had an effect on the ornamentation of royal hats.

After all the excitements life gradually returned to normal and, by August, Princess Christian and Emily were off for their spa visit. This time it was to Bad Nauheim, a little to the north of Homburg but still in the Duchy of Hesse-Darmstadt. Here they settled down to their routine of 'baths' and met their usual 'spa friends'. Prince Abby came quite frequently to see his mother. He was stationed nearby with his regiment. Both the Princess and Emily had taken their bicycles and so were able to widen the circle of places and people that they could easily visit. Emily in her new cycling outfit, recently purchased in Windsor,

> went to see about the Pss' photos and then joined a fellow cyclist, Lukie White, and rode hard through the two Morlea villages. Ran over a goose and got really upset. Came home in a crimson drip.

Poor goose, poor Emily. She had not yet mastered the art, which Fred had tried to teach her back in England, of controlling the bicycle going downhill while lifting her feet off the pedals.

Bad Nauheim was conveniently close to Friedberg where Grand Duke Ernie and his wife 'Ducky' were staying. This was one of their many castles and was set at the end of the village street, surrounded by impressive walls above a dry moat. On one occasion Emily had bicycled over to visit her friends among the Grand Duke's household; but, towards the end of August, she and Princess Christian were taken in a carriage to have dinner with the young couple. Emily was very fond of Ernie and knew he was a lively young man; but I wonder if she – and Princess Christian – were not somewhat surprised to play 'a wild game of puff ball after the meal'. Both she and the Princess were in their fifties, even if their host and hostess were thirty years younger. The marriage seemed to be going well at the time, and they had a beloved daughter Elizabeth. Emily met the little girl twice when she was brought over to have tea with her great aunt in Nauheim. Although the marriage did not last, on this visit the Princess and Emily found a close knit and happy family.

On the last day in Bad Nauheim in 1897, the Grand Duchess, Ducky, entertained her aunt and Emily once more, by taking them to the manoeuvres.

She accompanied the two older ladies most of the way but, when they got near the troops, Ducky was out of the carriage, on to her horse and away with the cavalry. She was a fine and daring rider and spent much time at Wolfsgarten with the horses she bred. The following day, Emily was on her way home. Just before she left, both she and the Princess were much saddened by hearing of the death of Louisa Brandreth – the Princess's friend and Emily's much loved aunt, from whose hospitable home she had set off so recently to watch the Jubilee procession.

CHAPTER THIRTEEN

To Russia

Emily left Princess Christian and Princess Thora in Frankfurt at the beginning of September 1897 and returned to England on her own. She found Alice at the Cottage going about her usual round, to Beaumont College, church services and helping people in the neighbourhood; this time the latter included 'staying with a Mrs Broham until she died'. Soon it was time to pack again and Emily and her bicycle were off on the train to Liverpool to stay with her Aunt Mary and Cousin Edward at Broad Green. Aunt Mary and Aunt Louisa had been sisters and, no doubt, it was a great consolation and comfort for Emily to be able to talk over Aunt Louisa's death. Healthy outdoor exercise was taken every day with Edward. He and Emily rode many miles around the district – to Sefton Park and Mossley and once into Liverpool itself to visit the Art Gallery.

This was followed by a fortnight's visit to Ireland with some of Gerry's friends and relations which brought Emily into quite a different set of people with very different interests: serious play acting, recitations, and 'Dante and Botticelli in the afternoon'. Emily had moved into a highly artistic world. It also gave her a chance to see some of the beautiful country around Castle Leix, the home of the de Vescis, and Killarney, before she finally returned to London on October 9th. Jeanne, her maid, met her at Euston Station and took the luggage while Emily went to Buckingham Palace with a 'dreadful sick headache', where she found the Princess and Princess Thora, recently returned from Germany, 'very nice and hearty'. After a rest, 'Pss Ch brought me tea in my room, [and we] discussed the tremendous plan of Pss Tora and I going to Russia in a fortnight'.

This had come as a complete surprise to both Thora and Emily. In a letter to her Grandmother, written from London about October 11th, Princess Thora says:

> You will have heard through Papa of Alix's invitation for me to go to Russia & that Mama has allowed me to go, it was such a surprise to me as I did not expect it in the very least, of course. I am looking forward to it immensely.[65] I think it will be most interesting & it will be so delightful to stay with Alix whom I have seen so little of since she married.

For Emily, her delight and excitement were immediately followed by the inevitable question, 'What shall I wear?' In her usual practical way she immediately set about shopping and visiting dressmakers and, almost every day for the next fortnight, there were tryings-on or some one coming with a new garment; 'Mrs Bucharles came with hats' one morning before Emily took Princess Thora to see about 'habits at Höhue'. There was still time, however, to go with Princess Thora 'to luncheon with Mrs Temple[66] … Pss Tora and I taken all over the [Lambeth] palace after lunch by two little chaplains' and to visit a Dr Hovel Parkin for Princess Thora to have her throat 'burnt with electricity'. Princess Christian gave Emily a muff and Princess Thora and Emily 'wound silk for Alix's penwiper'. At last the accounts were done, the Princess opened yet another bazaar, long talks with Prince Christle were enjoyed, the packing was completed, farewells were said, and a final dinner was taken at the Buckingham Palace Hotel. They were seen off at Victoria station in the evening of October 26th by 'the Pss, Alice and many gentlemen' and 'Got to Queenboro at 10.30 where the agent met us and we got safely aboard and started in a fog'.

Everything had happened so quickly that Emily felt as if it were all a dream and her sleep that night on the ferry was filled with dreams about what had happened since she last saw Princess Alix.

Emily and Jeanne saw Princess Thora into her cabin and, after Jeanne had arranged her clothes and slipped out, Princess Thora said:

'Emily, I do wonder what it will be like in Russia … and tomorrow we'll see Alix again. It isn't so long since I saw her in Germany but we had such a short time together … I did see little Olga again, and this time, the new baby Tatiana … the last time I saw much of Alix though, before that, was when she was staying with Grandmama before she was married and we played together on two pianos just before she left Osborne to go back to Wolfsgarten. That all seems very long ago … there have been so many

changes … Will it all be terribly grand? I wonder how Ernie and Ducky are managing … they always call these visits "the Russian invasions". Oh! I shall never sleep for all the excitement'.

'I am sure you will, my dear,' said Emily. 'It would be better if you did; it will be a long day tomorrow … I am just going up on to the deck and then I'll be in my cabin if you want me. Goodnight your Highness and sleep well.'

Emily closed the cabin door and, pulling her cloak around her, went on deck. Dense fog blanketed the whole harbour and only a few blurs of light could be seen. It seemed as if Queenborough, the Isle of Sheppey and even England did not exist. But the captain, who had sailed out into the estuary many times, knew his way, guided by the booms of the foghorns and the occasional lights on the buoys marking the channel between the mud-banks. The engine was stoked and added to the gloom with puffs of black smoke. The clunk and splash of the paddle wheel gently set the boat in motion.

Back in her cabin Emily got ready for bed, put her documents and money pouch with her brooch and watch in her leather dressing case – secure against the rigours of the long journey in its canvas cover – and, pulling the blankets around her, settled down for the night. The boat vibrated as the engine and paddles got moving into a steady rhythm and the churning of the water as the paddle-wheel revolved soon lulled her to sleep, with Princess Thora's words reverberating in her head.

'So many changes, so many changes, so many changes[67] *… Alix's head appeared from the steam of a bath smelling strongly of sulphur … she cried out … ' Oh! This horrid smelly water has made my ring all black' … And then she turned to her companion and said, 'I wish those people would stop staring at me and I can't get out of this wheel chair and run away … Oh Gretchen, push it fast, push it fast, push it fast … '*

And a train was gathering speed, as Princess Alix and Princess Victoria waved to Ernie and Ducky, while it carried them further and further from home and the familiar station at Darmstadt; carrying Alix away to Russia to join Nicky.

Victoria's face faded into Ella's; Serge was with her. Across the endless plain the train swept on and on and on. Then the winter light grew full of sun. There was Nicky who had come to meet his longed-for Alix. His smile was joyous but his eyes were sad and, when she reached Livadia, she knew the reason why.

The great man, once strong and bold and full of power, now grey with pain and illness, stood tall at the entrance door in full resplendent uniform to greet the beautiful Alix. He took her in his arms but his body felt frail and his breath shallow with exhaustion. Slowly he let her go and she walked with Nicky in a dream of love, through sunny rooms and sea-white light above the cerulean sea.

But always behind her shoulder, behind the shoulders of all in that fate-haunted palace the shadow of death hung in the air.

The shadow grew, became a cloud, filled the whole space, and was black.

Father Ioann, priest and confessor, the dying Alexander held in his arms, supported the spirit as bodily strength drained away …

The dark-haired Empress leaned over and kissed the dying lips …

The Tsar was dead. Long live the Tsar… and Nicky's voice called out, 'I feel as if I were dead too; the weight pushes me to the precipice, what can save me now? Oh! Russia'…[68]

Boom…boom…boom through the fog…toll….toll…toll…. the deep, rever-berating bells ring on and on and on and the train wheels jolt repeatedly over the gaps in the rails; the people stand at every crossing, bare-headed in sorrow…

An enormous crowd, crushed together in Peter and Paul's church, stand silent and still as the choirs, plaintive and monotonous, intone the solemn service.

The bells of St Petersburg call out to all: mourn his passing.

The crowds move to the bridges across the steel-hard waters silently slipping, silently slipping, silently slipping…

The colours change to white … catching the radiantly beautiful bride. Alix with diamond crown, and ermine-lined mantle of gold moves with simple dignity towards the Cathedral, through the Palace thousands, to wed her love, her one true love, her Nicky …

Rhythmic pistons, turning wheels, booming horns, gaining speed, gaining speed, gaining speed … crowds running, people shouting, children crying, rumours surging, people falling, bodies crushed in stampede.

Khodinka meadows seamed with blood. Indecision and bravado taint the newly crowned, tarnish the Tsar's holy dedication; scorn the sacrificial union of a young mother with her adopted peoples …

Warm sunlight began to finger its way into the cabin as the images of Nicky and Alix standing in coronation glory under the wide dome of the Cathedral, their faces radiating dedicated majesty, slowly fade …

Emily rubbed her eyes. The vibrations had ceased, voices called from the quay: they had arrived and day was here.

> Lovely bright and warm. Had a beautiful passage, calm as a millpond.

Gulls wheeled in the sunlit sky, their sharp eyes searching for any scrap of food and the harbour was a bustle of boats, big and small. Jeanne and the steward got the luggage on to the quay and porters seized it and stowed it away on the train to Cologne, as they had done so many times before. Princess Thora and Emily settled themselves into a carriage, hugging themselves with anticipation, wondering what the journeys in the next few days would bring. They were on their way to familiar, friendly Darmstadt to join the Emperor and Empress of Russia and go with them on the long unknown journey to St Petersburg.

They were greeted in Darmstadt by their old friends Fräulein von Grancy and Herr von Riedesel and quickly settled into their usual routines: the Princess with her cousins, and Emily calling on her friends and leaving appropriate cards. This time there were also cards for the Russian ambassador. They had time for two theatre visits and 'a smart luncheon with outsiders'. Then on October 29th, two days later, Emily wrote in her diary:

> Foggy and cold early, bright later on. Left Darmstadt at 10 o'C. A great assembly at the station of royalties and people to see the Emperor and Empress off. We established ourselves at once in our beautiful cabins. Luncheon at 12.30 with the Emperor and Empress and all the gentlemen. Princess Bariatinsky sat with me most of the day and we had tea together. Also Princess Thora sat with me. Dinner at 7.30. We came to bed at 10 o'C. Written in the new Russian Train.

Once more a 'Russian invasion' was returning from Darmstadt. This was just the latest of a long line of similar visits which had taken place throughout the nineteenth century, when one or other of the beautiful Hessian princesses, who had married into the Russian royal family, came back to visit her relations. This time it was Alix, born Princess Alice Victoria Helena Louise Beatrice of Hesse-Darmstadt, now Empress Alexandra Fedorovna of Russia, who had come with Nicky, Emperor Nicholas II, and their two babies Olga and Tatiana and a vast retinue of servants, to enjoy the hospitality of Grand Duke Ernie and his wife Ducky. These 'invasions' made formidable demands on the resources of the palaces, the Schloss and town but kept the family in close touch with each other.

Emily has pasted in her album an illustrated 'Fahrplan' in German and its

Russian equivalent (Plate 4). There are maps, and the time of arrival at, and departure from, every stop are given. Knowing how long each pause would be gave the passengers, on this long journey, the opportunity to 'run up and down' the platform as Emily and Princess Thora did at Korschen, Belaia and Luga. When the train was on the move, they visited each other in their cabins and sitting-rooms, and Emily began to get to know Princess Bariatinsky, one of the Empress's ladies-in-waiting, who was to play such an important part in her life while she was in Russia. Queen Victoria had an account of this first day on the Imperial Train from Princess Thora.

> I am going to have these few lines posted at the last german station we pass. I have got quite used to the motion of the train now & scarcely notice it; also we live just like in a house; dressing for dinner etc. Certainly it is the most wonderful train I have ever been in – & more than comfortable. We lunch at 12.30 & dine at 7.30 all together in the big dining saloon. Such funny food! They make me try all sorts of odd dishes, all of w[h] I quite like except the soups w[h] are horrid. There are dozens of men who walk about the passages, make one's bed & wait on one generally in high boots & small round astrakhan caps. They wear odd long coats with pleats behind; it is rather a becoming dress! Count Monravieff [sic] & Gen Richter are the two most agreeable gentlemen … the others look intensely Russian & do not speak much at meals … It is now getting dark & we shall soon leave this train & get into a still bigger one on the Russian frontier.

They woke to a foggy morning, but the sun soon broke through and they had a bright sunny day. Life continued unruffled: breakfast at 9, visits from Princess Bariatinsky and Princess Thora, lunch at 12.30. Princess Bariatinsky and Emily were photographed by Comte Muravieff (slight discrepancy between the two ladies' spelling) in the afternoon, followed by letter writing and tea. At the Russian frontier, the gauge changed and they moved into 'an even more lovely train'. Emily tells us:

> Bells rang and Cossaques [sic] in lovely uniforms received the Emperor. Crowds of officials changed the mountain of luggage.

We changed for dinner directly we got in and had dinner at the new time, 8.30.

After another whole day their journey is over. At precisely 7.35 in the evening the royal train completed its 1289 kilometre journey and arrived at Tsarskoe Selo, the royal village a few miles to the south of St Petersburg. There was a 'big reception of Cosaques in long, red uniforms and heaps of officers'. In her album Emily has pasted in a photograph, unfortunately only in black and white, of Baron Myendorff, Colonel of the Cossacks. He stands authoritatively in his ankle-length coat, gold braid on the sleeves and hem. The bodice of the coat is appliquéd with an intricate design of gold braid and dark material. A short sword hangs from his belt and he wears a high, brimless astrakhan hat. His tight-fitting, black leather boots shine with polishing. These brilliantly uniformed Cossacks and dragoons clearly impressed Emily.

Also in the album there is a newspaper clipping from the local French-language newspaper, quoting the *Official Gazette*. It names the Royal party who arrived on the train and the dignitaries who were there to greet them, their titles being given at length. Emily more simply records: 'The Emperor, Empress and Princess Tora drove from the station in an open carriage, then the babies'.

Colonel Myendorff, Colonel of the Cossacks whose uniform was much admired by Princess Thora and Emily.

Princess Bariatinsky and Madame Wassilitchikoff, who had met them at the station, came with Emily. The way from the station to the Palace was lined with Cossacks from the Emperor's personal retinue and troops from the joint battalion of the Guard. A fine sight it must have been – driving away from the station with the steaming train in the background and along the electrically-lit streets of Tsarskoe Selo to the huge glittering Alexander Palace. Emily ends that day quite simply with:

> Was taken to beautiful large rooms. The two ladies came and had supper in my room. I sat with them after and then came to my room and arranged a little.

As we have seen, 'Arranging a little' is a phrase that appears many times in the diaries. Emily had become very skilful at creating comfortable surroundings in different rooms in different parts of Europe – making the unfamiliar, homely. Here in Russia she did it again, creating a base from which to carry on her normal life and from which she set off to witness many grand occasions in spectacular surroundings.

All this had taken place in the dark. Emily had travelled to a new and mysterious country, had arrived amid the splendour and excitement of an Imperial return in a strange town, but she had seen little of the surroundings. Waking, as the low sun streamed into her new room on a fine bright morning, she breakfasted at the relaxed hour of 9.30. When she looked out of the windows, high up in the Alexander Palace, she saw the park bathed in the clear northern light. The golden leaves of the white-trunked birches brightened the scene and an army of gardeners was sweeping the paths. Later, she and Princess Thora went out in the grounds; this they frequently did in the mornings throughout their visit. Sometimes they met Alexandra and Nicholas and would accompany them and their dogs. One morning, soon after their bicycles arrived from England and had been 'tried out in the corridor', they met Nicky and Alix who immediately tried the bicycles. Nicky quite frequently writes in his diary that he bicycled to save time.

At first, Princess Thora and Emily kept to the formal gardens just south of the Palace, near the children's pond and the 'square island' garden surrounded with, and bisected by, canals. Emily has pasted a photo in her album showing two of the bridges crossing one of the canals. The Scotsman, Cameron,[69] who worked for Catherine the Great[70] in the later part of the eighteenth century, was responsible for much of the layout of the gardens and he designed the 'Chinese bridge' and the 'Chinese theatre' where, in the summer months, theatrical productions were given. Another of the photographs, taken during the summer, shows the yellow and white palace from across the children's pond. Awnings shade every window on this southern side of the building but a third photo shows the elegant classical northern face with its huge portico and double row of columns. Quarenghi,[71] the Italian architect responsible for many buildings in St Petersburg, designed the Alexander Palace for Catherine's favourite grandson, Alexander. He, however, preferred the flamboyant baroque of the Catherine Palace, set in the same large park a little to the east and only 'three minutes walk from here', as Princess Thora noted in a letter to her Grandmother. This was an immense building, much favoured by Nicholas I, but now, in Nicholas II's time, used mainly on ceremonial occasions. Nicholas and Alexandra found the Alexander Palace more homely and it rapidly became 'our Palace' in Emily's diary. Thora, writing to her Grandmother remarked 'that the house was very large and all the rooms which they have rearranged most comfortable'.

Although the invitation to visit Russia came in the first instance to Princess Thora, there is little doubt that Emily was also invited for herself – not just as a companion and lady-in-waiting to Princess Thora. On November 7th (October 26th Russian Calendar), a week after their arrival in Tsarskoe Selo, they all attended a

> church service at 11 o'C in the Chapel of the big Palace. An immense luncheon directly after in the big hall downstairs of all the officers etc. I sat next to the Emperor. Cercle after and I talked principally to the dear old priest.

Laconically stated, but what an impressive day it must have been for Emily. Starting with the church service, probably her first experience of the richly sensual Orthodox ritual with its processions and incense, magnificently robed priests and the deep sonorous singing filling the great baroque church. The light of innumerable candles glinted on the gold of the priestly robes and picked out the gilding of the decoration amid the smoky gloom of this grey November day.

Then they all walked through the magnificence of the Catherine Palace. The procession after the service would have taken them through a series of immense rooms: one hung with silk decorated with patterns of interwoven pheasants and swans; a suite of state rooms; the Chinese blue drawing room; rooms decorated in blue, green, and amber – the last lined with an immensely rich collection of Persian amber which had been acquired by Peter the Great. Through rooms with green pilasters or crimson pilasters: through picture galleries, their walls thick with old masters and, finally, down the ornate white State staircase to the Great Hall. Here, even on a dull November day, the gilded bas-relief and brilliant ceiling paintings would have glowed with priceless magnificence. A hall steeped in the extravagance of the Tsars and the immeasurable wealth of Russia.

Here was Emily sitting next to Nicholas II. The Emperor was slightly built, not very tall, with a kindly bearded face, a magnetic charm and 'a somewhat shy kindness which was all his own'. Emily, I am sure, was soon put at her ease and chatting away about her joy at seeing Alix again, the journey, the people they both knew in England and Germany, and the interesting time which awaited her and Princess Thora in Russia.

A 'cercle' was customary after the meal. The Emperor and Empress moved round and spoke with many, sometimes all, the guests. Sometimes the 'cercle' was very long; Emily's record was five hours! At her first, Emily talked mainly with the dear old priest. Probably this was the long-haired, long-bearded

Father John the 'dear old priest' whom Emily met and talked to on a number of occasions.

"Archipietr of Cronstadt" whose photograph appears in Emily's album. The Imperial family's life was interwoven with the Orthodox Church, and the Emperor and Empress were very dependent on their personal priests and confessors. As Princess Thora told her Grandmother, there was always a religious service on every festive occasion.[72] When Alix first arrived in the Crimea in the desperate last days of Tsar Alexander, the charismatic "John of Cronstadt", was there praying for a miraculous recovery of the mortally-ill Tsar. These were usually good and worthy men and they had considerable influence. When this was confined to the spiritual and religious life of the individual, all was well. Straying beyond this, particularly into politics, brought disaster. Emily enjoyed talking to 'the dear old priest', and it was repeated more than once. Her entry for that day, November 7th, concludes with

> Mlle Warsiltchikoff [sic: spelling of Russian names caused her some trouble] and I dined together and she asked the aide de camp up after. They sat with me till 1/4 to 10 I read when I went to bed at 10.30.

Emily had been invited to come to Russia with Princess Thora, the Emperor had shown her great courtesy at the luncheon in the Catherine Palace, and here is an example of Alix's thoughtfulness – making sure that Emily was not lonely and bewildered in a strange land. Throughout her visit, Emily was always accompanied by either Princess Bariatinsky whom she had first met on the Royal Train, Mlle Wassilitchikoff who met her on her first evening in Russia or, later, Princess Obolensky. They all belonged to the Empress's Household and had apartments in both the Alexander Palace and the Winter Palace in St Petersburg.

It was Mlle Wassilitchikoff who initially helped Emily with her Italian. Before she left England, Emily, realising that she might have time on her hands, despite having letters to write and other matters to attend to for Princess Thora, had armed herself with books to continue her studies of Italian. She had been doing this for some years, ever since the holiday in Florence and Sienna in 1891 with the Davidsons, when he had been completing his *Life of St Catherine of Sienna*. After this, she and Gerry had intermittently taken Italian lessons. She had been given a new stimulus, when staying in Ireland just before the news of the Russian visit broke. At Abbey Leix they had all been looking at a folio of prints of Botticelli's illustrations of Dante's Divine Comedy. The year before, 1896, an English language edition had been published of Friedrich Lippmann's original 1887, two-volume German edition and this was probably what they were looking at in Ireland. So now Emily was continuing her Italian in Russia and reading Dante's work in the original. On only her second evening in Russia, she noted 'dinner rather late. Relevayed and Dante after'. The next evening she 'read the second canto of the Purgatoria after dinner' and, a few days later, Madame Wassilitchikoff read Dante with her from her Benson's edition. Three weeks later arrangements were made for an Italian, Baroness Wolff, to come and help Emily and they read several Cantos of Dante together. In December, Emily learned that Dr Hirsch, the doctor, also spoke Italian. He arranged for a Mme Noto to come and give lessons and these continued for several weeks. Emily was good at languages and was fluent in French and German, so her studies in Italian gave her pleasure and she made great progress. The same cannot be said for her Russian, judging by the entries in the diary. Princess Thora, however, told her Grandmother that she had been working hard at the language and could understand 'everyday, sort of easy sentences'. During her visit Emily saw a number of Russian plays, but there was always someone such as Princess Obolensky to help her.

Mlle Wassilitchikoff (or K. Wass and finally Katousch as Emily later refers to her) became a great friend. She introduced Emily to many of her family and Emily visited them in their houses in St Petersburg. Katousch was much involved with the orphanage that was opened ceremonially by the Tsar on November 15th, the little Grand Duchess Olga's birthday. Both Emily and Princess Thora have left short accounts of this occasion and, in a cutting from the *Messager officiel*, there is a more fulsome one. Princess Thora, in one of her letters, told Queen Victoria:

> It was little Olga's birthday yesterday, there was a short service in the morning which is the custom here on all festive occasions. Alix took little Olga with us as it only last (sic) ten minutes or a quarter of an hour & she behaved beautifully & enjoyed the singing & tried to join in which nearly made us laugh.

Emily's entry reads 'we went in the afternoon to the "Olga Orphanage", a most successful function'. Princess Thora continues, calling it

> an orphan asylum for poor children which Nicky has built in

> commemoration of Olga's birth. They opened the buildings which had just been finished, it was a most interesting ceremony, there were chiefly only very poor people there & their joy at seeing Alix & Nicky was quite touching.

The orphanage was for children around St Petersburg of between six and fifteen years old, of both sexes, who were taught simple practical subjects such as gardening and cookery. The Emperor, Empress and Princess Thora were greeted on the steps of the building by the president of the Council of the Asylum, M Maitre de la Cour, Baron Wolff (possibly the husband of Emily's Italian teacher). A religious service was conducted by "M l'archiprêtre Jean Serguiew (de Cronstadt)": Emily referred to him as Père Jean the 'wonderful miracle priest', whom she had met at the Catherine Palace. After the service and the opening ceremony, the whole party toured the new buildings. Emily visited the orphanage twice more; on Katousch's name day when cakes were presented, and once when she had tea and 'saw all the children'.

This orphanage opened by the Tsar was a new addition to several similar institutions which cared for the orphans and foundlings in and around St Petersburg. The rapid industrialisation of the mid- to late-nineteenth century and the abject poverty of many of the workers resulted in vast numbers of homeless children. In fact, the economy of many of the surrounding villages depended on the hundreds of thousands of roubles paid out by the authorities to the peasants in these villages for the care of the foundlings. Sadly, the death rate of such children was appallingly high: the Institutions had a somewhat better record.

Again, it was Mlle Wassilitchikoff who took Emily to leave cards at the big palace, and then on to Pavlovsk about 10 miles south of Tsarskoe Selo. The 'Big Palace' as Emily always called the Catherine Palace, was a long, narrow baroque building of truly enormous size – over 300 metres in length. It was designed by Rastrelli,[73] probably the greatest architect working in Russia in the 18th century. A photograph in Emily's album shows part of the facade with its countless windows and white columns, set against a dark background, overlooking the courtyard. This was enclosed by curved one-storey buildings, the curves meeting at the magnificent gilded gates designed by Rastrelli. In the corner the onion domes and spires indicate the position of the Palace church where Emily had witnessed her first Russian Orthodox service. This was the imposing sight that Emily and Katousch drove past on a mild and sunny afternoon in November,

The Catherine Palace. The domes at the far end of this facade mark the position of the church where Emily heard her first Russian Orthodox service.

with the golden domes gleaming in the sunlight, on their way to a discreet side entrance to leave their cards.

Social custom placated, they drove to do some sightseeing. A short distance away was the Palace of Pavlovsk where they found 'Baronne Korff at home'. Pavlovsk was yet another Imperial Palace, built in the time of Catherine the Great by Cameron in the classical style and which she gave to her son Paul.[74] He lived there for a while before moving to Gatchina; but his wife, Mariya Fyodorovna, remained in residence for many years and so it became very much her palace. The central building was rectangular under a low dome with curved wings linking it to other substantial buildings around a large courtyard. Baronne Korff took them on a brisk tour of the interior showing Emily some of the outstanding rooms: Cameron's large dining room on the ground floor where the entire family of Paul, his wife and their ten children had sat down to meals – its fluted pilasters and moulded frieze and *trompe-l'oeil* ceiling, apparently extending the height of the room to the heavens, the Italian Hall on the first floor lit by the lantern windows in the cupola with its walls of imitation marble inset with Roman statues in niches. She would have appreciated the contrast between the rooms designed for Paul with their robust martial themes and those intended for Mariya decorated with musical instruments, flowers and fruit.

Emily would have been enchanted by the delicate decorations of the 'small' dancing room where, to the intimate music of flute, violin and lute, beautifully dressed young ladies of the Court would have danced minuets and chaconnes.[75] There was so much to see, so much to admire, so much to learn. Like most people who are sightseeing Emily was more than glad when 'Baronne Korff gave us tea'. With the day drawing in and darkness falling, the two ladies were driven back to the Alexander Palace through the edge of the forest of Pavlovsk. Workmen were trudging homeward in the dusk. They passed the barracks as they reached Tsarskoe Selo. Soldiers going about their evening duties were silhouetted in the lamp-lit rooms and there was the sound of hooves on cobbles and the steamy smell of the horses being bedded down for the night. In the darkness the warm glow from the villas and houses lined their way before they reached the comfort of 'our Palace'.

Both Mlle Wassilitchikoff and Princes Bariatinsky made a point of introducing Emily to many of the Court people who lived in the 'village' of Tsarskoe Selo. On her second day in Russia, Emily and Princess Bariatinsky 'drove afternoon and left cards'. The etiquette of calling and leaving cards was similar to that in England. However, it is set out clearly and firmly for the visitor in John Murray's 'Handbook for Travellers in Russia, Poland and Finland', published in 1870:

> Strangers are expected to make the first call, which is returned either in person or by card. In leaving cards on persons who are not at home, one of the edges of the card should be turned up. It is necessary to leave a card next day on any person to whom the stranger may have been introduced at a party. Those who are introduced to the stranger will observe the same politeness. Great punctuality is exacted at St Petersburg in the matter of leaving cards and entertainments and introductions.

One can see how Emily's time is much taken up with the politeness of cards; but it had its uses, for she quickly acquired a circle of acquaintances. It also accounts for the lists of names she often wrote at the end of the day – a reminder of those on whom to leave cards. As the diary develops, we meet the people of the town to whom she was introduced.

The von Hesse family became particular friends. He was a General, the head of the secret police according to the caption in her album (probably the palace security police), but he looks kindly with his round bald head and grizzled beard and moustache. Emily visited Mme von Hesse[76] several times and dined with them on November 20th. A few days later Mme von Hesse took Emily for a 'delightful drive in a troika[77] although there wasn't enough snow in some places'. She shared Emily's love of music. Towards the end of December, Emily and Princess Obolensky went to the von Hesse's house after dinner to listen to a M Zilotti playing the piano. The diary tells us:

> He played Tchaikowski [sic], Liszt, Rubenstein and a nocturne of Chopin, where he dreams that George Sand goes for a walk in the woods and dies and is brought back to him by the monks who lay her corpse at his feet and then he finds it is a dream and she still walks in the woods.

A unique passage for Emily – for a short time, perhaps, she was lost in the music.

In the early days, she and Princess Bariatinsky left cards on Mme Tolstoy, Dr and Mme Hirsch (he was the doctor) and Mlle Oderoff – who was the first to give Emily a ride in a sledge. Emily had tea with Mme Balascheff and was entertained by her on several occasions. They got on well, and it was she who visited Emily when she was kept in with lumbago and 'staid a nice long time'. Later, Emily walked to see Mme Balascheff and sat with her for three quarters of an hour which, as it is mentioned, was probably an unusually long time for polite visiting.

As the winter progressed, more and more sledge rides were made through the wide streets of Tsarskoe Selo lined with substantial villas built of wood with enclosed balconies, where those attached to the Court and the Royal circle lived when the Tsar was in residence. In the album there is a photograph of Tsarkoe Selo (apparently taken from a balloon), showing empty streets with only a few people walking and no vehicles. Two tall poles with prominent insulators are indications of the arrival of the telegraph and electricity in the town. It was reputed to be the first town in Europe to be completely electrified. A huge onion dome looms from the sepia distance and, away to the right, is a very long white building, probably the Catherine Palace.

Princess Marie Bariatinsky, one of the few close friends of the Empress, was with Emily off and on for some weeks, frequently lunching or dining with her in her room and visiting her for arrangements and chats. By the end of the

Russian visit, they had become close friends and she became 'Marie'. Emily got to know some of her family, one of the many noble families whose lives were interwoven with the Tsar's. On December 8th, after a long day of ceremonials connected with the Order of St George, Emily remained in St Petersburg with Princess Bariatinsky. However, Prince Galitzine, the brother-in-law, 'read French plays most interestingly and well'. Princess Galitzine, Marie Bariatinsky's sister, was the Grande Maitresse to the Empress. Emily frequently visited her and had dinner with her several times, once with Dr Hirsch as the only other visitor, and it was 'very pleasant'.

Emily had found her place in these new surroundings and enjoyed meeting members of the Household in much the same way as she did in England and Germany. She spent much time 'writing'. Some of this was business for herself or Princess Thora, confirming arrangements, writing letters of thanks and doing the accounts; some was writing home and to Cathy to tell them of her new experiences. Twice she wrote to Queen Victoria to give her news of her granddaughters and, nearly always, there was a rush to have letters ready for 'the Messenger'. She spent most mornings with Princess Thora but, in the afternoons Thora joined Alix – playing with the children, visiting relations or driving out with her and, once in December, going out with the whole family on snowshoes. In a lively letter to her Grandmother, Princess Thora gave this account:

> In the afternoon Alix & I usually drive together which is most amusing, their coachmen are padded till they look like cushions, they wear funny low hats & drive at a furious pace with their arms stretched out in front of them. You have no idea how curious it is till one gets used to it.

Sometimes, during November and December, Emily also was invited to luncheon with the Empress, especially if Nicholas was out shooting; afterwards they played with little Olga and the baby Tatiana. From Princess Thora's letters to her Grandmother it is clear that Alix enjoyed these quiet family lunches. As she said:

> We lead a very quiet life here & one can scarcely realise that they are an Emperor & Empress as there is, here in the country, an entire absence of all state. None of the gentlemen live in the

> house & the one lady on duty takes her meals in her own room, so one never sees any of the suite unless people come or there is some function.

This is corroborated by a note in Emily's diary for December 1st:

> Wrote all morning. M. Bariat came at 12.30. We were bidden to lunch with the Empress so she had her food upstairs. We played on the mountain with the baby after lunch.

There are two mentions of the 'mountain' in the diary. On November 22nd, she was sent for with Marie Bariatinsky 'to go on the "mountain". Very hot and exhausted'; and again, after lunch on December 1st, 'We played on the mountain with the baby'. This was a traditional source of exercise and amusement for children; a sort of switchback set up in one of the enormous corridors of the palace. Countess Choisell-Gouffier describing her visit to Tsar Alexander I's[78] Court says:

> At eight o'clock, on returning to the Palace, the first objects we saw were the two little Grand Dukes going down les *montagnes russes* at a great pace.

With very young children such as Alix's, it was perhaps more fun for the children than for the exhausted supporting adults. With Emily's love of children, however, it is clear that she thoroughly enjoyed her visits to the Royal nursery and the opportunity to chat to Alix and Thora in the old informal ways.

There is a charming photograph of Alix with her two children in Emily's album. It is dated November 1897 and signed by her with the addition of the two children's names. It was probably given to Emily together with the one of a young, handsome Nicholas, soon after she arrived in Russia (Plate 1). Alix is looking beautiful and motherly. Olga is a large, plump child with her hair combed into a top-knot above a square chubby face but, as Princess Thora remarked in a letter home, 'she is still very big but not near so fat as last year'. With a beloved husband, two little daughters, and being young and in good health, Alix looks supremely happy. As Thora remarked, 'I don't think I have ever seen two people who are so absolutely happy together'. There was every prospect that they would be blessed with a healthy son and heir before long. None of the anxiety and aggressiveness, which became so apparent in Alix's character in later years, and the desperate sadness which seared her once beautiful face, seems likely or possible.

When they came to live at the Alexander Palace, Nicholas and Alix had chosen rooms in the sunny, south-eastern corner of the building as their own and had decorated them in a style reminiscent of houses in western Europe with cheerful wallpapers and chintzes; water colours and engravings in simple wood frames hung on the walls; plants in pots, ferns, palms and aspidistras and great bowls of flowers brought colour and scent into the rooms during the long Russian winter. The curtains were draped and fringed, and every surface crowded with photographs of the family. At the time of Emily's visit, photographs of the babies would be taking their place alongside those of the family in Hesse and relations in Germany and far-off England. This somewhat 'bourgeois' taste was frowned on by high Russian society but it suited Alix and Nicholas well. Both had had somewhat spartan childhoods and it made them feel much more comfortable than the 'sparkling and overblown decor in the Russian Palaces'. Nicky had been encouraged in adopting this style by Ella, Alix's sister, the Grand Duchess Serge who wrote to him in May 1894 just before he set off to stay with Queen Victoria in England. She told him that:

> in England you will get delightful ideas and there are big warehouses where one can see ready rooms. Victoria [of Battenberg] must know all those places and where to find pretty chintz and then china for washstands.

She goes on:

> the English books are best for dressing [rooms], bedroom and boudoir ... [you could] get the pretty engraving (I think you can find it at Bygrofs or Gelton) called Darby and Joan painted by Sadler engraved by Bauchir; it is so simple and so lovely ... Try and see some fine private houses in London, ask Aunt Louise Lorne's advice she is a real artist, Alix can tell you and [will be] so pleased to help. Windsor is not pretty, I love the place but the style of rooms I do not like. Cumberland Lodge where Aunt Helena lives is oh so cosy.

Nicky and Alix followed Ella's advice: so it is little wonder that Emily felt so at home in 'our Palace'. To reach this oasis of family life, Emily may have been able to slip down some unobtrusive staircase and along a passage or two, or she might have walked though endless corridors and suites of rooms with traditional Russian decoration and passed the army of attendants who opened the doors, such as the 'Ethiopian, gaily and weirdly be-decked who mounted guard outside Nicholas's study'. From her diary, one has no idea that they were there; they were just taken for granted. But Dorothy Seymour, who visited the Empress in February 1917, mentions them in her account of the day. Even then, after three years of grinding war the rich trappings remained. Dorothy Seymour wrote,

> Went down to Tsarskoe Selo to see the Empress. Met by gorgeous officials, footmen, horses all white and prancing. Great state. At the Palace door two glorious footmen with huge orange and red ostrich plumes on their heads ... then taken through miles of palace and huge banqueting room. Door opened by a huge Negro.

It is one of the curiosities of Emily's diary that she never mentions the enormous number of people who must have been in attendance; very rarely does she even mention her own maid, Jeanne and, only once, on the lonely evening of Russian New Year, the name of the person who served her dinner. They were all an accepted and un-remarked part of palace life.[79]

Princess Thora commented on the quiet existence that Nicholas and Alexandra led: how they preferred to fill their days with the activities of secluded country life: enjoying each other's company, walking and driving in the grounds, meeting their relatives and playing with the children. Nicholas was especially fond of shooting, and the forests and parks around the palaces at Tsarskoe Selo, Pavlovsk and Gatchina were ideal for this. The '*chasse*' establishment with all the hounds and caged animals, including bears, which Emily visited with Frau Dietz was for organised shoots, when the animals were released and used as quarry for the sportsmen and hounds This was one form of sport: but, on other occasions, Nicholas was able to get some of the thrill experienced by many wildfowlers and sportsmen who go out after truly wild birds – geese, duck, snipe and woodcock. Perhaps he experienced some of the sensations that Levin did when he took Obolensky out shooting in *Anna*

Karenina: the silence of the winter dusk broken only by the twittering of little birds in the thicket; the excitement of the unmistakeable calls of game birds heralding their arrival; the moment before firing on the advancing dark shape and the pleasure of the retrieving dog bringing the limp warm body. Perhaps Nicholas was able to experience for a brief moment that curious combination: a love of nature and the achievement of the sportsman. It would have been a wonderful relaxation for someone in his position. He would have been able to shed for a short while the trappings, privileges and responsibilities of an Emperor and family man and return to the world of man the hunter. For a few brief hours he could, perhaps, enjoy the simplicity of the country life which, had fate dealt him different cards, he might have enjoyed for a long lifetime.

But it was not to be. The country life at Tsarskoe Selo, however desirable to Nicholas and Alix, was inextricably linked with the responsibilities and grandeur of St Petersburg. So their guests, Emily and Princess Thora, from their almost familiar base in the Alexander Palace, were taken to see the magnificent buildings and the pomp of the traditional ceremonies in the capital

CHAPTER FOURTEEN

St Petersburg and the Winter Palace

It was a cold grey day for Emily's first visit to St Petersburg, not perhaps the best for her first sight of this famed city. A certain excitement must have gripped her as the train from Tsarskoe Selo drew in to the Vitebsk station. Amid the bustle of the crowd, the noise of the train and the clouds of steam she and Princess Bariatinsky were met with a carriage and drove off through the traffic to do some shopping – a photograph album for Princess Thora and lace for Princess Christian.[80] The wide streets were full of carriages and carts, their iron-shod wheels grinding noisily on the cobbles or rumbling more quietly and smoothly on those streets that were paved with wood. The shouts of the drivers mingled with the jingle of harness as the horses tossed their heads and got their loads moving, their breath smoking in the cold air. The sombre grey day did little to lighten the greyness of the buildings, many of them of monumental size, the

The Nevsky Prospect with carriages and horse trams at the time of Emily's visit.

original pink granite stained and blackened by smoke Peter the Great's[81] edict that the palaces of the nobility should be painted bright colours meant that, where there was a palace, and there were probably about 4000 of them in the city at this time, there were welcome patches of colour, yellow, green, blue and pink to contrast. Their colour was heightened by the white and gold of the windows and the gilded decorations.

All this passed in a flash as Emily, busily chatting to Princess Bariatinsky, looked around her and tried to get her bearings as they made their way towards the Nevsky Prospekt. The great width of the famous shopping street and the teeming mass of people, well-wrapped up against the cold, who filled the pavements, may have astonished her but completing her commissions came first. She was out of the carriage and into the shops for her purchases – amazed by the wide choice of the beautiful Vologda lace and the luxury of the leather-bound albums. She completed her purchases, guided by her friend through the difficulties of the strange language, customs and money. Then off they went in the carriage to see some of the sights.

The diary records: 'Then to Nôtre Dame and Isaac's Church'. By Nôtre Dame, it is likely that Emily must have meant the Kazan Cathedral[82] which, at the time of her visit, still held the precious icon it was built to house. The icon had appeared miraculously in Kazan in 1579 and was known as Our Lady of Kazan. To reach the Cathedral, having completed their shopping, the two ladies would have driven up the Nevsky, over the Fontanka River and the Griboedov canal – their murky waters packed with barges – to this magnificent church modelled on St Peter's in Rome. They did not go inside but from their carriage they would have seen the two colonnaded arms curving towards the Nevsky and the fine statues of the two generals, Kutuzov and Barclay de Tolley, heroes of Tsar Paul who commissioned the building.

It was in this church that Nicholas and Alexandra had celebrated their nuptial mass after their marriage in the Winter Palace in those emotional times three years earlier.

From there, Emily was taken to see another spectacular church, St Isaac's[83], with its huge, high, gilded dome rising far above the massive square building. Each face had a portico supported by immense Corinthian columns and flanked by blind towers terminating in small colonnaded temples crowned with gilded domes. Intricate carvings filled the pediment of each apse. Along the roof tops stood huge classical and religious statues – a breathtaking spectacle which apparently left Emily unable to take in the great bronze statue of Nicholas I[84]

The Winter Palace. At the time Emily was in St Petersburg the Palace was painted dark red. The tower on the extreme left is a part of the building and was where messages from the Palace could be transmitted by heliograph to Tsarskoe Selo.

seated on his horse between the Cathedral and the Mariinsky Palace – an attractive pink palace, built for the daughter of Alexander I, which had formerly belonged to the Leuchtenbergs. Princess Thora spent much time with this family later in the visit.

Lunch called; and Princess Bariatinsky ordered the carriage to take them to the Winter Palace.[85] As Emily approached this great building for the first time, it looked dark and forbidding, its deep red walls sombre in the winter light. They would have driven around the immense 'Palace Square', an enormous open space used for parades and military spectacles, its vastness punctuated by the impressive Alexander Column. This monument had stood in the square for over fifty years as thanksgiving from the people of Russia to Alexander 1[86] for the defeat of Napoleon's armies. It was made of over seven hundred tons of Finnish granite and more than 2000 soldiers and workmen had been required to raise it into position but, such was its tremendous weight, this was sufficient to keep the column upright. On top, B I Orlovsky's sculpture – an angel carrying a cross – reigned majestic in the sky. The carriage drove to a side entrance of the Palace, and they went in through the vast doors, along endless high passages with footmen at each doorway, and into the intimacy of the Princess's room (Plate 4). Luncheon was served and they took a short rest before venturing out again into the damp chill air to see more of the sights of the city.

'Then after to the Fortress church where are all the tombs of the Emperors etc.' – the bare outline would later remind Emily of that afternoon (Plate 4). In their carriage they drove along the length of the Winter Palace and Hermitage buildings, over the newly constructed bridge across the wide Neva – its waters at this time of year still swirling past unfettered by ice, to the historic centre of Peter the Great's dream.[87] Even in the fading winter light, the elegant thin spire that topped the cathedral gleamed palely, piercing the dull sky. They crossed the moat and drove into the ancient fortress. Quickly they were out of the carriage, in through the great doors of the cathedral,[88] down the long nave gleaming with gold and rich carvings among the soaring columns. In the centre, a magnificently carved and gilded iconostasis carried their eyes towards the dome. To one side, behind an iron railing, stood a group of marble sarcophagi guarding the mortal remains of the Romanovs from Peter the Great onwards. Only his was adorned with flowers. The tombs were what Princess Bariatinsky had brought Emily to see and to pause for a moment's reflection. Of much less importance, but to Emily nevertheless vital, was leaving their letters home for the 'bag' at the English Embassy on their way to the Fortress. It was only a week since she and Princess Thora had left Darmstadt; the links with home and friends in England were still very warm.

When they returned to the Palace, Emily had time to think over all she had seen as she rested quietly in Princess Bariatinsky's room while the Princess was visiting a friend. Before they caught the train back to Tsarskoe Selo there was time to visit Princess Galitzine in her charming flat and to have a cup of tea. Back in the Alexander Palace Emily slipped into her usual routine and she ended the day by reading 'last night's canto of the Purgatoria'.

A week later, both Emily and Princess Thora were taken up to St Petersburg by the Empress herself. On this frosty morning the sun shone and the sky was blue with great towering clouds driven along by the high wind. The Neva reflected the blue, and the brilliance of the northern winter light enhanced the colours, although dust blew grittily along the streets and across the huge open squares. A carriage again met them from the train and they drove to the Winter Palace in time for lunch in the Empress's rooms. Then, fortified, they all set off to see the wonders of the Palace. They began in the Imperial family's own rooms, furnished in the bourgeois style so despised by St Petersburg society. Her rooms glowed with scented flowers which were her great love, and were decorated with icons and small pieces of the great Fabergé's craft. Did the Empress show Thora and Emily the wonderful Easter egg which at the touch of a catch opened to show the coronation coach?

Nicholas's gothic-styled library with its gallery panelled in dark wood formed a comfortable setting for his work. Unlike so many of the previous Tsars, Nicholas did not choose any of the world-famous paintings from the Hermitage to adorn the walls of his private rooms. Instead, he and Alix chose watercolours, engravings, and what connoisseurs consider second-rate paintings. Perhaps these brought back comfortable memories of Alix's home in Darmstadt or the private rooms of her Grandmother in Windsor and Osborne. No doubt Princess Thora and Emily found the rooms grand but curiously familiar.

Then they were off into the flamboyant brilliance of the state rooms which, unknown to Emily and Princess Thora in these early days in Russia, would form the stage for many of the ceremonies that they would later take part in. The light, reflected from the wide expanse of the river, streaming in through the huge windows was caught and refracted into rainbow colours by the chandeliers which hung in every room. Electricity had recently been installed, so the smoke of the thousands of candles was a thing of the past. Crystal chandeliers, bronze chandeliers or imitations made of intricate, gilded *papier mâché* hung beneath the elaborately painted ceilings. Their light lit the gilded carvings of the cornice and panelling and was reflected in the huge mirrors which filled the walls between the windows.

Treasures carved in marble, malachite, crystal, lapis lazuli and gold passed in a kaleidoscopic whirl as the visitors swept from room to room. They passed through immensely tall doorways – each door a symphony, reflecting the intricate mastery of the inlaid floors; swirling patterns and arabesques in a dozen different coloured woods. One room led into another making a great suite, with spectacular vistas along the river. Then to the top of the great Jordan staircase: an elaborate study in the art of marble carving – sturdy marble balusters, elegant shallow marble stairs and classical and romantic statues. Finally they reached the Hermitage where were housed the pictures and art treasures collected by successive rulers of Russia.

Here there was an unbelievable galaxy of pictures to see. Perhaps, on this first occasion, Emily was more interested in seeing the Winter Palace under the guidance of the Tsarina than examining the pictures, for, later in the month, she returned to the Hermitage[89] with Princess Bariatinsky 'to see the Rembrandts'. On this first visit, Emily left the Winter Palace after a lightning tour and returned to Tsarskoe 'by the 4 o'clock train' and 'Had tea on the way back'.

Later in the month, Emily went back with 'Bariat' to look at the

Rembrandts. These had been a treasured part of the Hermitage Collection for some considerable time but paintings continued to be bought: during the nineteenth century a fabulous collection of French art with many Impressionist paintings was being acquired. On her second visit, Emily would have had time to linger over some of the magnificent canvases of Rembrandt such as the *Descent from the Cross*, where the light falls on the stricken body of Christ, as it is lowered from the cross and on to the prematurely aged face of his mother. Rembrandt's ability to catch the character of the inner man and woman is seen in this epic painting. It is even more concentrated, with no narrative distractions, in the two pictures *Portrait of an Old Man* and *Portrait of an Old Woman* both painted in 1654. In these the careworn faces with eyes dulled by sadness and experience and the hands crossed in submission portray very moving images of old age. Emily often mentions, throughout the years of her diary, meeting some 'dear old lady' or man and so she would have taken particular interest in these two portraits. Although Emily, by her very nature and the nature of her job, never lets us know her inner feelings, there is no doubt that she was intensely interested in and sympathetic to people. She would have found a source of inspiration and reflection in every picture of this great collection. Like anyone who makes their way to particular pictures, Emily's eye would perhaps have been caught by the charming masterpiece of Leonardo da Vinci, *The Madonna with a flower*, in which a very young Mary is delighting the Christ child with a small plaything. Or possibly she caught a glimpse of the fan made of cast iron, so delicate that it looked like lace. The wealth of treasures was endless.

Emily visited other galleries and exhibitions during her visit to Russia. Among these was the charity exhibition of English pictures given by Grand Duchess Serge, Ella, as part of the 'Season' of Petersburg Society. Emily and 'Marie Bariat', as Princess Bariatinsky has become by January 22nd, went along and

> the Emperor, Empress and Princess Thora arrived soon after. All the English Corps dip. there. The Emperor bought an Alma Tadema and a Poynter and the Empress also bought two pictures.

The Emperor's choice of paintings tells us something of his taste. Alma Tadema and Sir Edward Poynter were both very popular painters in the late 19th century, both born in 1836. Alma Tadema, through his skills as a painter and his astuteness as a businessman, was able to lead a flamboyant and sumptuous life in St John's Wood in north London. Emily had met him on one occasion when she was dining with the Joachim family. He specialised in paintings of ancient Greece, Rome and Pompeii: eternally sunlit scenes in which well-nourished maidens in flimsy dresses with flowers in their hair draped themselves around pools and fountains on milk-white marble terraces above deep blue seas. Sir Edward Poynter had made his name with enormous canvases of historical events; his first great success had been *Israel in Egypt*. He was a very fine draughtsman and his skills found ample scope in his complex tableaux. Towards the end of the century, his paintings had become smaller and were of classical scenes, somewhat similar to those of Tadema. Sir Edward, in contrast to Tadema, had by the end of the nineties become more of an establishment figure; and, having been made Director of the National Gallery in London in 1894, was devoting much of his time to administration.

The day before Princess Thora and Emily finally left St Petersburg, Emily was given a chance to see a great collection of Russian paintings. After a very busy morning on February 25th, including going 'to Mr Clarke about money', she

> went out again at 2 o'C to join Katousch [Mlle. Wassilitchikoff] at the Palais Michel to see the Russian pictures. Many civil gentlemen took us round and Gd Duke George came a little before we left.

A lot is compressed into those few words.

Tsar Alexander III, who had made a conscious effort to bring the Slav nature of Russian culture to the fore, had begun to collect examples of Russian art with a view to opening a National Museum; but, because of his unexpectedly early death, it was left to his sons Nicholas, George and Michael to bring this about. In the year after he became Emperor, Nicholas bought the Mikhailovsky Palace, a beautiful cream and white building with an impressive facade of Corinthian columns. It was due to be opened officially as the Russian Museum on March 7th 1898 but Emily would miss this; so a special visit was arranged for her with the 'civil gentlemen' and Grand Duke George. In the short time available, they no doubt did their best to show her some of the highlights of the collection. Surely they would have taken her to see one of the oldest exhibits – the small 12th-century icon, *The angel with the golden hair*, and perhaps she got a glimpse of the 14th-century icon of Boris and Gleb, the two young princes of Kiev who were murdered by their elder brother. She might have been amused by the bronze of Tsar Paul, with his snub nose, and have remembered her visit to Pavlovsk. The impressive sculpture of Catherine the Great as Legislator by the early Russian sculptor, Shubin, and the matronly bronze of the Empress Anna and the Arab boy may well have caught her eye. The latter was the work of Carlo, the father of the famous architect Rastrelli, in whose buildings Emily had spent the last few weeks.

Many of the pictures were huge. She can have hardly failed to have been impressed, possibly overwhelmed, by the truly enormous canvas capturing the feeling and tension underlying the rich and dissipated life displayed by the inhabitants in the *Last Day of Pompeii*. This immense work by Bryulov,[90] who spent most of his life in Italy, was inspired by the opera of the same name by Giovanni Pacini. Another outstandingly impressive picture was *The Ninth Wave* by the prolific artist Aivasovsky. This painting shows the great wave at its apogee with the curve of water about to crash on to the shore. Some said that it foretold the fall of the Romanov dynasty but it is unlikely that such grim thoughts were expressed by Emily's guides. Finally, perhaps, she had time to look at the emotionally moving canvas painted ten years before by Vasily Polenov, of *Christ and the Adulteress* in which the feeling between the two main characters and the expressions on the faces of the surrounding crowd are brilliantly portrayed.

Emily didn't find time to do much painting when she was in Russia – the endless round of writing and visits filled her days; but fortunately she did manage a sketch from the window of Princess Thora's rooms in the Winter Palace. This overlooked the River Neva. Emily's sketch, done at moments snatched from the busy last few days, shows a very wintry scene looking north across the frozen river (Plate 6). This sketch gives us a rare glimpse, among Emily's impressions, of Russia beyond the Imperial circle. In the foreground, according to a marginal note by Emily, runs the electric tram – the open carriages packed with people. This is of some interest, because electric trams as opposed to horse trams were apparently not generally in operation in St Petersburg as early as 1898. Even two years later, none are recorded in a survey of the public transport in the city; but, by 1910, electric trams had become serious competitors of the horse-drawn vehicles: they numbered 525, whereas the numbers of horse-drawn ones had dropped from over 500 to 381. This decline was to continue until just before the outbreak of the world war, by which time there were three times as many electric trams as horse trams.

Beyond the tramline, horse-drawn sledges ply their trade. There were large numbers of these in the winter carrying goods and people, the long runners making for a much smoother ride on the packed snow of the streets, canals and rivers. Firewood, hay and huge lumps of ice cut from the river were among the wide variety of goods carried round the city.

The embankment of pink granite was built in the early years of the 19th century and marks the edge of the Neva. In the summer, the river would have lapped the embankment and, until less than twenty years before Emily's visit, this area was the main port of St Petersburg. The large classical building and the pair of curious pink columns which form the middle ground of the sketch show two important features linked with the port (Plate 6). The classical building, the Exchange built in 1810, was designed by T de Tomon. It was part of the grand plan initiated by Peter the Great in the early 18th century and carried through in the succeeding decades to make St Petersburg a great international port linking the hinterland of Russia with Europe and the West It was a bold and amazing concept and one which could only be achieved by an autocrat – to build an entirely new city on islands in the marshy delta of a capricious river in an uncongenial northern climate. But, such was the drive and power of Tsar Peter, that eminent architects from many countries of Europe came to design the buildings. Labour was conscripted from villages throughout Russia. Together they achieved this spectacular city. As it grew, industry and commerce developed. Gradually the strict plan broke down. Industries were crammed in amongst the original classical buildings. The design remained more intact in the area to the south of the Winter Palace – not seen in this view; but to the north across this eastern tip of Vasiliyevskiy Island one can see the mixture of churches, factory chimneys and other undistinguished buildings. These are across the Malaya Neva, a branch in the delta of the main Neva River and on the island to the north of the original Fortress of St Petersburg. Emily's sketch shows the long bridge linking the two islands.

Crowds of black-coated figures climb the steps of the Exchange. On the far side stands one of the flanking warehouses, built a little later than the Exchange, which proclaim the commercial activity. The remaining features of this group are reminders of the original port. The two tall pink columns were designed as lighthouses (Plate 6). They were part of de Tomon's original plan and were not only utilitarian but symbolic. The curious protuberances projecting from the trunk of each column are the prows of ships, hence their name, the Rostral columns, the rostrum being a prow. At the base of each column are groups of statuary. There are four in all, representing the four great rivers of Russia: the Volga, Dnieper, Neva and Volkov. Water transport was vital for the wellbeing of the country but rivers could be dangerous and fickle.

From the earliest days St Petersburg suffered periodic inundations. The whole of the area is flat, lying in the bends of the Neva as it makes its way from Lake Ladoga to the Gulf of Finland. One of the most disastrous floods which took place in 1824 formed the central drama of the poem the *Bronze Horseman* by Pushkin.[91] A visitor to the city at the time, Robert Lee, left a vivid picture of seeing horses and cows being driven up to the landings of staircases to try and save them from the rapidly rising waters. Less spectacular floods were fairly frequent. Even during Emily's short visit, there were two. On November 16th, she was prevented from going by train from Tsarskoe Selo to the capital because of the bad weather; she heard later that the city had been flooded, the Neva having risen, driven back by the high wind. And on January 26th a flood was caused by a tremendously high west wind; cannons were fired as warnings.

One of the most unusual events that Emily witnessed was the ceremony of the Blessing of the Waters. Perhaps this was based on ancient superstition but, more likely, it was because the religious life of Russia was so closely linked with natural phenomena. The ceremony took place on January 18th, soon after the Court had moved to St Petersburg for the Season. January 18th dawned fine and bright, bringing a sparkle to the winter which gripped the city. The wind blew light flurries of snow across the frozen river. By 10.30, all the ladies and gentlemen of the court, the Grand Dukes and Duchesses, and the Emperor and Empress were ready in their magnificent court dresses. The fabulous jewels sparkled in the morning sunlight. The great ceremonial procession moved off through the rooms of the Winter Palace: from the State Apartments, through the Concert Hall and the Nicholas Hall with their tall windows looking out over the river, through the Hall of the Field Marshals and the Great Armorial Hall. Each vast room glittered with a thousand lights reflected on the marble and gilt: each room doubled in size by the pier-glasses between the windows. Guardsmen in scarlet and white lined the route; orchestras and military bands played martial music and the national anthem.

The brilliant procession finally reached the Cathedral in the Palace, where a long and elaborate service took place with a liturgy particular to this occasion and many fine hymns. As the service came to an end, the clergy and choir still singing processed out of the Cathedral, preceding the Emperor and his entourage, back to the Armorial Hall, down the Jordan staircase and out on to the Neva itself. Here on the frozen river a small temporary wooden chapel crowned with a golden orb and cross had been built, and here, braving the bitter wind, in the presence of the Emperor, the clergy of the Orthodox Church blessed the River Neva. This was a man's affair. The ladies did not take part but watched from the windows of the Winter Palace. Later, water taken from the river during the ceremony was distributed to many places throughout Russia for use in blessings and baptisms as part of the ritual of Orthodox services.

Religion, the Tsar and Chivalry were all inextricably linked in the life of Imperialist Russia, as they were in many European countries until the twentieth century. In the ceremony of the Blessing of the Waters, religion dominated; but at the next great ceremonial occasion that Emily witnessed the military and chivalrous aspects were the inspiration.

While Princess Thora and Emily were still staying in the Alexander Palace, both were invited to the celebration of the anniversary of the founding of the second most important military order of chivalry in Russia – The Order of St George, Martyr and Victorious. On December 8th (Emily's diary)[92] they had an early start to the day; breakfasting at 8.15 in the dark and taking the 9 a.m. train to St Petersburg. Jeanne brought the luggage and after a short wait in Princess Bariatinsky's rooms a place was found for Emily to change. Her diary goes on: 'We all dressed in trains etc by 11.30. About 60 ladies in Russian Court Dress. The Empress and Gd Dss and Pss Tora all had pages to carry their trains.'

The Russian court dress mentioned by Emily was magnificent. The garments were full length, made of sumptuous materials enriched with jewels and embroidery. The colours were vivid and varied depending on the rank of the wearer; Maids of the Bedchamber, for example, were distinguished by embroidered green velvet robes. The style was strictly ordered and traditional. It was based on that of the Russian Court dress designated by an edict of 1834 in which the cut, colour, type of fabric and amount of embroidery was precisely stipulated. The dress was based on an open robe or full-length coat with a white satin underskirt and a very low-cut bodice with hanging sleeves. The skirt of the coat flowed into a train – again the length dictated by the wearer's rank. And, as Emily records, the Empress, the Grand Duchesses and Princess Thora had pages to carry their trains. Princess Thora, in a letter written to her Grandmother after a similar event – the swearing of the Oath of Fealty by Prince Boris on his Coming of Age – comments: 'We all wore evening dresses & orders at eleven in the morning which was rather terrible'.

The event on December 8th lasted most of the day. It began with a ceremonial procession through the rooms of the Winter Palace to the Cathedral where a special service took place. Emily's own comments are short and to the point as usual, but she has pasted into her album an official invitation or command from Gerasimov, the Chief Steward of the Chamber, and a cutting from the French language gazette. This amounts to four columns detailing with great exactitude who was to be present, where they were to stand in the rooms and their positions in the procession.

A translation of the official invitation from Gerasimov reads:

> The Court of HIS IMPERIAL HIGHNESS invites the following to be present at court:- Ladies in waiting, Ladies of the Bedchamber, Household Stewards, Maids of Honour, Gentlemen of the Court and other Noblemen.
>
> HIS IMPERIAL HIGHNESS is pleased to command that on the 26th of November, on the Feast Day of the Military Order of St George the Great, Martyr and Victorious, all the above mentioned persons and the Knights of the Military Order as well as soldiers and civil servants in the city, those in possession of a golden weapon decorated with diamonds and the military medal of the order, also Guards, Generals of the Army and Fleet, Field Officers and Staff Officers should assemble in the Winter Palace of HIS IMPERIAL MAJESTY at 11.30 in the morning for the prayer service.

It continues by saying which rooms the various categories of people should stand in for the morning ceremonies. It commands them to return at 5.30 to dine with HIS HIGHNESS in the Hall of Tsar Nicholas and ends by inviting the Knights of the Order of the Holy Apostle Andrew also to be present at the dinner and to wear the chain of that Order.

The cutting from the *Partie Officielle* or gazette for November 24th gives explicit instructions for the procession.

> When the various ranks of the Order are in their correct positions, both within the halls and facing the correct way, and the Chief Officer of the Court has announced this to the

> Emperor, the Procession headed by Chamberlains, will set out from the private apartments through the principal suites of rooms along the south side of the Winter Palace. As it passes through the great rooms it will be joined by those who are waiting in their assigned places.
> The Emperor, the Empress and Grand Duke Michel Alexandrovitch will be immediately preceded by the Lord Chamberlain and will be followed by the Grand Dukes and Grand Duchesses. Princess Victoria Helena will follow and a number of other Russian Princesses. The procession will pass through the Alexander Hall, the Picket Hall, the Armorial Hall, the Portrait Gallery to St George's Hall and to the doors of the Cathedral where their Majesties and their Imperial Highnesses will be received by His Eminence the Metropolitan of St Petersburg and Ladoga and by members of the Holy Synod and also by the clergy of the Court, who will present them with the Cross and Holy Water.

So it goes on, with the singing of *Lord Save thy Creation*, a special *Te Deum* in honour of St George and prayers for the Imperial family and the Russian Armies. After further kissing of the Cross by the Emperor and Empress, a blessing by the Metropolitan on all those who were present and a blessing of the flags and standards, the Clergy and Royal Ladies retired but the Emperor remained for the Retreat of the Standards.

As might be expected, Emily is rather more succinct:

> Walked through endless rooms and galleries all filled with officers and finally the poor people who had received the St George's Cross. Into the St George's Hall where there was a service with all the old standards and colours. Heaps of priests and a very large choir and a band playing hymns all the time. Procession back and then everyone dispersed.

Among the members of the Court who took part, the *Partie Officielle* mentions *Les Dames aux Portraits*. These were ladies, usually elderly, who

> wore on their corsages a miniature of their sovereign [quite

> often now deceased] framed with brilliants and who were zealous guardians of etiquette and living chronicles of Court life, and they cast a strict eye upon the bevy of maids of honour who were recognisable by the diamond monograms of the reigning empress on their left shoulders.

Princess Thora was one of the honoured guests at the dinner in the evening and Emily was also invited. She has left us her copy of the elaborate menu – one of the most magnificent pieces of her memorabilia (Plate 6). It was designed by V Vasnetov, a well-known Russian illustrator. Depicted in orange, blue and gilt, a vigorous young St George mounted on a rearing white horse with exuberant mane and tail plunges his spear into the mouth of a prostrate red-tongued dragon. A smaller, more lively dragon forms part of a scroll pattern at the bottom right. On the left of the page the initials of the reigning Tsar, H II, an orange and black ribbon of the order behind a cross, the double-headed eagle of the Romanovs and the date 1769 form a symbolic design gracefully framing the list of dishes for the feast.

These show a strong French influence. They include Dvina Sturgeon in Champagne, French Fatted Fowl, Strasbourg Pâté and Montmorency Punch. The meal was taken to the accompaniment of music provided by the court orchestra and the 'musical choir of the Preobrazhensky regiment'.[93] Emily's companions were 'two dear old admirals' and the meal was followed by a 'prolonged cercle'. So ended a long, long day in which she not only watched but took part – a day of traditional Court pageantry. It was events such as these that Nicholas continued to attend, in later years, even when he and Alix lived almost entirely at either Tsarskoe Selo or Peterhof and only came to the capital for special occasions.

Enough of tradition and grandeur: December 8th hadn't yet ended for Emily. She changed her clothes and set off with Princess Bariatinsky to visit her sister and there met a 'Caucasian Princess with a strange history' – sadly never elucidated. The evening ended with Prince Galitzine, her hostess's husband, reading 'French plays, most interestingly and well'. But she had to leave before the end to catch the '12 o'C train back to Tsarskoe Selo'.

In the early months of their visit Emily used the train for the 14-mile journey from Tsarskoe Selo to St Petersburg very frequently. The Imperial family also used the train whenever they had engagements in the capital. Emily ends her account of a December evening with:

> We all went to the theatre. The Emperor to the French play with the Grand Duke Paul. The Empress and Pss Thora to the Opera – one by Glinka. We came away early and a good while before the end and waited long at the station and relevéd with the Emperor and the gentlemen. Got back very late.

This line was built in 1837, sixty years earlier, in the fever of enthusiasm for railway building which swept across Europe. It was a comfortable and easy link between the Royal 'village' and the Imperial capital. Construction of the railway between St Petersburg and Moscow began in the 1840s and was completed in 1851 but, at this time, only a very small part of the vast Russian Empire was served by rail. Travel was still mainly dependent on the rivers: the roads were very poor. In 1857, railway construction was opened to private enterprise and changes in the tariff on imported iron and steel encouraged industrialisation and railway building.

The possibility of a railway linking Siberia with European Russia had been discussed as early as the 1850s but it wasn't until the 1880s that it was given serious thought. There were several reasons for this change. Firstly, there was serious overpopulation in parts of European Russia and periodic famines devastated large areas: migration to Siberia was encouraged, for it was extremely rich in mineral and other resources; but the journey was very hazardous and many died on the way – a tenth of adults and a third of the children. Secondly, there was the strategic aspect. The opening of Siberia and improvement in communication would enhance Russia's influence in the Far East. Vladivostok was founded in 1860 and, despite its harbour being ice-bound for a third of the year, was the main Russian naval base on the Pacific. Yet it was over 12,000 miles from Russia's main naval base at Kronstadt on the Baltic. Over the years many schemes were put forward, some possible, some hare-brained. It was only when Tsar Alexander III became interested in the matter in the late 1880s that things began to stir. A number of sections, such as the Central Siberian Railway, had been built east of Moscow but there were still immense gaps. In 1891, however, Nicholas, while on his tour in the Far East, laid the foundation stone of what would become the eastern terminus of the Trans-Siberian Railway and a new impetus was given to the undertaking.

This is the background to Emily's short note on December 16th:

> Had Signora Noto after but only for a short time as I went to Mme Hesse to see a Panorama of the Siberian Railway … A good many children and people to see the Panorama. Came away after tea. Walked home.

It sounds rather as though the Panorama was on show in the Hesse's house. As General von Hesse was the chief of security for the Imperial family, this is possible. As usual, Emily is glad of her cup of tea! One can imagine the interest of the 'people' and the excitement of the children as they looked at the brightly coloured pictures of the route as engines steamed their way through distant lands, passing through miles of primeval forest, over huge rivers, through distant mountains and across the endless vistas of Siberia. Perhaps the explanations gave some idea of the tremendous task which had been undertaken: cutting through hundreds of miles of virgin forest; constructing rafts of trees woven together to take the weight of the ballast and rails, so that trains could pass safely across the treacherous bogs; and blasting a way through the mountain sides. Perhaps the captions touched on the bitter cold of the winter, the mud of the spring, the heat of the summer and the myriad insects that attacked the workers who suffered, besides, incredible hardships with sparse food and the minimum of shelter. Men had to undertake nearly all the hard physical work, for it was almost impossible to find enough fodder for horses in this land of trees.

By 1897, the railway had reached Irkutsk. The way to the east, to link with the line from the Pacific coast, was blocked by Lake Baikal with its mountainous southern shore. Over thirty tunnels and an ascent of 3400 feet had to be constructed before the line was eventually complete, and this was not achieved until 1904 – 05. But 1897 saw a remarkable feat. The link across the continents was completed with the building of a special ship by the British firm, Armstrong Whitworth. The ship was designed not only to carry a train but also as an icebreaker. The parts were shipped from England and brought to the terminus of the western section of the railway at Irkutsk by train, then hauled on sledges to the edge of the lake and rebuilt into this unique vessel. The link was completed. Although the lake was ice-covered for half the year, the ferry was made in such a way that she could drive herself up over the edge of the impeding ice: a screw at the bow then pushed out the water under the ice; the combined weight of the ferry and its cargo broke the unsupported ice; and the boat dropped back into the water. The action of the screw sent the lumps of ice out through the channel behind the ship. And so the train continued on its way. Even after the overland link was completed the ferry continued to be used for through, fast mail, as it was quicker than the tortuous, steep route through the mountains.

Emily had sent off letters by the 'Messenger' that morning. But no doubt in the next few days when she was 'writing', she told Gerry, Alice and Cathy about what she had seen in this glimpse of a Russia beyond the royal world of Tsarskoe Selo and St Petersburg.

CHAPTER FIFTEEN

Ice Hills and Imperial Balls

Being a guest of the Emperor and Empress meant, inevitably, that Emily's life in Russia took place in the sphere of the Imperial Household but she was not neglected by the people of the 'English Embassy'. From her diary it appears that there was little contact with other foreign communities – although she did meet one lady from the German Embassy – or that she saw much of the British people who lived and worked in the capital. She and Princess Thora did, however, have one brief chance on February 19th. After writing letters to Queen Victoria and Princess Christian in her room that afternoon, she 'went with Pss Tora to the English Embassy to meet the English colony. Were there nearly an hour'. This was probably so that the 'English' – this must have included the Irish and particularly the Scots, who had a long tradition of working in Russia – could meet the Princess, a granddaughter of their Queen. It is noticeable that Emily throughout her diary always uses 'English', as was customary at the time, where now we would say 'British'. It appears that, in Russia, the segregation of the different nationalities into 'colonies' was of long standing; although European nationals had been welcomed to the city as traders, financiers, architects and engineers in St Petersburg, ever since its founding by Peter the Great in 1703. In the papers kept by the Blessig family who emigrated from Strasbourg at the end of the eighteenth century and prospered throughout the nineteenth, it is clear that the Germans formed a close-knit community and usually married within their own national group.

A fortnight after their arrival, Emily and Princess Thora went by train to a service at the English church in St Petersburg. Emily records that there were many officials at both stations and that Mr Goschen and Mr Russell met the Princess at the church. They went to this church several times during their stay and it is later that we learn that Mr Watson was the resident clergyman. It was he who – as Thora told her Grandmother – held a service on December 25th to celebrate Christmas. The Princess wrote to her Grandmother on the 28th:

> My dearest Grandmama,
> My most loving thanks for your charming present & the little card I received by the messenger on Sunday. It was so strange spending Christmas away from home & also it not being really Christmas here. Emily & I went to church as I had asked the clergyman to have a service.

Unusually, the actual church was on the first floor of the building and Mr Watson lived on the ground floor. The pillared hall of the church was decorated in the modern Art Nouveau style with the columns decorated with William Morris-type lilies.

Other members of the 'English Delegation' who became Emily's acquaintances were the Hubbards and their children, both while she was staying in the country and after she moved to the Winter Palace. Mr Hubbard was ill and confined to his bed when Emily dined at their house on the Russian Christmas day. It was a large party. Emily went in to dinner (nearly always noted) with Mr Watson and sat next to Mr Desgras whom she got to know well on the return journey from Russia. He also was the one who eventually got Emily out on to the 'Ice Hills'. An expedition had been planned for some time once the winter had really set in but on the first afternoon chosen Emily called it off, pleading tiredness. In her final week in Russia, however, she went

> at 2 o-clock to the English Embassy. Sir Nicholas came to sit with me in my carriage and talk a little and Mr Desgras came with me to the ice hills. He took me down twice and I was terrified but gradually got used to it. The rest of the embassy and a good many others came … Hubbards too.

There is no record of Emily ever going on a toboggan in Britain; perhaps she had before the diary begins. She was a keen skater and had had two brief attempts in Russia but the ice hills were a new experience. In the very flat landscape of St Petersburg these roller coaster slopes, often starting from elevated platforms built out from elaborate wooden pavilions, were entirely man made. Blocks of ice and quantities of snow were built into ranges of hills and valleys and flooded with water to make an exceedingly fast switch-back ride – terrifying or exhilarating depending on the bravery of the traveller. Lady Londonderry's experience back in the 1837 is graphically described. She was taken by sledge to a place where a large party was assembled.

> All the young dandies were there in a kind of Esquimaux costume, eastern caps, embroidered gauntlets, short jackets and furs, *tous brignant l'honneur de conduire les dames*. A temple was erected with steps to ascend and at a certain distance the same opposite and from each of these was a descent of smooth nearly vertical ice perpendicular of from sixty to eighty feet.
> Immediately after we arrived … I was half pushed, half lifted into a large sledge that stood in the middle of the temple. In this were three persons on each side who supported themselves by pushing against each other's backs.
> I was told to shut my mouth, sit quiet, hold my tongue and not be frightened, assured there was no danger, and down they pitched us. It is impossible to conceive how dreadful is the shock … I neither breathed, nor saw, nor heard. there was mist before my eyes and a singing in my ears … *Il fallait revenir*, therefore I climbed up the opposite steps to the second temple and returned in like manner, half dead, but satisfied with having accomplished this wonderful exploit.

Emily admits that she was 'terrified but gradually got accustomed to it'. Whether she enjoyed it is uncertain but at least she was able to say she had experienced the 'ice hills'. Whether Princess Thora was taken out Emily does not say. Thora, however, gives a delightful description of sledging with the Imperial family in the grounds around Tsarskoe Selo. In a letter to her Grandmother towards the end of November she writes

> The sledging which has now begun is most amusing, one looks like a large parcel when one is packed into the sledge as the amount of furs one wears is marvellous. The only sort of hat one can wear is a fur cap which is most comfortable, last night we went out sledging by moonlight at eleven o'clock, you have no idea how delightful it is as they drive very fast & have no bells so one flies along quite silently over the snow.

Sir Nicholas O'Connor, who had sat talking to Emily in her carriage before the trip to the ice hills, was the Ambassador. Emily met him and Lady O'Connor many times and Lady O'Connor visited her in the Winter Palace. He gave a dinner in honour of Princess Thora in January, mainly for the English Community to meet the Princess. Emily had had to consult the Princess about the seating plan for this some days before and Thora appears to have enjoyed the occasion. A little later on February 10th there was a grander affair.

> Pss Tora came to talk to me until dressing time and I had to hurry. Dined at the English Embassy. The Emperor and the Empress, Vladimirs and a good many other royalties and society. 42 in all. Afterwards the Balalaika band played and there was a dance and supper, sitting down and hot. The Emperor and the Empress went away before supper. Pss Tora and Gd Dss Vladimir staid till after and we left at 1 o'C. A very successful entertainment.

This was something of an achievement. In a letter to her Grandmother, written soon after she arrived in Russia, Thora had written, obviously in response to a request from the Queen: -

> As to what you say about Alix & Nicky seeing so few people, Victoria & Irène both begged me to try & persuade Alix to have a few more, occasionally, & I have done my best I think she quite knows how important it is [that] she should get to know more of the society but the truth is she & Nicky are so absolutely happy together that they do not like to have to give up their evenings to receiving people. I do really think however they will do more now, we are actually going to have a little dinner to which some outsiders are coming which is quite a new departure & we have also dined out once or twice lately with various of the family to which also other people were invited which they had never done before. Nicky enjoyed it so much that I think it is perhaps the beginning of a rather more social life. Of course it is difficult for Alix & I must say she does try her utmost and she does the honours at the big functions

quite charmingly.

In a letter written soon after the dinner at the Embassy in her honour Thora wrote again to the Queen and said:

> I dined at the English Embassy one day last week as they were most anxious I should do so, it was not a large dinner but I made the acquaintance of some very charming people. Sir Nicholas O'Connor has asked Nicky & Alix to go there one evening which I am very glad off [sic] as I fancy they have been to none of the Ambassadors at all yet & it would be a beginning. Alix, though she was very alarmed beforehand, does all the honours quite beautifully and every one is so delighted as they say she was so shy formerly. I think she is now beginning to feel quite at home here which of course makes it easier.

Emily noted in her diary a few days after the dinner and 'successful entertainment' that she and Princess Thora talked deeply. Was it on the same subject that was worrying the Empress's relatives?

The trouble was that Alix's innate shyness combined with her dislike of the brittle, showy society, so full of gossip and intrigue – and the sort so strongly condemned by her girl-hood mentor, Miss Jackson – made such occasions abhorrent to her. In addition, her total devotion to Nicholas and their children plus her own increasing ill health gave her every excuse for avoiding Society. On the other hand this behaviour provided Society with an armoury of reasons for criticising her. It has also been pointed out that her pregnancies often coincided with the Season – another reason for withdrawing. Yet, as her cousin Thora, who knew her so well and was also shy, said 'she carried out the honours quite beautifully.'

Alix may not have liked the people who made up St Petersburg Society but she really did love – in perhaps an idealised way – the peasant people of Russia. Writing to one of her sisters after the coronation Alix said that the ceremony had seemed a kind of mystic marriage between herself and Russia and in her heart she now felt herself to be not only the Empress but also the 'Mother of the Russian people.' And this continued throughout her life. And, at least in the early days, these people loved her. Princess Thora's account of the opening of the Olga Orphanage bears this out.

The loyalty and respect of the armed forces were vital to the Emperor's and Empress's wellbeing. As mentioned in the previous chapter, Nicholas and Alexandra were always guarded by select contingents of the army or navy and Nicholas probably felt more at ease in their company than in any other except that of his own family. He expressed these feelings to his mother in more than one letter. In August 1897, after a very trying visit from his cousin the Emperor of Germany, Nicholas wrote to his mother saying how much he enjoyed being with the troops, and that being with them was 'one of the genuine consolations of my life now!' It seems that Alix, too, was happy among the ordinary soldiers. After Emily and Princess Thora had been in Russia for about a fortnight they witnessed one of the colourful parades of the Hussars stationed at Tsarskoe Selo. One morning Emily went with

> Mlle Wass to the manège [indoor riding school] for the Huzzar's fête ... A most beautiful and interesting sight. With a religious service first and then the Emperor walked past the whole regiment while they uninterruptedly shouted and then there was a double march past the Emperor and Empress.

Two days later a similar event took place in St Petersburg in the fine classical manège built early in the nineteenth century. This time there was a display with 'wonderful quick marching'.

One of the many events that were crowded into the Russian Christmas Day took place in the manège in Tsarskoe Selo. After a long morning service and luncheon the Imperial party proceeded to where the resident troops were assembled and the Empress gave each soldier a present from the 'immense Christmas tree'. Then the soldiers danced and sang.

By the time Christmas – whether western or Orthodox – arrived, Princess Thora and Emily's visit to Russia had been extended. This had all come about quite quickly. Late in the evening of December 10th, probably just about the time they would have been preparing for their return to England, Emily and Thora discussed the rumours that she had heard about 'plans in high places'. The diary continues:

> December 11th. Snowed a good deal. 9 deg. frost. Had lumbago which took me in the night. Went to breakfast but had to give up going to Petersburg and spent the day in my

room very stiff and doubled up. The Empress sent me an embrocation and a hood for dining out, *baschulich*. K Wass came in and out to me. Pss Tora came to sit with me and told me of the alterations to plans and that we are to stay a long time yet.

No indication of surprise, delight or even possible disappointment. The next day Dr Hirsch the palace doctor came and 'prescribed and talked Italian', and started Emily on the road to recovery. Soon she was out and about again, going to St Petersburg to 'Mr Clarke's bank for money' and to the Bazaar with M Bariat where they spent a long and tiresome time completing the Christmas shopping for herself and Princess Thora. Life settled back into the busy routine but inevitably the question of clothes raised its head again; for now they were both going to be in Russia during Christmas and the Season. Just before the end of the year and before the Orthodox Christmas festivities, the 'dress-maker came and a great deal of trying-on took place'. There were several more visits throughout the rest of their stay and Emily's 'grey silk was done up' and, once, she purchased some more 'stuff for a gown' in a 'selling-off place'.

As Princess Thora remarked to her Grandmother, it seemed very odd being away from home at Christmas but it had its compensations. The Imperial family celebrated not only their Russian Christmas which fell on January 6th by the western calendar, but also December 25th. The Dowager Empress who had been born Princess Dagmar of Denmark and was the sister of Princess Thora's aunt Alexandra, Princess of Wales, continued to celebrate the western date. She invited Nicholas, Alexandra and Thora to dine on the 25th at Gatchina,[94] her country palace where her late husband Tsar Alexander III had preferred to live. Emily went too. She had visited Gatchina once in November when Herr Dietz, a master of hounds 'in charge of everything to do with *La Chasse*, had shown Emily, Madame Hesse and her children around the stables, kennels and the menagerie, including the bears. After this fascinating and extensive visit they returned to the Dietz's house where they all drank hot chocolate. It was just about this time that one of the bison, which had been freed from the menagerie some nine years before, had flown into a rage and killed two of his fellows. Now his fate was sealed. Nicholas ordered his death and Misha,[95] Nicholas' younger brother had been directed to carry out his execution with the help of Dietz.

Christmas Day December 25th was more peaceful: for Emily there was dinner with the Dowager Empress's household, Princess Bariatinsky, Princess Obolensky and Mlle D'Ecaille, probably a lady-in-waiting to the Dowager Empress. On December 31st a more intimate dinner took place. As Emily wrote: 'We went to the Gatchina with the Empress and Pss Tora. Dined there only ourselves and Mlle D'Ecaille'.

In her letter of December 28th to her Grandmother, Princess Thora related not only that they had dined at Gatchina but also that 'Alix and Nicky prepared a tiny tree for me which was most dear of them but they said they kept their real presents for me till their own Christmas.' She goes on to say that, at that time, they were 'all very busy choosing presents for all their people & the officers on duty here, the soldiers etc. tables full of things it really is a sight to see them all'.

Emily didn't open her presents from home until the 26th when the Messenger arrived with a great packet of letters. Rather forlornly, she wrote: 'looked at parcels and presents all evening and alone'. But this didn't last for long. She was soon back to her usual busy round and on January 5th Christmas Eve 'The Empress had a Christmas tree in Pss Tora's room and presents. Quite lovely ... staid quietly here. Talked to Annie [one of the maids], looked at the presents and dawdled around. The servants came in after supper to my tree and have things. Mrs Orchard came too.' This was the Mrs Orchard who had been in the Grand Duke of Hesse's Household for many years and had come with Alix when she moved to Russia. Emily had been at Wolfsgarten in 1891 when they had all celebrated Mrs Orchard's twenty-five years with the family. Christmas Eve ended with Princess Thora coming into Emily's room late at night to show her the wonderful presents she had received at the family gathering at Gatchina.

By January 11th when Princess Thora next wrote to her Grandmother, all the Christmas festivities were over.

> On Christmas Eve we went to the Gatchina where there was first a service, the chapel is a very fine one and was lit up with hundreds of candles, all the priests also held candles & the choir too, the singing was quite beautiful & most impressive only as the service lasted over an hour and one stood the whole time it was rather exhausting. After that there was the Bescherung [present giving], five immense trees & all the tables round them in a beautiful room which was quite white with marble pillars.

> Every body received an immense quantity of most beautiful presents, the empress very kindly gave me a beautiful umbrella handle & a nephrite vase with silver, we then dined & returned here [Alexander Palace] where we had our own Bescherung. Alix & Nicky gave me so many beautiful presents I was quite overcome; amongst others a lovely diamond & turquoise brooch, a diamond & emerald ring & diamond pins for the hair, an Empire buckle, some charming water-colours & quantities of other things they really spoil me dreadfully.

She ended by mentioning that there had been a 'most curious ceremony' at the end of the Christmas Day service to commemorate the final departure of Napoleon from Russian soil on Christmas Day 1812.

The unbelievable wealth of jewellery of the Tsars and the aristocracy was frequently remarked upon by travellers to Russia and it was during the glittering St Petersburg Season that the most ostentatious displays were seen. The Opera, the Ballet, sumptuous dinners and social occasions were all places for showing them off but above all it was at Dances and Balls where there were the greatest opportunities.

After the momentous decision that their visit to Russia should be prolonged, it was clear that Princess Thora needed to be equipped to take part. Her clothes were immediately seen to. Even before the wonderful Christmas gifts, the Empress had given her cousin a most beautiful brooch. But there was still the dancing. It seems that Thora was uncertain about the mazurka step. The usual brief note appears in the Diary for January 10th:

> After luncheon Pss Wassilitchikoff and daughter came to see Pss Tora and we went down and Myendorff shewed Ps Tora the Mazurka step and the Empress played.

The note may have been brief but with its help in later years Emily was able to conjure up that warm and friendly afternoon when she and Tora had been able to talk with Alix as they had in the old days

The door was opened for them and there sat Alexandra at the piano. Outside the afternoon with snow clouds looming was becoming bleak and dark but in the room the light glinted on the Empress's hair and the fire burned warmly in the grate. On the

piano, sheets of music lay scattered and, as they came in and after the rather formal greetings, Alexandra handed some manuscript music to Emily and said:

"Oh! You left this the last time we were singing. Would you like it back?"

"Oh! Yes. Thank you, your Imperial Majesty", said Emily; "I wondered what had happened to it. Princess Thora and I were thinking of practising it again in a day or so".

"Now," said Alexandra, "Let me introduce you to Colonel Myendorff. Perhaps you have met him before; he was on the train when we came from Darmstadt. This time he is going to make sure that you can all do the mazurka step correctly. Have you got your dancing pumps? Good. Over to you Colonel."

Colonel Myendorff stepped forward thanking Alexandra and turned to the ladies: Princess Thora, looking a little nervous, Emily unruffled as ever, and Princess Wassilitchikoff holding her daughter's hand.

"Now, Ladies. Stand in a line behind me and I'll show you, slowly, how to place your feet. The music will be in three time and I'll call out, One and Two, Three as I move. Without the music first and quite slowly. One and Two... Three..., One and Two... Three..."; and so they all tried, slowly moving round the room behind the Colonel. Alexandra sat and watched, her hands over the keys, ready to begin playing as soon as the pupils gained confidence. She began, slowly at first and then quicker until she reached the full speed. The Colonel called a halt. Slightly puffed and a little pink in the face the ladies were glad of a pause and Alexandra said:

"That was fine. When you get your breath we'll try again, first with Colonel Myendorff leading, then he can drop out and you continue round the room on your own. Are you ready?"

She started playing again, her graceful body swaying slightly to the rhythm of the music and her hands dancing over the keys. The Colonel stepped aside and the ladies went on. Once or twice the youngest hesitated but a kindly word from the Colonel got her going again and Princess Thora moved steadily along, gradually relaxing and becoming more supple, and responding to the nuances of her cousin's playing.

"Do you think I'll be all right Alix?" Thora said as she sat down on a chair beside the pianist. "It is such a while since I did the mazurka and I had quite forgotten it but it is coming back. How about you Maria?" she said turning to Princess Wassilitchikoff's daughter.

"I have seen my sisters doing it but they are always so impatient and will never teach me. Thank you, Colonel Myendorff. I can go home and show them now how it is done by a really good dancer. Thank you ever so much your Imperial Majesty. I am sure they never imagined that I would have had the Empress to play for me."

"Now Maria, I think you have said quite enough. Don't go and brag to your sisters, you are just a very lucky girl."

Turning to Alexandra, Princess Wassilitchikoff with a deep curtsey said: "Thank you very much, Your Imperial Majesty. We are most grateful and hope that we shall not disappoint you and our teacher when we go to the next Ball".

With that the door was opened for the Wassilitchicoffs and they and Colonel Myendorff left the room.

"Stay a little longer Thora," said Alexandra. "Come, Emily, come and sit by the fire and we'll have a few minutes to talk before the children are brought in. It has been so lovely having you both to stay and this afternoon reminded me of those wonderful carefree days we had at Romrod. Do you remember?"

"Oh! Yes," said Thora,

"We had such fun when we were all in the old castle together and your father was alive and we had all his soldier friends in to meals. And Emily and Fräulein Grancy did so much sketching."

"Oh! Yes Emily; did you ever finish your sketch of the old castle?" said Alexandra.

"Yes I did, in pencil; I never painted it. I pasted it into my album and I have some rather good snapshots of the party that summer. There is one of everybody standing on the wooden balcony and one with them outside the front door. Oh! Yes, and there are one or two of the manoeuvres; some of the cavalry officers and one with me in the carriage. You both rode with officers, do you remember? I have also got a lovely photo with the two of you. Oh! It has been so nice to see you both together again."

"Emily, you must show those to Alix sometime," said Thora; and at that moment the door opened and in came little Olga[96] *in a great hurry saying*

"Mama, Mama. Look at my new doll!"

She was followed by her nanny and a nursemaid who carried baby Tatiana.[97] *As she ran the brightly coloured doll slipped from Olga's hand and a cascade of wooden pieces fell on the carpet.*[98] *Emily, Thora and the nanny rushed to pick them up; collecting the red-cheeked faces and the prettily painted 'barrels' and putting them back one inside the other. The completed matrioshka was given back to the little Grand Duchess.*

"Goodbye Alix and thank you, I'll do my best," said Thora, as Emily whispered to her, "Come Thora I think it is time for us to leave ... Goodbye Ma'am."

As they walked along the corridor, past the staircase to the children's rooms, Thora turned to Emily and said "Do you remember the time we learnt the mazurka step at Balmoral, that autumn when Ernie came?" "Yes," said Emily, "and we had such a successful dance afterwards, and her Majesty laughed so much and made us all dance until we were quite exhausted. It gave her so much pleasure." "Oh! Yes. I remember that, and do you know that she told me then that she had been taught the step years and years before, before she had even got engaged to dearest Grandpapa. And I think her teacher was one of Nicholas's great-uncles!" Emily was much impressed and said "How extraordinary! And here you are learning it again in one of Nicholas's palaces and with dear Alix playing for us. What a delightful afternoon." And so they both returned to their rooms and the next engagements.

The 'Season', held in the weeks before Lent, was the time for Balls and Dances. Perhaps this is why Princess Thora was invited to stay the extra time, perhaps it was because Alexandra found it so refreshing and comforting to have her as a visitor. Who knows? There is little doubt that Thora was enjoying her cousin's company and revelling in the luxury of the Russian Court and thrilled to have the chance to enjoy the fun and splendour of the St Petersburg Season. Or perhaps her Grandmother had not given up hope of finding her a husband – Thora was twenty-seven by this time – and had instructed her other granddaughter the Empress to try. But in a letter to Gretchen written at the time Thora was in St Petersburg, Alix confessed that although Thora was much liked she had been unsuccessful in finding a suitor.

Princess Thora's Season began quietly with the Grand Duchess Vladimir's *thé dansant pour la jeunesse* at her palace. Emily's comment was: 'Very pretty and many pretty girls. I danced several contredances in a bonnet'. A 'contredance' was the equivalent of the quadrille – a dance in sets. Ladies often wore hats in the evening; Nicholas's comments to his mother on the hats worn by the Kaiser's wife, Augusta Victoria, the previous summer were pretty scathing: 'in particular the hats she wore in the evening were frightful'. Perhaps it was correct for Emily to dance in a bonnet. The Grand Duchess Vladimir, Marie Pavlova,[99] originally from the German principality of Mecklenburg, was the third-ranked lady of the Empire, taking precedence immediately after the two Empresses. She was the leader of Society at the time and was, in character, everything that Alexandra was not. She was energetic, poised and devoted to gossip and intrigue. Together with her husband,[100] she turned their house just along the Neva from the Winter Palace into a glittering court. The St Petersburg Season opened with her great Charity Sale, which was held for four days in the Hall of the Nobility. Her husband, Grand Duke Vladimir, was an uncle of Nicholas being the son of a younger brother of Tsar Alexander III.[101] Vladimir was Commander of the Imperial Guard but his real interests lay in the Arts. He was President of the Academy of Fine Arts and Patron of the Ballet School. Later he became the protector of Diaghilev, the great exponent of Russian Ballet in the late 19th and early 20th centuries. These two, the Grand Duke and the Grand Duchess, gave the most splendid receptions in all St Petersburg.

The *thé dansant pour la jeunesse* perhaps bore similarities to the *Bal Blanc* which was given for young ladies in white, with their chaperones of suitable rank, dressed in sombre shades of black, grey and purple, sitting on stiff chairs around the room. There was a master of ceremonies who controlled the dancing – which was mainly quadrilles and cotillions. For the latter, the mazurka step was also required and the figures were very similar to the quadrille. In addition the dancers offered each other gifts of flowers, balloons, rosettes or miniature bells. Great loads of flowers – jonquils and carnations – were imported from the south of France giving a feeling of innocence and springtime to the occasion.

The *thé dansant* was followed the next night by something entirely different. After a very busy day, dashing about and meeting people, Emily wrote:

> half dressed before dinner and finished after. We went down with the other ladies at 9. The Ball a most wonderful sight but a fearful crowd and badly managed in many ways for comfort and crowding. A wonderful sitting down hot supper for everybody. Got upstairs a 2 o'C. Went to supper with Ad. Arenief. I talked to all the Ambassadors and lots of people I knew.

Now the newspaper report:

> A huge, brilliant ball was held yesterday, January 12th (Russian calendar) in the great halls of the Winter Palace. 3,700 were invited. The Ball was opened with a polonaise. His Majesty the Emperor made the first circuit with her Majesty, the Empress Alexandra Feodorovna, and the second with her Royal Highness the Infanta Eulalie of Spain: Her Majesty the Empress with the Ambassador of Turkey: His Majesty took the third turn with the wife of the English Ambassador and her Majesty

> with the Ambassador of France.
>
> Their Majesties and members of the Imperial Family also took part in the dances that followed.
>
> In the interval between the dances the wives of the Ministers of China and Japan and Society Ladies had the honour of being presented to her Majesty the Empress in the concert hall.
>
> A little after midnight their Imperial Majesties and their guests took supper in the Armorial Hall. Her Majesty the Empress took a place at the middle of the table having, on her right hand, the Turkish Ambassador and, on the left, the Ambassador of France. During the supper His Majesty the Emperor moved around among the guests at the supper tables. The Ball lasted until 2 in the morning.

Neither of these accounts gives much idea of the brilliance of the occasion. Emily was more impressed with the 'sitting down hot supper'; and the newspaper account wallows in protocol. But it is interesting to note who were the most honoured guests. The Turkish Ambassador was the doyen of the diplomatic corps; the French had loaned vast sums of money to Russia; delicate negotiations were in hand with China and Japan in regard to Port Arthur, a vital warm-water port which, it was hoped, would become the eastern end of the Siberian railway.

Massie gives a vivid account of a very similar ball given by Nicholas's parents only four years earlier. His mother, the Empress Maria Feodorovna, revelled in Society and sparkled at Imperial Balls. Despite Alexandra's very different character, early in Nicholas's reign the old ways prevailed. This excerpt gives an idea of the brilliance of the 1894 ball.

> Traditionally the finest balls were those given by Their Majesties at the Winter Palace. No Palace in Europe was better suited for formal revelry. The Winter Palace possesses a row of gigantic galleries, each as wide and tall as a cathedral. Great columns of jasper, marble and malachite supported high gilded ceilings, hung with immense crystal and gold chandeliers. Outside, in the intense winter cold of a January night, the whole three blocks of the Winter Palace would be flooded with light. An endless procession of carriages drew up, depositing

passengers who handed their furs or cloaks to attendants and then ascended the wide marble staircases, covered with thick carpets. Along the walls baskets of orchids and palm trees in large pots framed huge mirrors in which dozens of people could examine and admire themselves. At intervals along the corridors troopers of the Chevalier Gardes, in white uniforms with silver breastplates and silver-crested helmets, and Cossack Life Guards in scarlet tunics stood rigidly at attention.

The three thousand guests included court officials in black, gold-laced uniforms, generals whose chests sagged with medals from the Turkish wars, and young Hussar officers in full dress with elkskin breeches so tight it had taken two soldiers to pull them on. At a great court ball, the passion of Russian women for jewels was displayed on every head, neck, ear, wrist, finger and waist

An Imperial ball began precisely at 8.30 in the evening, when the Grand Master of Ceremonies appeared and tapped loudly three times on the floor with an ebony staff, embossed in gold with the double-headed eagle of the tsar. The sound brought an immediate hush. The great mahogany doors inlaid with gold swung open, the Grand Master of Ceremonies cried out, "Their Imperial Majesties," and hundreds of dresses rustled as ladies sank into a deep curtsy. This announcement in 1894 produced the appearance of a tall powerful, bearded man, Tsar Alexander III. Beside him, in a silver brocade gown sewn with diamonds, her famous diamond tiara in her hair, was his dark-eyed Danish wife, Empress Marie. The orchestra broke into a polonaise, then as the evening progressed, a quadrille, a chaconne, a mazurka, a waltz. At midnight in adjacent rooms, a supper was served. While demolishing lobster salad, chicken patties, whipped cream and pastry tarts the merry-makers could look through the double glass of the long windows to see the wind blowing gusts of fine powdered snow along the ice-bound river. Through clusters of tables, the Tsar, six feet four inches tall, ambled like a great Russian bear, stopped here and there to chat, until 1.30, when the Imperial couple withdrew and the guests reluctantly went home.

Such was the ball given during the Season of 1884, Tsar Alexander III's last. He was dead within the year. That in 1898 was very similar and, although Emily's account hardly does it justice and she rarely says that she enjoyed an occasion, she must have enjoyed and certainly been impressed by this one. There was an unusual amount of 'relevé' the next day with others who lived in the Winter Palace. After escorting Tora to a French play that evening, there was a supper with 'loads of people, princes and princesses and an unknown old man. Card playing and talk went on until supper at 12 o'C, I had brown bread and milk' and 'came away at 12.30.' There was plenty of opportunity to talk over the events of the previous evening without leaving the shelter and comparative warmth of the palace on a freezing night for the French play had been performed in the Hermitage Theatre at the eastern end of the great building. On the following nights there were more plays and 'a very pretty ball at the Grand Duchess Vladimir's'; another ball in the Winter Palace which was 'most successful ... table covered in red flowers and every conceivable delicacy.' Emily stayed till past 1 o'clock.'

There was a second and slightly smaller Imperial Ball on February 1st. Emily has pasted a newspaper cutting, the musical programme and the supper menu into her album. The menu was entirely in French and many of the dishes originated from that country – yet again, examples of how pervasive French influence was in St Petersburg. This had been the case for two centuries. In the early years of the 19th century, the aristocracy took pride in speaking French to such an extent that many of them could barely speak Russian. And, despite the efforts of previous Tsars to emphasise the Slav roots of Russian life, Peter the Great's vision for Russia to become European in outlook was deeply rooted in the upper echelons of society. French and English were the languages of this court which made Emily feel very much at ease and able to get on with the members of the Household and others she met in Russia.

The cutting from the French newspaper tells us that their Majesties took part in the dances, the Ball beginning with a waltz played by the court orchestra. Supper took place between midnight and 1 o'clock, in halls transformed into magnificent winter gardens. Emily was frequently much impressed by the way parts of the Palace were made into wonderful gardens and palm courts which banished the bleak winter weather. During the supper interval, Nicholas, as was customary, walked among the guests and spoke to many but Alexandra was left sitting between the ambassadors of Turkey –

again – and Austro-Hungary. It must surely have been an ordeal for a shy, twenty-four-year-old Empress: but, diplomatically, protocol must be followed and good relations were critical. Turkey held the gateway for most of Russia's grain exports through the Dardanelles and the Straits of Constantinople, and Russia had just signed an 'entente' with Austro-Hungary on the subject of the Balkans, as ever an explosive and unpredictable area, in the hope that for the time being this perennial question might be 'put on ice'.

Both Alexandra's mother-in-law and her sister Ella sparkled on these great occasions and spectacular balls. It was said that, at those given by Ella and her husband Grand Duke Serge,[102] Ella retired half way through and reappeared in a yet more beautiful gown and yet more dazzling jewels. But, for Alexandra, they were a duty that had to undertaken and became increasingly irksome as her health deteriorated. The imperial balls continued for a few more years after Emily's visit but, when the longed-for heir was eventually born and found to be so vulnerable and frail, the Emperor and Empress withdrew, only coming to St Petersburg for essential ceremonies linked to tradition and religion. The last great imperial ball – according to Prince Michael of Greece the last great festivity of Imperial Russia – was given in January 1903. It was a magnificent spectacle. The guests were commanded to come dressed in costumes of the 17th century. Nicholas came dressed as one of his ancestors, his favourite Tsar Alexis Michailovich, and Alexandra came as his wife, Nathaly Navishkim. The photographs in Prince Michael's book show the Tsar in a long brocaded and embroidered coat over a high-necked tunic of similar opulence and, on his head, an embroidered, high-crowned hat with a deep black rim. The Empress was resplendent in an even more gorgeously brocaded kaftan, ornamented with huge cabochons from the imperial treasury. On her head she wore a copy of a crown of the period, encrusted with many precious stones, and her necklace, made in a great hurry by the jeweller Fabergé, contained one of the largest sapphires in the world. There was one further great ball in 1913 to celebrate 300 years of the Romanov dynasty, but the spontaneity and sparkle had begun to fade.

The dances and balls that Emily attended were all during the 'Season' when the court moved to the capital, but her visits to theatres took place throughout her Russian visit: she went to the theatre over twenty times. Theatre-going was often rather more a social occasion than because of deep interest in the play: when they were still at Tsarskoe, she often had to leave early in order to catch the train. Probably her happiest visits were when she went with one of the ladies-in-waiting. The majority of the plays were in French, for instance *La Jalouse* which was 'excellent and funny'; but she managed seven in Russian. Princess Obolensky helped her to understand the first; she enjoyed this one, but her comments were not always favourable. On December 16th, for instance, she saw one which was a 'benefit' and attended by Grand Duke Serge, Grand Duchess Elizabeth (Ella) and Grand Duke Vladimir who were probably patrons. This performance was dismissed as: 'A very long 5 Act and stupid piece ... which lasted till nearly 1 o'C.' Evidently this time she had to remain until the end! A much more satisfying performance was seen just before she left, when her great friend Katousch, the von Hesses and Emily went to 'a real Russian play, very good and exciting'.

Most of the theatres she went to probably necessitated a carriage drive wrapped up in warm furs; the performance she attended on December 17th of *Le mari de la debutante* had to be left early as the snow was becoming too deep for the carriage horses to negotiate. On only one occasion were they able to walk to the theatre, when Prince Gargarine and Emily had been dinner guests at the Hendrikoffs, and the theatre was just next door. 'Our Royalties were there'; so they went round on foot. Once they were established in the Winter Palace, they could make an indoor – but none the less quite long – walk to the Hermitage Theatre: they didn't have to leave the shelter of the great building. Emily wrote in her diary for January 28th:

> Dined at 7 o'C. Dressed after. First of the series of Ermitage plays took place. All assembled in the theatre by 9.30 and the Royalties all came in at the last. A French play by Scribe, '*Le Diplomate*' and a short bit of ballet. Tea in between the two and supper after to which I went with Mr Hartong. All over at 1.30.

This beautiful little theatre with its classical auditorium within curved walls enclosing the semicircular seating of red velvet made a wonderful place for intimate productions. Elaborate golden cyphers of the Emperor's initials embellished the stage curtains and there was an air of luxury and comfort which added richness to these occasions.

Emily frequently went to plays when she was in London but the wealth of opera which she experienced in Russia was a revelation. Tchaikovsky had died only four years before, in 1893. Many of his works were being performed that Season in St Petersburg. She went to *Eugene Onegin*[103] no less than three times but made no comments (the first time she had great difficulty with the spelling). She also saw his work *Pique Dame* or the Queen of Spades which had its first production in 1890 and was based on a poetic novel of Pushkin. *Iolanthe*[104] was much enjoyed but the *Demon* by Anton Rubinstein[105] was 'very dull'. Mozart's *Don Juan*, the alternative name for *Don Giovanni or the Rake punished*, was performed as a benefit for the National Schools. It was done in Russian and 'the box was full of ladies who are patronesses'. Many, if not most, of the theatres and actors and actresses had their patrons at this time and Emily went to several 'benefits', one of which was 'for an actress on her 25th anniversary for which all the Royalties were present'.

The ballet performances she saw did not please her much; in one she 'nearly slept' and at another, a benefit for a male dancer, there were just 'different scraps of ballet'. *Cedrilla*, however, 'had very good dancers and for the 'new ballet *Raymonde* ... the box was full of people, many people in waiting ... It was very pretty'. Theatre visits were mainly social occasions: to see the new productions and to be seen.

Music was always her first love and Emily gives much more detail about the two concerts she went to. In early February, she went with Katousch to a concert given by the acclaimed Spanish violinist, Sarasate.[106] The new lady-in-waiting to the Empress, Princess Orbeliani, went with her. Emily noted the programme: 'They played Schubert's *Der Tod und das Mädchen*, [the] quartet D Moll, posthumous, then the *Kreutzer* and then a good many Spanish dances which were far and away the best'. She heard one symphony concert at the Conservatoire when she went with some of her Embassy friends, the Goschens and Mr Desgras.

> A Herr Richter played a viola with the orchestra by Berlioz. Then there was a Smetana orchestral thing and then a Rubinstein piano and viola and I came away and caught the 10 o'C train.

Rubinstein was a Russian composer who had recently died, and perhaps the Berlioz was *Harold in Italy*, because Berlioz wrote very little for solo instruments and orchestra. She also went to the last of three Concert Balls. 'Went to supper with Mr Hohler'. So it sounds as if, this time, the music was secondary and that it was again, mainly a social occasion – and with Emily it always sounds as if the meal and the name of her supper companion were more important. But this was probably so that she could remember to thank them the next day – an important part of social etiquette.

CHAPTER SIXTEEN

Important Days and the End of the Visit

Most visitors to St Petersburg complained of the weather especially in the winter. It was dark, damp and cold. Wherever she was, Emily recorded the weather for each day and her observations in Russia make interesting reading, bearing out the impression given by other travellers. Throughout the winter the number of frosts increased each month from ten in November to twenty-three in February. The days when it was snowing varied from twelve in November to eight in February. But in November snow was followed by a thaw; in February there were only two days with thaw and thirteen with a bitter wind and Emily frequently complained that she was very cold, even on the infrequent days when the sun shone. In general it was the sudden changes that were so unpleasant and, before the roads were macadamised, they became a morass of mud. Thora writing to her Grandmother said that the greatest drawbacks were darkness descending at three in the afternoon and the sudden changes from intense cold – 36° of frost and a high wind – to thaw. Sometimes the streets were just sheets of ice and the horses fell – which 'made me quite sick'.

When Emily was first in the city, she moved about in carriages and the normal conveyance for ordinary people was a small, four-wheeled horse-drawn vehicle. In her album there are photos of some of these with their curious high wooden yokes. Princess Thora gave a good description of the well-wrapped-up drivers in a letter to her Grandmother. Once the snow was deep enough, carriages could be replaced by sledges: both might be used depending on the state of the roads. Once, Emily came back early from a shopping expedition in early February, 'as it was too cold to keep the carriage out longer'. But on February 19th: 'I drove with Pss Tora in the sledge between 12 and 1 o'C. Went the other side of the river – over the bridge – almost into the parks on the island and back over the Neva itself on the ice'.

Sledges became the vehicles for moving people and goods as soon as the snow was consolidated; often a much more comfortable ride than on the rough roads and muddy tracks.

So the weather was always mentioned at the beginning of each diary entry but was soon forgotten in the excitements of the day. Some of the occasions were great public events but others, equally part of the Imperial calendar, were the celebrations of the Name Day of an individual – more personal, but in the case of the Imperial family celebrated with great pomp. This – the anniversary of the Saint on which a person was baptised – was very important in the Orthodox religion, more so than the day of birth. November 26th, or November 14th (Old Style), was the Name Day of the Empress Mother and it was also the third anniversary of Nicholas and Alexandra's wedding – a very important day indeed which according to Emily was celebrated with a 'big service and ceremony' in the Catherine Palace in Tsarskoe Selo. It was followed by a 'big luncheon. Lots of ladies from Petersburg came.'

A month later, on December 17th, they went by train in the evening to St Petersburg, to be ready for the next day. The diary records for December 18th (6th Old Style)

> We all went down at 9.30 and assembled for the Te Deum[107] and Mass for the Emperor's name day. The Empress Mother and all the family there. Went to the big manège at 12 o'C for an enormous parade. A very large luncheon after and a very long 'cercle' after that and everyone nearly died of fatigue. It was all over by 3.30. We had stood for more than 5 hours. Changed dresses and came back to Tsarskoe and got here at 5 o'C. Had tea with Marie B. Pss Tora came in. The Empress Mother arrived and brought a weeping lady with her who wished to dine with M. B., so I dined alone.

Emily realised the significance of the presence of the Empress Mother at the Te Deum and Mass for Nicholas's cousin, Grand Duke Konstatin Konstantinovich, (KR)[108] it was a matter of the greatest importance. He wrote

> After the parade there was a large luncheon in the Nicholas Hall. The Empress Marie appeared here for the first time since the death of the Emperor; the two Empresses sat side by side.

It was over three years since the death of Alexander III; and yet, even after the period of court mourning, this vivacious and popular Empress had not been seen in public with her daughter-in-law. Their close relationship began under the most inauspicious circumstances, and these exacerbated the almost universal problems of mothers and daughters-in-law. At first, Alexandra felt great sympathy for the bereaved Marie, and Nicholas tried to comfort his mother by dutifully dining with her and sitting with her in the evenings. He also was dependent on her, having had so little preparation for his new role, and he turned to her frequently for help, particularly for political advice – which Marie was happy to give. She little realised how much Alexandra resented this. To Empress Marie, Alexandra was still the awkward young German girl and Nicholas her darling 'school boy' son. She, Marie, had spent over ten years as the wife of the Tsarevitch, before she became Empress; plenty of time to learn the ways of the Russian court. Alexandra had been plunged straight in. And, for the first months of their married life, Nicholas and Alexandra had to share the Anichkov Palace[109] with his mother while a suitable place was made ready for them. So, not only did Alexandra have to accept that her mother-in-law took precedence over her on all public ceremonies, as protocol decreed; but, in the early days, she had to live in the other's palace and compete for her husband's attention. Not only this: Marie was very reluctant to give up certain crown jewels that traditionally belonged to the reigning empress. Public scandal was only just avoided by Nicholas's repeated remonstrances. At last Marie handed them over; but by then Alexandra hardly wanted to wear them. Tension between the two women ran high.

The change in her life, the very sudden transition from a young unmarried girl to wife of a reigning monarch, was difficult for Alexandra and her moods would swing from loneliness and despair to intense joy and thankfulness. There was some improvement in the spring of 1895 when she and Nicholas moved to Peterhof[110]– on the Baltic some way west of St Petersburg – and Marie left Russia for a long summer visit to her Danish relations. When Alexandra found that she was pregnant, there was great rejoicing. Her sister, Ella, came to stay with her and the two young women were able to enjoy each other's company, following familiar and gentle pursuits while at the same time Alexandra could devote herself to planning her first real home in the Alexander Palace[111] at Tsarskoe Selo. Her mother-in-law returned full of good will and longing to see her grandchild. Even the birth of a daughter, Olga, rather than the hoped for heir didn't dampen the spirits of the family.

Two years later, suffering from illness during her next pregnancy, Alexandra may again have been longing for a young woman's company, as Nicholas was always so busy with his responsibilities. In the spring her sister Irène, Princess Henry of Prussia, came; and then late in the year an invitation was sent to her favourite cousin Thora. So it had come about that in the autumn of 1897 Thora and Emily had left England to spend these four fascinating months as the guests of the Emperor and Empress. There is no doubt that Thora's presence made Alexandra happier and more self-assured, and the Season of 1897–98 was considered to be brilliant. Thora, for her part, had enjoyed herself immensely. Quite early on in her visit she told the Queen

> I cannot tell you how much I am enjoying my stay here & now that I have got to know every body of course it is much nicer as it is rather shy work to come into the middle of a large family & a strange court where one knows nobody, but they are all so kind & easy to get on with. They are so civil to me I feel quite overcome. I always sit next to Nicky at the big dinners & am made to go before most of the Grandduchesses which fills me with shyness.

While in Russia, Thora spent most of her time with Alexandra and her children and, as mentioned earlier, Alexandra made sure that Emily had companions during her visit. In addition to Princess Bariatinsky and Mlle Wassilichikoff who were with her off and on throughout the four months, Princess Lili Obolensky became a more constant companion when they were in the Winter Palace. Emily was also frequently accompanied, especially on shopping expeditions, by Mlle Schneider. She took Emily to the bazaar where a wealth of exotic goods could be found and twice they visited the 'Seliniogradoh' [sic] – which sounds as if it were a department store. On their first visit they couldn't do any shopping as all the rooms were being changed. The second time Emily was still unable to get all she wanted – 'only the embroideries'. The first mention of Mlle Schneider in Russia was when she was having 'trouble with a sock' and Emily gave her advice on knitting. She gave Emily and Princess Thora a few Russian lessons, but it doesn't sound as though these were continued. She had been in England in the summer of 1894 to teach Alix Russian, during the time when Queen Victoria had made herself responsible for all 'Alicky's arrangements until she was taken to Russia'; and she had accompanied Alix on her visit to Harrogate.

In later years when Nicholas had abdicated Mlle Schneider remained very loyal to Nicholas and Alexandra. She continued as a tutor along with Pierre Gilliard in the 'band of captives' who remained with the family at the Alexander Palace, Tsarskoe Selo in 1917, and later in Tobolsk. When they were finally moved to Ekaterinburg, Nicholas and Alexandra chose among others: Countess Hendrikoff, whom Emily also met on several occasions in 1897–8; Mlle Schneider;[112] Pierre Gilliard, whose book became one of Emily's most precious possessions; and Dr Botkin whom Emily met when the Russian royal family came to Friedberg in 1910. When the group reached Ekaterinburg, Mlle Schneider was separated from Nicholas, Alexandra and the children, and was imprisoned but later released. Unlike some of her fellow prisoners, who were also released and later rescued by the White Army, she was executed in September 1918 by the Bolsheviks in Siberia, as was Countess Hendrikoff.

Soon after the Christmas and New Year celebrations the court moved from Tsarskoe Selo to St Petersburg to be in the capital for the 'Season'. As the last days in the country approached there was much leave-taking of the residents and of those who were not going to St Petersburg; much packing of clothes and belongings and, more vexing, much discussion about whom to tip and how much. This was a subject that always exercised Emily considerably whenever leaving a place whether with her 'Royalty' or not. On this occasion Marie Bariatinsky gave her guidance. They moved to St Petersburg on January 12th 1898.

> Lots of people to say goodbye at the station. Came straight to my rooms. Jeanne was very badly and everybody much upset as there was no housemaid or anyone to do anything. I made my own bed. Had a very bad headache. I sat with Pss Tora while she dressed to go with the Majesties to the Empress Mother for New Year's Eve. All the ladies went to their homes and relations. I had dinner alone. L. Obolensky came to sit with me having done her church before going to her parents till midnight.

Not the happiest of starts in the new place but soon they got into the swing of more grand occasions and processions through the state rooms of the Winter Palace.

Towards the end of January 1898, on the day when the court had been giving an official luncheon in honour of the German Emperor's birthday, Emily met 'the new little Pss Orbeliani who made her first public appearance in waiting'. This young lady was an orphan from the Caucasus and Emily's remarks make one feel that she thought the princess needed mothering. A few days later they were together again.

> Left cards and notes at many places. Got back soon after 5 o'C and had milk and bread with Pss Orbeliani who came to my room. Marie Bariatinski [sic] came to say goodbye to me as she left altogether after 6 o'C. Pss Orbeliani had dinner with me and we went to the Opera, 'Don Juan' in Russian for the benefit of the national schools. The box was full of ladies who were patronesses.

The princess appears a few more times in the diary having meals or going to the theatre with Emily. Perhaps Emily's comments give the wrong impression; for in these early years at court Sonia Orbeliani was 'high-spirited, an excellent horse woman and a fine musician'. Alexandra became very fond of her, enjoying her cheerfulness and intellect: she took her to her heart. This was made abundantly clear when Sonia fell desperately ill while accompanying the Russian royal family to Darmstadt in the autumn of 1903. They were there for the wedding of Alexandra's niece Alice, the daughter of her sister Victoria and Louis of Battenberg, to Prince Andrew of Greece. Despite the wedding festivities and the needs of her own family – and the disapproval of her German relations and the Imperial suite – Alexandra nursed Sonia like her own child.

Sonia was suffering from an incurable spinal disease and gradually wasted away over the next decade. Alexandra did all she could to alleviate her pain and earthly ills and to prepare her for the life to come. The invalid lived in rooms close to those of the Grand Duchesses and Alexandra visited her every day when she went to the children's rooms. Sonia died during the war in the hospital at Tsarskoe Selo where Alexandra was nursing wounded soldiers and the Empress missed her sorely.

Emily's last two weeks in St Petersburg were a whirlwind of activity, seeing as much as she could of people and places before their departure date finally came. The snow had become sufficiently deep for sledge rides to be taken, although unpleasant if it was actually snowing, to see new parts of the city. She attended more concerts – on the 14th 'a delightful' one with a Beethoven quartet, a Schumann quintet and Schubert opus 163. She went to the theatre to see *Le Barber de Seville* in four acts by Beaumarchais with Lili Obolensky, and with the von Hesses and Katousch to see a 'real Russian play. Very good and exciting', and a third and final visit to *Eugene Onegin*. She saw previously unvisited parts of the Winter Palace with Mr Hartong, being particularly impressed with the beautiful 'Winter Garden or Palm House' where the grim Russian winter was banished in a wealth of tropical greenery. She enjoyed 'teas' with the Princess Galitzine, maitresse of the court. On the 24th, she 'went out at 2.30 and paid endless card-leaving calls and writing down and ended up by going to see Countess Hendrikoff'. She collected money from Mr Clarke at the bank, went on the ice-hills with Mr Desgras, visited the 'Palais Michel to see the Russian pictures' and even had time to go with Princess Thora to two dances, including a dinner and dance at 'Pss Helene of Altenburg'. Squeezed into this social whirl were last-minute shopping expeditions. One day she went 'after luncheon and got basket things, things for the maids and red stuff' and on another she bought 'wedding presents for A Ponsonby and Bessie Mead. Also some silver things'. In between, there were quiet moments with Princess Thora, when they sat quietly and 'wound silk for penwipers'.

Perhaps the busiest day was February 16th when she lunched with people from the Embassy, 'came back for a tub' and then set off with Katousch

> to the Institute at 'Smolsky' [sic] for 400 girls under Pss Lieven. Went all over it into the different classrooms: heard lessons and lectures. Assisted at the dinner at 6 and ate 'Kacha'. Heard three girls play harp, piano and sing.

A breathless visit.

The Princess Lieven whom Emily met at the Smolnyi Institute was Princess Elena Alexandrovna Lieven (1842 – 1915) who came of a family that was well known to the English Royal Family. A previous Princess Lieven who had been present at (Queen) Victoria's baptism in 1819 was the wife of the then Russian Ambassador and, when the 18-year-old Victoria ascended the throne, it was Princess Lieven who remarked on her 'aplomb and air of command'. In 1898, Emily saw 'lessons and lectures' in Princess Elena Lieven's Institute for the education of the daughters of the nobility. Perhaps one of these was a dancing class similar to the one in a magnificent book *Photographs for the Tsar* produced in the early years of the twentieth century. Here, in a large room lit by innumerable candles and huge candelabra, under the watchful portraits of the founder Catherine II and other benefactors, stand eight lines of girls in four long sets. Their hair is in buns, they are wearing long, white dresses with aprons and holding hands in pairs, and are being instructed by a stout lady in a severe dark long-skirted suit. The pupils are caught poised in stillness waiting for the music to begin.

She was back at the Winter Palace by 6.20, just had time to call in and see Princess Thora before dressing – putting on her best dress – and driving with Katousch to the

> Chérémétieff dinner at their beautiful Palace. The Emperor's mother, Emperor and Empress and many Grand Dukes and the huge Chérémétieff family ... A choir sang all through dinner and after dinner there was the Ballalachia [sic] band and an interlude for singers in the middle. Left at 11.15.

As Emily was there, Princess Thora was certainly among the guests; and how pleased she would have been that at last Alexandra was dining out with other families. It really seemed as if Thora's urging backed up with advice from Alix's sisters was at last encouraging the young Empress to go out into Society. Perhaps this would stem some of the ill-natured gossip; but unfortunately the good intentions came to little. Alexandra fell ill.

The very next day, the 'Empress was in bed with a bad cold'. Worse was to follow. The following day, February 18th, Emily had a 'very disrupted day as the Empress ill and Pss Tora not allowed to see her. I was with Pss Tora most of the day'. Later on 'Much fuss about the Empress ... Had my dinner in interrupted scraps. Dr Hirsch finally pronounced measles'. No reports on the Empress for the next two days but Thora herself was 'badly with cold and very low in her mind' and at 5 o'clock she was still 'very badly and sorry for herself but got better gradually.' Was Thora also going down with measles? Had she also caught the disease from Ella who had been visiting? Or was she feeling miserable because this wonderful trip into fairy land was coming to an end? Ella had certainly recovered very quickly and been allowed to visit. Not so poor Alexandra. Emily's report for the 21st was 'Empress had a bad day with high fever and strong rash at last. Temperature diminished towards evening'.

The programme to entertain Princess Thora had to be altered as she was no longer able to be with Alexandra for most of the last week of their visit. Nicholas's relatives, the Leuchtenbergs, were called in to help and for several days Emily took her to 'the Duchess of Leuchtenbergs' who lived in a 'distinguished old mansion' on the English Embankment, a little to the west of the Winter Palace. The Duchess of Leuchtenberg at this time was the second wife of Prince Eugene Maximilianovich Romanovsky, 5th Duke of Leuchtenberg. They had had to sell his old family home, the Mariinsky Palace near St Isaac's church in the early years of their marriage. She was an amazingly attractive lady even being described as a 'femme fatale'. Tsar Alexander III had granted her the title by special decree. He was the second Emperor to honour her with a respected title, for Alexander II had made her Comtesse de Beauharnais in the year when she and Prince Eugene were married. She was not perhaps the sort of lady that Princess Thora was used to associating with but probably a most entertaining companion.

Emily had a farewell audience with the 'Empress Mother' – who was 'very gracious' – nearly a week before leaving St Petersburg but she left going to say farewell to Alexandra until the very last moment. The tips had been given, again after much consultation, the packing had been completed and Princess Thora escorted to say goodbye to 'the old Grand Duchess Constantine'.[113] Emily got back to her room just before 1 o'clock on February 26th and then she 'went in to see the Empress, wrapped myself in a large white sheet, as I could not change my dress before luncheon. She was much beloved. She was weak and had a nasty cough but better altogether'.

This was probably the most intimate moment that Emily had with Alexandra in the whole visit. The Empress was in need of sympathy and comfort from her old friend; perhaps their feelings were nearer to those of the Darmstadt and Wolfsgarten days when Alix was the motherless child. Emily would have been so worried about Alexandra for measles was a very serious illness and Alexandra so easily succumbed to illness. She could and did make heroic efforts when someone else was ill; but, if exhausted, pain and illness overcame her and she readily became an invalid – perhaps as a refuge from some of the difficult situations that she found herself in. Nevertheless, her illnesses were real: but they could all too easily be the excuse to retreat into her private world. Within cosy family gatherings or with old friends from her early days the serious shy and aloof Alix could become the warm loving person of her childhood.

It was sad that Emily's last visit was under these circumstances; for, by her invitation, Alexandra had given Emily a wonderful time, showered her with kindness and gifts and deepened their love and understanding. In her darkened bedroom Alix would have been surrounded by her precious icons – the essential sacred images, the 'gateways to God' – and no doubt she would have spoken to Emily of her faith and how much it meant to her. Emily would have been a sympathetic listener, for she had seen how much conversion to Roman Catholicism had meant to her sister Alice and how its precepts guided her life. To Alexandra, the Orthodox faith and its teachings which she studied extensively were inextricably bound up with her love for Nicholas and his unique position as Tsar of all the Russias, chosen by God to be His representative on earth. Her *raison d'être* was to bear his successor. This may all have been strange to Emily but it would have deepened her understanding of this shy, misunderstood young woman.

Back from the Empress's rooms, Emily joined Thora and Nicholas for luncheon and the afternoon was a 'fearful bustle' of farewells. A quick visit to the Vladimirs and 'streams of people to see Pss Tora, and all came to see me first' Lily Obolensky went to the station with Emily where they found:

> All the gentlemen in full uniform and Embassy too. The Emperor brought Pss Tora to the station and saw us off. Mr Desgras was with us. Soon settled in. Had food in the restaurant wagon at 7. All sat in my compartment after. Parted at 9.45. I did accounts and wrote diary before settling in.

They travelled all through the night, and walked in the sun at the last Russian station – at about midday. The snow ceased when they left Russia and they continued through Germany reaching Berlin about 10.30 at night. They had retired to bed as they were so tired; and so Sir Frank Lascelles who had come from the Embassy was unable to see them. Emily found that having Mr Desgras with them made the journey much easier; he ordered the meals and generally smoothed the path. She mentions the time change – 'gained or rather lost two hours. Got to Ostende at 1.30 English time. Were half an hour late. Had an excellent passage. Sat on the deck in the sun.' They were in London by 8 p.m. Princess Christian, Else and Major Martin were on the station to meet them. 'Pss Tora hastily presented Mr Desgras and we parted. We drove quickly to Paddington and came down by the 8.20. I went with them to C. Lodge and then they sent me home. Very sad and empty without Alice who had gone off in the morning to join Pss Louie at Southampton to go to Geneva'.

What an anticlimax! No one except the maids to tell of all her journeys and excitements, all the friends she had made, all the great ceremonial occasions she had taken part in. But next morning she found the crocuses and snowdrops were out in the garden and the birds were singing. Her Russian friends were very much on her mind and on this lovely mild day after going round the garden she sat down and 'wrote frantically all morning to all the Russian people to go by the messenger'. In the evening Gerry arrived. So there was: 'Wonderful and joyful relevage all evening and quite late'.

CHAPTER SEVENTEEN

From One Century to the Next

How glad Emily was to share her reminiscences with Gerry; a grand revelage. Here was another person who would in the future pick up her inferences and enjoy her spontaneous recollections; someone who could be part of this new Emily. The feel of Russia, the smells of the streets and palaces, the sound of the language, the winter light on the river would fade all too quickly, only to be awakened by chance remarks and brief glimpses. None of this tinge of sadness would have shown when she had a long conversation with the Queen, who was 'most beloved', a few days after she returned. She was able to tell the Queen of her time and its excitements; of how her granddaughter and family were getting on, what the new baby Tatiana was like and whether Olga was less fat. There would have been special anxiety about Alix's measles. Uppermost in the Queen's mind would be this concern for Alix's health but soon she would be asking whether there were signs that Nicholas and Alix were at last playing their leading part in the social life of the Court. Fortunately, for the time being this could be pushed aside with the excuse of Alix's illness. Neither the Queen nor Emily was to know that Alix would suffer complications and that the illness would drag on for so long. Nicholas, writing to his brother Georgy at the end of March, over a month after Emily had seen Alix on her sick bed, was bemoaning the fact that 'the effects of Alix's rotten measles, [meant that] yesterday [March 28th] was the first time, [that] she went out for a walk in the garden'. By then the Season in St Petersburg was over, Lent was upon them and another opportunity to appear more in Court Society lost; all Thora's cousinly advice had come to nothing.

Thora would have told her mother, who was at Cumberland Lodge when they returned, about their fascinating experiences. Emily and Thora saw much of each other in the early days of March. until Thora too succumbed to measles, probably a legacy from her cousin. Before this, later in the day on which Emily had been summoned to the Queen, the princesses and Else had a real session with Emily at Cumberland Lodge looking at photographs and mementos. The next day a Mr Birkbeck was at a friend's house in Windsor and he and Emily 'had a good deal of Russian revelage'. But gradually Russia became part of the past and the life of Windsor, Cumberland Lodge, the Cottage and London took over. Beacons from Russia flared now and then; collecting an Easter egg which Alix sent her via Cumberland Lodge; going to Goodes the china shop in London to get a saucer for Frau Schneider; pasting cuttings and photographs into her album and, much later, writing to Signora Noto who had encouraged her Italian during that Russian winter. She doesn't usually, at any time in all her letter-writing, mention to whom she wrote, but does note on several occasions that she wrote to the Empress.[114] And then there were the Christmas and Easter cards signed by Alix and her increasing family, which continued to come over the years. Now, we can see them carefully preserved in the back of Pierre Gilliard's book (Plate 6-16): the links with Alix might have been tenuous but they were unbroken.

Gerry's presence at the Cottage ensured that Emily was soon swept back into the musical world of London. Within a month of her return they went to six concerts, including the last Pop concert of the season, after which she and Gerry joined the Joachim quartet at a friend's for a supper party that went on until '1-oC and was most cheerful'. A few days later, the Joachim family came down to Windsor and stayed the night at the Cottage. They arrived at 6.15:

> Some Bachs [sic] were played before dinner. Joachim, Shem and Gerry all reading. Dinner was not over until 10. Then cards until 11 o'C and Bach again till nearly 12.

The next day,

> Ellie [a maid] gave Uncle Jo his breakfast. We had ours when we got back [from church]. There was lovely playing most of the morning. Spohr's violin duets. After a big luncheon, siestas were taken and then we went for a little walk to the Obelisk pond… and they all left at 5.15.

This was in all in the house full of the young Liddell children and rather different from the visit of some years previously.

There were two private concerts, one in the house of the Henry Joachims at which Eugenie Schumann, one of the Mendelssohn family, and Gerry's sister-in-law Shem, as well as the artist Alma Tadema, were present. Emily no doubt told Tadema that the Emperor had bought one of his paintings at the exhibition in St Petersburg in January. That evening after supper Shem played first with 'Uncle Jo' and then as part of a trio with Joachim and Leonard Borwick who later became a well-known concert pianist. Emily revelled in this type of intimate music with fine musicians. But there were also huge concerts, such as the one next day at the Crystal Palace, when she 'got good seats in the gallery' with Susan Baring. Susan had been one of Queen Victoria's ladies-in-waiting who became the wife of Sir James Reid, the Queen's physician – somewhat to the consternation and discomfort of the monarch. Susan and Emily were good friends and they frequently saw each other – including bicycling together in Windsor Great Park. After the marriage Emily frequently visited the Reids and watched their young family growing up in London.

Joachim and his quartet were back the following year and gave a series of Pop concerts in February, much as they had done for the past thirty-seven years but on June 1st 1899, there was a very special performance at the

> 'Philharmonic'. Joachim played the 'Beet.' concerto. He was presented with [a] gold laurel wreath. Gerry and I went round to the artists' room after.

And so the musical life went on – with many concerts in London and the annual seasonal performances of the Christmas Oratorio and Messiah in Windsor, in which Emily and Gerry usually sang. In the early autumn of 1900 Emily went to the Birmingham Festival of Music and among other pieces heard the

> *Dream of Gerontius* and *The Song of Hiawatha* in three parts by Coleridge Taylor. [Samuel Coleridge-Taylor 1875-1912. Violinist and composer, son of an English girl and a West African doctor practising in London]. The composer came forward after and was a black boy'.

Undoubtedly the most accomplished musician among Emily's friends was Shem who was married to Fred, Gerry's brother, and was by 1901 the mother of three boys. The diary entry for July 13th 1901 tells of Emily's return, with a 'racking headache', to London, after clearing up the house in Broad Green,

Liverpool, of her aunt Mary, who had died in March that year. In the evening, she went round to the Liddell's flat and saw all the family. She ends the day saying

> I staid on to dinner and came away a little past 10-oC very tired but better, Shem was feeling the heat a great deal – but cheerful and a great dear.

Then – pencilled in below – 'This was the last time I saw Shem'. Three days later, telegrams announced a crisis and, despite the efforts of three doctors and two nurses trying to bring on the birth, the baby was still-born and Shem died a few hours later, early on the morning of the 17th. Emily was soon round at the flat and 'found Fred quite wonderful – Gerry of course with him.' As the day went on, more and more relations arrived. Emily as usual was 'writing'; a 'cross for Shem was bought at Harrods' and the older boys, Cecil and David were brought from school. The next day Emily was in the thick of arrangements for the funeral and the boys and their clothes. She was at the flat when

> The men came very soon and took dear little Shem down the stairs. Agnes [Shem's sister] and I followed and they put the shell in the outer coffin and little Guy's [the youngest boy] flowers inside.

The burial was on the following day at Brookwood and they all went down by train to the Necropolis station. 'It was a beautiful service so simple and just what Shem would have liked. The heat was awful but the place looked beautiful'. This is one of the rare occasions when Emily lets down her reserve. Shem had a very special place in her affections and she loved the Liddell family. But not quite all of them! After the funeral Emily and two friends returned to Windsor and, in the evening, went to see Nell Liddell who lived down near the Thames. They found her playing croquet 'and we thought in all ways she was a "loser" and she never even asked after Fred'. A very uncharacteristic outburst from Emily. Shem's death would have reminded her of her sister Mamy's death, fifteen years before: giving birth in those days was a hazardous undertaking.

As so often happened, the Cottage became a refuge for the bereaved, and

Alice and Emily rearranged the house so that Fred and the boys could have a home. The flat in London was given up; Fred learnt carpentry and Emily knitted many pairs of socks for young legs. For the next few years her life and that of the family were closely intertwined, even when Fred found houses to rent in Windsor and Eton. All seemed to thrive, and one of the great benefits were the lovely long holidays which Gerry, Emily and the Liddell family spent with Nina and Charlie Balfour at Newton Don near Kelso in the Borders. There they enjoyed croquet, bicycling, fishing, shooting and great picnics to Smailholm Tower and down by the Tweed at Chesters. It was at Newton Don that Emily 'tried Nina's free-wheel bicycle and had a fall getting off' but next day it was better after lowering the seat. By May the next year she had a 'free-wheeler' of her own.

During all these times Emily was never far from the Christian family and had periods in-waiting with the Princess. She also saw the young princesses frequently at Cumberland Lodge or over at the Cottage. They had all become intimate friends and spent many hours talking and sharing experiences. Throughout the nineties, Marie Louise spent long periods at Cumberland Lodge or with her Hesse cousins or travelling abroad, as on the occasion when Emily returned from Russia and Alice Loch was away with Marie Louise in Genoa. Emily recorded that they had many long talks together whenever they met. Whether the princess's increasingly unsatisfactory marriage was discussed is never vouchsafed, but Emily must have had more than an inkling that all was not well. Sometimes the princess was looking very unwell; sometimes her nerves were much on edge and explosions were not far away. In her autobiography, Marie Louise admits that there were faults on both sides, and that she and Aribert might inhabit the same building but hardly saw each other except to put a 'public face' to the marriage. When the Boer War broke out in the autumn of 1899, Germany sided with the Boers and tensions and hostility to Marie Louise living in Berlin increased, especially as her brother Prince Christle was serving with the British force in Natal. The antagonism distressed her, and a 'series of bad colds', had a serious effect on her health. Her family doctor ordered a change of scene. A journey to America and Canada was suggested. Aribert was in favour but was not pleased when Marie Louise also wanted her Grandmother's approval; and she incurred further wrath with another lapse in etiquette, when she failed to consult the German Ambassador in Washington but communicated directly with the British Embassy.

So, in the late summer of 1900, after an interesting and varied visit in the

United States, she moved to Canada. She had been staying in Ottawa with the Governor, General Lord Minto, and Lady Minto, and was just about to board a train to travel across the Rockies to Vancouver, when a cable was received – uncoded – demanding the immediate return of Marie Louise to Germany. Her father-in-law was exercising his right under a law of Anhalt, his petty German state, to annul the marriage. Marie Louise was saved the ignominious return to Germany by another cable – this time encoded – which soon followed, from Queen Victoria to Lord Minto: 'Tell my granddaughter to return to me. V R'.

Louie arrived back in the bosom of her family at Cumberland Lodge after a very uncomfortable and hot journey from Ottawa to New York and across the Atlantic. On October 5th 1900, Emily, having just arrived home from the concert in Birmingham, found a telegram from the Princess 'to say I was to join Pss Louie on Sunday at the Palace and to take her to Cologne on Monday'.

On Sunday, 7th of October, Emily

> found Pss Louie at Buckingham Palace. Major Martin [the Comptroller of the Christian Household] still here but soon left. Pss Louie and I talked for two hours and then she dressed. We went to luncheon at the Club. Walked back. Colonel Cowans came in the afternoon and staid to tea. I wrote letters. We dined at the Club and had a carriage. Strummed on the piano in my sittingroom after getting back.

Next day after buying gloves, books and food, they

> dined at the Club and Colonel Cowans with us. He came to see us off and also Major Martin. We went a new way to Port Victoria as the Queensboro' pier is not yet remade. Had food on board and remained on deck a short while as it was so beautiful and then went to bed.

Tension may have been growing but so far they were on familiar ground. This time, however, they only went as far as Cologne.

> It was a 'lovely day like summer… went straight to the Hotel du Nord. Dressed and tidied and went down to luncheon. Saw

> Geheimrath Justizrath[115] Hegnel and Dr. Silberstein at another table. The former came up and introduced himself. Pss Louie and I walked in the hotel garden after and watched a large wedding. There was a lawyer interview from 3 till ¼ to 6 and we then went out and had coffee and bought a few things. Supper at 7-oC and then the lawyers again from 8 till 11-oC Very satisfactory but most exhausting.

They breakfasted at 9.30 next morning and then

> dawdled around and went out a little. Hegnel had luncheon with us. We went out for a little but it was too wet to remain. Gehm. Hegnel came again soon after 4-oC. We had food at 5.30 and started again by 6.23 train to Flushing.

One catches a little of the apprehension which gripped the two – the princess, perhaps relieved that at last her unhappy marriage and the hostile atmosphere of Berlin were about to end, but also depressed by the inevitable feeling of failure and the disapproval of Society. For Emily it was a new departure. Although she did occasionally deal with legal matters at home, she had always had Alice or one of her male relations to consult. Here, she was on her own as adviser and supporter of the princess. It was, as she remarked, satisfactory but exhausting – emotionally, having to conduct the negotiations in a foreign tongue, and bearing such responsibility. But it was all done in her usual efficient and unflappable way.

On the ferry from Flushing she met a friend from her St Petersburg days – Mr Goschen, who was meeting his son from South Africa. Their arrival in London was considerably delayed as the boat nearly went aground in the thick fog. When they finally reached Buckingham Palace, they found Princess Christian newly returned from Balmoral, and spent the afternoon searching the shops for a cape for the Princess; at last finding one at Dickens and Jones, and so back to the usual round. They all remained in London for the next week. Another Privy Counsellor from Germany, Geheimrath Gerling, came twice to tie up the loose ends with Emily, the first when Emily was having 'a real [sic] bad sick headache.'

At last, all was ready for the final break with Anhalt. Towards the end of November, Marie Louise asked Emily to go with her to Berlin to collect her possessions and close down her affairs. The annulment of the marriage was completed by December and, from December 14th until the 20th, Emily and Louie were in Berlin. When they arrived off the train, Prince Christian was there to greet his daughter and took them to the Schloss where they were to stay. The next day

> December 15th 1900. Dull cold day. Breakfast at 9.30. We went very soon after to Tempelhoferufer with the Prince. Found Herr Knobloch and Justizrath Fränkel there. Dr. Silverstein came very soon and Esther v. Behr. A most trying time. We found most of the silver and valuable china had been taken to Dessau. The maids came and packed clothes. Lists were made of Pss Louie's silver things.

These tiring and difficult jobs had to be interrupted to visit the Empress of Germany at Potsdam. She was taking a deep interest in all that was happening to her husband's cousin and, the next day when she was in Berlin, 'the Empress saw me before she left [for Potsdam] and was charming about Pss Louie and everything'. Then Emily flew back to Tempelhoferufer to see the 'Maples man about packing the things' and, finally that afternoon,

> Sat with Pss Louie when I came back. She was much agitated at having to break to the Prince about staying on with her till Thursday according to the Emperor's wish ... but it was all received quite well.

Another visit to her old home the next day found the lawyers already there when they arrived; but,

> when they left we worked hard and got the furniture moved with Parminter's help into the two drawing rooms. Pss Louie looked through lots of drawers etc. Her box of private letters was returned to her and taken by Parminter to be deposited at the Eng. Embassy

The princess found time to present Herr von Arnim with his 'Victorian Order' before they went by the 7.05 p.m. train to Potsdam to have supper with the Emperor and Empress … who were both very kind'.

Packing up continued for the next two days; but the important decisions had been made, and both Emily and the princess had time for some shopping and visiting friends in the capital. Finally, on the 19th, after rushing off in a fly to say farewell to the Empress at the Potsdamer Bahnhof, they were back at the house to see Herr von Knobloch locking up and taking the keys. At the Schloss that evening more friends came to see them including Joachim 'which was very nice'; and the von Arnims came to dinner. At last on the 20th they were ready to leave.

> Lots of people came to see Pss Louie off and brought flowers. We had a very long day's journey and were terribly tired. I had lumbago and didn't know how to get from the train to the ship. Rather a rough passage but none of our party were ill.

The princess and Emily were back just in time to complete preparations for Christmas. The Cottage rang with the laughter and games of the young Liddell family who were staying for some time. They all sat up to see in the New Year and the new century … wondering what changes it would bring.

For over sixty years of the 19th century Queen Victoria had been on the throne and all those at the Cottage, and most of the people in Britain, would never have known another monarch. Now in her eightieth year, she was definitely an old woman. Her strength had been declining as the century drew to a close and she could be difficult with her family and those around her. Once, late in June 1898, when the Queen was entertaining guests at the Castle, Emily, who had 'had a very nice dinner', noted that 'great silences prevailed'. The Queen felt it her sacred duty to continue her work but she made few public appearances – an exception being the laying of the foundation stone for new buildings at the Victoria and Albert museum on the 17th of May 1899, which carried on the good work of her long-gone but never-forgotten dear Albert. On the occasion of her 81st birthday the local madrigal society, in which Emily and Gerry sang, performed a Birthday serenade in the courtyard of the Castle and the Queen came to the window to acknowledge their homage. But much of her time was spent in the seclusion of her homes – Windsor, Osborne or Balmoral – and Princess Thora was a frequent companion and confidant.

The outbreak of the Boer War in South Africa in October 1899 shocked the nation. The news in the autumn was very bad. The British forces in South Africa were totally inadequate. The Boers, infuriated with their treatment by Britain, invaded Cape Colony from the Transvaal and Orange Free State. They laid siege to Mafeking, Kimberley and Ladysmith for many months. Families began to receive the dreaded telegrams announcing wounding and death; Emily notes that North Dalrymple was wounded and that Sydney Earle, a relative of her Aunt Lizzie, was killed on November 30th. Only after a truly disastrous week in December of that year, when three relieving forces were defeated, did volunteers from Britain and the Dominions of Canada and Australia, combined with the invincibility of the British Navy, ensure that sufficient troops were poured into the battles under the leadership of Lord Roberts and Lord Kitchener. The tide began to turn. The relief of Kimberley on February 15th, Ladysmith on the last day of the month and finally Mafeking on May 16th were all cause for rejoicing, but it was the scenes on 'Mafeking night – an orgy of relieved feelings' as G M Trevelyan puts it – which remained in the memory for many years.

In the early months of the new century, 1900, the Queen broke her seclusion and came to London: to see and be seen by the people, inspect her troops and visit the sick and wounded. On March 8th, she made a spectacular visit to Buckingham Palace. The route along which she drove from Paddington station to the Palace was 'filled with people anxious to give their venerable Sovereign a hearty welcome' and, down Constitution Hill, 'the mass of humanity grew larger and larger forming up in ranks ten deep near the Palace'. So wrote *The Times* correspondent. Many members of the Royal family, including Princess Christian and Princess Thora, with Emily and several friends were waiting in the Palace ready to greet the Queen. At the Royal entrance in the courtyard, where the members of the Houses of Parliament were waiting, the Queen was received by the Earl of Hopetoun, the Lord Chamberlain, and members of the Cabinet.

> And then it was that the Lords and Commons found that cheers and bows were an insufficient expression of their feelings. The Queen was descending from her carriage, and in another moment would be out of sight, and so, without stopping to consider precedent or etiquette, they, one and all burst forth with "God Save the Queen" so that the walls rang again. Answering cheers broke from the crowd outside, and so, with song, with

cheers from all estates of the realm, their Queen and Empress passed into her Palace.

The Times reporter again.

Emily's diary is brief and in Italian – which she was practising at this period! She lists Gerry, Lady Jeune, Mrs Thynne, Agatha and Beryl among those waiting in the Palace, She writes that she went to the luncheon room with the Princesses at 12.30 to see the Queen, who arrived at 12.45 to be greeted by 'an immense and enthusiastic crowd; members of both Houses of Parliament sang "God Save the Queen".' Her album has several photos of the crowds, including one of the black- coated Members of Parliament raising their top hats as the carriage comes through the archway.

The Queen driving into Buckingham Palace on March 8th 1900 receiving the acclamation of the Lords and Commons.

The Queen returned to the Castle that night. Two days later, Emily was present when the Queen drove in a carriage with Princess Christian and Princess Beatrice to the Victoria Barracks Windsor to inspect 'a detachment of 100 men, in their khaki equipment, who were being despatched to reinforce the 3rd battalion of the Grenadier Guards in South Africa'. The newspaper cutting assures us that 'It was not in any sense a formal inspection, but rather a gracious and kindly visit to say "Good-bye and God speed": a certain degree of formality, however, is apparent in the accompanying photograph!

On a further four pages of the album, newspaper photographs and columns of print in ecstatic prose describe the Queen's journey by train from Windsor to the Royal Arsenal at Woolwich on March 22nd. Emily also records the day, fortunately in her rather more understandable English, although it is still in her 'Italian period'.

March 22nd 1900, Thursday.

> Grey dull raw day ... We had luncheon at 1-0C and I went after with the Queen, Pss Christian, Pss Tora, Louisa Antrim. Major Legge, Col Davidson and Sir Arthur Bigge to see the Herbert Hospital at Woolwich. A wonderful and most interesting sight. Talked to lots of the men. Got back to Windsor at 7. Had tea in the train coming back. Writing and running around. Dined with the Household, all the men. Joined the Queen and Ladies. Bessie played ...'

At the bottom of the next page in the diary she noted: 'Wrote the account of the expedition to the Herbert Hospital to put into the Queen's diary' – one gathers more interestingly than in her own; for a day later she dined with the Queen who was pleased with her contribution.

Among the cuttings from the newspapers and drawings of the occasion by Mr J Sanderson Wells, Mr T Walter Wilson and Mr Begg, there is in the album a detailed sketch map, produced by the Royal Artillery Institution in Woolwich and printed in gold of the Queen's route from the Royal Arsenal to the Herbert Hospital. The crowds were immense: 20,000 workmen were gathered at the arsenal; they had a half-day holiday, with pay, at the Queen's command; 40,000 citizens filled Beresford Square and then – along the route to the hospital, up the hill and on the Common,

> From the roofs, from the windows, from every point in fact upon which it was possible for a human being to gain a foothold, a human being waved a loyal welcome.

The Queen's open landau passed the Royal barracks, the house where General Gordon was born and the monument of the Prince Imperial.[116]

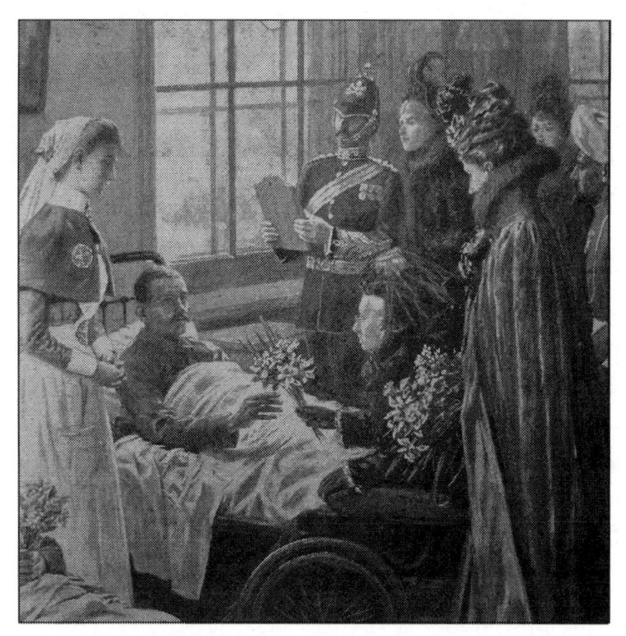

Queen Victoria visiting a wounded soldier from the Boer War, March 22nd 1900 in Woolwich Hospital.

Several thousand school children, nearly hidden in their flags, waited at one point.

> Here there was a momentary halt, and her Majesty leant towards the side of the carriage, bowing and smiling to her little subjects. A tiny girl dressed in khaki came forward somewhat shyly and offered a bouquet to her Majesty.

The main reason for this journey was to visit the sick and wounded at the hospital. There are two touching prints in the album of the chubby-faced old lady, spectacles perched on her nose, sitting in her wheelchair speaking to the patients. She offered them bunches of flowers and words of thanks, cheer and encouragement, watched by Princess Christian, Princess Thora and her suite, including Louisa Antrim and Emily, while a helmeted and ceremoniously dressed medical officer read out the man's name and experiences. In all she saw 274 of the 554 patients. Quite a feat. And there was still the return journey to make through more cheering crowds. As the newspaper reported,

> The road was kept by troops and every available man had been turned out to cover the four miles between the hospital and Blackheath station. Shooter's Hill road was quite impassable; the heath was black with people as far as the eye could see. As a rule Her Majesty is greeted in the heart of a city or in the heart of the country. Yesterday it was the turn of the suburbs which gave her welcome and a splendid welcome it was.
> The Queen and the Princesses reached Windsor a few minutes after seven, [after an hour's journey] and drove straight to the castle in a closed carriage.

The Queen's involvement with her troops continued into the summer and there are photos of her greeting and inspecting the naval brigade on its return from the siege of Ladysmith on May 2nd. Earlier, when writing about the news of the raising of the siege, which Emily would have learnt from the telegraph at Cumberland Lodge, she notes that:

> Lord Dundonald entered the town last night [February 28th] and Buller went in today. The garrison was living on ½ lb of meal and a little horseflesh. Buller's troops require complete outfit of boots and clothing before they can move.

The Queen held garden parties at Buckingham Palace – at the end of June, at which Paderewski played, and at the beginning of July. The former was the last time Emily saw the Queen and the latter was the Queen's last grand public occasion, although she still continued to inspect returning troops.

As the year 1900 drew to a close, the Queen's health gave cause for concern; her autumnal visit to Balmoral hadn't worked its usual magic. 'This time it was different; her insomnia and general wretchedness had left her weak and apathetic' according to Sir James Reid. It was on January 18th that Emily first heard of real worries. She had been out in the morning when the two young princesses had called at the Cottage and left a message saying they wanted to see her immediately. She went over to Cumberland Lodge and found them 'dreadfully anxious about the news from Osborne.' Emily was in London the next day and saw Princess Thora off to Osborne from Waterloo station. The following day she had a better account of the Queen and, on returning to Cumberland Lodge, found Alice still with Princess Louie.

> Continuous better accounts came throughout the afternoon and evening. The Emperor had got down there … the Queen was taking more nourishment and had slept, perfectly comfortable and happy and quite clear. Pss Thora had seen her twice. The Prince went out riding and came home late.

On Tuesday 22nd,

> The news was not so favourable early and continued to get more and more serious. It is Prince Christian's 70th birthday. Alice came over morning. A telegram came from the Prince of Wales summoning Prince Christian to Osborne. He left at 12.30 and would arrive at soon after 7-oC. Pss Louie, Pc Abby and Colonel Cowans all took him to the station … About 5-oC came a message to say the Queen was sinking slowly and at 7-10 we got a telegram from Pss Thora "Dear Grandmamma just passed peacefully away. God help us all" Princess Louie very good and brave. We sent some telegrams.

So an era had ended. But the present must be attended to. Prince Christian had gone off to Osborne to be with the Royal Family; but Prince Abby and Princess Louie were left at Cumberland Lodge. They, particularly the princess, turned to the Loch sisters for consolation and support. Emily was at the Lodge with her and, the next day, Alice also came over; she, too, was a much cherished companion and support. Emily says:

> Prince Abby was sent for to meet Prince Christian in London who was there for the Privy Council to give the oath of allegiance to the Prince of Wales as King Edward VII. He came down to dinner. Heard Pss Christian and Pss Tora are well. Pss Louie and I went for a drive after luncheon. Wrote a little. Talked and worked after tea and dinner. Many sadnesses.

Everyday tasks, drives in the park, walks to the Cottage and talking to Alice and Margie, who was staying, relieved some of the tension and brought respite from the many, many letters that had to be written, both by Emily and the Princess. There were constantly changing plans about Louie and Abby going to Osborne. Eventually, a week after the Queen died, they did get there, just for one night. The following evening the princesses all arrived back at Cumberland Lodge – Thora very tired. Many German relations came to stay and suitable mourning clothes had to be acquired and tried on. Saturday February the 2nd, the day of the funeral, arrived and, although this has been related in many books, it is perhaps worthwhile seeing it through Emily's eyes.

> Rain early – cleared later till 4 – then rained again. Prince Christian with all the other gentlemen went off to London by 8-oC. Pss Tora, Pss Louie, Major Martin and I went down to Windsor at 12-oC. Crowds of people on the road walking down. Drove through the Frogmore grounds up to the castle. Left the princesses there and I walked down with all the other ladies to St George's. Were placed in the Choir. Waited nearly 3 hours. The service was quite beautiful and the whole procession and sight. I was quite close to the coffin in line with the Duke of Connaught, the King and the Emperor. A most beautiful satin pall embroidered at the R School of Art was over the coffin with the Royal Standard and the Crown. An immense crowd of foreign Royalties and representatives. On arriving at the station after the coffin had been placed upon the gun carriage one of the horses kicked over the traces and so the picked 200 blue jackets in 5 minutes undid them and drew the carriage themselves which all said was a wonderful sight. After the service I took Ly Bids home. Got hold of Gerry and we went up to the Castle for food. A wild confusion. Came back and waited at Ly Bids with nice revelage. Carriage fetched me. I waited with Harriet [Phipps] in her room. Came home with Major Martin having lost the others. I dined quietly with the princesses. Pss Christian so wonderful.

Two days later Emily was again deeply moved. First when she was taken into the Memorial Chapel at St George's to see 'the Queen's coffin with the officer guards and all the masses of beautiful flowers' and later in the afternoon when she 'went on the leads to see the last sad and most beautiful procession of taking the darling Queen from the Memorial Chapel to Frogmore. It was most beautiful'. Emily was very sad. It wasn't only the loss of a beloved Queen but the loss of someone who had been a friend of her family for many years. Inevitably she would have been reminded of her mother who had died nearly twenty years before and the Queen's comforting support at that time.

Edward VII had waited so many years to become sovereign. Perhaps this mood infected everyone, for changes and clearing up of the old regime began almost at once. Emily and Gerry were with Lady Biddulph in her apartment at the Castle a few days later when Sir James Reid came in to say goodbye and they all had a long 'relever'. In the middle of February, the new King opened Parliament in great state. The family were staying at Buckingham Palace and after breakfast Emily:

> Sat with Pss Tora. [Then] wandered with her into various rooms. Dressed and had luncheon at 12.45. A large household. All started to the opening of Parliament at 1.15. I, Lady Sophia, Minnie Cochrane and May Egerton all went in a "coach" after our psses. They took their seats on each side of the throne and we stood behind them. The House was crammed. The King and Queen Alexandra came in at 2.15 in their red velvet and ermine robes and she wore the Queen's little diamond crown. She minded dreadfully having to do it and looked lovely and very sad. It was a very interesting ceremony. We got into our carriage directly and sat and watched the procession go away with the enormous painted gilded coach and 8 cream horses.

Many of the diary entries in these early weeks of 1901 show how much Emily was with the family. Princess Thora took up painting again and there were many hours of reminiscence and recollection. Emily often remarks how well Princess Christian was bearing up and how frequently she was down at the Castle, often staying till quite late in the evening, helping Princess Beatrice whose life would be changed more that anyone's.

The two sisters spent hours sorting their mother's clothes and small possessions and, at the beginning of March, Emily was given two

> remembrances of the Queen. A locket which turned out to have been given by Pss Christian herself with Pss Thora's baby hair of

> a fortnight old in it. Also a little Almanach the Queen had always carried in her pocket of her first jubilee year in 1887. I value them more that I can say.

On March 7th the three princesses from Cumberland Lodge 'went down to the Castle to see all the Queen's costumes that she had kept since she came to the throne. Her wedding dress and the one she wore at the first council and many others'. Princess Christian and Princess Beatrice hoped that their mother's great collection of dresses could 'be sent to the S Ken Museum, if possible.' It was.

Not all was looking back. The Queen had left Schomberg House in Pall Mall to Princess Christian and almost immediately the family began to take an interest in it. This house, number seventy-eight on the south side of Pall Mall was named after Marshall Schomberg who had lived there for a short while at the end of the 17th century but who died in 1690 at the Battle of the Boyne. Emily visited the house for the first time with Thora and Princess Christian on February 16th and throughout the year there were many visits to see how the workmen were getting on. Later, choosing furniture from Cumberland Lodge to be moved to London, buying new carpets at Hamptons, furniture at Maples, and choosing a tea-set at Goodes all helped the Princess to make a setting for her new and more independent life. A year later, after a tiring day of decision making, they had their first meal in the house – always something to be noted in the diary – when the Princess and Emily had tea in what would become the equerries' room. April 14, 1902 was the day of the great unpacking. Prince Christian came to lunch on the 17th and the drawing room was arranged on the 18th. By the 20th all was ready to entertain the Prince of Wales (later George V) and family to tea in considerable splendour.

At the end of April, Sir Henry Trotter and Sir Edward Bradford lunched at Schomberg House to be 'consulted about Coronation safety. They tried to find a passage through at the back and we all scrambled about the back garden and wall' which ran along the side of the Mall. As the end of June approached, more preparations were being made; the streets were decorated and the capital was *en fête*. On Sunday June 22nd:

> The whole day from 8-oC in the morning till quite late at night a ceaseless stream of vans and conveyances crammed with sight seers and foot passengers passed ... most orderly and quiet.

Princess Thora went to Mrs Bell 'for her to try on her coronation gown. It is quite beautiful.' Emily was among the many guests at the dinner at Buckingham Palace the following day. Presentations of the foreign suites were made to Queen Alexandra but the King was too ill to attend. The next day, the news of his operation for 'perityphlitis', as Emily calls it, (peritonitis), threw arrangements into confusion and there was much to-ing and fro-ing among the relations who had come for the event. Fortunately, throughout the day, there were good reports of the King and, as history relates, he was well enough for the ceremony to take place on August 9th.

While the changes in domestic affairs were going on for Princess Christian, Princess Louie also was looking around for her own establishment. Early in August 1901, she went up to London with Major Martin to see about a house. When she returned to Cumberland Lodge, she had long talks with Emily; but this house proved either to be unsatisfactory or temporary, for on November 8th the Princess was all day in London again house hunting 'and thinks she has found one'. By March 7th, although not yet living there, Princess Louie spent the day at the house with her friend Mary Hughes, and Emily was helping in the search for housemaids and a cook. All was ready by April 4th for Princess Thora to visit her sister with Emily and take tea.

Having been a constant companion to the old Queen, Thora now became more and more her mother's confidant and companion. Princess Christian continued unabated her activities to help the poor and sick. Her crèche, nurses' home and nursing institute, home for crippled boys, and many others in and around Englefield Green and Windsor, were not forgotten. But, now that her own residence was in London, it was even easier for her to be able to devote time to the sick and needy in the metropolis. She had been engaged in this work for many years. There is a letter from Emily to Sir Henry Ponsonby, dated February 14th 1887 in which she tells him of the Princess's great hope that the Queen will really go to the East End of London. 'She feels it will do such an immensity of good'. Emily continues with:

> I know what it would mean to Princess Christian if the Queen would take her on the occasion but H.R.H. won't ask it & said it would not do even to mention it through you. So I don't know what would happen if she knew I was mentioning it entirely of my own idea but I thought (if you thought it would do) that when you heard matters arranged & discussed you

> might perhaps put in a word in case a favourable opportunity should come.

This somewhat convoluted note gives some idea of Emily's concern for the Princess in her great love and devotion to the people of the East End: and this continued throughout her long life. As *The Times* reported, many years later at the time of the Princess's death, 'Her life was devoted to good works among the poor and afflicted. So frequent, during her more active days, were her visits to hospitals and other institutions in east London that she came to be known among the people there as "Our Princess"'.

Thora herself also undertook much charitable work but she had many other interests. She, like her father, was devoted to the animals at Cumberland Lodge, showing great attention to the dogs, her cats and kittens; a beautiful grey Persian cat was poisoned causing much anguish. She began to take considerable interest in the gardens at the Lodge and Alice quite often came over to give advice. She rode with her father and very occasionally went hunting. She also took up painting again and played tennis, squash racquets and table tennis. A new enthusiasm by 1904 was golf. Early in March that year, a 'golf man' came to Cumberland Lodge to see about 'the ground for golf here'. By the end of the month Princess Thora and Emily were on the golf links at Sunningdale, 'swinging and driving' and, a few days later, they were both taking lessons at Ascot golf links. By 1906, Thora played a round with Colonel Wray, a member of her mother's household, and, during a visit to Yorkshire, Thora and Emily played with Lord Cecil Manners at the Rotherham and District Club in Thrybergh Park where their efforts were reported in the newspaper.

The excitement of new vehicles was in the air and Thora was full of enthusiasm. On going to London at the beginning of February 1904, she was met by Nona Kerr at the station and 'sent straight in the motor to Pss Louis of Battenberg'. Back in the country on February 26th, while Princess Christian spent all day down in Windsor at her Nurses' Home, [117]

> Pss Thora and I went to luncheon with Lady Cathcart and then went in the Mercedes motor which has been lent them to the Ascot Hospital and then all over the country and to Bagshot and back to the Wheatsheaf in an hour ... Sir Reginald lent me his big fur coat'.

By April that year, it appears that the Christians had an electric vehicle in London. On April 27th Thora and Emily went out calling on their friends and relations 'in the electric' and then 'twice round the park'.

A new century was on its way with its excitements and uncertainties. But 1904 was the year that Princess Christian could not help but look back. It was the year when she made her pilgrimage to see the last resting place of her beloved son Christle.

Princess Christian, Emily, Sir W. Taylor and Princess Thora in a car in 1905.

CHAPTER EIGHTEEN

Royal and not so Royal

Princess Christian's eldest son, Christian Victor, was her first born child and he had entered the world at Windsor Castle in 1867. He had a conventional upper-class upbringing. Educated at Wellington College, he was destined for a career in the British Army. His younger brother Albert on the other hand followed his German relatives, being adopted as heir by one of them and serving in the German Army. Emily had known both the boys from their schooldays and became particularly fond of Christian Victor, who was always referred to as Prince Christle. He was a pleasant and friendly young man, getting on well with his family, school friends and fellow officers – among other activities he organised cricket matches at Cumberland Lodge which were watched on long summer afternoons by Emily and other members of the

Prince Christle.

household. He was sensitive to his mother's moods; it was he who encouraged her to take up photography when she appeared to be suffering from a bout of depression. When stationed at Aldershot, he frequently paid quick visits to Cumberland Lodge and on these occasions Emily often remarked that they had long and pleasant chats. He was popular with all the family and Queen Victoria was especially fond of him.

As mentioned earlier, Prince Christle served in the Ashanti war in 1895 and survived, unlike his uncle Prince Henry Battenberg. In 1898, he was again called to return to Africa – this time to a very different part – Egypt. The diary records that on July 21st 1898

> Prince Christle arrived at 4.30 [at Cumberland Lodge]. Great agitation about his going to Egypt. He drove with the Pss and me after tea. Many conflabs with everybody, principally in my room. He went back to Aldershot after dinner.

The agitation continued the next day – 'telegrams about Pc Christle going to Egypt'. The following day, Saturday, both before and after the Princess and Emily attended a 'fearfully grand wedding' in London, there was much agitation and many telegrams. Major Martin came down from London especially to discuss Pc Christle's affairs' and Colonel Eliot was also there. However, by late on Sunday evening, all was settled.

> Major Martin went to Aldershot and came back about 9-o'C after a most successful day and interviews with Duke of Connaught and Prince Christle. All is settled for the latter to start for Egypt on Wed. Aug 4th.

What was happening in Egypt that was so urgent and important? In the early 1880s a charismatic Islamic fundamentalist claiming to be the Mahdi[118] gathered a vast army of followers, the Dervishes, challenged the power of British, and occupied Egypt. He succeeded in wiping out a 10,000 strong Egyptian army led by a retired British officer which had been sent to suppress him. In 1884 the British Government sent General Gordon to the Sudan – this only after considerable hesitation due to his colourful and unconventional past behaviour; but he had served in the Sudan in the 1870s and so knew the country. Now he was to proceed to Khartoum with orders to evacuate the

English and Egyptian troops stationed there. It appears that Gordon interpreted his orders idiosyncratically and was determined to hold the city; as a staunch Christian he was determined to 'smash the Mahdi' – the rebellious Moslem. But events turned out differently. Knowing of Gordon's self-induced predicament, the British government under Gladstone hummed, hawed and hesitated about sending relief. Months passed, food ran low; Khartoum was surrounded and besieged. At the end of January 1885, five months after his arrival, the city fell and Gordon was hacked to pieces two days before the relieving army reached the scene. The Queen and the British public were horrified. For many years – for two or three generations – Gordon was regarded as one of the great heroes of the Empire. 'The way in which Gordon sustained his position is one of the marvels of history' wrote the author of an encyclopaedia article in 1931. His fate was not avenged for thirteen years.

In the late 80s and the 90s, Egypt, having nearly collapsed into bankruptcy, was showing signs of economic recovery, thanks to a massive loan negotiated and administered by Evelyn Baring.[119] But the increasing prosperity and Britain's rule were again threatened from the south by the Mahdi's successor, the Khalifa. His armies had advanced far north towards Cairo. The British government, determined to be rid once and for all of this threat, ordered Kitchener, Sirdar (Commander in Chief) of the Egyptian Army, to invade the Sudan and vanquish the Khalifa's army. The task appealed to Kitchener[120] for he had admired Gordon and success in this campaign would avenge his hero's death.

It was to take part in Kitchener's campaign that Prince Christle, whose regiment was the 60th Rifles, was summoned, as a member of Kitchener's staff. The decision having been taken, the family set about helping to get the Prince ready; Emily bought him chocolate; the Princess paid a visit to Aldershot to say a last farewell and see the Duke of Connaught. The Prince made his farewells to the household and his dogs at Cumberland Lodge. This was going to be a quick visit to Egypt and so he didn't take his dachshund with him as he had done to India. There *Schwartzchen* had become a great favourite with the men and had always looked 'so proud in his khaki coat trimmed with red.' He said a quick goodbye to his sister Louie in London, just before she and Alice set off to stay with the Queen at Osborne.

The Prince was in time for the battle. Kitchener decided to challenge the might of the Mahdi state at Omdurman, their city on the banks of the Nile, close to Khartoum. Winston Churchill, who as a young cavalry officer had managed to get himself into the fray, gives a graphic account of the battle. In *My Early Life* he describes his hasty journey to be there in time and the light-hearted atmosphere.

> This kind of war was full of fascinating thrills ... Nobody expected to be killed. Here and there in every regiment or battalion, half a dozen, a score at the most thirty or forty, would pay the forfeit; but to the great mass of those who took part in the little wars of Britain in those vanished light-hearted days, this was only a sporting element in a splendid game.

Perhaps those who were wounded, those who succumbed to fatal diseases and the more sensitive may have felt rather differently. Prince Christle was evidently one of these; he wrote 'anyone with a humane heart' would be 'very gravely impressed with the terrible nature of modern war.' By all accounts the battle that finally took place on September 2nd 1898, despite some initial successes by the Dervishes (Emily's cousin Douglas Loch[121] who had a signals post on a ridge where they could monitor the advance of the enemy army was nearly engulfed by an unseen column of Dervishes) was a massacre. The Mahdi's armies lost ninety percent of their men. It has been estimated that in three hours of fighting fifty-five men were killed per second.

> It was a battle where two civilisations clashed: on the one side, a horde of desert-dwelling Islamic fundamentalists; on the other, the well-drilled Christian soldiers of greater Britain, with their Egyptian and Sudanese auxiliaries.

So writes Niall Fergusson with a hundred years of hindsight. In five hours the battle was over, the 'burning religious zeal' was no match for the deadly metal of the Maxim guns.

By October 11th 1898, the Prince was back in England and Emily had the chance of a long chat with him. No doubt he told her of his experiences in Egypt before he set off for Ireland the next day. This can only have been a very short visit, for he and Emily were again enjoying a 'revelage' a fortnight later.

It was nearly a year later, in October 1899, that the Prince left the country again – this time to South Africa for the Boer war. On October 5th, Princess Thora and Emily went to the 'Stores' and 'bought many things for Prince

Christle.' The following morning, on a gloomy grey day, Emily and '*mia famiglia reale*' (she was in her Italian phase), with the Duke and Duchess of York, saw the Prince off on the 11.40 train to Southampton. In the following months, news of what was happening in South Africa came to Emily from the telegraph at Cumberland Lodge and the newspapers. All seemed well with the prince. After many early reverses in the campaign, events began to go better for the British and by June 1900, Pretoria, the capital of the Transvaal, was in British hands. Christle, writing home to a friend in July, said that he had got through six fights from Colenso and Spion Kop to Allman's Nek and that he hoped soon to back in Ireland with his battalion. Lord Roberts who was in command, however, wanted Prince Christle on his staff. The first hint of any anxiety about the Prince came to Emily when she joined the Princess at Buckingham Palace on October 22nd. 'They heard that Pc Christle had enteric but is doing well'.

Two days later:

> The Princess got a telegram from Lord Roberts[122] says [sic] Pc Christle was seriously ill but no complications and admirably nursed and doctored. It quite overcame the poor Princess and she did not come down at all but had a little food in her room.

The next day he was 'progressing favourably'. Mr Fripp,[123] the artist, came to see the Princess and cheered her up considerably. Throughout all these days of anxiety Emily only reports the facts. Her thoughts, however, must have turned to what had happened to Henry Battenberg in the Ashanti campaign and what her sister had told her about 'enteric' in India. One wonders at her amazing emotional self-control – even in the privacy of her diary. Her whole concern was with the poor Princess. The following day's news was perhaps not quite so cheerful. 'Prince Christle had had a good night, his pulse and respiration rather quicker: his temp lower'. On the 27th after a quick visit to London, Emily learned that the news was very bad and, in the evening, this was confirmed when Colonel Cowans 'came down at 7 –o'C and brought a rather worse report. The Pss sent for Mr Fairbank who rather comforted her.' There were 'more bad telegrams' the next morning and Emily spent the whole day with the Princess and they did not go out at all.

> All the Louis Battenberg family came up. Pc and Pss Louis sat with Pss Christian. I took Nona and all the children to my room.

They did not stay tea. Pss Louie did my fortune with cards after tea. A better telegram came saying Prince Christle no worse and some symptoms better which was a gt. relief. I sat with the Pss and wrote in between whiles.

On Monday 29th October:

Prince Albert arrived from Germany about 12-o'C. We had bad accounts of Pc Christle in the morning. Sent for Mr Fairbank. Received about 4-o'C a telegram from Pss Thora [with the Queen in Balmoral] to say Prince Christle has passed quietly away that morning. Pss Victoria of Battenberg came up from Frogmore with Nona and the Pss remained until 7.30 when Pc Louis fetched her away. Pss Christian came down to tea and was quite wonderful tho' breaking down every minute. Telegraphed for Dr. Thorne who came down at 11-o'C. Prince Abby waited to see him. Very late writing. Special messenger from Lord Lansdowne.[124]

So ended the life and career of one of Emily's 'family': a charming young man in the prime of life and a favourite of his grandmother. The Queen wrote to Dr Reid saying 'I feel quite crushed' and many said that it was news of Prince Christle's death which hastened the decline in the Queen's health. She returned from her holiday in the Highlands without the usual rejuvenation of her spirits. Three months later she was dead.

For Emily there were immediate things to cope with. Inevitably there were all the telegrams to read, letters to write, visitors to receive. The family and friends rallied round the Princess; she was especially 'delighted' to have Constance Gordon who also helped Emily 'immensely'. On the last day of the month Emily and Princess Louie were in London early to meet Princess Thora who returned from Balmoral. Prince Christian arrived from Germany and they all travelled down to Cumberland Lodge.

All the poor family met. Alice came in the afternoon and saw them all. Many interruptions so could not write till I came to bed and then wrote 18 letters.

The following day there was a memorial service for the Prince in St George's Chapel. Prince Christian, Prince Abby and Princess Thora all went but 'Pss Christian staid quietly at home and Ps Louie with her'. The chapel was full and Emily thought the service 'a very nice one'. The Princess sat in Emily's room in the evening and all seemed peaceful but the next day tensions among the family surfaced and, although Emily does not let us know the details, 'there were fearful *péripéties* in the morning but after some explosions it got much better and the day became peaceful and pleasant'. The tragedy was reawakened for the Princess when she received a letter on November 3rd written by Prince Christle giving an animated description of a cricket match in Pretoria in which he had made thirty and sixty-nine runs. In a letter to a friend he had mentioned that he had been bitten by a mosquito. He thought this and the cricket match had brought on a fever but it was nothing much. How poignant at the time – but how she would have cherished that letter as the days went by! It must have been a sad moment when Princess Thora and her father went 'to fetch Prince Christle's dogs and I went to meet them. We got soaked.' Perhaps some calm and tranquillity was restored when they talked it over in the evening in Emily's room.

The Prince's belongings were returned some time later in the month and 'Pss Christian gave me Prince Christle's prayer book and Testament that he had had with him all the campaign.' In the event of his death Christle had asked that his body should remain where he died as was the case with the other casualties. He never at any time, school, University or in the Army, wanted to be 'elevated above his contemporaries' if he had not earned it by his own efforts.

Other important events for the Christian family were soon crowding in: by December Princess Louie and Emily were in Berlin closing her house; and in January the anxieties about the Queen's health and ultimately her death added to the emotional stress. By the beginning of March the strain was beginning to tell. The first hint that a change was on the way was on the 6th when someone 'came from London to arrange about the journey.' By the 14th, Princess Christian, Thora and Emily were all set to go, and that evening saw them at Calais installed in a *salon lit coupé*. Very comfortable but much too heated. We had food at Laon at 7 o'clock, very nasty and dear'. They travelled to Milan through some very wintry weather.

Heavy snow storm as we came over the St Gothard. It had been lovely as we passed round the Lake of Lucerne. The snow was very deep and several avalanches had come down. Very wild and cold. Turned to rain as we got further down and the lake of Lugano was quite blotted out.

They were met and looked after by the Consul in Milan and had time the next morning to see the Cathedral before setting off for Florence. Here their old friends the Crutchleys met them and Emily was soon back into the routine of 'setting up home' in rented lodgings. So began their holiday, visiting many of the places that Emily had seen on earlier visits with the Davidsons. Thora took up her painting again and the Princess had many friends to see. The weather was unkind, wet and cold, but on the whole it was a restful period except for two disturbing letters, one from Mr Fairbank who had been such a comfort to the Princess when Prince Christle died, and one 'about expenses'. Perhaps this was why some of the pieces of furniture that the Princess had chosen were found to be too expensive to buy and bring home.

Somewhat restored by April 20th, they were off again, this time to visit Empress Vicky, extremely ill with cancer, at Friedrichshof. After a long and tedious journey, the Princess and Emily arrived at Kronberg station at six in the

Empress Vicky (signed and dated May 5th 1901): looking well but she only lived for two months after Princess Christian's visit that spring.

evening. 'The Princess went up to see the Empress the minute we arrived'. There were many people that Emily knew from the past. Deta Perpocher was at the station to meet them and they caught a glimpse of Princess Mossy and her husband Prince Fischy, whose wedding Emily and the princesses had attended in 1893. Count Seckendorff, another friend and member of the Empress's household dined with them on the first evening. The Empress had been gradually fading with the dreaded illness since before her mother's death. In the New Year of 1900 she could no longer keep it a secret from her daughters and they did all they could to nurse her and shield her from the unkindness of the Berlin gossip. But before long her drastically changed appearance made secrecy impossible. It was then that she discovered how much she meant to her friends and relations, particularly her brother Bertie and his wife Alexandra, her sisters and daughters. The house was filled with children and grandchildren to such an extent that Count Seckendorff was of the

> opinion that his mistress' sufferings were not lessened by the hordes of children and relations that filled the Schloss, which he described as half hotel, half hospital. But Vicky's letters and diary only express pleasure at the kindness of her family and friends sitting with her, and reading to her, holding her hands and wiping the tears away when she lost control.

Those who came to stay were encouraged to enjoy themselves. Emily paid visits to old haunts: the old castle where she had stayed when the Schloss was being built, Homburg and Frankfurt to the shops, tea with the von Dieshaus family at Rettershof. Deta Perponcher took Emily to the Saalburg, the frontier camp of the Roman Empire which was quite near and where the vigorous restoration, carried out under orders from the Kaiser, was making remarkable progress. She was 'shown all over it by the Jacoby son and his father who came later.' Dr Pagenstecher, the eye specialist in Wiesbaden, was visited, this time for Emily to get a pair of spectacles. Bridge was the diversion in the evenings and both Emily and the Princess took part. Princess Christian quickly learned the game and 'played until ¼ to 11. I till 12'. And two nights later Emily made a grand slam!

Soon after they arrived, 'there was a terrible explosion and fire at a village near Höchst of benzine. Herr v Reischach bicycled over to see and met many wounded and heard 50 were killed'. The next day, Emily accompanied Deta

Perponcher to the hospital at Höchst to enquire after the wounded on behalf of the Empress.

Princess Christian spent most of the time with her sister and, almost as soon as they had arrived, decided to extend their visit by ten days – 'so everything must be altered'. Sometimes the Empress was well enough to take a drive, but on other days she was too weak and the two sisters sat and talked in her room, a bunch of flowers sweetening the air by the open window. Occasionally Emily read *The Times* to her and also, just before they left, she read Louis Botha's pamphlet about the Boer situation. It must have been a sad leave-taking for Princess Christian, knowing as she did that her sister only had a short while to live and that this was the last time she would see her. It was only the Empress's tremendous spirit which kept her going for another two months in this house and garden –a memorial to her dear husband, who had never had the opportunity to put into practice the liberal ideas which she had done so much to instil in him. Both Emily and Princess Christian would have looked back with tears not far from their eyes at the amazing building standing among trees in their early summer glory as they said farewell and drove off with Princess Vicky and Herr von Reischach to the station.

Back in England the various memorials to Prince Christle were beginning to take shape. Some were purely ornamental – such as the window designed for the Park Chapel which Emily had spoken about with Archdeacon Baly in January. Early in June she saw 'Fuch's model of the monument to Prince Christle in Bray chapel' and later in the month she and Gerry saw the actual statue when they went to 'Macdonald, 373 Euston Road to see Prince Christle's monument'. The statue of the prince was eventually placed at the foot of the Hundred Steps just below Windsor Castle and was unveiled on 6th November 1903. Emily, Cathy and Jeanne joined Princess Thora for the ceremony. It remains as a reminder of this young man, very much a son of Windsor, who lost his life in far-off South Africa (Plate 6).

The Princess was keen that more practical memorials should also commemorate her son. The original nurses' home for the accommodation of 'District Nurses' had been enlarged by the acquisition of neighbouring properties. Emily was with the Princess when she visited the new properties on February 3rd 1903 and was shown round by Miss Robins. Four days later, she was there again when Sir William Taylor who was advising the Princess came to see the place. He came several times in the next few weeks and on April 14th 'Pss Christian went to a meeting of doctors at the Home about starting a Nursing Home for patients'. A little later the Princess also consulted a Miss MacColl at 51 Welbeck St about setting it up and then the work went ahead. In February 1904 there was much activity: committee meetings, inspections and acquiring equipment. On the 22nd of the month, Emily and the Princess were in London searching for teapots. Harrods proved unsuccessful; we 'could find none nice'. They moved on to Elkingtons where they were *given* 'six at £2 each as it was for Prince Christle's Memorial Nursing Home'. To make sure all was well, the Princess spent all the 26th at the Home and then, on the 27th of February 1904, it was finally opened with

> a very nice little ceremony. The Dean read the prayers, Mr Tower the lesson and the Archbishop [Davidson] gave the blessing. Crowds of Doctors, Clergy and nurses there. Everyone went all over the home and then had tea. All left at 5 o'C. The Princess staid on later and went up at 5.30 to the workmen's dinner which she gave them at the White Hart. 164 men, all Hollis' except 4. She thanked them all for the work they had done.

It was a typically thoughtful gesture of the Princess. The nursing home was immediately in use and about a fortnight later the Princess was down at the Home seeing 'old General Anderson who was with his son who came to the Home with a fractured skull but who is getting on all right.' Later in the year Princess Thora herself became a patient, when she was taken ill and finally had to have an operation which left her 'weak and poorly' for some time.

The Nursing Home was up and running and was a practical memorial to Prince Christle: it also furthered Princess Christian's own interests but once again it was in Windsor. In contrast, on April 11th 1904 Emily accompanied the Princess to Suffolk, to Bury St Edmonds, where

> We started at 1.30 with Yeomanry escort and drove to the Bury Barracks for luncheon ... Afterwards the Princess planted a tree and then listened to speeches and presented medals and then visited and opened the two Suffolk regimental homes in mem. of Prince Christle.

In March the year before, the Princess had spent a weekend in Oxford with the President of Magdalen College where Prince Christle studied before he

Victoria Falls seen from the 'Blondin' where now the bridge crosses the river.

joined the Army. On Saturday when they arrived, the Princess, the President, Mrs Warren and Emily spent an evening reminiscing about Prince Christle. The book which Mr Warren had written about the Prince had just been published,[125] and on Sunday evening Emily 'read the life in my room till dressing time. Quiet evening and revelage'. This was all part of the healing process for the Princess: around this time thoughts of travelling to South Africa, and seeing her son's grave and the places where he had passed his last few months, were beginning to take shape.

It was not until August 1904 that Princess Christian, Princess Thora and Emily accompanied by Admiral Fullerton and Sir William Taylor started on the journey to South Africa. They travelled in comfort on the *Walmer Castle* where staterooms had been suitably adapted – Emily had been to inspect them earlier – and had a very pleasant and enjoyable voyage out. Emily devoted a whole album to this trip; and so we have a collection of memorabilia and many photographs recording the events.[126] Some of the photos are formal groups but there are many 'snaps' taken by one or other of the party. Although the authorities recognised that the Princess's visit had sad origins, nevertheless it was one of the most royal occasions on which Emily attended her Princess. There were welcoming crowds as soon as the party reached the Cape and these

'The Blondin' (the workmen's 'cage') crossing the river just below the Victoria Falls with many of Princess Christian's party on board but not the Princess.

continued wherever they went. Special trains were provided by the Cape Government Railways, the Central South African Railways and the Natal Government Railways, each of which supplied lavishly decorated timetables of the various journeys. Sheaves of flowers, speeches of welcome and presentations of local worthies marked every stop. Foundation stones were laid, hospitals were opened, the Pss's special hospital train inspected, garden parties attended and innumerable hands shaken, nurses introduced and addresses from 'Loyal Women' acknowledged.[127] Special attractions were laid on, such as visiting Cecil Rhodes' house, the de Beer diamond mines at Kimberly and the gold mines near Johannesburg. They visited the Victoria Falls and rode across the Zambezi in the workman's cage or 'Blondin', suspended hundreds of feet above the river in the position where the bridge was about to be built. Princess Christian did not venture in the Blondin but kept her feet firmly on the ground and her hat protected from the constant spray with a large umbrella.

Many of the places visited, especially in the Transvaal, were the battlefields of the recent war, 'where all was explained' and the graves of the fallen honoured. The newspaper cuttings from the *De Volksstem* show how carefully the words had to be chosen to describe the visit in what was still a tricky

Princess Christian with her feet firmly on the ground by the Victoria Falls

situation. Even so, the welcome to the Princess was very enthusiastic. This no doubt was because the underlying reason for her journey touched the hearts of many, especially mothers who had lost their sons in the recent fighting. The most important part of the journey was to visit Prince Christle's grave in Pretoria. The authorities showed great sensitivity, and Princess Christian's first visit was made in the privacy of the early morning, so that she could see it alone. Later in the day she returned with others and was able to say a last farewell before boarding the train and continuing on her long pilgrimage. Despite the kindness and thoughtfulness of her hosts, the tour was exhausting and Princess Christian was very tired by the time she returned to Cape Town.

Emily for one, however, was sad to leave a country where she had made many friends. She had found so many reminders of her uncle Henry Loch, who had been Governor of the Cape and had died in 1900, and of his wife Aunt Lizzie, and had been able to meet Agnes Skinner, the sister of dear Shem. She had seen a new country with a different climate and scenery. Although she deplored the heat and the dust, she marvelled at the 'curious outcrops of rocks' and revelled in the tropical lushness of the Victoria Falls. The occasional drizzly damp days had reminded her of Scotland. By the time the two princesses and their party were back on the return sea voyage they were all ready for a rest.

No dances or sports are mentioned this time. The weather turned very rough and cold. Seasickness took its toll and there were 'fiddles on the tables' for several meals. The heavy swell kept up for many days and they spent much of their time in their cabins. At last on October 29th they were back in England, disembarking at Southampton. Major Martin came to meet them and

> told us of the great excitement of the last few days and of the near shave of war with Russia as they had fired on our fishing boats, killing and wounding a good many men. Mr Balfour had made a thrilling speech last night in Southampton and it had calmed down or we might have run into gt. danger on our way home.

But all was well; they were safely back. Emily's diary again records the precise time of train departures and their arrival at Cumberland Lodge. On their first afternoon at home, the Princess was off to see Miss Robins and find out how the Nursing Home was getting on, and Alice came to Cumberland Lodge and stayed to tea.

Earlier in the year Emily and Alice had also suffered a grave personal loss; in July their sister Cathy had died, leaving a great gap in their lives. She had returned seriously ill from India, having suffered a stroke over two years before, and was sent back by ship with a Miss Oram. Rather pathetically the two older sisters hired a fly on March 28th 1902 and

> Cathy arrived [at Windsor Station] with Miss Oram. She was lifted out and when the train left was carried over the line and put in the fly. We got up to the Cottage at 10 to 6 and she had a good tea and went to bed.

For the next two years, with fluctuating hopes of a complete recovery, the sisters' lives revolved round Cathy's health. Sometimes all seemed well and they had great fun – a lively holiday in Wales and a Mediterranean holiday with the Deverells. But in June 1903 she had her final board at the India Office. Emily

> went in with her to the room and saw Sir William Hooper who was charming and the other doctors who came later. It was the final decision about C not returning to India and about her pension. She was wonderful.

It was a sad blow. Catherine Grace for most of her life had been wholeheartedly devoted to nursing. Now she was deemed incapable of carrying on and the truth had to be faced. Princess Christian had asked her to serve on her Reserve Nursing Board. A few other committee involvements helped to give her some interest and keep her going but a year later her health began to fail very seriously. By the last day in June 1904, it had come to the point where Alice and Emily sat with her as she gradually got weaker. The 'doctor could do nothing for her' and she 'finally went away from us at 1.45, very quietly.'

On July 5th 1904:

> A dull quiet day, we made a lovely lily bunch for Cathy tied with R R C ribbon. Gathered roses. Beautiful wreaths came all the morning ... Eckford and Lusher were busy all morning decorating the grave at St Judes ... the men came at 2-o'C and took little Cathy down. We put the coffin on the trolley drawn by the little white pony ... covered with lovely flowers. We walked to St Jude's with her and all the servants came too. All the relations and friends met us at the Church. Aunt Lizzie, Evie, Molly, William, Ruth, Helena and Arthur Nicolson came back with us to tea.

This was the end of the life of their youngest and talented sister who had brought such fun into their lives and had extended their knowledge of the world by her lively and vivid letters from India. As usual only the practical aspects of Alice's and Emily's loss are recorded: 'getting black things', 'looking through and dividing C's things', 'things sent for probate' and, by the end of July, Emily had visited Mr Gosford to remake her will.

Meanwhile there were several other changes on the domestic front. It had often been remembered in the family that Alice had said that she kept a 'pickle shop in Windsor': but for the first twenty years of the diaries there is no mention of such a place. There had been hints throughout the 90s that additional earnings would not come amiss. The sisters had, as routine, let the Cottage for two or three months in the summer for many years but, in 1901, there is an entry noting that 'Gerry got up early and cycled into Windsor to take Alice's Malmaison pinks to Tilt and she sold them all'. And there are several entries saying that 'flowers were packed': the garden was making its contribution. On September 30th 1902, however, comes the short statement: 'Heard that the Chutnee [sic] business was secured for Alice and Mrs Stevens'. The next day 'Alice went down in the morning to see about the Chutnee business' and, on the 4th; she 'went in the 'bumble' to Windsor to pay in the cheques and take over the Chutnee business. She met Ly Evelyn Riddell at the house and mixed and saw into it all'.

Two days later Alice went down early in the morning and spent hours at the Chutnee shop and didn't get home until 3 in the afternoon. Although Emily took a keen interest in the new business – on November 1st she:'looked over papers and accounts with Alice after dinner' – she does not appear to have visited the establishment until mid-November. Then, she and Freda Biddulph, who was staying at the Cottage after her mother's death, were in Windsor one afternoon and 'walked to see Alice at Chutnee House' which was at 13 Church Street, very close to the entrance to the Castle. By early 1903, buses were running regularly between Englefield Green and the town; so it became easier for the sisters to get up and down, and much easier for Alice to get to the shop. Not only was 'Chutnee Castle', as Emily came to call it, a business, but it became quite a social centre; so many of their friends were intrigued by the enterprise and came to visit, including Thora and Louie and, later on, Aunt Lizzie Loch and her daughter Evie. As time went by, Emily began to get drawn into the business and, in May 1903, she was making 'Chutnee lists after dinner with Alice'. In June that year there was a large bazaar in London in which many of Emily's friends, including Princess Louie, were engaged. She was up on the 9th helping to prepare the stall and on the 11th, having tidied up at the Club, she

> went on to the bazaar. Gerry already there. Lots more pots from May Watts [second wife of the artist, George Frederick Watts] and Alice's chutnee arrd. I sold pots till 5.45.

Perhaps to celebrate the first anniversary in November 1903, there was a tea party at Chutnee Castle to which all the people at Cumberland Lodge went – 'Gerry was also invited. Cathy, Alice and Mrs Stevens there – quite successful'. The ' pickle shop' was a reality and went on to be a success.

November 1903 saw another change in Alice's life. On the 5th Emily wrote

> Alice was fetched by Mr H G [Huntley Gordon] in the motor before 8-o'C to go and hear the result of the pole.[sic] She had triumphant victory. 333 to Mr Grey's 58.'

Alice had been elected District Councillor for her ward and, four days later, 'started at six for her first Rural District meeting in Egham'. All her work – and good works – in and around Englefield Green were bearing fruit. Alice became a hard-working member of the Council. She often used her tricycle to get to meetings.[128]

Throughout her life, from 1883 onwards, Emily's time was a mixture of her own affairs and those of the Princess. When away with the Princess, Emily devoted her time to the Princess's needs; when she was at the Cottage, the demands of Cumberland Lodge were often intertwined with those of her home. Among the buildings around the Cottage there was a laundry; often the case with many big houses. Mrs Sharratt the wife of the groom was in charge for many years. As time went on, more washing from other friends' households began to be taken in. Presumably a small charge was made, but it was mainly a service to friends. Even so standards had to be high. In April 1899, Emily: 'Went to the laundry about cut linen but got no light on the subject'. And she was back there a few days later; there had been other problems over the years and matters were coming to a head. After talking it over for some time with Alice and her brother-in-law, William Deverell, it was decided, late in 1900, to make changes and also for the laundry to provide some financial return.

On the day when she had attended the memorial service for Prince Christle, November 3rd, she went down to the laundry 'to arrange about new laundry plans with Mrs Sharratt and Polly'. On December 7th, according to Emily's 'Epitome', they 'started paying laundry with Mrs Munro'. Mrs Munro had made her entrance. She did not sound as if she were the easiest of characters to deal with; moreover, the changes didn't please those who had been in charge before. Mrs Munro and her son Robert arrived at the Cottage on the 7th and were taken down to the laundry by Polly. Next day Emily had 'a great deal of running around and fuss about the laundry. At the end of January Emily paid Mrs Munro her money but there were still 'bothers and difficulties'. Thora and Louie went to visit the laundry a month later and luckily 'Mrs Munro [was] more cheerful'. After a while, it was decided to add two more rooms to the original building, and this generated a good deal of aggravation and required frequent visits to sort out problems. Then there was the new machinery. Emily and Alice 'studied laundry catalogue' in July 1901; later, in August, while in London, she and Gerry visited 'Bradford's together in a cab and I saw about Laundry machine'. On the 8th: 'The man from Bradford's laundry machine came down to meet us and settle about the laundry arrangements. Much consultation.' In spite of all this personal service, things did not run smoothly. On October 10th, Emily fussed around all morning about the machines which arrived and [were] carried into the laundry but could not be put up.' With a lot more 'running around' they were installed a week later, but not before Emily had had to telegraph from Cumberland Lodge post office to get something done, for the 'man from Bradfords never turned up'. This all happened at the time when the Princess and Thora had come back from a visit to Osborne, the Prince had returned from Germany and they were all anxious to inspect Schomberg House in Pall Mall and make plans for its refurbishment.

By late October, although new machines had been installed in the laundry, all was not running smoothly. Emily wrote for October 24th

> Wet day. Went over to the Cottage after breakfast [She was staying at Cumberland Lodge] ... Found a good many tiresomenesses at the laundry. A new hard water sistern [sic] wanted ... the shirt ironing machine does not do for the small shirts.

Mrs Munro proved rather mysterious – perhaps there had been a disagreement with Mrs Sharratt; for, on December 13th that year, 1901, Emily 'went down to the laundry and Mrs Munro and got her and Bobby off in their fly at 10.45 after she had pasted up her door and given me the key'! After much consultation around the family they did decide to go on: enlarge the buildings, get bigger and better machines, amalgamate the old and new buildings and make it into a going concern and Mrs Munro did return. Other workers, not always satisfactory, were taken on. Even in 1904 it still was not completely right. Over-optimistically Emily wrote on February 4th: 'Went out with the Princesses and then ran across to the Cottage. The machines all in working order' but, by the 7th, she and Cathy went down to the laundry and Mrs Munro complained that the 'big machine won't work yet' and on the 11th she again walked over to the Cottage and found that 'the big machine not yet put right. It is most despairing'; even after being mended it was still found to have done 'shocking bad work'. Perseverance continued and by midsummer all appears to have been running smoothly. A Miss Cook was asked to take over the book keeping – price lists had been determined by Mrs Munro; and they had taken out accident insurance – there had been an accident at the beginning of 1903. Maybe Emily learnt more when she visited the Kelso Steam Laundry with Charlie Balfour when staying at Newton Don in August – she would certainly have looked it over with a discerning eye.[129] Thus at last she was able to leave with an easy mind when she and the Princesses set off on their tour to South Africa.

CHAPTER NINETEEN

Growing Unrest – the End of the Victorian Period

Emily's links with Russia were essentially personal; her continuing friendship with the Empress – the exchange of cards, small presents and letters – and her 'penfriend status' with the growing Grand Duchesses. Her visit in the late 90s had, however, made her more aware of what was going on in that distant country and some of these public and impersonal events are recorded in her diaries in the early years of the 20th century. In 1904, on February 7th, after a fairly humdrum Sunday at Cumberland Lodge where she was in-waiting, Princess Christian telephoned her friend Lady Jeune in London and heard that 'the Russian and Japanese ambassadors had left the two Courts and hostilities might begin at any moment'. On the 13th she noted: 'Heard of more Russian ships being taken and one blown itself up' and again, two months later, in April: 'News, evening, of the loss of a large Russian battleship with the Admiral and 700 on board.' And Major Wray's greeting to Princess Christian's party when they arrived back at Southampton on October 9th 1904 had been full of consternation about the Russians firing on the British fishing fleet in the North Sea and the near shave of war with Russia.

Compressed into these few brief references was the disaster of the Russo-Japanese war. In the late 90s and early years of the 20th century, the Russians had been consolidating their position in the Far East by securing warm-water ports at Port Arthur in Manchuria and Chelumpo on the Korean peninsula, thereby linking Port Arthur with the Trans-Siberian railway at Mukden. At the same time, the Japanese, after being catapulted into the 'world' by Commodore Perry in 1853, had quietly and purposefully transformed their fighting forces. They were now poised to resist any power that thwarted their aim of acquiring colonies and safeguarding the homeland. They had successfully taken on and beaten China in war over the Korean peninsula in 1894; and by late 1903 they were ready to contest the Russian presence in that part of the world. Complex negotiations had been going for some months between Russia and Japan about the integrity of Manchuria and Korea while at the same time safeguarding their respective interests in these two countries. It was known that relations were frosty. Xenia, Nicholas's sister wrote in her diary for January 1st 1904 (Russian style):

> After morning service everyone looked on with interest as Nicky talked to the Japanese! Afterwards Nicky told us that he had said to the Japanese that Russia wasn't just a country – but a part of the world and that in order to avoid a war, it was better not to try her patience, or else it would end badly.

And she continued on the 25th of January

> War has been declared ... terrible ... In one telegram it says that Kurito, the Japanese Ambassador was recalled from St Petersburg before Russia's answer was received.

This is not surprising if one believes that, as early as October the previous year, Togo, the commander-in-chief of the Japanese Imperial Navy, informed Ito, Chief of the Naval General Staff, that war would soon break out between Russia and Japan. By January, one hundred Japanese ships were ready to face the Russian fleet at Port Arthur. By February 4th the Japanese negotiators reported that 'we are obliged to conclude that the Russians do not want peace'. On the 5th Togo received the Imperial order; on the 6th he sailed against Port Arthur and on the 8th made his successful attack, sinking two battleships and putting five Russian cruisers out of action. Another unit of the Japanese fleet attacked the Russians at Chelumpo and landed an army. Only then did the Japanese declare war. This was their way of undertaking hostilities: fight first, talk later.

Another major disaster followed in March when the battleship *Petropavlosk*, on which the commander of the Russian Fleet was sailing into battle, was blown up by a mine and nearly all the officers and crew were killed. It was a disastrous blow to the Russians and Xenia commented that 'Mama and Nicky were terrible upset'. At the time the Empress was suffering from flu and was also pregnant with her long awaited son who was eventually born in July. His arrival was one of the few bright spots in the black year of 1904. Olga, Nicky's younger sister, recollected in her memoirs how happy the people looked when the news was announced, although the nation was really in the depths of depression because of all the disasters in Manchuria.

Wilhelm, Nicky's cousin the German Kaiser, wrote to him soon after the birth of the Tsarevich. Mingled with sentimental congratulations were sturdy advice and opinions. The letter also hints at the impossibility of an Asian nation being better armed and more successful than one of the current 'great powers'.

> There is no doubt to me that you will and must win in the long run but it will cost a lot of money and many men ... Of course the operation of the field army will be easier and will give better results as soon as the Baltic fleet will have arrived on the scene and forced the Jap Fleet back into their ports, restoring the command of the sea to you, now lost by the inefficiency of the admirals in command of the naval forces at Port Arthur.

The Kaiser's advice may have been right but the outcome was quite the opposite. The Russian Baltic fleet set sail for the Far East, a journey of thousands of miles round the Cape of Good Hope, in October 1904. As Emily learned when she returned from South Africa, the nervous, trigger-happy Russians fired on Hull trawlers fishing on the Dogger Bank, thinking that they were Japanese torpedo boats. The fleet's performance when they reached the Far East was no more propitious. On May 27th 1905 their ships were surrounded by the Japanese fleet in the Straits of Tsushima and practically annihilated – four thousand killed and nearly eight thousand captured. As KR wrote in his diary for May 16th (old style) 'How terrible, what a disgrace and how much sorrow.' This terrible disaster really signalled the end. There was no hope of the Russians regaining the initiative. Port Arthur and Mukden had fallen in March. In all she lost around 400,000 men and, at the peace negotiated at Portsmouth, New Hampshire in the United States, despite the diplomatic skill of Witte the Russian foreign minister, Japan gained the right to Port Arthur and Dalny; the Manchurian railway came into her sphere of influence and she gained valuable fishing rights. Manchuria was restored to the Chinese. Russia, however, escaped paying any indemnity and KR considered that Witte had achieved a considerable diplomatic victory. He concluded his diary entry by writing:

> Nevertheless there is nothing joyful about this peace, crowning as it does such an unfortunate war for our forces. Not only does the peace bring no joy, but it is rather frightening.

In June a mutiny broke out on the *Potemkin*, one of the ships of the Black Sea fleet.

These events were part of the escalating forces of revolution that had been simmering for years. Nicholas wrote in his diary on January 9th (old Style) 1905: 'A terrible day! There were serious disturbances in Petersburg as a result of workers wishing to reach the Winter Palace. The troops were forced to open fire in several parts of the town; there were many killed and wounded. Lord how painful and how sad'. The shock to the Imperial family that day was nothing to their feelings on February 4th (old Style) when a revolutionary conspirator finally caught up with Nicholas's uncle, Serge. Emily's diary for February 17th ends:

> Heard when we got back that Grand Duke Serge had been killed by a bomb under his carriage in Moscow,

This time, the public event came close to Emily's personal links with Russia. Grand Duke Serge was the emperor's uncle and was married to the beautiful Ella, Alix's older sister. Ella's photo in Emily's album is of one of the loveliest – she was tall and slight of blonde colouring with features of extraordinary fineness and purity. She had eyes of grey-blue on one of which there was a spot of brown, and the effect of her glance was unusual. Although Emily did not see so much of her as of the younger children, she admired her. When she and Alix had discussed Russia, long before Alix's marriage, the talk was based on Alix's visits to her sister in Russia. As a young girl, Ella had fallen for Serge and, despite Queen Victoria's deploring the prospect of 'her beautiful grandchild' marrying a Russian, Ella had got her way. She had settled in Russia married to one of its richest men; but they had no children and some of the comments from her Russian relations indicate that that it was not a happy marriage. Sandro, Nicky's brother-in-law, husband of Xenia, described Serge in his memoirs as obstinate, arrogant and disagreeable. He was also incompetent – it was under his governorship that the tragedy on the Khodinka fields occurred at the coronation. Sandro despised his condescending grimace when exaggerating his St Petersburg drawl, as he addressed Ella as 'my child'. She was

Princess Elizabeth (Ella)

too proud to complain and stayed by his side for nearly twenty years, her loyalty undiminished by the passing of time, and her sorrow adding a spiritual halo to her beauty.

Although it was not obligatory for Ella to convert to Russian Orthodoxy, she did so and, as she grew older, became deeply religious to the extent that Serge considered her almost unbalanced. But her religion appears to have stood her in good stead when the horrors of the assassination blew her husband to pieces.

KR wrote in his diary for February 5th:

> After lunch she [Ella] heard a loud noise from inside the rooms, as when snow falls from the roof, only louder, and she immediately thought that something terrible must have happened: it flashed trough her mind that Sergei could have met with an accident … Ella quickly put on her hat and coat and set off in the direction of the noise.
> On Senate square, before the Nikolski gates, there was already a crowd of people. They did not want to let her pass, but she pushed through to the place where the remains of poor Sergei

> were lying – part of the torso and a leg, a blown off hand, pieces of body and clothes.
> She fell on his right hand and took off the rings. Her face covered with the blood of the victim. They found pieces of the gold chain, on which his cross and medallions had hung. She rummaged around in the snow, which for a long time afterwards continued to give up small bones and bits of cartilage, pieces of the body and splinters from the carriage.
> Ella arranged for a stretcher from her Red Cross organisation, on which the remains were placed and covered with a soldier's coat. All this was done in front of her. She ordered the stretcher to be taken to the Chukov monastery.
> Her calmness and goodness, her submission to the will of God, and her lack of anger are striking and deeply moving. How glad I am to be with her, the only one of the whole family.[130]

The unrest in the country and the fear of assassination had made virtual prisoners of the Romanov family. Many were forbidden to travel. Nicholas and Alexandra and several others were at Tsarskoe Selo. Only a few were allowed to get to Moscow to be with Ella in this time of grief. Not only this: even those in St Petersburg were forbidden to attend the requiem masses in the Kazan or St Isaac's cathedrals. Some relatives from abroad came however: among them Grand Duchess Marie (Duchess of Edinburgh), Princess Victoria of Battenberg and Grand Duke Ernie of Hesse-Darmstadt and his new wife Eleonore

It was a year later, in 1906, that Emily first met Eleonore. At the end of August that year, she was at Bayreuth with a large party of friends including Gerry and Guy Liddell. They were there to hear performances of several Wagner operas including Tristan and Isolde. Emily had heard this opera two years earlier; at the time, she wrote 'am quite sure I hate it'. On this occasion though, she thought she 'disliked [it] less than the last time'! The diverse group of people at Bayreuth sounded quite intellectual and a good deal of reading went on. On the 15th there was:

> Some reading aloud of the Bernard Shaw Valkure … We started at 3.30 for the theatre which began at 4 o'C and only got there just in time. Gerry and I sat in our usual places. Tea in the first interval and supper in the second.

As usual, meals were very important to Emily but this time she was fortunate. For in the theatre restaurant she met 'Duke Ernie [who] greeted me most heartily and asked me to go and stay at Wolfsgarten'. So, at the end of the month, she set off on her own in a *Schlafwagen* to travel overnight from Munich to Darmstadt. Refreshed by coffee at Darmstadt, she took another train to Langen and was met by

> Fräulein v Rotsmann [a new acquaintance] with a charming open carriage and a break for my box. Had to wait a long time for it. Hastily changed for 9 o'C breakfast after which the Gd Duke came to find me and presented me to the Gd Duchess and then he shewed me all his changes and improvements and we releved much.

Emily had not stayed at Wolfsgarten for many years. She and the princesses had seen the ducal family in Friedberg in the late nineties and had had meals with the first Grand Duchess in the castle. Whether Princess Christian or Emily had had any idea of the problems of that marriage the diary does not tell; but, by the turn of the century, life for Ernie had become almost impossible – according to letters to his sister Victoria Battenberg. Grand Duchess Victoria Melita was more interested in riding her pedigree horses than being sociable with the people of Darmstadt. In December 1901, after Queen Victoria's death, this – her last arranged marriage and particularly significant to Princess Thora – ended in divorce.

What a lot of 'revelage' there must have been for Emily and Ernie. So much had changed. Ducky had remarried; his adored daughter was dead and now lay with her mother, brother and sister in Rosenhöhe; and he, Ernie, was married to Eleonore and a new baby was on the way. There were many happy memories from the past, and these were brought sharply into focus when 'they went to the house in the wood where we cooked our own lunch and had it there'. Back to the days nearly twenty years before when he and Emily had made shortbread. Now, in the new more tranquil atmosphere, there was a chance for Emily to get to know Eleonore. Next morning, they sat out in the garden and had a long talk before Emily caught her train.

Emily and Princess Thora were back in Germany for a holiday with Ernie and his family a year later – 1907. At first they stayed in Wolfsgarten. By now, motors were giving much greater freedom of movement. While there, they

Nicholas and Alexandra with their family, card sent to Emily with best wishes for Christmas 1906.

were now able to go to the theatre in Darmstadt and back in the evening. The party then moved to Friedberg and followed the manoeuvres to the north. Later they drove over and stayed at Heiligenberg where Princess Victoria Battenberg entertained them at her family home. Prince George, her elder son, after being with the party for much of the time, returned to Dartmouth where he was a naval cadet. 'Poor little Dickie[131] was cross and complaining' after his brother left and when he wasn't allowed to take his dog 'Scamp' out driving'. Princess Victoria had recently been in Russia with Nicholas and Alix, and she and Emily had a 'long talk about Russia all the evening' on September 22nd. Emily had heard something of events in Russia and had a recent photograph of the family, bringing Xmas wishes. The family was now much larger, and those she had known as babies back in 1898 were pretty little girls of eight and ten. They had been joined by Maria, Anastasia and the little boy Alexei – in the photo still in skirts.

Princess Victoria had been so saddened during her visit by all the disasters which had struck the Romanovs that it was 'only in the faces of the four winsome little girls' that she had seen any happiness while staying at Peterhof. This brief happy interlude is described by KR in his memoirs when, in August 1906, 'we went to visit the Empress' sister Victoria Battenberg who was with Ella in Illinskoe and is now starting a second week with their Majesties. Their four daughters came into the room and also, to the great joy of our children, the two year old Tsarevich. After going round the tea table and greeting everyone, he climbed on to his mother's knee'. After tea 'our boys and the imperial girls had a wonderful time romping round with him on the floor. Ours were delighted.'

More often it was the problems that were apparent. There were problems with Nicholas's relations forming unsuitable liaisons and marriages; there were increasing signs of political unrest despite the Emperor having made a conciliatory speech at the opening of the Duma; always there were fears of assassination. Emily would have been particularly anxious to hear about Alix and how Ella was managing after Grand Duke Serge's assassination. Perhaps Victoria told Emily about Ella's increasing religious devoutness and how she had given up her place in society and set up an order of nuns to help the poor and sick. Alix's health was not good. She suffered from pains in her legs, back and head, and her heart was beginning to give cause for concern. The young Tsarevich would have been mentioned; but whether Victoria knew how easily Alexei could be bruised is debatable. The child's condition was kept a closely guarded secret but the anxiety that it was causing must surely have been seen by a loving sister. By this time, the Empress was depending more and more on Grigory Rasputin, who had been introduced to her two years earlier, to calm and soothe the pain of her little boy.

Emily went abroad again for a quick visit to Oberammergau[132] in June 1910 to make sure that everything would be satisfactory when she took Princess Thora to the play later in the year but on August 22nd at the end of a very warm close day, Emily and Princess Thora were off to Germany again. They were on their way to stay with Grand Duke Ernie and his wife Eleonore. The journey was easy by the well-known ferry and train. By four in the afternoon of the next day Thora was being greeted by her cousin and Emily was back with her old friend Fräulein von Grancy. Time had moved on but the warmth of the greetings had the comfort of long practice. Now, however, a motor sped them on their way to Wolfsgarten and they were soon installed in their rooms; Emily's was below the Music Room where they had spent so many happy hours in the past. There were two quiet days at Wolfsgarten – except for Emily's old enemies the 'gnats' who were out in force. In the last line of her diary entry for August 25th there is a hint at what is to come: 'All the heavy luggage was sent off to Friedberg'.

This was to be no ordinary holiday in Hesse. This time there was a special invitation for Princess Thora and Emily to join in the visit of the Russian Royal family to the Empress's home country. Ernie and Eleonore were no doubt delighted that the family was coming to them again but their great entourage and the responsibility for their safety must have taxed resources to the limit. As we have seen in the years since Emily and Thora were in Russia – and especially since 1905 – the threat of assassination to the Tsar and his family had greatly increased. Friedberg, a small town to the north of Frankfurt, boasted a fine castle with ancient walls towering above a moat. The site had been chosen by the Romans for a fort – their baths still remained within the fortress. In the intervening centuries owners had strengthened the fortifications, built towers and robust gatehouses with drawbridges and other deterrents. Inside the walls a village of houses – some half-timbered, some stone, some stucco, of various ages and set at all angles – had been built around a jumble of small squares and culs-de-sac. On the east side of the road, which wound its way from the gateway at the top of the slope from the town to the northern gate, stood a handsome creamy-pink stucco mansion, 'the Schloss' of Emily's album. Here in this fine 17th-century house the Russians would be safe. There was an air of graciousness about the place. The large irregularly spaced windows were framed with terracotta stone. Three tall wings each edged in terracotta stood forward from the lower two-storeyed body of the house. The roof of each gable-end was lightened by amusing scrolls and curlicues which swooped upwards like well-waxed moustacios (Plate 7).

Two days later, August 27th, the diary continues:

> Lovely fresh day. Left Wolfsgarten at ¼ to 10 in three motors and got to Friedberg before 12 o'C. Everybody went all over the rooms to see how they were disposed. I am up near Frl. v Grancy. Got unpacked and wrote all afternoon. The Gd Dk and Dss arranged all the rooms for the Emp and Empress. After tea, which we had on the terrace, the royalties and Georgina [an additional companion to Thora] went to Nauheim. Frl. v Grancy and I did shoppings and then back through the *Anlagen* [park]. We had dinner also on the terrace and played parlour croquet evening.

One can imagine the excitement of finding their rooms in this large unfamiliar building; running up and down the staircases, peeping into this room and that – all newly cleaned and painted, with fresh hangings and well-

Arrival of the Russian Royal Family at the Schloss in Friedberg Castle on August 30th 1910

beaten carpets. The Empress and Emperor were to be in rooms on a lower floor: the Empress's health had been causing much concern in the last few years. A year or so before in a letter to her daughter Tatiana who was always very solicitous about her mother's health, Alix had written that she was just beginning her eighth week of being ill; and this wasn't the only time that she had to retire to her bed. As a result, the Empress could not walk well and had to use a wheelchair. The younger Russian Grand Duchesses would have been put near the nursery wing, where Edey, the nurse employed by Eleonore, slept with her two young princes.

Thora was near Olga and Tatiana. They were almost young ladies by now: Olga fifteen and Tatiana two years younger. Earlier in the year, Tatiana had written to her mother asking if Olga could, at the Alexander Palace, have a room of her own. Space had also to be found for Prince and Princess Andrew of Greece and their family. Princess Andrew, Alice, was the eldest daughter of Victoria Battenberg. She appears in Emily's album as a young child in the family group on the steps of Wolfsgarten in 1891. She had been married in 1903. For a few days the Empress's other sister, Irène, and her son Waldemar were also resident visitors.

August 30th was the great day when the Russians arrived. Emily went out shopping in the morning for Thora and the Grand Duchess and got back about 12 o'C. Then:

> The Russian Royal Family arrived at 3.30. The Gd Duke and Dss and all the people in waiting went to the station to meet them. Pss Thora and I and the little boys saw the train pass by and then met them on their arrival at the door. We had tea in the dining room with all the ladies and gentlemen and the Royal people out of doors on the terrace.

While the new arrivals settled themselves in, Emily and Fräulein von Grancy went for a walk, coming back by the town where Emily bought post cards. She ends the day;

> The empress did not come to dinner and the others went to sit with her. We waiting people went to the drawing-room and played bridge.

For the first day or so of the visit Alix was tired and didn't leave her rooms very much; her family went to sit with her in the evenings. The older Grand Duchesses, Olga and Tatiana, however, were up and ready to go out the very first morning. Emily and Thora were there to take them shopping. They were driven over to Nauheim in a motor and had a great time looking around the shops. Word got around amongst the other shoppers and soon they were 'rather mobbed and so we dashed into the *Anlagen* to get away from the crowd.' This did not worry Olga and Tatiana who, when they returned to the Schloss, hurried in to their mother and told her all about the jewellery they had seen: such different settings from the ones in Russia and such beautifully cut stones. Next morning, Emily was summoned again and was off with them to several jewellers' shops. 'They chose heaps to be inspected by the Empress which we took back with us. Were rather pursued by the crowd and saw the Emperor among the people.' Security appears to have been very relaxed and so different from Russia. Later in the visit Princess Thora and the Empress motored to Nauheim one afternoon. They got out and went around the town looking at the shops with Thora walking beside Alix's wheelchair. 'They shopped and were not recognised by anybody' wrote Emily.

There were plenty of games to entertain the younger members of the party.

All the children at the Schloss in the castle at Friedberg
playing with the Victoria on September 6th 1910.

'Bumble Puppy'[133] arrived on their second afternoon. It was immediately unpacked and played. On September 6th after lunch, 'there were great games in the courtyard with the bigger children dragging the Victoria with the little ones in it and photos taken.' Emily has left us a photo in her album of the four dark-haired Grand Duchesses in their white knee-length dresses – even Olga not yet in long skirts – and black stockings standing to the side and the Tsarevich and Princess Alice's two little fair-haired girls seated in the carriage. A white-dressed adult stands on the landing at the top of a double stair in front of the door keeping an eye on things. This might be 'Nona' Kerr mentioned several time by Emily – in fact she had been shopping with Nona and Dickie earlier in the day. There is one other person in the group. At the front of the Victoria is a boy of about ten in a suit and a wide stiff white collar – unnamed by Emily – but who is probably 'Dickie, whom Emily had been with earlier in the day and had met as a small unhappy child at Heiligeberg back in 1907.

There are also some snapshots in the album which show the crowd of nurses and prams with their various royal charges: the nurses with boaters and the babies with wide-brimmed straw hats. In contrast, Alexei, in sailor suit and hat, squints into the sunlight from his specially adapted bicycle pushed by his

The younger children out for a stroll with their nurses and Alexei on his specially adapted bicycle with Derevenko.

sailor guardian Derevenko. One of the most informal and charming photos is one of Grand Duke Ernie's two sons and the Tsarevich sitting on a grassy bank looking rather solemn. A marked contrast to the two snaps – pasted just above in the album – of the two young princes George Donatus and Louis laughing, as they stand, all muddy with bucket and spade, on a heap of sand or mud beside a lake.[134]

Afternoon relaxation was often an expedition to a beauty spot. In the past this had been taken in a carriage; but now that 'motors' were well established and somewhat more reliable these were used; making it possible to travel further afield. But the nearer more familiar places were not neglected; two days after the photographic session in the courtyard, on a warm sunny afternoon, the whole party set off in six motors for an expedition to the Feldberg.

> We got out at the foot of the hill and 1 hour and 20 minutes walk up. Rather a fear that it would be too much for Frl v Grancy but she did it. We walked about a little on the top and then had a splendid coffee meal in the restaurant at 6 o'C. Most

The Tsarevitch, Alexei, with his cousins Donatus and Louis the sons of Grand Duke Ernie and Eleonore This card was also sent by Alix to Emily with best wishes for 1911.

George Donatus and his brother Louis enjoy bucket and spade work in the mud.

> of them walked down again. Frl v Grancy, Mlle Beitzen, the three younger Gd Dss and I came in the Gd Duke's open motor. The others joined us. We did not get back to Friedberg till 8.20. The empress came up after dinner.

There is a photograph of another similar expedition when:

> The whole party of 19 went in 5 motors directly after luncheon to Münzenberg, most beautiful ruins. We walked about and went to the top of a high tower. Fürstin Lich, the Gd Dss' sister in law, with her girl and boy met us there. We had beautiful spread of coffee, cakes etc in the village inn outside place when we came down and got back to Friedberg at 5.15. A most lovely expedition.

There they are in the album, nearly a century later, caught by the camera lens sitting on bentwood chairs on a wooden deck under the trees outside the Gasthaus. Nicholas, sporting a fine moustache and beard, turns towards us with Thora on his left, very upright with a dark hat and stiff expression. To his right,

The whole party on an expedition in 'motors' take coffee at Munzenberg .

Alix leans back in her chair looking at the camera rather mournfully from under a wide-brimmed hat. Opposite her across the table sits her brother Ernie. Emily is tucked in at one end of the table, upright in her high-collared dress. Eleonore and some of the other ladies have long scarves draped around their shoulders, no doubt to anchor their large hats when the motors got up speed.

These were expeditions for the grown-ups; but the one to Lich – the Grand Duchess, Eleonore or 'Onor' as the family called her, was a Princess of Solms-Hohensolms-Lich – was one where the children also went. 'They all played games. The Emperor tearing about also'. Their host and hostess the Prince and Princess Solms-Lich, had five children. One can imagine the great fun that all the young ones had – the Russian Grand Duchesses so rarely met children or young people – rushing about and playing games, especially when some of the younger grown-ups such as Nicholas joined in. He really seems to have thrown himself into the carefree atmosphere of the holiday. On one evening, they played hide-and-seek in the dark and, while it was played, just before Emily and Thora left, 'the Empress and even Frl v Grancy joined in it.' By then Hesse was beginning to work its healing magic on Alix. Emily wrote for that final evening:

> We dressed early and at 7 o'C the Russian singers sang for an hour. It was in the dining-room and we all sat in the next room with the folding doors open. The empress came in for it. She looked lovely.

The visits which the Russian royal family made to Hesse usually lasted for several weeks and often there was some special occasion for them to take part in. In 1897 when Princess Thora and Emily had travelled out to join them in Darmstadt before going to Russia, Nicholas and Alix had come, among other things, to lay the foundation stone of the Russian church which was being built for them when they visited Darmstadt. The church was in the park of the Mathildenhöhe – an Artist's colony which was very much the brain child of Ernie, built on the land which had belonged to an ancestor, Ludwig III. The foundation stone of the church was laid on four railway wagon-loads of Russian soil, so that it stood on part of the Mother Country. The Emperor and Empress returned to Darmstadt for the formal consecration in 1899, and again in 1903 when it was used for the wedding of Princess Alice of Battenberg and

Prince Andrew of Greece. While Emily was in Friedberg, however, she noted that on Sunday September 4th:

> Everybody went to their respective churches. Even the Empress to Nauheim Greek Church. Pss Thora, I, Dick, Nellie and Pss Alice's English nurse to our church.

Evidently, on this Sunday it was too far for the Empress to travel to the Russian church in Darmstadt but she did later in the visit. This was last time it was used by Nicholas and Alexandra: by 1911 Livadia was ready for them and they took their holidays on the Black Sea.

One of the special occasions in 1910 was the Grand Duchess's 39th birthday. Emily had to borrow a white dress for it. On September 17th

> We collected before breakfast to give our presents and good wishes. The Empress came also. She also came to luncheon. All the Lich family came over and Pss Louise of Battenberg, Dickie, Nona and Princess Andreas. We had games all the afternoon in the garden with the whole party. The empress came out for the whole time and gave prizes. I won a buckle for finding an apple blind-folded … In the evening Frl. v. Grancy and I were asked to sit with the Empress down stairs. [While the family played hide and seek in the dark].

Emily had many opportunities of talking to Alix – once when they had lunched together she was 'charming and full of talk'. It is clear from her memorabilia – the cards and letters that she has kept – that Emily became much closer to the Empress during this visit. Emily's caring instincts were always aroused by someone's ill health and, although there was little she could do for Alix in this respect, she did over the years to come not only write letters and send small presents, but bought one or two things for Alix and sent them out to her. She probably had less opportunity to talk with Nicholas, but was present on one hilarious occasion when the party went to visit Schloss Braunfels Solms.

> A most wonderful castle on the top of a hill over the town. The old soldier at the gate refused to believe it was the Emperor of

> Russia and the Grand Duke and was most amusing but had to give in when told to announce them and the whole party to Pss Braunsfels Sohms. We all went in. We saw the most wonderful clothes and vestments which were said to have belonged to the Heilige Elizabeth and afterwards worn by Richard Coeur de Lion then made into priests' vestments. Also beautiful clothes of 200 years old belonging to an ancestress.

After this amusing and fascinating afternoon they left the castle at 5.30. Their journey home was much delayed as two tyres burst. There were compensations – for Emily anyway; while repairs were being made, they stopped for 'delicious coffee' in Garten Wirtschaft. They didn't reach Friedberg until after eight and 'the children [were] dreadfully tired'. Much earlier that day Emily had read to Marie and Anastasia while they drew, so she was also getting to know the younger members of the family – and probably their governesses and nurse maids.

One evening, not long before Thora and Emily left:

> dinner was late as an architect was shewing plans to the Emperor and Empress of a new house they are building in the Crimea and the Empress was busy with it from 5.30 till 8 o'C.

This was an exciting undertaking in a beautiful part of Russia and it seems quite likely that Alix had told Emily about this new house when they lunched alone. At last, instead of having to take over an historic building which she and Nicholas had done so often before, they were having one built exactly to their wishes. They had chosen a site, at Livadia, where there were many magnificent palaces set in luxuriant woodland (Plate 7) – on the slopes above the Black Sea, yet not too far from the city of Yalta. The climate was warm and sunny – Alix's doctor, Dr Botkin, who appears in photographs of the Friedberg visit – had recommended that she should spend more time in a warmer climate. It was in a part of Russia so very different from St Petersburg and the north and one that everyone enjoyed: the sea, the luxuriant flowers and above all the wonderful climate. Discussion and planning had been going on for some years. Older palaces had stood on the site but in 1904 after inspecting the 'Big Palace' which had been there for over fifty years, it was decided to demolish it and build something completely new. N P Krasnov was chosen as the architect; it was

Livadia, in 1911, Nicholas and Alexandra's palace of white limestone on the shores of the Black Sea not far from Yalta.

probably he who was discussing the plans with Alix and Nicholas in Friedberg. It had been decided that the building should be white, light and airy and a place for recreation; it was to fit harmoniously with the dense woodland, and yet let in the sun and have views of the sea. Krasnov chose the Italian Renaissance style but interpreted it in a modern manner. Local white limestone was to be used for construction and for decorative work. He not only designed the building but also much of the furnishing and decoration.

Perhaps that evening, once he had given a report on how the building was progressing, it was these points, including the chairs for dining-room, the carving of the fireplaces and monograms in the children's rooms, which were being discussed. Time was pressing. The 'official founding' of the palace had taken place on April 23, 1910 – only six months before – and all construction work had to be completed before September 14 1911. Not long to complete a building of 116 rooms and a large patio which was to be planted with roses.

It was done in time. In Emily's album there is a Christmas and New Year greeting on a postcard from 'S J', possibly a governess who had been with the Grand Duchesses in Friedberg, with a photo of the new Livadia dated 1911. Apart from the greetings, the writer says that all the children are well and she is glad that they will soon be returning to Tsarskoe because she wants to be home in Moscow for Christmas. It is recorded that Nicholas and Alix spent time in their new palace in 1911 and that they were thrilled with the place. Nicholas wrote of his first impressions to his mother:

> We don't find words to express our joy and pleasure of having such a house, built exactly as we wished. The architect Krasnov is a remarkable stalwart – just think that during 16 months he built the palace, a big suite-house and a new kitchen. What is more, he has wonderfully laid out and decorated the garden all around the new buildings with our excellent gardener, so that this part of Livadia had gained much. The sights from every point are so nice, especially of Yalta and the sea. The rooms have a lot of light, and you remember how dark it was in the old house.

The family were able to enjoy the enchanting place three more times before the darkness of the 1914 war changed everything.

No such foreboding would have been in Emily's mind as she took her farewell of Alix the next day. The rest of the house party had gone off to the Frankfurt Zoo but Emily and Princess Thora had lunch with the Empress and no doubt expressed regrets at parting but anticipated meeting again before too long. 'The Empress gave me a beautiful amethyst pendant' wrote Emily and she promised to look for a bag for Alix in London. This was almost the first thing she and Thora did the next morning after they had arrived back at Schomberg House … 'to Asprey to choose a bag for the Empress'.

Princess Thora and Emily had enjoyed their holiday in Friedberg during the period between the death of Edward VII and the coronation of George V. King Edward died quite suddenly on May 6th 1910. Emily who was at the Cottage had telephoned the Princess that evening and had been told that the King 'was hopelessly ill'. Next morning Emily heard that he had died at 11.45 p.m. George, Prince of Wales, had become King. There are some touching letters between George V and Nicholas II. These two cousins were so very similar in appearance and possibly temperament; they both enjoyed country life and were keen shots. One lived in a relatively peaceful, established constitutional democracy – although politics in England was fairly volatile at the time – but the other, an autocrat, out of touch with his people, had been precipitated into a period of simmering revolutionary change which escalated beyond control. At the time of Edward VII's death they were sensitive to each others' predicament and sympathised deeply. Nicholas wrote to George as soon as he heard the news

> Dear Georgie,
> Just a few lines to tell you how deeply I feel for you and the terrible loss you and England have sustained. I know alas! by experience what it costs one. There you are with your heart bleeding and aching, but at the same time duty imposes itself and people and affairs come up and tear you away from your sorrow.

Later in May George replied

> My dearest Nicky,
> These three weeks have been terrible, my heart has been nearly breaking and at the same time I have had to carry on all my duties and bear my new responsibilities and see so many people to arrange all the last sad ceremonies and entertain William, 7 Kings and numerous Princes and Representatives from practically all the countries of the world.
> I saw Sir Arthur Nicolson today and he told me of all your kindness and sympathy which touched me deeply …

Clemmie's father Arthur Nicolson who became Lord Carnock had been in touch with both monarchs in his diplomatic capacity. This somehow brings the family closer to the tragedy. Emily was one of those able to be in St George's Chapel for the funeral service and she confirms that there was: 'A most enormous concourse of Foreign Emperors, Kings and Princes and attendants in brilliant uniforms. The service lasted about ¾ of an hour. I went after to see where Edward VII's coffin was lowered into the vault'. Her entry for May 20th ends:

> Fred Liddell came home from London. He had been on guard at Westminster Hall 3 days and nights and then walked by the coffin all the way in the Procession to Paddington.

Much that happened the following year was happier for all the Royal

Family. They were all involved in the celebrations: on May 16th, June 10th and June 22nd. Memories of Queen Victoria resurfaced in May when her great memorial which now stands outside the gates of Buckingham Palace was dedicated with due pomp and ceremony. Emily went with Lady Lugard to the Mall 'in the motor' and they were 'there a whole hour beforehand and were among everyone one knew. The ceremony was very grand. The German Emperor and Empress and all the royalties were there'. (It is interesting how the Kaiser always gets a special mention). Later that afternoon she visited 'Mrs. Bell to try on my dress for the coronation … very satisfactory', then to 'Sloane St to see about my coronation shoes at Gerretts'. She returned to the Cottage after all this royal gallivanting and ends the day with: 'Alice went to the council meeting'. The next day she was back to visiting the people in the cottages but was called away as her fluency in German was useful with so many foreign visitors at the Castle. Her life continued to be its mixture of royal and mundanely humdrum.

June 10 saw the great ceremony of the Investiture of Edward, Prince of Wales, with the Order of the Garter. An ancient order and a very young Prince – Emily calls him 'the little Prince of Wales'! She and Gerry had tickets for the service with seats in the nave of St George's Chapel but Sir Walter Parratt the organist took them to the organ loft so they had a splendid bird's eye view.

> It was the most lovely sight. All the Knights, the Princes and King and Queen and Officers of State walked from the Castle after the Installation to the Chapel for the service and sat in the choir in their own stalls in their full robes, the Queen in hers. A beautiful service.

Once again Emily has pasted a cutting from *The Times* into her album. It goes into great detail and gives a vivid picture of the occasion. It noted all who took part in the procession and, among the Royal Knights, it lists Prince Christian of Schleswig-Holstein. So he was well enough to take part; his health had not been very good in recent years and he was getting to be an old man.

There was quite a build-up of excitement for June 22. Emily and Gerry were in London the day before; and Gerry, whose arrangements never have the precision of Emily's, at the last moment had her 'plans all altered and she is going into the Abbey and many arrangements to be made accordingly'. Is there a slight air of exasperation? Emily, however, had a quiet evening and Nellie her lady's maid was able to try her 'hair arrangement for tomorrow'. She had to be up very early next morning, 5.45, and had great difficulty getting to Schomberg House through the masses of traffic.

> Had breakfast at eight. Went to the Abbey by ¼ to nine. Waited in the annexe talking to masses of people. Formed up when our Princesses came. I had a very bad seat but Major Martin kindly gave me his next to Mrs D C [another of Princess Christian's ladies-in-waiting] where I saw beautifully. It was a most beautiful and impressive sight and service done by the Archbishop [Randall Davidson]. A sermon by Archbishop of York [Lang]. King George and Queen Mary were everything one could wish. It was over by 2.30. It took some time for everyone to get away. I went back with to Schomberg House and had food by 3.30. All the guests left then. Pss Louie brought me back.

The next day they watched the processions through London and among other spectacles saw the King and Queen in an open carriage drawn by six cream-coloured horses. In the afternoon on the spur of the moment Emily with some of the Liddell family went to the Horse Show at Olympia. In the evening back at the Cottage she found Alice rushing off to present prizes and 'went down to see Mrs Paterson after dinner'. Mrs Paterson was one of Emily's perennial problems. She had some years before been a resident in one of the Loch's cottages, had gone off to London and got into financial difficulties – Emily among other things had had to write to a pawnbroker. A spell in a Home of some sort in Devon had brought some respite for Emily but now in 1911 Mrs Paterson was back in one of the cottages again. Emily certainly spent as much time trying to sort out Mrs. Paterson's affairs as she did for the Princess or for any of her more intimate friends such as the Liddell family.

Her duties as a lady-in-waiting meant that, for at least two to three months each year, Emily was with the Christian family; more and more of her time was spent with Princess Thora. She did, however, continue to accompany Princess Christian from time to time escorting her to meetings in London as she had done for many years and occasionally going with her to something really special. October 9th 1911 was one of these days. The Princess had been honoured by being asked to launch the new battleship, the *King George V*. There are photographs in the album showing the enormous hull on the stays, the mighty vessel gliding down the ways, the crowd around the Princess as she launches the ship and the great battleship sailing far off into the misty distance, attended by her tugs. Emily was clearly most impressed. She wrote:

> Left Claremont for Portsmouth. Pss Christian, Pss Victoria [as she now often calls Thora]. Capt Hankey and I went by train from Esher and arrived at 11 o'C. Met by Admirals Sir William Moore and Tait with motors. Went to the Dockyard and straight to the launching 'Booth' where there were crowds of people. The huge ship – Dreadnought *King George V*. There was short religious service and then the Princess christened her after which the blocks were knocked away by hundreds of men – then they were called out; the Princess severed the cords with chizel [sic] and hammer – the weights dropt and almost the same second the huge ship moved and slid down into the sea. It was wonderful.

They went back to Claremont[135] that night but the next afternoon they motored to Frogmore. 'Tidied and unpacked. The maids had come over in the

Frogmore from across the Lake, Princess Christian's home for some of 1911-13.

morning. Mr Forrest came to see the Pses after tea about the C Lodge plans, which they approved'.

What had been happening? In 1911 it was decided that the Princess's home, Cumberland Lodge, should be wired for electric light to replace the old gas system. As so often happens once the fabric was uncovered it was found that much more needed to be done. The old building was found to be riddled with dry rot and was deemed a great fire risk as there was so much dry and rotting timber. It was decided to rebuild the inside of the house at an estimated cost of £10,000 and the family was asked to move out. This was why, when the Princess returned from Portsmouth that evening, they went to Frogmore – which had once again become the Christian family home. They expected to be able to return to Cumberland Lodge after a year and thought they would have it as their home for the Princess's lifetime; by November 1912, however, rumours were beginning to circulate that this was not to be. In considerable distress, Emily wrote to Lord Stamfordham George V's private secretary saying:

> It has just come to my ears that the London authorities – Woods & Forests or Board of Works, I don't know exactly which – consider they are re building Cumberland Lodge for some other

The long room opening on to the garden at Frogmore as it was when Princess Christian was living there in 1911-13.

Royalty, presumably the Duke of Teck,[136] & as they consider that Prince Christian has not much longer to live!! That a double change would be irksome to them.

My object in writing to you is this. If the King or other less high Personages do not intend Princess Christian to stay on there after the Prince's death (be that near or far off) I think some thing ought to be found out & that they ought to know. It would come with a truly dreadful shock if it burst upon them when that sad event takes place. They are making their plans in re-furnishing & arranging what they believe to be their permanent home at Cumberland Lodge. Would it be possible to find out the King's pleasure & intention with regard to this – & either to silence the London office people – or to break it gently to my poor Princesses? Ys sincerely Emily E Loch

Emily's anguished appeal was quickly acted upon and within a few days she had a letter from Stamfordham confirming that:

When Cumberland Lodge is finished Prince & Princess Christian will occupy it and no one but HM himself has anything to do with the future occupancy of the house. The Woods and Forests or any other official Body had better save themselves the trouble of making arrangements about what, HM holds, does not concern them. The King was so glad to hear that Prince Christian was better.

A final letter from Emily on this matter does show how some of the confusion may have arisen. Some years previously, Princess Christian, who had little financial understanding, had become worried by 'ways & means'. She had thought that it would be more economical for her to give up Cumberland Lodge and have a smaller country residence after the Prince's death. It was however pointed out to Princess Thora who was party to these discussions that there would be many costs attached to living in a privately-purchased house whereas these were in the case of Cumberland Lodge met by the Crown. It appears that in 1912, unknown to Emily, Princess Thora had been directly in touch with the King. So one way and another King George V settled the matter satisfactorily for the Christian family. They were able to have

Cumberland Lodge which Princess Christian looked upon with affection as home for her lifetime.

The illness of Prince Christian which had given rise to all this anxiety had first begun some years before and had stimulated the Prince to set some of his affairs in order. In the autumn of 1906 while in Germany he met one of Emily's cousins, David Loch. In his diary, David noted for October 7th: 'Pc C very pleasant and quite ordinary'. The Prince evidently liked David sufficiently to invite him to join the Household at Cumberland Lodge and help the Prince sort out his papers. David arrived on January 1st, found that the family were 'all very nice and not in the least stiff and formal', and that the papers were in 'fearful confusion'. He was at Cumberland Lodge most of the early part of 1907 and by May was able to write in his diary, in German, 'have brought in order the papers about Princess Louise's divorce from Prince Aribert of Anhalt. A sad story. A[ribert] most tricky. Must have been a fine fellow!' David's note goes on to say that the Prince told him about some scandal which had been hushed up concerning anonymous letters, a Herr Gunter and various accusations – all unresolved.[137] The entry ends with a conversation held a short while later, concerning what should be done with the papers after the Prince's death. The Prince said: 'All those concerning Princess Louise are to go to her. The Princess (Christian) says I should leave the rest to Princess V. At all events they are never to go to Ernst Gunther or Prussia'. And so the matter ended.

David appears to have got on very well with the family; Princess Christian wrote to several people including Lord Burnham of the *Daily Telegraph* to try to help David to get a job – he wanted to be a journalist and did eventually, although warned against it as a career by Valentine Chirol. He rode with the Prince in the Park and noted that the Garth was the Prince's hunt and accompanied the Prince to meetings including one in London at which 'HRH made a very successful speech about hogging and docking'. David frequently played golf with Princess Thora and occasionally Emily helped to make up a foursome. The family gave him presents when he left Cumberland Lodge in August But he came back in the autumn when 'the Prince [was] very seedy in bed and I moved papers from PA room', and Emily notes that he 'did a letter' for the Prince on November 1st. After this, David came back for short visits and went over to see the Prince whenever he, David, was staying at the Cottage.

For much of 1907 the Prince had been in good health. On April 10th of that year he celebrated his 50th day out hunting in one season – the first time he had achieved this – and was very pleased with himself. He frightened the Princess and Emily that evening as he did not return until 8 o'clock … no doubt he had been celebrating. Despite being seventy-six, the Prince continued his programme of country pursuits and visits to Germany as he had done for many years but, by April 1908, Emily recorded that he was 'not well with a severe liver chill'. He recovered fairly quickly and there is no mention of his health again until Princess Thora and Emily returned from a lively visit to Lord Beauchamp near Malvern at the end of September that year. Princess Christian was abroad but Prince Abby had just come over from Germany. Thora and Emily arrived at Cumberland Lodge to find the Prince ill in bed where he had evidently been for some time. Dr Barron was in charge of the patient and as soon as they arrived back Emily telephoned him 'and he came to see Pss Thora and tell her what he thinks.' There is an almost daily record of the Prince's health; sometimes, usually after a good night, 'the Prince is better' and then there is a setback and he is again in pain. Another nurse was engaged in early October and Dr Barron brought in another doctor for a second opinion on the 8th. They prescribed 'thin food' and the Prince was to remain in bed for a fortnight. Two days later, at last, the Princess returned from abroad, unannounced to the Prince, and stole in secretly 'at ¼ to 1 in the morning,

The Schloss at Glücksburg one of the houses in Schleswig Holstein where Prince Christian lived as a child and which Emily visited in 1886.

terribly tired … and not a sound was made.' The Prince remained in bed and the Princesses continued their normal occupations; Princess Christian going to various meetings, the Nursing Home and her friends and Thora playing golf almost every day, often at Sunningdale, and undertaking a number of engagements such as visiting a children's convalescent home and attending a League of Mercy meeting.

In late October 1908, the hunting season was about to begin and the Prince became agitated when he realised what he was missing. On the 24th, a cold but fine day, the Prince got up early and was ready to inspect the hounds which Mr Gosling brought round to Cumberland Lodge for him to see. On the first day of November, he was very worried because he wouldn't be fit to attend the opening meet of the season the next day, but he got better and two days later he and Princess Christian went out for a drive. A week later the two princesses accompanied him in a carriage to the meet at Wentworth. As 1908 drew to a close he seemed to be on the mend; but the improvement did not last. By the time Emily was back with the family in March 1909 the Prince was again suffering pain and sickness and Princess Thora was getting very agitated. Again he recovered and was sufficiently well by November to be out with the Hunt and enjoyed a 'splendid gallop'. In December he was shooting with King George although it made him very tired.

From the time when Emily and Thora came back from Malvern, Emily was seeing much more of the Prince and getting to know him much better. There are many entries noting 'sat with the Prince'. Sometimes he was 'very cheerful and talky'.

In later years she drew on her recollections of how:

She had sat with him after dinner one October evening, by the flickering light of the fire. She had shown him the pretty brooch he had given her back in 1886 when she had accompanied him, the Princess and Prince Christle on their nostalgic visit to his old home in Schleswig-Holstein. The brooch with its flowers of horse chestnut set his memory off and he recalled the pleasure of seeing 'old Cille', his nurse from the far off days, when he had been a little boy running about the long corridors of the great houses: Gravenstein, his home, standing by the lake; Augustenburg with its great courtyard and hundreds of windows and the exciting towers and turrets of the Schloss of Glucksburg. He remembered climbing up and looking out of the windows high up in the towers and seeing the boats on the lake and watching the storks on their nests among the chimney pots. He remembered how they had all sat in the Princess's room when she was ill soon after they arrived and how he had told Prince Christle of the wonderful life that had been his family's before the war with Prussia. How Bismarck and Prussia had seized the land and castles from Denmark and turned his family into landless wanderers.

Together they recalled the greeting that had been given him when they got out of the train from Hamburg and into a steamer accompanied by officials and an old man of over 90 who had known Prince Christian's father. How pleased everyone was to see him again! How, when they arrived at Gravenstein, they had been greeted with salvos of cannon-fire. How gentlemen in white ties, white gloves and evening clothes had welcomed them at two in the afternoon. There had been speeches and applause, and little girls in white dresses and flowers everywhere. Oh yes! And there had been fireworks in the evening; the bursts of many coloured lights reflected in the calm waters of the lake. And there had been singing – all the old songs from his childhood.

"And you told me of your family's history," Emily reminded him.

"And I had a wonderful time watching the country people arriving by boat and carts with their children and dogs for the Fair held near the castle. One day I wandered off by myself when the poor Princess had to keep to her bed and collected the most delicious blackberries. Poor Princess! She had such horrible neuralgia[138] *while she was there; and do you remember the evening when a Doctor from Flensburg had to be sent for and we treated her with mustard leaves?"*

On our way back we visited Princess Calma[139] *and saw her tiny baby. And then we visited the Schröder's*[140] *wonderful farm near Hamburg. It all seems so far off now ... the flames flickered on the walls ... the Prince dozed off in a cloud of old memories.*

As the century moved on the Prince's health continued to be worrying: sometimes he was well, sometimes confined to bed. In Emily's album there is a photo of him looking frail, wrapped in a thick winter coat in front of Frogmore, probably in 1912 – 13. Later, in a 1913 photo, he is up on horseback again, as well-seated as ever. The background looks like the stables of Cumberland Lodge. So they got back to their old home.

The outbreak of the war in 1914 must have been a terrible time for almost all the royal family; and for those such as the Christians who had their nearest relatives on different sides of the conflict it must all have seemed so senseless and almost unbearable. The diary entries give some idea of the build-up of tension; previously international politics had only been mentioned once or twice – Emily and the Linde family had had long discussions as early as 1908 about the relations between England and Germany. But it wasn't until July 27th 1914 that Princess Christian sent for Emily saying that their plans were all upset and they wouldn't be able to go abroad because of the war scare. In the next few days the Princess was over at the Cottage almost every evening to discuss the situation. Fred Liddell found the Stock Exchange shut on August 31st – 'a thing never known in English history before' wrote Emily rather dramatically. That evening all those at Cumberland Lodge were anxious and unhappy about the war news 'which is very serious'. Two days later Emily wrote 'the cabinet was divided about the advisability of England going to war. It will be horrible if we shirk. Germany has declared war and France is mobilising'. Emily was called into Cumberland Lodge in place of Dorothy Seymour, Fred Liddell was summoned back from Ireland, where he had just gone, to take on the Cumberland Lodge business, Baron and Baroness Schröder came to the Cottage the day war was declared (August 4/5), and 'were very unhappy about their boy and everything.' It wasn't until the 14th August that a way of getting letters to Prince Abby in Berlin was found. England declared war on Austria on August 12th, and on the 15th the Austrian Embassy was closing, so Count Mensdorff 'would take some letters over.'

As the reality sank in to those at Cumberland Lodge, they each responded in their own way. Emily became even busier writing letters and got drawn in more closely with the domestic business of the Lodge; later she ran a recreational 'Hut' for the troops in the Park causing her daily wrestling with the accounts. The Princess was immediately occupied in meetings about nurses, hospitals and medical supplies. Princess Thora became deeply involved in the affairs of the YMCA, the League of Mercy, and Soldier and Sailor Welfare Societies. Patriotism was in the air and the battles were closely followed. The mounting lists of casualties brought the horror close to home. On August 6th, 'the pses were at Farnborough with the Empress [Eugènie] to see Prince Maurice before he leaves for the war' and, on September 28th, the Epitome tells us that he was killed. The same day Freddy Bemelmans the son of Clemmie Nicolson, Emily's cousin, was also killed. The weariness had not set in, but the slaughter was beginning on both sides. Prince Abby remained in the German army. Grand Duke Ernie was deeply unhappy – as he mentioned in a letter to his sister Alix.

One event brightened those dark days. On July 5th 1916 Prince Christian and the Princess celebrated their Golden wedding. This was the first in the Royal Family since 1811. To welcome in the New Year that year the Prince gave Emily a delightful photograph of himself and his horse and dog ... 'the three friends'. Perhaps this shows the Prince at his most natural and contented.

New Year greetings to Emily for 1916 from Prince Christian
with his 'friends', his horse and his dog.

He and Princess Christian had had a long marriage. Each had their own interests; each had their own friends and companions but each respected and needed the other. On July 5th that year there was a thanksgiving service in the Park Chapel and a modest luncheon for sixteen – of which Emily was one – at Cumberland Lodge. In the afternoon a special messenger arrived to present the Princess with the gold medal of the British Red Cross Society, and Queen Mary and George V drove to Cumberland Lodge to congratulate his aunt and uncle. The Prince was looking well despite his eighty-five years.

He continued well throughout much of the following year but in the autumn although he still managed to get out shooting – on September 14th he got a stag, his last – it seems that he had nurses at night. Most of his outings were in the carriage, once or twice with Emily 'all through the Forest which was lovely', once with Princess Louie to do 'parish work', and frequently with the Princess. Near the end of September they went out for a quick turn in the Park before lunch and got involved with a mock battle between the Life Guards and the Coldstreams. Their horse became very frightened and nearly overturned the carriage and the Princess had to get out and implore them to stop; refuge was found for the Prince in a neighbouring house until all was

Park Chapel in Windsor Great Park near Cumberland Lodge where the Christian family and Emily attended Sunday services for many years and where Prince and Princess Christian held a thanksgiving service for their golden wedding anniversary on July 5 1916.

quiet. On October 10th the princesses and Emily moved to Schomberg House; Fred Liddell brought the Prince up the next day. By now his health really was giving serious cause for concern, often with bad nights. On the 20th he was better but had a disturbed night, not surprisingly as there was an air raid on London and a bomb fell in Piccadilly Circus. Other doctors were called in and one decided to sleep in the house. All these changes were very upsetting for the Prince and on October 22nd Emily was compelled to write to the Sub-dean of the Chapel Royal, the Reverend Canon Edgar Sheppard who was a friend of the Prince and had often visited him:

> Dear Pop,
> Could you come up tomorrow morning? Princess Christian is so anxious to see you & for you to see the Prince. He is not at all well & they are all very worried about him. He is really not well but in addition he insists that he is going to die because they would bring him to London. He always said it would be so & therefore he intends to die! This is a despairing frame of mind & the Princesses think that if you could influence 'mind over

> matter' they would be so grateful.
> The Doctor is to sleep in the house & they are to have three nurses now – & altogether it is very disturbing & yet they say the condition lies a great deal in his own hands.
> Could you come tomorrow about 11.30 as the Prince would be 'see-able' in the morning & Pss Christian also wants to see you & will you have luncheon here at 1.30.
> In haste for post,
> Yrs affect
> Emily E Loch
> Could you telephone through the Castle?

And then, written across the letter, 'of course no one knows they are anxious about the Prince'.

Whether the doctors were wrong and only the Prince was right will never be known. Pop duly came – and he thought the Prince was very ill. But by the 27th although he seemed better in the morning, 'he had a failure in the afternoon and took leave of them all'. He lingered on until the next day; Princess Thora sat with him nearly all the time, holding his hand. In the late afternoon the Sub-dean was fetched just in time to pray for him and bless him. 'We all stayed there till the last'.

The usual rush of people, letters and condolences filled their next few days. The Princess rallied wonderfully. The Prince's body was taken back to Frogmore where the Canadians kept vigil for the last night. The next day the cortège set out for St George's Chapel with the coffin on a gun carriage and pall bearers on each side.

> Fred Liddell carried the Prince's crown and Colonel Hankey the insignia. The princesses and we in waiting followed in two carriages. The foresters, Mr Forrest and Mr Lloyd completing the procession. Nearly 5000 troops: Coldstreams, Lifeguards, Household Brigade, Canadians, 60th Rifles. The King met the procession at the entrance to the town and joined in the walking to St George's Chapel. It was a most beautiful service arranged by the Prince himself … the congregation included the Prince's own friends, servants, Park people and children according to his wish.

The Prince was back in Windsor and near the Great Park where he had had so many wonderful days and which had been so important to him during his lifetime.

This Prince, who had seemed so dull to Queen Victoria's children back in the 1860s; who came from a family which had suffered much from the Prussians in the past, whose surviving son was separated from him by the war, had far outlived many of his detractors. He had gained the affection of the people of Windsor. The Ranger appointed by Queen Victoria in 1866 departed: another player on the Victorian stage had made his exit.

CHAPTER TWENTY

Revolution and Evolution

In 1921, Pierre Gilliard published his memoir of the thirteen years he spent at the Court in St Petersburg with the family of Nicholas and Alexandra. His book became one of Emily's most treasured possessions. Over the years, particularly since the happy holiday she and Princess Thora had spent with the Russian Imperial family in Friedberg, she had had some correspondence and exchange of small presents with Alix, Olga and Tatiana. She had put away the pretty cards they had sent her for 'Xmas' and New Year – Tatiana particularly wanted to see Emily again (Plate 10). At first these would have been just charming reminders of the family kept in a bundle in her desk, expecting to see the family either in England or Germany before too long. As war clouds gathered and the storm finally broke, their significance became greater: but still, in the early days of the war, she probably thought all would settle down after the conflict and travel between the countries would resume. At least Russia and Britain were on the same side even if the festering wound of Germany was ever present. Gradually she must have become aware of the great unrest in Russia, especially after March 1917. How much she was aware of what was happening to Nicholas and his family, then and during the next 15 months, is unknown – but probably very little. Since then, those months have been assiduously studied and we who know what the end was to be, are still appalled by the events at Ekaterinburg. For those who knew and loved the Emperor, Empress and all their family, at the time, the news of July 16th 1918 must have come as an unbelievable bolt from the blue. How much more precious the little cards and letters would have become to her.

When she began to look back on her life in the late 1920s and drew up her 'Epitome', Emily also collected the cards and letters together and pasted them into the back of Gilliard's book together with a couple of prayer poems from a copybook once in the possession of Grand Duchess Olga at Ekaterinburg.

It is clear from the condition of the book that Emily read it many times. Gilliard gives an interesting and intimate insight into the life of the Imperial

Family. He had come first, in 1905, as the French teacher for Olga and Tatiana, having spent some time teaching in the family of one of Nicholas's cousins, the Leuchtenbergs. It was this family that had looked after Tora when Alix succumbed to measles in 1898. At first Alexandra accompanied the two little girls to their lessons – Pierre Gilliard remarks that during the very first lesson he felt that it was he who was being examined. After a few months, however, Princess Obolensky, Emily's friend from 1898, came instead of the Empress. Gilliard felt more relaxed with her but the Empress continued to keep a very close eye on the lessons. He was astonished to find that instead of the haughty, cold person that he had been led to expect Alexandra was just a mother devoted to her family and determined to play an important role in their upbringing.

It was in February 1906 that Alexandra brought the 18-month old Alexei for Gilliard to meet for the first time. He was deeply moved by her pride and happiness with her beautiful baby son but he also noted her anxiety and fear for the life of her little boy. As the years went by the younger Grand Duchesses joined the French classes. Gilliard then began to realise how much the happiness of the whole family depended on the state of Alexei's health. Only very gradually did he learn that the boy had haemophilia and suffered terribly from pain and fever whenever a haemorrhage occurred. The illnesses were never spoken about by the mother or father. Gilliard gives a vivid and moving account of how, on one occasion when the child was in fearful pain and with a high temperature, the Empress, because there were guests, carried on as if nothing was happening. But then he saw her escape down the corridor, her face contorted with anguish, and rush to comfort her suffering child. There was little that the doctors could do and the Empress began to put her faith more and more in the mystical healing powers of Rasputin.

Gilliard gives a description of perhaps the last really happy, carefree day that Nicholas was able to enjoy with his son. This was in May 1914 when the family was staying at Livadia. The weather was brilliant, Alexei's health was good, there was snow on the mountains and there was time. It was decided that the 8th of May should be the day for an expedition to go up the 'Pierre Rouge' on Mount Jaïla. A small party set off in two cars. The Emperor, Alexei, Gilliard and an officer from the Standart in one; the ever present Derevenko and a cossack in the other. They passed through magnificent pine forests and out on to grasslands where snow still lay in great drifts. Alexei was able to run, slide and roll in the glittering snow and for once allow full play to his natural boyish spirits; and he had a ready companion in his father. Even then, however, caution could not be forgotten and Gilliard realised that, although Nicholas never spoke of his son's illness, it was something which never left him. But this expedition, devoted to his son's happiness, was one of the rare occasions on which Nicholas was able to behave as a simple mortal: he became relaxed and refreshed.

By 1914, Olga was nineteen years old and no doubt the age-old routine was being put into practice once again: finding a suitable husband for the hand of the eldest daughter of the Tsar. In June, rumours were beginning to circulate that Grand Duchess Olga Nicholaievna was to be betrothed to Prince Carol of Roumania. Olga herself had not been told this officially and her father had said that she would not be forced into a marriage she didn't like. One day she cornered Pierre Gilliard alone and asked him to tell her the truth and reluctantly he nodded assent that a marriage was contemplated. To which she replied that she did not want that and she did not want to leave Russia. When he pointed out that she would be able to return home whenever she wanted, she said that this marriage would make her a stranger in her own country. Firmly she concluded '*Je suis russe et veux rester russe*'! Her feelings were quite clear. Russia and the unity of the family meant more than anything.

After a polite visit by sea to Constanz, where the family were entertained for one day by King Ferdinand and Queen Marie, daughter of Alfred, Duke of Edinburgh, the Russians moved on to Odessa and the idea of the marriage was postponed. Olga had got her way. As Gilliard points out in a footnote: if she had been married, she would have escaped her terrible fate.

Excerpts from Emily's diary gave an idea of how the build-up to the First World War affected the family at Cumberland Lodge. From July 29th onwards the events seemed to be on a different level. It was no longer going to be a conflict between a couple of countries in some remote part of the world but 'there was grave apprehension about a universal war.' From then on, she felt that the situation was much more serious. And she was right. After Austria sent an ultimatum to Serbia late on July 24th – a month after the assassination of Archduke Francis Ferdinand, heir to the Austrian throne – the Russian government, determined to back Serbia, tried a policy of conciliation but the newspapers became more and more violent in their condemnation of Austria's behaviour and, despite telegrams flying east and west and many anxious discussions among statesmen, Germany declared war on Russia on August 1st. There is a list of the dates of the various declarations of war in the diary: first Germany on Russia, then Germany on France, Great Britain on Germany,

France on Austria, Great Britain on Austria and, on August 23rd Japan on Germany. It was indeed a universal war. The European countries were embarking on the general war they had been studiously avoiding for 99 years. What a changed world would emerge and the changes would be most marked in Russia.

Emily's immediate concerns at the end of July were getting a passport for a Miss Hennery who had just come to stay, discussing what was happening to the people she and the princesses knew in Germany and helping Princess Christian with her nursing and Red Cross matters. How the Imperial family in Russia was faring, however, cannot have been far from her thoughts. She had become deeply interested in what went on there and had developed a love for things Russian; by coincidence on July 23rd and 24th she had been to two Russian operas. She ends the entry for July 24th by remarking that the applause was most enthusiastic for the orchestra and in particular for the conductor.

It was as people, rather simple unpretentious people in their daily lives, that Emily knew the Russian Imperial Family. Nevertheless her innate respect for and love of royalty probably played its part. She had seen Nicholas quite frequently in his gentle family role but, during her stay in Russia she had, on several occasions such as the Blessing of the Waters and the great feast of St George, seen him in his imperial role, as Tsar of all the Russias.

The French ambassador in St Petersburg during the tense days in late July 1914 was Maurice Paléologue. He was unusually close to Nicholas. The President of France had just paid a successful State visit and France and Russia were bound by Treaty to assist each other in cases of aggression. France was Russia's ally when Germany declared war on her. For these reasons, Paléologue was the only foreigner invited to attend the Tsar's proclamation to his people on August 2nd. The Ambassador in his memoirs gives a dramatic and moving account of the occasion.

> It was a majestic spectacle. Five or six thousand people were assembled in the huge St George's gallery which runs the length of the Neva quay. The whole court was in full-dress and all the garrison were in field dress. In the centre of the room an altar was placed and on it was the miraculous ikon of the Virgin of Kazan.... In the tense, religious silence, the imperial cortège crossed the gallery and took up station on the left of the altar. The Tsar asked me to stand opposite to him as he desired, so he

said, "to do public homage in this way to the loyalty of the French ally."

Mass began at once to the accompaniment of the noble and pathetic chants of the orthodox liturgy. Nicholas II prayed with a holy fervour which gave his pale face a moving mystical expression. The Tsaritsa Alexandra Feodorovna stood beside him, gazing fixedly, her chest thrust forward, head high, lips crimson, eyes glassy. Every now and them she closed her eyes and then her livid face reminded one of a death mask.

After the final prayers the court chaplain read the Tsar's manifesto to his people – a simple recital of the events which have made war inevitable, an eloquent appeal to all the national energies, an invocation to the Most High, and so forth. Then the Tsar went up to the altar and raised his right hand toward the gospel held out to him. He became even more grave and composed, as if he were about to receive the sacrament. In a slow, low voice which dwelt on every word he made the following declaration:

"Officers of my guard, here present, I greet in you my whole army and give it my blessing. I solemnly swear that I will never make peace so long as one of the enemy is on the soil of the fatherland."

This was followed by ten minutes of wild cheering in the hall which was taken up by the crowds along the Neva. In the Winter Palace square there was 'an enormous crowd with flags, banners, ikons and portraits of the Tsar.' When the Emperor appeared on the balcony the entire crowd at once knelt and sang the Russian National Anthem. As Paléologue says:

to those thousands of men on their knees at that moment the Tsar was really the autocrat appointed by God, the military, political and religious leader of his people, the absolute master of their bodies and souls.

Soon after the beginning of the war, Emily began to note each day in her diary the events in Belgium, France and Russia and the naval battles. The information was probably gleaned from Cumberland Lodge; for example on August 13th she had:

> heard of the battle of Haelen in which the Belgians repulsed the Germans. Mr Lamdin, [the steward at Cumberland Lodge] spoke on the telephone that there had been a cavalry encounter between British and Germans but no result known. Also through the American ambassadors in Berlin, Copenhagen and England that Prince Albert was safe and well in Berlin.

Her reports are very patriotic and possibly rather sceptical about the French 'More French successes announced – if true' for August 14th. But on September 1st she was more gullible. 'Heard on eye-witness authority that the Russians had passed through Scotland and England on to France and were at Havre, we having conveyed them from Archangel in 5 days.' On the 3rd, a single line: 'A big Russian victory over the Austrians'. So continue the short notes: the swinging to and fro of the battles, the fall of Antwerp, the sweep towards Paris, and the encounters between the German and British Fleets. Increasingly, however, she becomes more and more aware of the terrible loss of life. By October 12th: 'Desperate fighting – but it is believed that the Germans are weakening. Frightful slaughter on both sides.' Her war note for September 22nd begins:

> News of Naval disaster. Three of our cruisers the *Hogue*, the *Crecy* and the *Aboukir* sunk this morning by German submarines. It is hoped a good many saved ... Ned Bouverie on the *Hogue* but saved and landed in Holland.

On October 29th, as noted in the last chapter, Freddie Bemelmans and Prince Maurice were killed, the latter dying from wounds received in the retreat from Mons. The next day she reports another victim of the war – not death this time but reputation. The indiscriminate tarring of anyone of German origin and with a German name had forced

> Prince Louis of Battenberg to resign and Lord Fisher appointed in his stead. All the papers full of praise of Pc Louis for sacrificing himself to the good of the country. Lord Fisher is 73 years old.

Three days later, she noted that the chief of staff at the Admiralty had also resigned as he would not work with Lord Fisher. One can sense Emily's astonishment and dismay at these announcements. She knew Prince Louis' wife, Victoria, well and quite often had long talks with her; she had stayed in Prince Louis' home, Heiligenberg, during her visits to Germany.

'The hysteria which gripped the country in the early days of the war, much encouraged by the sensational papers and magazines against anyone with connections with Germany was one of the blackest pages in our history'. Such was the assessment of Violet Asquith in later years; at the time her father was the Prime Minister. The apparently indestructible power of the German armies and their many successes at sea sinking so many British ships in which this country took such pride and which were thought to be invincible, made people in all ranks of society turn on those who had any connections with the enemy. Emily does not overtly mention this in regard to the Christian family. Perhaps this was because the family were little known in the country and kept a low profile. Prince Christian had taken to heart the admonition given him during the 1870 war between Germany and France when he had wanted to go off and fight. The Queen, his mother-in-law, had firmly told him that he was a member of the English Royal Family now and his allegiance lay with England. Also, circumstances had made him have his home in this country although he travelled nearly every year to Germany. Even so, some of his personal income came from Germany: Fred Liddell in the early months of the war tried, unsuccessfully, to get money out for the Prince. But, as far as the diaries go, the Christian family did not suffer from the hysteria. The Battenbergs were not so fortunate.

Prince Louis Battenberg held the highest office in the British Navy as First Sea Lord, but he still retained his home in Germany and, until hostilities broke out, still had close links with that country. Despite his obvious loyalty to the Service in which he had made his career, he became a target for malicious rumours. Public opinion, desperate at the disastrous loss of warships during the first three months, needed someone to blame. It found a scapegoat in this senior officer with a German name. Winston Churchill, not the easiest of people to get on with, was his political master. Battenberg had worked successfully with him for over two years; together they had built up the Navy. When the hysterical campaign became impossible to ignore and Churchill's position as First Lord of the Admiralty was jeopardised, it was he who had the task of asking Prince Louis to resign. According to his letters to Prince Louis he, Churchill, much regretted it. He delivered the ultimatum on the very day when the Prince heard of the death of his nephew, Prince Maurice. The Battenberg family were loyal in their service to Britain. Churchill's request for his resignation hit Prince Louis when he had had many months of severely hard work and was suffering from the after effects of gout. He was utterly shattered by the request but acquiesced with great dignity and, as Emily remarked in her diary, all the newspapers were full of praise for Prince Louis sacrificing himself for the good of the country.

Throughout the autumn Emily kept up the war notes. On several occasions there are 'Russian victories', then repulses, 'then Russia and Germany preparing a desperate struggle in Silesia', 'great battle impending in Poland, 'rumours of a tremendous Russian victory in Poland', 'Russian success still firmly rumoured', 'curious silence about war news', 'they say the Russian victory is sure', 'the Germans say they have taken Lodz', 'the German's taking Lodz most likely true but no real importance as it is an open town and can be avoided by the Russian army.' Next day 'Lodz capture confirmed. Great rejoicings in Berlin. Russians don't seem to mind as strategically they can manage better round another way; it is a large, open and unfortified town and so of no military use', 'the Russians successful in Poland. Very little news from Belgium.' Several days have 'no war news', and the year ends with 'Polish news good'. The tragedy of the terrible losses, the prevalence of rumours and the use of 'spin' by the authorities are all there.

It is perhaps as well that Emily had other matters to fill her time. Visiting the wounded with Princess Christian in the hospitals that sprang up in many big houses, and running the YMCA hut on Smith's Lawn. The laundry had expanded considerably needing staff, coke for the furnace, a delivery van – one tried had a gas balloon on its roof – and weekly bills to the customers. The grounds of the Cottage were enlarged into a small farm with poultry, cows and pigs. It was a move towards self-sufficiency. Food was becoming very scarce, particularly after the chilling announcement from Germany in January 1917 to neutrals 'of a policy of unrestricted naval warfare from February 1st; all sea traffic to be prevented in wide zones around Great Britain, France, Italy and the eastern Mediterranean'. So the crops of vegetables, the cows and their calving, the number of piglets in a litter and the state of the beehives all became matters of importance. All these undertakings not only filled her days but they all required constant keeping of accounts. Almost every evening Emily did some account or other.

The Liddell family are frequently mentioned. Since the death of Shem in 1901, Emily had acted as a surrogate aunt culminating in the Loch sisters altering the Cottage and part of the laundry into a house for Fred and his three boys. The boys in 1914 were now young men and Emily was deeply interested in their enlistment. David the eldest and Guy the youngest joined as ordinary 'Tommies' soon after the declaration of war but, during 1915, they both obtained their commissions and were joined by Cecil who had previously been in the Diplomatic Service. So by July 1915 Emily was able to write 'All three Liddells in khaki.'

Her links with the Russian Imperial family were kept up. We have of course none of her cards and letters to them but there is evidence that these were sent and that sometimes small gifts were exchanged. Both Alix and the children sent cards for Xmas and New Year in 1912, 1913 and 1914 – the last from Livadia. There were Easter cards in 1914 and 1915, the first from Olga and the second from Olga and Tatiana (Plates 11-14). In January 1915 Alix found time to write a letter (Plate 8).

> Dearest Emily,
> Warmest thanks for your dear note. I was so pleased to receive it. Every word from a dear old friend warms the aching heart. I did not write to you for New Year as we were visiting hospitals all over Russia. And then I was put to bed again as my heart was in such a very bad state after the great fatigue. I still cannot recover and cannot work in the hospital. My friend Ania Wiroahoff (whom you saw at Friedberg) [more usually spelt Vyzubora] had terrible railway accident. She was buried under the smashed wagon – with great difficulty they got her out. The left leg is broken in 2 places and the cheek bone and the rest of the body much crushed. We took her to our hospital and is looked after by those with whom we worked all these months; all friends around her. I nursed her too the first three days and then once more heart so bad that must lie quietly. She needs looking after the whole time, rubbing her back, lifting the leg and so on, all things which I ought not to do, but when another has pain you crush under your own suffering – but such a weak heart will not let me do all I wish tho' my will is strong and kept me up (with much

> medicine) and above all trust in God. What times our dear countries are going through, such a mercy you are with us. Work is our saving. How much Thora also does. God bless you 1000 kisses fr. Yr. own Alix.

This short letter on pink paper was so precious to Emily. It told her much of what was happening to Alix. How she threw herself into her war work. Nursing the sick, actually doing the nursing herself, until her weakened body gave way. Her tenderness with Ania who had in fact been very difficult towards the end of 1914 when Nicholas was away with his troops. Ania had become over the years a clinging friend of Alix. It is reputed that it was through her that Rasputin first became such an influence over the Tsar and Tsarina. On her head fell much of the opprobium aimed at Alexandra. Some thought her a scheming woman: others considered her rather stupid and merely a vehicle, a go-between. Pierre Gilliard wrote:

> She became the Tsarina's lifelong confidante, and the kindness the Tsarina showed her made her her lifelong slave. Madame Vyrubova's temperament was sentimental and mystical, and her boundless affection for the Tsarina was a positive danger, because it was uncritical and divorced from any sense of reality ...... Madame had the mind of a child, and her unhappy experiences had sharpened her sensibilities without maturing her judgement.

Emily did not mention her in her accounts of the Wiesbaden visit but Ania had been there. It is possible that she is among those photographed in the group which visited Munsenberg that year.

It was later in 1915, September in fact, that Nicholas, against the judgement of many around him, assumed supreme command of his armies. Emily noted this in her diary. Paléologue in his memoirs gives a first hand account of how he heard of the Tsar's decision from Sasonov, the Russian Foreign Minister; first in non-commital official tones and then because they knew and trusted each other, Sasonov continued in confidence: 'I can certainly admit, *cher ami*, that I greatly regret the step the Emperor has just taken'. After saying that the reasons put forward by the ministers against this step at the beginning of the conflict are now even more relevant, as it would take months to reorganise the army and supply it with the means to fight successfully, Sasonov continued:

> Isn't it terrifying to think that henceforth it is the Emperor who will be personally responsible for all the misfortunes with which we are threatened? If the inefficiency of one our generals involves us in disaster, it will be not merely a military disaster but a political and social one at the same time.

Paléologue was intrigued to find out why the Tsar had taken this step and, after many enquiries, reached the conclusion that it was partly that he considered himself to be a sort of Christ who should shoulder all the troubles of his country and sacrifice himself, and partly persuasion on the part of Alexandra and Rasputin that it was his religious duty to put himself in supreme command. Anna Vyrubova said that Nicholas had told her that a scapegoat was needed to save Russia and that he would be that person. 'God's will be done.' An appeal to religion was the all powerful weapon which Rasputin used to influence the Empress and the weapon that she, in her turn, used to influence the Tsar in all his decisions.

From 1915 Emily's handwritten records of the battle events were replaced by short newspaper cuttings from the *War News*. Her own life had become more and more busy and there was only time to scribble down her daily record of her own concerns. Throughout 1915 she was desperately worried about her great friend Gerry who had a succession of serious illnesses and operations for the removal of gall-stones. Gerry was away for months on end in hospitals and nursing homes in London. She only returned to the Cottage just in time for Christmas in 1915.

There was a card from the four Grand Duchesses late that year, and another card of a winter scene with evening light in a snow-covered orchard brought Alix's wishes from Tsarskoe Selo (Plate 15). It was dated Nov. 24/Dec. 7, 1915. She wrote:

> Dearest Emily. I send you my warmest Xmas wishes and every blessing for 1916. God grant the New Year may bring this terrible war to a glorious end for the Allies. Have terrible much to do and then heart gets again worse and cannot work in the hospital. The emp and Alexei come off and on fr Headquarters front and from inspecting the troops. Ernie and Irène are well, our R sister saw them. An affectionate kiss fr. Yr loving Alexandra.

There are few notes in the diary about what was happening in Russia in 1916 but there is a card from Alix with a colourful picture of a hospital train in Russia sending best wishes for 1917 (Plate 16) and the rather despairing message:

> Dear Emily. I send you my best love and wishes for Xmas and New Year 1917. I think so much of you all and all dear old friends. Ones heart is so full of sorrow but faith in God's mercy keeps one up. A kiss fr. Alix

The last card in the collection, a winter woodland scene with two figures, is undated but it is pasted in after the one with New Year wishes for 1917 and so it was probably sent early that year. Emily had evidently been able to send a small present (Plate 15).

> Affectionate thanks dear Emily for yr. Sweet smelling Xmas present wh. it was most dear of you to have sent me. A loving kiss from the children and I send many kisses. Fr Alix.

This was the last time Emily heard from Alix.

Dorothy Seymour, mentioned in an earlier chapter, a very distant relative of Emily who had for a short time been a lady-in-waiting to Princess Christian, spent several months at the end of 1916 and the beginning of 1917 in St Petersburg or Petrograd as it was called by then. She has left a vivid account of those times most amusingly illustrated. Dorothy was working as a VAD in a Red Cross Hospital based in the palace of Grand Duke Dimitri Pavlovich – she has a minute sketch of him being taken away to imprisonment in December 1916 as he was implicated in the murder of Rasputin.[141]

Rumours about the death of Rasputin and the impending revolution were rife and continued unabated as the tensions in the city grew in the early months of 1917. It was during this time on February 4th that Dorothy was able to get down to Tsarskoe Selo for a short visit to Alexandra and Grand Duchess Olga. She found the 'Empress quite lovely, wonderfully graceful, lovely eyes and colouring, very human and a sense of humour'. 'Grand Duchess Olga in nurse's dress, pretty eyes, nice little thing, very pleasant and informal. Sat and talked for nearly two hours. Is evidently a pacifist, and War and its horrors on her nerves – whole room and place heavy with tragedy. Can believe anything of Rasputin's influence there'.

On more than one day Dorothy's diary records that the revolution is imminent, and for March 8th she has a page with the title 'Revolution begins'. Her sketches show the nursing staff, bread queues,[142] the Cossacks riding people down on the Nevsky and an officer's sword being taken from him and flung into the Fontanka (Plate 16). Despite orders to the contrary, she went out into the streets and saw the mobs surging hither and thither. She was in danger from the indiscriminate firing and she had to run the gauntlet of machine guns when trying to reach the nurses' home. She saw the people kneeling outside the Kazan Cathedral, imploring the Cossacks not to fire on them, the looting of the Astoria hotel and the murder of Baron Stachelberg. Their hospital was in the thick of street fighting and eventually the mob broke in.[143] The nurses were forced to treat their wounded and hand over twenty-five suits of clothing at the brandishing of a sword but they were also presented with bottles of looted wine. The place was in confusion, the Duma met, Ministers resigned. The regiments of Guards were too revolutionary, so the Cossacks were called in but by March 13th the last remnant of the Imperialist regime, isolated in the Winter Palace, gave in and the Revolutionaries formed a Government. There were plans to murder the Empress. 'No one knows where the Emperor is'. Muliakoff's announcement in the Duma that Alexei should be Emperor with a Regency was met with uproar. By March 15th, 'food getting very low, everyone at the Hotel Europe without food all yesterday'. And she had a very unpleasant twenty-four hours without food on the day the Tsar gave up his sword to the Army[144]. By the 18th the Red flag was hoisted over the Winter Palace and the Imperial emblems in the streets were destroyed. The Revolution had taken place.

The Red Cross some days earlier had ordered the closure of the hospital and dispersal of the patients. Then it was up to Dorothy and the other nurses to get out of the country – not an easy task when her passport had got lost in a Government office. Eventually on March 24th they were able to go. There is a final small sketch of the nurses laden with suitcases walking at 6.30a.m. to join the Ambassador's train bound for Sweden.

Meanwhile Alexandra had been kept in isolation, as a virtual prisoner at Tsarskoe Selo. After Nicholas abdicated, it was expected according to Dorothy that he would join her and the family there and wait for a chance to get out of the country. But it was not to be. He and his family began their long and uncertain period of imprisonment. This began in the relative comfort of the Alexander Palace and quite a large number of their household remained with them including Pierre Gilliard, Dr Botkin and Fräulein Schneider.

Emily's increasingly busy life went on. She makes no mention of the Imperial family until July 16 1918 when she pastes in the daily newspaper account with its bare last line, 'Ex-Tsar Nicholas II murdered'. It wasn't until she wrote the Epitome that she recorded the full horror. 'The Tsar Nicholas II, the Empress, Cesarewitch and all four Grand Duchesses, Olga, Tatiana, Marie and Anastasia murdered at Ekaterinberg.'

According to Princess Marie Louise's memoirs, the Christian family were told of the fate of Nicholas and his family by King George himself when he came to lunch at Cumberland Lodge. He didn't want the announcement to be made public until Thora, who was not at home, had been told. There were others who were intimately involved, none more so than Victoria of Battenberg the eldest of the Hesse sisters. She was staying in her house on the Isle of Wight. Marie Louise volunteered to take a letter from the King bearing the news as she was just about to go and stay with her cousin. When Victoria heard, the two cousins did not 'talk at great length about it at all there was so little one could say. The horror of this ghastly tragedy was too overwhelming for mere words, and just the ordinary expressions of condolence seemed utterly out of place.' Marie Louise stayed with Victoria for some time and the two princesses found solace in hard work: they spent the next three weeks gardening.

For most, the war dragged on to its weary end with some very worrying times and many more casualties. The Liddell brothers were back on French soil – always an anxiety for Fred, Gerry and Emily. But there were brighter moments. On January 23rd 1918 all four Liddells, the three boys, two of whom had been awarded the Military Cross, and Fred, who received a Royal Victorian Order, were decorated by George V. There was a tremendous bustle that dark, foggy morning to get all four Captains Liddell off to London for the investiture. Emily in her turn was awarded the MBE for her work with the YMCA huts.

This was a cause to which Princess Thora devoted much of her time. Sometimes Emily saw wider aspects of the YMCA when she went with the Princess on inspections of YMCA centres and huts in London, Aldershot and elsewhere. On the other hand, throughout 1916, 1917, and 1918, Emily with

The YMCA hut, one of many around the country where the soldiers and others on active service could enjoy refreshment and recreation. This was used by the Canadian Foresters at Egham

her friends from around Englefield Green worked almost every day in the YMCA hut on Smith's Lawn. Emily's talents at meticulous planning were invaluable. She and her helpers were 'at the coal face', preparing food and drinks for the men and providing parcels for those about to set off on long journeys to France. Her skills as a business woman were called upon when she set up a Savings Bank for the men. There were anxious times when withdrawals exceeded deposits but they usually balanced in the end. Arranging transport for helpers and entertainers was another perennial task. Princess Thora had done much to see that there was entertainment for the men in the evenings. Lecturers, concert parties or cinema films were arranged. Films were the most popular; these went well, provided the electricity generator worked. Emily was seventy years old by 1918, so it is not surprising that often she became very exhausted and was delighted when she could take a day off. But she persevered and continued to be concerned with the 'Hut' until well into 1919, by which time it had been taken over by the Canadian YMCA. Then she turned her energies to the Red Triangle Hut in Englefield Green which was allied to the YMCA and was for recreational purposes in the village.

At last on November 11th 1918 she was able to write in red ink in her diary: 'Armistice signed – Hostilities cease.' She went on:

> It was announced [in the hut] that the Armistice was signed and no more hostilities. The bands played and we decorated everything with flags – there was great excitement and thankfulness. Cpt Smith came in to say he would like a thanksgiving service at 6 with the band ...... The service only began at 6.30 and was beautifully done and a crowded hut.

Throughout these years, Emily went into waiting three times a year and continued to accompany Princess Christian to meetings and hospitals. Often she also attended Princess Thora. During this time the Princesses were more often at Schomberg house than at Cumberland Lodge. In early 1918 Woods and Forests became concerned about this and began questioning the use of the building but Fred, who had become the Princess's man of business, was able to announce on February 28th that 'Woods and Forests [had] given in about Cumberland Lodge and Princess Christian staying there.' By early 1923,

Emily Loch and two of her helpers dressed for work in the YMCA Hut during the 1914-18 War.

however, Fred and Mr Lloyd were again discussing the disposal of Cumberland Lodge. By that time the Princess had decided to remain in London.

It was while Emily was in waiting in the spring of 1919 that there was a ceremonial march past of the Guards up the Mall celebrating the war's end. Schomberg House was an ideal place for seeing this and many guests were invited to watch. Emily as usual was concerned about food. On the cold wintry morning of March 22nd,

> Pss Thora and I went in the motor to buy cakes at Gunthers for the guests ...... everybody began to arrive soon after 1.15 to see the Guards march past. We managed on the balcony with most of the four windows in the Princess' sitting-room. A most welcome meal of cakes and sandwiches and hot coffee after it was over. It was a wonderful sight headed by the Household Cavalry marching on foot and then every batt. of Guards, machine guns, ambulances driven by the men who had been out the whole war. Two cows also who had been all thro' the war. It lasted 1½ hours.

It was a few days later that Princess Thora met 'the Russian lady-in-waiting who was with the Empress and the family till within 2 months of their murder', and invited her to tea at Schomberg house 'to talk about it'. This was probably the first time Emily heard any details of the Imperial family's imprisonment. First at Tsarskoe Selo, where she would have been able to visualise them in the Alexander Palace – although under very different circumstances from those in which she had seen them: now surrounded by guards and restricted in where they could go. Then their removal to Tobolsk, to the east of the Ural mountains, away in Siberia, with only a few of their servants and officials. The long train journey was quite comfortable and the prisoners were treated with some dignity, for the guards had been chosen carefully and were reasonable men. This continued at first in the Governor's house in Tobolsk. It had been cleaned and painted for them, but Nicholas and his family were not allowed to leave the house, except occasionally under a strong armed guard to go to church. There was not much space but Nicholas and Alexandra had a bedroom and the four Grand Duchesses shared one room. Alexei had his own room with his sailor-servant next door. There was a sitting room for Alix and a study for Nicholas, and a large hall in which, as restrictions became more severe, a portable church was erected.

Pierre Gilliard and some of the personal servants were in the house with the family. Countess Hendrikoff and Mlle Schneider and the gentlemen-in-waiting lived in a house across the street but had meals with the family. The family were confined to the kitchen garden for fresh air but at first the others were allowed to walk in the town. In time, however, this was forbidden. Alexandra and the tutor continued to give lessons. There was some relaxation with books – Janet Adam Smith in her biography of John Buchan mentions that Olga enjoyed *Greenmantle* – but there were many hours of boredom and anxiety. The news of the Bolshevik revolution at first made little change in Tobolsk. The soldiers allowed the family some relaxation of the rules for Christmas 1917 but, in the New Year, they became more repressive and lack of funds brought new difficulties: rigid economies had to be undertaken. Some of the servants were given money to return to Petrograd; the rest worked for very reduced pay and everyone joined in paying the household bills. Food became frugal and simple but occasional gifts were allowed from some nuns.

In April a new powerful Bolshevik envoy arrived from Moscow. Soon, it became apparent that he intended to take Nicholas away; no one, not even the previous officer in charge, knew why or to where. Alexei was very ill with another haemorrhage and could not be moved. After an agonising time, Alexandra decided to go with her husband; Dr. Botkin and Marie went with them. The family was divided. Olga was left in charge of the housekeeping; Tatiana of her brother – with Dr Derevenko's help; Anastasia, the other ladies, Mr Gibb (the tutor) and M Gilliard also stayed. The first group had a horrifyingly uncomfortable journey overland to Tioumen to reach the railway. It was impossible to travel by river, as they had done before, because of the ice. They were then taken to Ekaterinburg, a mining town in the Urals, which was in the hands of the Bolsheviks. Here their journey ended and they were imprisoned in the house of the engineer Impatieff. This house was much smaller and all views from it were blocked out. The family was allowed little communication with the outside world and they hardly knew where they were. They had scant news from Tobolsk and few possessions. This was to be their home during the hot months of May, June and July 1918. Their treatment by the guards became increasingly harsh and demeaning. Late in May the party from Tobolsk arrived. Pierre Gilliard gives a grim account.

The second party was able to travel by river to the railhead at Tioumen and then on the train to Ekaterinburg, where they arrived on May 22nd. Gilliard was separated from his pupil when they got on the train and had to travel in a fourth-class carriage. Soldiers guarded them for whole journey and they arrived in the middle of the night. The train stopped some distance from the actual station. Next morning, several cabs came alongside the part of the train where the children were. Gilliard, from his carriage window, saw Nagorny[145] carrying Alexei followed by the three girls each struggling with a heavy suitcase. He tried to get out to help them but was brutally pushed back into his carriage. It was raining and Tatiana struggled past through the mud carrying her little dog. Nagorny came back to help her but he too was kicked aside. A few moments later the cabs set off for the town. At least there would have been a brief moment of relief when the family was reunited.

Poor Gilliard was very distressed. He and the others were forced to wait in the train for several hours and he feared that he would not see the children again. He was particularly perplexed and upset at the arbitrariness of what was happening to the members of the suite. He saw Countess Hendrikoff, Mlle Scheider and one of the Generals being led away as captives whereas he and Baroness Buxheovenden and a few others, after much anxious waiting and speculation, were told that they were no longer needed and were free. He couldn't understand what was happening.

In the days that followed he managed to get in touch with the Swedish and English consuls to see if anything could be done to help the prisoners. The consuls believed that they were in no immediate danger but they hadn't taken into account the very fluid situation as the armies of different allegiances moved around the neighbourhood. He was not allowed to see or speak to the family, although Dr Derevenko and Dr Botkin had asked if he could join his pupil. 'It had to be referred to Moscow'...and the request was eventually turned down.

After a month, during which the fourth-class railway carriage had been their lodging, Gilliard and others were ordered out of the district and sent back to Tioumen. Here chaos reigned with refugees pouring through the town. Although Gilliard had obtained a permit to travel, all the trains had been requisitioned for troop movements. The remnants of the Imperial suite probably only survived because they were swamped in the mass of refugees. Gilliard was still in Tioumen when the newspapers reported that posters had appeared in Ekaterinburg announcing that 'Nicholas had been sentenced to death and executed during the night of 16 – 17 July. The Empress and the children had been evacuated and placed in safe place.' A few days later, Ekaterinburg fell to the anti-Bolsheviks and Gilliard was able to return to the town. His visit to the Impatieff house soon convinced him that mass murder had taken place. He was horrified that the children had shared their parents' fate and over and over again repeats: 'Why the children? Why the children?' In the next few months he learned more; he examined the forest clearing with the mine shaft and saw the few sad relicts of the family's possessions. Then, amidst the disturbances which engulfed the whole of Russia, he had to leave with great sadness in his heart.

Some of this Emily would have read in Gilliard's book. How much she and the princesses learned from the Russian lady we don't know; nor does Emily mention what her name was. We know from various accounts that Mlle Schneider and Mme Hendrikoff were both with the Empress until quite near the end. Both were shot. Baroness Sophie Buxhoeveden was ordered to leave Ekaterinburg and the district of Perm within a month of arriving there. She survived to write an account first published in 1928.

Perhaps the princesses learnt more from 'Mr. Preston the English consul from Ekaterinburg' who came to tea on February 15th 1921. 'He told [us] about the murder of the Csar and family as he was there then'. Uncertainties remained, and they remained for the rest of the century. Now at last, what was left of the bodies of the family, after all the atrocities, can rest in peace: in 1998 they were interred in the cathedral of St Peter and St Paul in St Petersburg beside the other Romanovs.

As peace became established the lives of the princesses and Emily returned more or less to normal. In 1922 Emily joined them at Schomberg House at the beginning of October and they settled into the usual routine of meetings for both princesses. Emily accompanied Princess Christian to an SOS African meeting on the 3rd, a South African Emigration meeting on the 4th, a Red Cross meeting for the Russian Relief Fund and for starving refugees in Greece on the 10th and the Leper Colony on the 30th. Princess Christian presented 'certificates of gratitude' to a lady and gentlemen at the Lord Roberts' workshops on the 18th and so it went on. There were usually drives in the afternoon round parts of London and occasionally short walks. There were dinners and luncheons with relatives, including George V, and friends. For most of the time the Princess was well but she did complain about her eyes late in the month and consulted Sir R Cruise. She had 'palpitations' in early November which brought a flurry of doctors but she got over them quite quickly and only missed one engagement.

Emily begins 1923 with 'Elise telephoned that Pss Christian has had another slight heart attack and then she telephoned herself.' Emily did not see much of the Princess until she went into waiting on April 10th when she found the Princess 'not too good and faint'. She did seem rather poorly but managed to go with her daughters to see Queen Mary's Dolls' House in which they were all very interested – Princess Thora had sat for Mr Hickley for the painting of a minute portrait in October the previous year. She was also able to attend the wedding reception at Buckingham Palace of the future George VI and Elizabeth Bowes-Lyon on April 26th.

Two days later she was complaining about her head. Early in May she suffered another slight heart attack and a nurse was engaged. She was better by the 18th and was cheered up by being driven to Kensington Palace to stay with Princess Beatrice for ten days. Emily and Thora visited her each day from Schomberg House where they were living. Princess Christian's birthday fell during this period: good wishes and flowers poured in but the only visitors allowed were her daughters and her brother, the Duke of Connaught. Two days later, Thora brought her back to Schomberg House and she seemed 'brighter and better'. That evening, Emily after dinner in her own room 'sat afterwards with the Princess till she went to bed at 9.15. She was full of talk of old times.'

Next morning the Princess fell into a coma and, a little over a week later on June 9th, she died. 'We were all with her'.

This daughter of Queen Victoria about whom so little is recorded had been Emily's patron and friend for over forty years. She had introduced her to Emperors and Empresses, Kings and Queens, in the courts in Britain, Germany, Sweden and Russia. She had widened Emily's horizons. The Princess had been patron or president of 123 organisations and had worked hard with imagination to lessen the hardships of women, children, the underprivileged and the sick. She had devoted many hours to the welfare and training of nurses and had established hospitals. She had great skills with her embroidery and had encouraged the arts with her School of Art Needlework and her support of the Bach Choir. She had friends from the highest in the land to the poorest: she had become known in London's East End as 'Our Princess'.

She had had her own problems about which Emily's laudable discretion only allows us to speculate. These had been overcome. Emily had joined the household in the high Victorian era which to many seemed as if it would continue for ever. Together the Princess and Emily had adapted to great changes. They had evolved a way of life to cope with increasing economic pressures, reduced incomes and the conditions of post-war Britain. They had played their respective roles in the shadow of war. They had accepted and embraced the changes in technology: in communication from telegrams to everyday telephoning, from light with oil lamps and candles to gas and electricity, from carriages, dog carts and flys to motors and taxis, underground trains and buses. Although Princess Christian had to confess to young Tommy Poore, an avid collector of bus tickets and Emily's great-nephew, that she had none: she had never been on a bus. Against this background of momentous change the essential qualities of kindness, love and loyalty, integrity and discretion remained.

Above all the Princess had made a loving and closely-knit family, and now it was to her bereaved daughters that Emily's attention turned. Emily records with evident relief that the ever-practical and thoughtful King George V, on the very day of the Princess' death, told Princess Thora and Princess Marie Louise that Schomberg House was theirs, allaying any possible anxiety. But the protocol of death demanded that 'every other Royalty came all day [and] the poor Princesses [were] quite overwrought'. Emily did her best to comfort them. There were endless letters and telegrams to answer. Emily had a team of helpers including Nella du Cann, the Princess's current lady-in-waiting, and Dorothy Jackson as Dorothy Seymour had become after her marriage to an army officer whom she had nursed during the war.

On the evening of her death, the Princess's coffin was carried from her room in Schomberg House by ten Guardsmen 'all over 6 feet tall' to the chapel of Marlborough House. There, vigil was kept all night by the Kilburn Sisters. The Princess had even instructed that they should be 'fed and rested' in a nearby house. Emily ends her entry for that day with:

> Mr Nixon took the service when the soldiers brought her in, where we left her, the Sisters guarding her. Sat a little with Pss Thora before going to bed. Only we two in the house.

The sadness and loss seeped in once the busyness of the day was over.

The Princess's funeral was held at St George's Chapel Windsor five days later. Until then, her coffin remained in London and Emily made several visits, remarking after one at 10 o'clock at night 'the four sisters there like people in a Dutch picture'.

The Quest was to discover how Emily Loch came to know the last Tsarina of Russia. The story has unfolded. Emily knew Princess Alix from her childhood to her murder. The journey, guided by Emily's diary, has led from a quiet English village near Windsor Castle through the Courts and Spas of Germany to the capital of one of the great Empires of the world, Russia. It has spanned the end of the Victorian era and approached the age of modern technology. It began when monarchies dominated much of Europe and moved to a time when the power of the people was flexing its muscles. But it is the men and women, many, many of them, from Emperors and Empresses to laundry women and grooms who in their daily lives, with their loves, hopes, fears and deaths make the story. Emily in her gentle, unchanging integrity has been our guide.

Until her death in 1932 Emily remained in close contact with Princess Thora who continued to live at Schomberg House and was joined by Princess Marie Louise. There they made a centre for music. Prince Aribert continued to live in Germany, where he farmed the estates he had inherited until his death in 1931. Princess Thora and Emily visited him twice in the twenties. Princess Thora survived the Second World War including the bombing of Schomberg House and died in 1948. Princess Marie Louise, the last of the Christian family, lived to attend the Coronation of Queen Elizabeth II and died in 1956.

The Players

Notes

1 Queen Victoria had written to her grand-daughter Victoria Battenberg on the 11th of the month saying: 'And I am very depressed. How I dread the week after next and how I wish it was months and years off! The nearer the fatal day approaches the more my invincible dislike to Auntie's marriage (and not to dear Liko) – increases. Sometimes I feel that I could never take her to the Marriage Service & I wish I could run away and hide myself'.

2 By 1871, Princess Christian, often referred to by her nickname 'Lenchen' by the Queen, had slipped from favour. Writing to her eldest daughter on May 6th 1871, the Queen having mentioned her misfortunes with her babies goes on to complain of Lenchen's minor ailments 'cold upon cold and unbecoming stoutness' and continues saying her husband pampers her and does not understand how to manage her.

3 The Queen shared their love of dachshunds and in 1878 requested that a pair should be sent to her by Crown Princess Vicky from Germany. Her great friend John Brown greeted her on a January afternoon, in 1878, with the cheerful news 'here are two dakels [sic] come – bonnie dogs'. Dackel is a colloquial name for Dachshund.

4 The Princess began at an early age. A fire-screen with a circlet of appliquéd flowers can be seen at the Swiss Cottage, Osborne House, made by Princess Helena when she was fourteen.

5 See Chapter 6; Princess Christian and Emily's visit to Prince Sandro.

6 Queen Victoria's Journal. Royal Archives, 20 May 1886

7 It is said that Princess Christian interceded with George Loch as he lay dying that Catherine Grace should be allowed to take up nursing.

8 In 1878, Alice received an Honourable Mention for an un-mounted fan in the Fan Makers Exhibition.

9 Duvellroy was a Paris firm which had a branch at 197 Regent Street. To complete the fan they would have taken the 'leaf' or 'mount' which had been decorated by the artist and pleat it (usually) and fix it to the 'ribs', the upper part of the sticks. The bunch of sticks would be held together at the pivot and the fan could be revolved round this. Two guards would be fixed to the outer sticks to protect the delicate structures inside. Materials varied greatly depending on the importance of the fan and the cost. Dedicated

craftsmen would produce the most intricate designs on the sticks, pivot ends and most especially the guards. In the case of Alice Loch's fan in the Royal Collection the decoration is painted on fine gauze and the sticks and mounts are mother of pearl.

10 According to Wilson, 2005, it was only in 1907 that the Qualification of Women's Act allowed women to sit as Councillors, Aldermen, Mayors or chairmen on County and Borough Councils.

11 The poet Shelley in 1814, after the collapse of his marriage with Harriet Westbrook, eloped abroad with Mary Godwin and spent several months touring round post-Napoleonic Europe before returning to England. They then spent a few months at this cottage in Bishopgate, chosen for its healthy climate, considered suitable for someone, such as Shelley, who was suffering from consumption. He remembered his time at the cottage as very happy and in 1816 published his poem *Alastor* which brought him to critical notice. It is also believed locally that Mary Shelley wrote *Frankinstein* here. This seems unlikely as the work is dated 1818 and they only stayed at Bishopsgate for a few months.

12 Henry Loch, was Governor of the Isle of Man from 1863 to 1882

13 Papers in the Public Library Victoria, Australia, (Letter Book NGV PRO 5863/p/0000)

14 Mattei: a form of alternative medicine based on the work of Conte Cesare Mattei. In 1888 R M Theobald published an English translation of Mattei's *Electrohomeopathic Medicine*. The Count claimed that Electrohomeopathy was a sort of 'restorative nutrition given under the form of medicine' and that the therapeutic agents (called electroids) act on the blood and give the organism the power to cast off the 'morbid, injuring elements'. Emily's Diary 14/8/1892: 'long discussion on Mattei and Homeopathy with Dr. Reid.' His (very concise) diary records nothing of this.

15 The custom of calling gave a structured form to social intercourse Very exact details about the correct way of calling is given in 'The Lady: a magazine for gentlewomen' of about 1871. The lady's visiting card was printed in small, clear copper plate without embellishments. The card was oblong 3.5 inches long. Her name was in the centre and her address in the left hand corner. Husbands and wives should have separate cards; a husband only left his on bachelor friends. In the actual calling the etiquette was as follows: Calls were delivered in person or by a manservant from the carriage, never posted. If the recipient was not 'at home' three cards should

be left, one for the lady and two for the husband, and if a grown-up daughter living at home a card should be left for her. Alternatively a corner could be turned down to indicate that the call was made to all If the recipient was 'at home' the visit should not take more than half-an-hour and when the visitor left, she placed two cards on the hall table, not in the drawing room and not in the card-basket, nor should they be offered directly to the hostess. A card left at a farewell visit had PPC (pour prendre congée) written in the corner

16 A letter from Emily Loch to Dr Reid, dated November 30th 1885.

17 Abdul Karim when appointed was 24 years old, slim and clever and soon ingratiated himself with the Queen. She understood that his father was a doctor in Agra but investigations by the members of the household in the 1890s found he was an apothecary at the gaol, but this was not a matter which worried the Queen. Ideas of his own importance grew. The Queen created him 'the Queen's Munshi' or secretary, particularly in matters concerning India. Antagonism among the Court and Government grew against the Munshi with the Queen always taking his side but they eventually considered him a bore rather than a danger, although he could have had access to confidential matters. He survived all the efforts to remove him as long as the Queen could take his part.

18 More than twenty years earlier in 1861, Elizabeth Wied, as Carmen Silva was then known, was being considered as a possible wife for Bertie, the Prince of Wales, by his mother and eldest sister. The reports from Princess Vicky were not encouraging: although she spoke excellent English, her German was not very refined and her *esprit de conduit* and royal bearing (at the age of 17) not developed.

19 It has been suggested by a medical person that the Princess may have been suffering from trichiasis, (in-growing of the eye-lashes) which is treated by cautery either with silver nitrate or electricity

20 This book, written and illustrated by 'Miss Brown', Catherine Grace Loch, was published by Bickers and Son, Leicester Square, London, and is based on a diary kept by Cathy Loch of the journey made with Florence Leveson Gore (daughter of the Duke of Sutherland) and Miss Bragge in 1876. The title and the idea follow that of Richard Doyle's book *The Foreign Tour of Messrs Brown, Jones and Robinson* published by Bradbury Evans, Whitefriars, London, in 1855.

21 The Marquess of Lorne, Princess Louise's husband was appointed Governor

of Canada in 1878. In 1880 the Princess was injured in an accident in a sleigh and later was involved in a railway accident in the United States.

22 Princess Louise decorated some of the rooms in Rideau Hall, the Governor's residence in Ottawa, with paintings of apple blossom, very similar to the paintings of Alice Loch.

23 Such 'Tableaux vivants' were favourite occupations of Queen Victoria's family and frequently were very elaborate affairs requiring authentic costumes.

24 Pablo de Sarasate born in Pamplona 1844, died 1908, world famous violinist and composer of music for that instrument.

25 Perhaps Emily meant a form of French Billiards which is played on a pocket-less table with three balls, a red and two white and confined to cannon play, or carom, as it is usually termed from the French word *carombolage.*

26 In one of Emily's albums is a faded sepia print of this expedition, showing the party riding through the trees.

27 It was the custom in the Royal families to set out the presents on tables for birthdays and at Christmas time.

28 Tsar Alexander II had rather more liberal views than many of the Tsars including his successor Tsar Alexander III. He was blown up by a bomb in St Petersburg on March 1st 1881. The place of his assassination is marked by a remarkable, multi-domed church finished in 1907 named The Church of the Resurrection of Christ'.

29 No letters from Cathy to her sisters have been found but the quotations and information are taken from *Catherine Grace Loch, A memoir*, Published by Henry Frowde, London, Edinburgh, Glasgow, New York and Toronto in 1905 with a introduction by Field-Marshall the Earl Roberts at the invitation of Surgeon-General Bradshaw who edited the book. The memoir is dedicated to the 'Members of Queen Alexandra's Military Nursing Service in India'.

30 Miss R A Betty succeeded Cathy as the senior Lady Superintendent of Nursing.

31 Empress Vicky wrote to her mother in October 1890 saying that Emily Loch was in Berlin with them and how much her daughters were enjoying having Gerry Liddell and Conga Bigge to play the pianos with them. The four girls were able to perform pieces for 'eight hands'.

32 One of Emily's bilingual words. Knieper is German for bar.

33 Queen Victoria had hoped that Princess Alix would find Prince Eddy a suitable suitor and she was very disappointed when Alix turned him down. She wrote to her granddaughter Victoria Battenberg in early 1889 asking if nothing could be done to get Alix to change her mind and for some time the Queen continued to have hopes that Alix would not be lost to Russia which she considered a dangerous country 'totally antagonistic to England'. But Alix would not change her mind. After being turned down Prince Eddy became engaged to Mary of Teck but died soon after the announcement of the engagement. She subsequently married his brother who became King George V.

34 Dessau, the capital of the small Duchy of Anhalt, absorbed in the German Federation, lay about 60 miles south-west of Berlin.

35 The Dell was a large house with a park on the east side of Wick Lane in Bishopsgate, Englefield Green. The Loch's Cottage was almost opposite and their land lay between Wick Lane and the boundary of the Great Park.

36 Game of poker.

37 Pope Joan is a card game for three or more players. It is played for counters on a specially designed board.

38 Catherine of Sienna (1347-80) member of the Dominican third order. Played a part in restoring the Papacy to Rome from Avignon. Canonised in 1461.

39 'Little Alice' was Princess Victoria Battenberg's daughter. Twelve years later in 1903 she married Prince Andrew of Greece in Darmstadt with great family rejoicing. Both Nicholas II and Alexandra were present and by some it was considered to be 'the last time that gaiety could triumph over tragedy and war'.

40 Baron Riedesel zu Eisenbach, the other on the right Dr Hugo von Leohardi. Both were stewards of the Hesse Court. Riedesel later became ADC to Grand Duke Louis.

41 Baroness Wilhelmine von Grancy

42 There is a discrepancy between Emily's diary for October 1891 and the account given by Richard Hough in Louis and Victoria. On page 155 he refers to Prince Ernie and Princess Victoria Melita staying at Balmoral in October 1891. Queen Victoria was enchanted with their liveliness. Here she thought 'was a marriage made in heaven' and she encouraged them to be together as much as possible. This is from a letter in the Broadlands Archives (BA, QV to VMH , Queen Victoria to Princess Victoria of Hesse) dated

October 22, 1891 but there is no doubt that it was Princess Helena Victoria (Thora) and Prince Ernie who were at Balmoral in October 1891. From other letters quoted by Hough in relation to the possible marriage of Prince Ernie and Princess Melita, dated March 29,1893 (Darmstadt Archives,VMH to Grand Duke of Hesse) and Septemberb 24, 1893 (Broadlands Archives, QV to VMH) it seems quite likely that Prince Ernie and Princess Melita were at Balmoral in the autumn of 1892.Their marriage took place in April 1894.

43 There are many references to the preparation of a Christmas Tree and in the earlier years this always occurred after December 25th and as in this case after New Year.The fashion for sending Christmas cards came in the late 1880s. In Emily's family the presents exchanged were quite small and inexpensive.

44 Miss Simpson had trained a a nurse in the Edinburgh Royal Infirmary.

45 From Emily's account it sounds like a form of Grandmother's footsteps but rather more energetic.

46 After Victoria, Ella and Irène had all left home on marriage, Queen Victoria was anxious that Alix should have another companion, other than Miss Jackson, who by 1887 the Queen described as having 'bad health, hard ways and crabbed temper'. Gretchen von Fabrice joined the Hesse household in late 1888 and continued as a pleasant and satisfactory companion to Alix for many years.

47 The Queen always liked her grandchildren, but particularly her granddaughters, to have a quiet visit to her before their marriage so that she could instruct them in the intricacies of the married life.

48 The 1910 Baedeker lists about half a dozen ladies' clubs.The Green Park Club was at 10 Grafton Street.

49 Aunt Michem, Maria Pavlovna (1854-1920) was the wife of Vladimir, brother of Tsar Alexander III.

50 Farrah's Original Harrogate Toffee, Established in 1840 and still sold in silver and blue tins saying 'Every Packet bears the makers Signature.'

51 The New Gallery was at 121 Regent's Street.

52 Emily's spelling. In other books he is Profeit. He managed the domestic arrangements at Balmoral.

53 Clewer, once a separate village, now part of Windsor lies west of the Castle, slightly upstream and about 6 miles from Bishopsgate, Englefield Green.

54 Emily along with many in the Victorian age had a fascination with, and

great faith in, the efficacy of Electricity. The 1928 Everyman's Encyclopaedia gives galvanism as a term applied to the method of the alleviation of pain and cure of disease by means of a current of electricity; alternating current was considered to be the best for therapy.

55 There is a fan of Alice Loch's, in the possession of the Loch family, decorated with sprigs of hawthorn flowers, which was commissioned by the Queen in the last years of her life. Alice left a note with the fan (see Plate 3).

56 A Fly was a quick covered travelling carriage with one horse available for hire usually from a livery stables.

57 It was polite etiquette for people to sign a suitably grand book in a royal residence when they were staying in the district or on special occasions. Emily mentions doing it many times or accompanying people to do it.

58 Stanford, Charles Villiers. Born in Dublin in 1752, died London1924. Composer and choral conductor.

59 In the mid-nineteenth century guns on ships became much more powerful and the vessels required greater protection. At first iron plates were added to the hulls of wooden ships but in 1860 *HMS Warrior*, the first iron-built ship was launched with 4½ inch iron armour plating backed by 18 inches of teak. In later ships iron and finally steel formed the hull.

60 Dreadnouht had been used as the name of ships in the British Navy since Elizabethan times. The most famous in the Victorian and Edwardian periods was *HMS Dreadnought* with ten 12-in guns launched at Portsmouth on February 10th 1906. The term 'dreadnought' was used loosely to mean the great steel ships of the British navy in the period before 1914.

61 Willy Brown was the brother of the much better known John Brown who had become a close companion of the Queen after the death of Prince Albert, much to the disquiet of the Queen's children. Emly noted John Brown's death. March 27th 1883 in her diary.

62 Dame Albani, stage name of a Canadian singer, Mlle Lajeunesse, born in Quebec in 1851. She appeared in London in 1872 in opera. Later changed to oratorio and sang before many European monarchs. Edward Lloyd (1845-1927) English tenor. In the 1860s was the solo tenor at the Chapel Royal and from 1888 was principal tenor of the Handel Festivals.

63 From 1570 till 1878, Cyprus was part of the Turkish Empire. In 1878, as a result of the Treaty of Berlin, the administration Cyprus was handed to Great Britain. Britain annexed the island completely in 1914 soon after the

outbreak of the First World War.

64 War had broken out between Turkey and Greece in April 1897and the British government and public were horrified at the 'Armenian massacres' carried out by Turkey. As Longford (1964) says 'Europe was again shuddering under the horror of Turkish mis-rule. Queen Victoria wanted to remonstrate but was dissuaded from doing so by Lord Salisbury.

65 As we have seen, Princess Thora and Princess Alix had become great friends, and this is remarked on by Baroness Buschoeredin, a special friend of the Tsarina in her later life. Both in their youth suffered badly from shyness which in the Victorian period was considered very bad manners and carried an almost religious stigma. Both the cousins overcame it later in life but appearing in public was often a great strain.

66 Mrs. Temple, wife of the Archbishop of Canterbury, Frederick Temple (1821-1902) who had been appointed Archbishop the year before.

67 In Emily's dream the events which had overtaken Alix were quickly evoked. The urgent summons by Nicholas that she should join him in Russia meant that there was none of the usual pomp and ceremony for the journey of the Tsarevitch's betrothed. Alix's sisters took it in turn to accompany her on the long train ride across Europe to join the Imperial family in Livadia in the Crimea. She found Alexander III in the last stages of his illness. He died within a week of her arrival and Nicholas' mother became the Dowager Tsarina Marie Fedorovna. There was the long train journey carrying the late Tsar's body from the Crimea back to St Petersburg, the funeral, followed a week later by the marriage of Nicholas and Alexandra. For the first few months of their married life Nicholas and Alix lived in the Anichkov Palace, the home of Nicholas' mother. A year later their coronation took place in Moscow. Alix's arrival and marriage, already coloured by the death of Alexander III, was further spoiled by the catastrophe of the Khodynka fields where hundreds of thousands had assembled to celebrate the coronation in a great feast Rumour spread that the there were insufficient supplies. The crowds stampeded, hundreds were killed and thousands injured. Ill-conceived advice from Nicholas' uncles, that the celebrations should continue, only compounded the tragedy and ill-feeling. The masses of simple Russians took the disaster as an omen that the reign would be unhappy; the more sophisticated used it as an example of the weakness and shallowness of the young Tsar and his 'German woman'. Nicholas' efforts to help the injured and pay for coffins for the dead did little to dispel these

feelings.

68 Nicholas felt and was totally unprepared for being Tsar. His father had kept almost all the reins of power in his hands. As late as 1892 Nicholas remarked that he had been made a member of the Finance committee which was a great honour but not much pleasure.... 'I never suspected its existence' and when it was suggested that Nicholas should be appointed president of the Trans-Siberian railway, his father was astonished and said that he was still absolutely a child and only had infantile judgements. 'How would he be president of a committee?' (Massie)

69 Charles Cameron (1740-1812)

70 Catherine (II) the Great 1762-96)

71 Giacomo Quarenghi (1744-1817)

72 Rituals were essential for the Orthodox Religion. From birth, every major event in the life of a religious Russian, even to purchasing an estate, entering the civil service and many more were blessed by a priest.

73 Bartolomeo Francesco Rastrelli (1700-71)

74 Paul (1796-1801)

75 The chaconne was a moderately slow dance in 3/4 time.

76 Mme von Hesse was probably Marie Grancy in the household of Princess Alice of Hesse who married General von Hesse in 1871.

77 Troika was a sledge or wheeled vehicle drawn by three horses abreast

78 Alexander I (1801-25)

79 In addition to the servants inside the palaces there was an army of soldiers and police whose job it was to ensure the safety of the Tsar and his family. Under the command of the Palace Commander there was the Sovereign's personal escort and the combined battalion of the Guard plus sentries in the palace and park. There were also the Palace Police who watched the neighbouring streets and supervised the coming and goings of all attending audiences. Special guards were active whenever the Tsar and his family were travelling

80 Lace was a very special feature of Russian life and in the past was used in many garments. It formed an important part of a girl's trousseau. It was made in many parts of the country and had distinctive patterns. In the 19th century a new centre was developed near St Petersburg in the Kirishy region but the biggest centre was in Vologda province. At the beginning of the 20th century about 40,000 lace makers were involved.

81 Peter the Great, founder of the city which once again bears his name,

reigned from1682 to 1725.

82 Completed in 1811, although the project was first conceived in the reign of Emperor Paul (1796-1801). The architect was Andrey Voronikin.

83 There were many engineering problems associated with the construction of the St Isaac's church, particularly the weight of the massive granite columns. As a result the building was not consecrated until 1858, forty years after the architect Auguste de Montferrand (1786-1858) had begun work.

84 Nicholas I (1812-1855)

85 The Winter Palace designed by Rastrelli (1700-71) in the 1730s in the reign of Empress Anna (1730-40) but extensively enlarged, again by Rastrelli, in the 1750s for Empress Elizabeth (1741-61). Reconstructed after a disastrous fire in 1837 to the Rastrelli designs.

86 Alexander I (1801-1825)

87 The Peter and Paul Church lies in the Fortress which occupies the small island of Zayachiy, one of the many islands lying in the Neva river as it approaches the Baltic Sea.

88 The Cathedral of St Peter and St Paul is very unlike early Russian churches: it was designed by D Trezzini and completed in 1733. The thin golden spire was the tallest structure in St Petersburg at the time of Emily's visit.

89 The large building loosely referred to as the Winter Palace by Emily and used by the Imperial family as their winter dwelling included the Palace itself in addition to the Large and Small Hermitages where the magnificent art collections of the Tsars were displayed.

90 Karl Bryulov (1799-1852) *The Last Day of Pompeii* was painted in 1830-32.

91 Pushkin, Alexander Sergeievitch (1799-1837) Russian poet. Author of *Boris Godounov* and *Eugene Onyegin* and many other works.

92 The Russian calendar differed by eleven days from the British, thus December 8th, in Emily's diary would have been November 26th, Russian Style.

93 The Preobrazhenskiy regiment was the first regiment of the Imperial Guard and the Tsar was always its Colonel. It was the most powerful of the regiments established by Peter the Great.

94 Gatchina lies about 50 km south of St Petersburg. In the mid 18th century Catherine the Great gave it to her lover Grigory Orlov and on his death it passed to her son Paul. He remodelled it into a building which resembled a barracks with outlying walls, a moat and sentry boxes. This was perhaps the building's appeal to Alexander III and his wife Maria Fyodorovna, Nicholas II parents, who fled there for reasons of security after Alexander II's

assassination and funeral. The Dowager Empress continued to use it long after her husband's death.

95 Misha, Mikhail (1878-1918), brother of Nicholas II

96 Olga, Grand Duchess born in 1895. Died 1918.

97 Tatiana, Grand Duchess born in the year of Emily's visit, 1897. Died 1918

98 Russian nesting dolls noted in Orlando Figges, *Natasha's Dance*, that Sergei Maliutin, in 1891, while working in the folk-craft workshops at Talashkino, developed the Russian Nesting Doll or Matrioshka based on the Japanese nesting dolls. These became so popular that soon the myth became established that they were ancient Russian toys. The author has in her possession one of the Japanese dolls with a fierce expression and long mustachios.

99 Maria Pavlovna, the elder, (1854-1920) 'Aunt Michen.'

100 Grand Duke Vladimir (1847-1909) brother of Alexander III

101 Tsar Alexander III (1854 -94)

102 Grand Duke Serge, Sergei, (1895-1905), brother of Alexander III and therefore uncle to Nicholas II.

103 The first professional performance of *Eugene Onyegin* was in 1881 at the Bolshoi.

104 Iolanthe or the Peer and the Peri, comic opera by Gilbert and Sullivan first performed in London 1882

105 Anton Rubinstein (1821-94) .Settled in St Petersburg in 1858. Founded the Conservatory.

106 Sarasate, Pablo Martin Melitón (1844-1908). Spanish violinist and composer.

107 In the Service book of the Holy Orthodox Church the liturgy for the 'Great office of Thanks giving (*Te Deum*) for the occasions of solemn thanks giving' is detailed. There are twelve parts beginning with asking for forgiveness of sins, continuing through psalms, a litany, prayers and hymns culminating in asking for long life of the Tsar.

108 Grand Duke Konstatin (KR) well known poet,died 1915. Son of Konstatin (1827-92) brother of Tsar Alexander II

109 The Anichkov Palace in St Petersburg lies near the Nevsky Prospekt and the Fontanka river. It was begun in the reign of Empress Elizabeth (1741-61) and altered by succeeding sovereigns. During the reign of Tsar Alexander III it was the scene of many glittering balls hosted by his wife, Marie Fyodrovna, now the Dowager Empress.

110 Peterhof, a very grand palace on the Gulf of Finland named after Peter the Great. Building took place in the reign of Elizabeth when court life became more opulent and reached its zenith in the reign of Catherine the Great (1762-96). Nicholas I (1825-55) built a smaller and simpler palace in the park at Peterhof which was much favoured by later Romanovs such as Tsar Nicholas II and Alexandra.

111 The Alexander Palace, a classical building , stood in a large park in Tsarskoe Selo, the village about fourteen miles to the south of St Petersburg. It was the residence where Nicholas and Alexandra spent much of their time and one that they felt was really home.

112 During the 1914 war Emily was able to send £5 to Frau Schneider through the good offices of Princess Margaret of Connaught who married the Crown Prince of Sweden.

113 'Old Grand Duchess Constantine' was probably Alexandra of Saxe-Altenburg who was married to Grand Duke Konstantin brother of Alexander II. She had been born in 1830 and died in 1911.

114 Some time after she had left Russia, Emily was consulted by Princess Bariatinsky, on behalf of the Empress, about engaging a permanent nurse for one of the children (Communication via Marion Wynn from C Zeeprat).

115 Geheimrath Juztizrat - the King's Privy Counsellor.

116 The Prince Imperial was the son of Napoleon III who married Countess Eugénie de Montigo in 1853. His father, Napoleon III was soundly defeated in the Franco-Prussian war of 1870. Empress Eugénie and her son sought refuge in England. Napoleon joined them there in 1871, after a period of imprisonment by the Prussians and died in 1873. The Prince Imperial was killed in the Zulu war of 1879. Empress Eugénie remained in England and became a friend of Princess Christian and other members of the Royal Family.

117 The Princess had spent many hours over the years concerned with the Nurses' Home which was beside Clarence Crescent in Windsor.

118 The Mahdi, Mohammed Ahmed (c 1843-85) was one of several ' Mahdi' over the centuries, who assumed the role of the promised Messiah of Islam, apparently promised by Mohammed but not mentioned in the Koran.

119 Evelyn Baring was a member of the banking family. Later created first Earl Cromer.

120 Kitchener, Horatio Herbert, Viscount of Khartoum and Aspall. (1850-1916)

121 Douglas Loch was serving in the Signal corps in Kitchener's army and had

to set up heliograph stations on the few hills and vantage points so that the movements of the Mahdi troops could be watched. In a letter to his parents, dated 5.9.98, from Omdurman, he gives a graphic picture of the battle on Friday September 2nd . He was just getting out his camera to take a photograph of 'the Dervish line, with the shells bursting over them, advancing towards the British troops when the cavalry officer who was standing with him shouted out "Look out". 'I turned and saw the overlapping part of the line [not the part he had been observing] coming over the higher ridge of Helio Hill not 500 yards away. We mounted and cleared, not much too soon. Keeping well to the flank we got into the Zeriba [a defensive structure of thorn bushes by the River Nile]. It was a real fine sight to see the whole crowd gradually advancing carrying about 200 banners. The infantry now opened long range volleys and the maxims started giving them fits. They halted about 1000 yards from the Zeriba'.

122 Lord Roberts, first Earl Roberts (1832–1914). From December 1899 was in command of the British forces in the Boer War. Ably supported by Lord Kitchener and the largest force Britain had ever placed in the field he reversed the disaster of the first few months and by June had entered Pretoria, the capital of the Transvaal.

123 Charles Edwin Fripp (1854–1906). Artist who painted for Queen Victoria and her family.

124 Lord Lansdowne (1845–1927). A member of the Cabinet from 1895–1906; until 1900 Secretary of War and then Foreign Secretary.

125 Prince Christian Victor. *The Story of a Young Soldier.* Edited by Herbert T Warren and published by John Murray. The book was dedicated to the officers and non-commissioned officers of The King's Royal Rifle Corps. It was compiled from letters to Prince and Princess Christian, Queen Victoria (given to Princess Thora), the Duke of York (George V) and Prince Christian Victor's cricket book, shooting book and diaries.

126 Among the cuttings in Emily's album of South Africa is a column from *The Diamond Fields Advertiser* which notes that 'a skilled attendant is accompanying Princess Victoria … It is said that she had asked that great preparations of cameras, plates and film be made so that she may take home a great number of photographs of her travels in South Africa'.

127 The Princess' visit took place just over two years after the war ended and memories were still bitter, particularly in the Transvaal. A newspaper article which Emily has pasted in the album exhorts people to behave with

graciousness to their royal visitor; the first member of the Royal Family ever to visit this part of the British Empire. She also includes the report of the Guild of Loyal Women in the Transvaal in which the President of the Graves Fund of the Guild (of which the Pss was patron) after expressing the loyalty of the members, points out that the ties of love and suffering bind women throughout the Empire from the highest to the lowest.

128 See Note 10 (Chapter Three)

129 The Balfours and some of the neighbouring families had set up the Kelso Steam Laundry a few years before. It lasted for nearly a hundred years.

130 After the murder of her husband, Ella founded a religious nursing order, the only one in Russia. She lived quietly close to the nuns' convent where they nursed the poor and ill of Moscow, and always wore the grey robe of the order. She was murdered during the early days of the revolution; her body, thrown down a mine shaft at Alapaevsk, was rescued by Father Seraphim, and placed in a coffin. He accompanied the coffin through Siberia and Manchuria to Peking and then on to Shanghai, Hong Kong and Colombo to Port Said. There Louis and Victoria of Battenberg met the coffin and escorted it to its final resting place on the Mount of Olives.

131 Dickie was the future Lord Louis Mountbatten.

132 Oberammergau is a small village about forty miles south-west of Munich in Upper Bavaria. A Passion play has been performed there at intervals since 1634 when a vow was taken by the villagers after a severe bout of plague. Emily had been before 1910 with Gerry and other friends.

133 The Encyclopaedia of Sports, Games and Pastimes (c 1935) describes 'Bumble Puppy' as a childen's game for two or more. A pole, not shorter than 10 feet is firmly planted in the ground. From the top of the pole an old tennis ball in a string bag is suspended from a stout cord to within about 3 feet of the ground. The first player holds the ball out and hits it with the racquet. The aim is to wind it round the pole before the other player is able to hit it back. If more than two players take part, sides must be taken. This seems the most likely form of Bumble Puppy to have been used. The OED describes a totally different game, more like an out-door of bagatelle. E M Forster in *A Room with a View* has the ball being hit as high as possible over the tennis net and being allowed to bounce.

134 The two sons of Grand Duke Ernie and Eleonore, George Donatus (born 1906) and Louis (born 1908) survived the 1914-18 War. Donatus, the hereditary Grand Duke married Princess Cecile, the daughter of Princess

Andrew of Greece (Alice of the Wolfsgarten photographs) in February 1931. His father Grand Duke Ernie died on October 9th 1937. Louis' marriage to Margaret Geddes (daughter of Lord Geddes) was planned for that month but postponed until November 20th. The family of the new Grand Duke took off in a plane from Frankfurt to attend the wedding on November 16th. The Party included Onor (Eleonore), now a widow, the two sons of Donatus , the best man and the boy's nursemaid. They were all killed when the plane crashed in fog at Ostend Airport, the only scheduled stop on the flight to Croydon where Louis was waiting to greet them. The wedding went ahead, privately, the next morning at the suggestion of Victoria Battenberg and then the newly married couple left for Ostend and Darmstadt and buried their relations at the Rosenhöhe mausoleum.

135 Claremont was the residence of the Connaught family.

136 Queen Mary came from Teck. The Duke is probably her brother.

137 Duff (p159) mentions that Princess Marie Louise nicknamed 'Mrs Aribert' by the German court, 'arrived in time to be caught up in the web of anonymous letters which tangled the German Court in the 'nineties, letters which purported to know every secret behind every closed bedroom door'.

138 Neuralgia, pains in the face and head, was a very frequently mentioned. It was almost a fashionable complaint in the Royal Family.

139 Princess Calma was Prince Christian's sister who had married Duke Ferdinand of Glücksburg in 1885

140 Relations of Baron Schröder the near neighbour of the Loch's in Englefield Green.

141 The murder was planned by Prince Yussoupov (born 1887) to take place in the Moika Palace in St Petersburg. It appears to have been a rather botched affair and eventually Rasputn's body was pushed through a hole in the ice of the frozen Neva.

142 The food supply in the city was getting very short. Throughout Russia it was scarce but St Petersburg being so far from the grain growing areas was dependent on supplies coming by train. This simply did not happen as so many of the trains were occupied in supplying the troops at the front. The lack of food proved critical.

143 The Staff had identified the palace as a hospital by displaying Red Cross flags which they had made out of sheets and the cloth from Father Christmas's gown

144 This was the day the Tsar abdicated. It took place on the train bringing him

back from the front which had been diverted to Pvosk. Nicholas abdicated first in favour of Alexei and then, six hours later, of his brother Grand Duke Michael also handing over

145 Nagorny had replaced Derevenko, who had left the Imperial family, as Alexei's carer.

Royalty

Queen Victoria, 1819-1901: married Albert (1819-1861) Prince of Saxe-Coburg in 1840

The Children of Queen Victoria and Prince Albert

Victoria (Vicky) 1840-1901: married Frederick/Friedrich of Germany/Prussia. 1831-1888. He became Emperor Frederick III (1888). She became Empress Vicky.
Albert Edward 1841-1910: married Alexandra of Denmark 1844-1925. He became King Edward VII (1901-1910).
Alice 1843-1878: married Louis IV of Hesse-Darmstadt 1837-1892.
Alfred (Duke of Edinburgh and Saxe-Coburg Gotha) 1844-1900 married Marie of Russia 1853-1920
Helena (Lenchen) 1846-1923: married in 1866 Christian of Schleswig-Holstein 1831-1917.
Louise 1848-1939: married Marquis of Lorne 1845-1914.
Arthur (Duke of Connaught) 1850-1942: married Louise (Louischen) Princess of Prussia 1860-1917.
Leopold (Duke of Albany) 1853-1884: married Helena Princess of Waldeck-Pyrmont 1861-1922.
Beatrice 1857-1944: married in 1885 Henry Battenberg 1858-1896.

Grandchildren of Queen Victoria and Prince Albert

Children of Victoria, Empress Vicky and Emperor Friedrich III

William (Willy) 1859-1941: Kaiser Wilhelm II 1888. Married Augusta, Dona, of Schleswig-Holstein-Augustenburg, niece of Prince Christian.
Charlotte 1860-1919.
Henry 1862-1929: married Irène of Hesse-Darmstadt.
Victoria (young Vicky or Moretta) 1866-1929: married Adolphus, Prince of Schaumburg-Lippe.
Sophie 1870-1932: married Constantine, King of Greece.
Margaret (Mossy) 1872-1954: married Frederick Carl of Hesse 1893.

Children of King Edward VII and Queen Alexandra, mentioned in the text

Albert Victor, Prince Eddy, Duke of Clarence and Avondale, 1864-1892.
George, 1865-1936: married Mary of Teck. King George V 1910-1936.

Children of Princess Alice and Louis IV of Hesse

Victoria 1863-1950: married 1884 Louis of Battenberg 1854-1921.
Ernest Louis (Ernie) 1863-1937: became Grand Duke of Hesse-Darmstadt 1892. Married (i)Victoria (Ducky) daughter of Alfred Duke of Edinburgh 1894, Divorced 1901. Daughter Elizabeth 1895-1903. Married (ii)1905 Eleonore of Lich 1871-1937. Their children were George Donatus 1906-1937 and Louis born 1908 married Margaret Geddes 1937. All near relations killed in air-crash on way to wedding. Louis became the Hereditary Grand Duke of Hesse-Darmstadt.
Elizabeth (Ella) 1864-1918: married 1884 Grand Duke Serge of Russia 1857-1905.
Irène 1866-1935: married 1888 Henry of Prussia brother of Kaiser Wilhelm II.
Alix (Alicky)1871-1918: married 1894 Nicholas II of Russia 1869-1918.

Children of Alfred, Dukeof Edinburgh and Gotha and Marie of Russia, mentioned in the text

Marie (Missy) 1875-1938: married Ferdinand 1856-1957 King of Roumania.
Victoria Melita (Ducky) 1976-1936: married (i) Ernest Louis (Ernie) 1863-1837 of Hesse Darmtadt; divorced 1901. Married (ii) Kyril 1876-1938, cousin of Nicholas II.

Children of Princess Helena and Prince Christian of Schleswig Holstein, Prince and Princess Christian

Christian Victor(Christle) 1867-1900.
Albert (Abby) 1869-1931: inherited estates in Germany and title from uncle of Schleswig-Holstein-Sonderburg-Glücksburg.
Helena Victoria (Thora, Tora, Toria) 1870-1948.
Marie Louise (Louie) 1872-1957: married 1891 Aribert (1864-1933) of Anhalt; marriage annulled 1901.

Children of Arthur, Duke of Connaught and Louise Princess of Prussia

Margaret 1882-1920: married Crown Prince Gustav of Sweden in 1905.
Arthur 1883-1938.
Victoria Patricia (Patsy) b 1886.

Children of Princess Beatrice and Prince Henry Battenberg, mentioned in text

Victoria Eugenie (Ena), born 1887: married Alfonso XIII of Spain in 1908.
Leopold 1889-1922.
Maurice 1891 -1914.

The Battenbergs

Alexander of Hesse 1823-1888 married Julie, Countess of Hauke.
Their children were Princes of Battenberg.

Louis 1854-1921: married Victoria of Hesse; took the name of Mountbatten 1917.
Alexander (Sandro) 1857-1893: briefly Sovereign Prince of Bulgaria 1879-1885; became Count Hartenau 1889; married Johanna Loisinger 1889.
Henry (Liko) 1858-1896: married Beatrice of Great Britain.
Francis Joseph (Franzjos) 1861-1924.

Children of Victoria and Louis Battenberg

Alice b 1885: married Andrew of Greece, 1882-1944 in 1903.
Louise b 1889: married King Gustav of Sweden.
George, Marquess of Milford Haven.
Louis (Dickie) 1900-1979: Louis Mountbatten, first Earl Mountbatten of Burma; last god-child of Queen Victoria; married Edwina Ashley in 1922; killed in Ireland by IRA bomb 1979.

The Russian Imperial Family

Alexander II of Russia 1855-1881: married Marie of Hesse 1824-80.
Their children included:

Alexander III 1845-94: married Dagmar (Marie) of Denmark 1847-1928.
Vladimir 1847-1909: married Maria Pavlovna (the elder 'Aunt Michen') 1854-1920.
Sergei 1857-1905: married Elizabeth (Ella)of Hesse 1864-1918

The children of Alexander III and Empress Maria Feodorovna included

Nicholas II 1868-1918 married Alexandra Feodorovna (Alix) 1871-1918 in 1894.
George ('Georgy') 1871-1899.
Xenia 1875-1960.
Olga 1875-1960.

Children of Nicholas II and Alexandra Feodorovna (Alix)

Olga 1895-1918.
Tatiana 1897-1918.
Marie 1899-1918.
Anastasia 1901-1918.
Alexis 1904-1918: Tsarevitch.

Other Relations of Nicholas II mentioned in the text

Konstantin (KR) whose diaries are quoted was a nephew of Alexander II.
Nicholai Nicholaevich, uncle of Nicholas II. Commander-in-chief from the beginning of the 1914 war until replaced in 1915 by Nicholas II. Named as successor on Nicholas' abdication.

People mentioned in the text

People appear under the name by which they are first mentioned in the text and also under their surname.

Abby. See children of Princess Helena and Prince Christian of Schleswig Holstein.

Albany, Duchess of. Helena of Waldbeck-Pyrmont. 1861-1922. Married Prince Leopold 1853 -1884 who suffered from haemophilia.

Albert Edward. Edward VII. See Queen Victoria's children.

Alexander. Prince 1886-1960. Became Marquess of Carisbrooke. See children of Princess Beatrice and Henry Battenberg.

Alexei, Tsarevich. Son of Nicholas and Alexandra. Suffered from haemophilia.

Alexis Michailovich 1629-76. Tsar from 1645-76. Well educated and devout. Nicknamed 'the meek Tsar'. Nicholas II's favourite Tsar.

Alice. See Loch.

Alice, Princess. See Queen Victoria's children.

Alix, Princess. Alexandra Fedorovna. Tsarina of Russia. See children of Princess Alice and Louis IV of Hesse.

Alma Tadema 1836-1912. Very successful Dutch artist who settled in London in 1870.

Anastasia, Grand Duchess. See children of Alexandra Fedorovna and Nicholas II.

Andrew, Prince, of Greece. Married to Princess Alice. See children of Victoria and Louis Battenberg.

Ania Vyrubova. Friend of the Tsarina.

Aribert, Prince. Son of the Duke and Duchess of Anhalt, a small Duchy south-west of Berlin. Married to Marie Louise 1891, divorced 1901.

Aunt Louisa. See Brandreth.

Aunt Mary. Sister of Catharine Loch and aunt of the Loch sisters. Lived at Broad Green near Liverpool. Had a son Edward, Emily's cousin.

Balfour, Charlie and Nina. Of Newton Don near Kelso. Nina was the niece of Gerry Liddell.

Bariatinsky, Princess. A lady-in-waiting to the Tsarina. Remained a close friend for many years. Variously referred to by Emily as Marie, M. Bariat and Bariat. A regular companion while Emily was in Russia and a correspondent after Emily returned to England.

Baring, Susan. One time lady-in-waiting to Queen Victoria. Married Sir James Reid.

Beatrice, Princess. See Queen Victoria's children.

Betty. Miss R A Betty. Great friend of Catherine Grace Loch.

Bidds. Lady Biddulph. Widow of Sir Henry Biddulph who had been Keeper of the Privy Purse and died in 1878. Lived in Henry III Tower, Windsor Castle. Daughter Freda and son Victor.

Bigge, Arthur. Appointed in 1888 Assistant Private Secretary and Assistant Keeper of the Privy Purse. Became Queen Victoria's Private Secretary after Sir Henry Ponsonby. Later became Lord Stamfordham. Had a fine singing voice.

Borwick, Leonard b. 1868. Pianist, pupil of Clara Schumann. Many performances with Joseph Joachim.

Botkin, Dr Physician to the family of Nicholas II and Alexandra. Remained with them until the end at Ekaterinburg.

Brandreth, Louisa and Edward. Aunt and uncle of the Loch sisters; he was the brother of Catharine Loch. Louisa Brandreth died on August 27, 1897. Lived at Elvaston Place, London.

Catherine Grace (Cathy). See Loch.

Cecil Liddell. Son of Fred and Shem Liddell.

Charlotte, Princess of Prussia. See children of Empress Vicky and Emperor Friedrich III.

Chirol, Sir Valentine 1852–1929. Traveller and journalist. For 12 years Head of the Foreign Department of *The Times*. Authority on Asiatic affairs.

Christian, Prince. See Queen Victoria's children.

Christle. See children of Princess Helena and Prince Christian of Schleswig Holstein.

Clemmie. Mary Clementina Marion Nicolson. Born 1851. Daughter of Admiral Sir Frederick William Erskine Nicolson and Mary Clementina Marion, daughter of James Loch. Clemmie was sister of Arthur Nicolson, first Lord Carnock, and aunt of Harold Nicolson. Married 1884 Baron Bemelmans and lived in Strasbourg.

Cohausen, Emma. A native of Wiesbaden and great friend of Emily.

Connaughts. See children of Prince Arthur, Duke and Duchess of Connaught.

Constance Gordon. Daughter of Colonel George Gordon and companion of Princess Christian.

Cowans, Colonel. A member of Princess Christian's Household.

David Liddell. Son of Fred and Shem Liddell.

David Loch. See Loch.

Davidsons, Randall (1848–1930) and Edith (Edie), daughter of Archbishop Tait, Dean of Windsor (1882) and Domestic Chaplain to Queen Victoria. Bishop of Rochester (1891). Bishop of Winchester (1895) and Archbishop of Canterbury (1903).

Desgras. A member of the British Embassy in St Petersburg who accompanied Princess Thora and Emily Loch on their return journey from Russia.

Derevenko. Sailor-carer of the Tsarevich. Deserted the Imperial family before their murder. There was also a Dr Derevenko with the Imperial household who remained with them in exile.

Deverell, Margaret (Margie) 1875–1968. Niece of Emily Loch. Daughter of William Deverell and Marion Clementina Mary Loch. Trained as a pianist in Germany. A pupil of Clara Schumann. Married Edward Poore. Mother of Tommy Poore.

Deverell, William Henry. Married Marion Clementina Mary Loch. Father of Molly Margie, Harry and Helena. Lived at 52 Onslow Square, London and Bossington, Stockbridge, Hampshire.

De Vesci, Lord and Lady. Lived at Abbey Liex, Ireland.

Dickie 1900–1979. See children of Victoria and Louis Battenburg.

Dorothy Seymour. See Seymour.

Douglas Loch. See Loch.

Dowager Empress Marie Feodorovna. 1847–1928. Born Princess Dagmar of Denmark. Widow of Alexander III, mother of Nicholas II and sister of Alexandra, Princess of

Wales, later Queen Alexandra. Remains returned to Russia on September 28, 2006 and interred in the Peter and Paul Cathedral, St Petersburg.

Ducky. Princess Victoria Melita. See children of Alfred, Duke of Edinburgh, and Marie of Russia.

Edwards, Sir Fleetwood. Keeper of the Privy Purse after Sir Henry Ponsonby's stroke which occurred on January 7 1895.

Eleonore. Wife of Grand Duke Ernie, his second wife, married 1905. See children of Princess Alice and Louis IV of Hesse.

Elizabeth. Queen of Romania. Called herself Elizabeth Carmen Silva. Married to Carol I of Romania.

Ella. Elizabeth, Grand Duchess Serge. Sister of Tsarina Alexandra. Married to Grand Duke Serge, uncle of Nicholas. See also children of Princess Alice and Louis IV. Murdered 1918. Made a Saint of the Orthodox Church early in the 21st century.

Ellie. Amalie Weiss. A fine singer. Wife of Joseph Joachim.

Else Blücher. Native of Wiesbaden who became a constant companion to Princess Christian.

Ely, Lady Jane. Wife of third Marquess of Ely. Member of Queen Victoria's household for many years. Developed a strong bond with the Queen as she was also a widow.

Emily. See Loch.

Emma von Cohausen. Lady-in-waiting to Princess Charlotte of Prussia. Home in Wiesbaden.

Ena. Princess Victoria Eugenie. See children of Princess Beatrice and Henry Battenberg.

Ernie. Prince of Hesse. See children of Princess Alice and Louis IV of Hesse.

Evie. See Loch.

Fairbank, Mr and Mrs. Friends of Princess Christian for many years. Queen Victoria considered him a very good dentist. According to the *Medical Departments of the Royal Family (1896),* W. Fairbank Esq. was Surgeon in Ordinary.

Frazer, Alice. An acquaintance who was a frequent visitor to the health spas. She also had a house in London and appears throughout the years of the diaries.

Frazer, Hugh. Son of Alice Frazer.

Fred Liddell. See Liddell.

Freda. Daughter of Sir Henry and Lady Biddulph.

Fritz (Frederick). Friedrich III of Prussia. See Queen Victoria's children.

Galitzine, Princess. Sister of Marie Bariatinsky. Grande Maitresse to the Tsarina.

George Donatus. Son of Grand Duke Ernie. See children of Princess Alice and Louis VI.

George Loch. See Loch.

George. Grand Duke (1871-1899). Brother of Tsar Nicholas II.

Gerry. See Liddell.

Gilliard, Pierre. Swiss tutor of the children of Nicholas and Alexandra. Remained with the Imperial family throughout their imprisonment until Ekaterinburg. Survived and wrote memoirs including *Le tragique destin de Nicolas et de sa famille.*

Goldbech, Herr. Vice-consul in Frankfurt.

Gordon, Colonel George. Equerry to Prince Christian. Lived at Royal Lodge. Windsor Great Park.

Goschen. A member of the British Embassy in St Petersburg.

Grand Duke Paul 1860-1919. Uncle of Nicholas II.

Gretchen. Baroness von Fabrice 1862-1922. Trained as a teacher. Came as governess to the

Christian children in1884. Later joined the Household of the Grand Duke of Hesse, being appointed special lady-in-waiting to Princess Alix in 1888. Companion to Princess Alix until Alix became Tsarina in 1894. Returned to Germany and married General von Pfuhlstein in 1898.

Guy Liddell. Son of Fred and Shem Liddell.

Helena. Princess Christian. See Queen Victoria's children.

Hendrikoff family. Associated with the Court at St Petersburg and Tsarskoe Selo. Countess Hendrikoff remained with the Imperial family in Siberia. Executed by the Bolsheviks in 1918.

Henry, Prince of Battenberg. See Battenbergs.

Hesse. Herr von Hesse and Mme. Head of the Palace Security police at Tsarskoe Selo. It is probable that Mme was of the de Grancy family from Hesse Darmstadt.

Irène. Princess of Hesse Darmstadt. See children of Princess Alice and Louis IV.

Jackson, Miss Margaret (Madgie) Hardcastle Jackson. Staunch Protestant, conservative. Governess of the Hesse princesses especially Princess Alix. On retirement was given a grace and favour establishment by Queen Victoria.

Jeanne. Lady's maid to both Emily and Alice Loch.

Jeune, Lady. Friend of Princess Christian and wife of Sir Francis Jeune, an eminent judge. She moved much in military circles and frequently met the Adjutant-General.

Joachim, Joseph 1831-1907. Virtuoso violinist and composer. From 1862 till his death appeared regularly in London. Teacher at the Berlin Academy of Arts 1868. Founded the Joachim quartet 1869, playing much music by Brahms.

John of Cronstadt. Orthodox priest. Closely associated with the Imperial family. Made a Saint of the Orthodox church early in the 21st century.

Kenmare, Lord. Had estates in Ireland, near Killarney.

Kitchener, Herbert Horatio 1859-1916. Field Marshall. Commander-in-Chief of the British Army.

Knoops. Family who lived in Wiesbaden, owned a riding stables and had children much the same age as the Princesses Thora and Louie.

KR. Konstantin. Cousin of Nicholas II. Nephew of Alexander II.

Leopold, Prince. See children of Princess Beatrice and Henry Battenberg.

Leuchtenberg, Duke and Duchess. He was Prince Eugen Maximilianovich Romanovsky. 5th Duke. She was his second wife and looked after Princess Thora when the Tsarina fell ill.

Leveson Gower, Lady Florence. Daughter of the Duke of Sutherland and friend of all the Loch sisters. Married Henry Chaplin, a gambler and spendthrift. Florence died young.

Liddell, Fred. Brother of Emily's great friend Gerry Liddell. Married the violinist Shem Skinner. Father of the Liddell boys David, Guy and Cecil.

Liddell. Colonel George Augustus Liddell 1812-1888 and Mrs Liddell. He had been Deputy Ranger of the Park. Lived at Holly Lodge, Windsor Great Park. She died 1883. Parents of Gerry and Fred.

Liddell, Geraldine 1855-1948. Briefly lady-in-waiting to Queen Victoria. Life-long friend of Emily Loch. Sister of Minnie Liddell who married Charles Balfour of Newton Don and of Fred Liddell who married Shem Skinner.

Lieven, Princess Elena 1842-1915. Ran an institute for education of the daughters of the nobility in St Petersburg.

Lizzie, Aunt. See Loch.

Loch family

Alice 1840–1932. Eldest daughter of George Loch. Lived at The Cottage, Englefield Green near Windsor.

Catharine (Mama). Daughter of Joseph Pilkington Brandreth. Married George Loch 1836. Mother of Alice Helen, Marion Clementina Mary, Emily Elizabeth and Catherine Grace – the 'Loch Sisters'.

Catherine Grace 1854–1904. Youngest daughter of George Loch. Qualified as a nursing sister and served in India for most of her career.

David. Distant cousin of the Loch sisters. Descended from Francis Erskine Loch, youngest brother of James Loch, Emily's grandfather.

Edward Douglas b. 1873. 2nd Baron Loch of Drylaw, son of Henry Loch.

Elizabeth (Lizzie), Lady Loch. Wife of Henry, first Lord Loch of Drylaw. Daughter of Hon Edward Villiers. Aunt of the Loch sisters and twin sister of Lady Lytton. Lived at Elm Park Gardens, London.

Emily Elizabeth 1848–1931. Daughter of George Loch. Lived at The Cottage, Englefield Green, near Windsor. Lady-in-waiting to Princess Christian from 1883 till the Princess's death in 1923. Author of the diaries.

Evie. Evelyn, daughter of Henry and Lizzie. Married Lord Bernard Charles Gordon-Lennox.

George. 1811–1877. Eldest son of James Loch of Drylaw. QC and MP for the Northern Burghs 1868. Married 1836 Catharine (died 1886), eldest daughter of Joseph Pilkington Brandreth of Liverpool. Commissioner for the Stafford and Sutherland Estates with and after his father. Father of the 'Loch sisters'

Henry Brougham 1827–1900. Youngest son of James Loch and brother of George Loch. He was Governor of the Isle of Man 1863 – 1882; Governor of Victoria. Australia 1884–1889; Governor of the Cape and High Commissioner for South Africa 1889–1895. Created Baron Loch of Drylaw 1895. Married Elizabeth Villiers in 1862.

James 1780–1855. Father of George Loch. Agricultural improver and administrator. Commissioner to the Duke of Sutherland. Member of Parliament.

Mama. Catharine Loch.

Mamy. Marion Clementina Mary.

Marion Clementina Mary (Mamy) 1845–1885. Daughter of George Loch and Catharine Brandreth. Married William Henry Deverell and had four children: Mary Catherine (Molly), Margaret, Henry (Harry) and Helena. Died at Helena's birth. Lived at 52 Onslow Square, London and Bossington, Stockbridge Hampshire.

Londonderry, Lady. Made a tour of Russia with her husband and son in 1836–7 and kept a lively journal.

Lorne, Marquess of. See Queen Victoria's children.

Louie. See children of Princess Helena and Prince Christian of Schleswig Holstein

Louis b. 1908. Son of Grand Duke Ernie. See children of Princess Alice and Louis IV.

Louis IV. Grand Duke of Hesse-Darmstadt. Husband of Princess Alice and father of Victoria, Elizabeth, Irène, Ernie and Alix.

Louis. Prince of Battenberg. See Battenbergs

Louisa, Lady Antrim. Lady-in-waiting to Queen Victoria. Related to Gerry Liddell and married to Lord Antrim.

Louise, Princess of Lorne. See Queen Victoria's children.

Louise, Princess of Prussia. Married to Arthur, Duke of Connaught. See Queen Victoria's children.

MacLaggan, Dr Thomas John. Graduated MD Edinburgh 1850. MRCP London 1882. Physician in Ordinary to Prince and Princess Christian. Lived at 9 Cadogan Place, London. Author of several medical papers including '*Rheumatism, its nature, pathology and successful treatment*'.

Malet, Sir Edwin Baldwin 1837-1908. British ambassador in Berlin 1883/4-1895.

Mama. See Loch.

Mamy. See Loch

Marcia Dalrymple. Lived in Windsor Great Park and frequently helped Princess Christian. She had a brother, North, who was attached to the Christian Household.

Margie. See Deverell.

Marie Louise (Louie). See children of Princess Helena and Christian of Schleswig Holstein.

Marie, Grand Duchess. Third daughter of Nicholas and Alexandra.

Martin, Major. Comptroller of the Christian Household.

Maurice, Prince 1891-1914. See children of Princess Beatrice and Henry Battenberg.

McNeil, Sir J. An official in Queen Victoria's household.

Mendelssohn, Franz. One of the family of the composer Felix Mendelssohn.

Mossy. Princess Margaret. See children of Empress Vicky and Friedrich III.

Munro, Mrs. In charge of the laundry at the Cottage for many years.

Munshi, The. Abdul Karim. Joined the Queen's household in 1887.

Myendorff, Baron. Colonel in the Cossacks and member of the Imperial Household.

Nassau, Duke and Duchess of. Had estates near Wiesbaden. He had been a fellow student at Bonn University with Prince Christian.

Nicholas. Tsar Nicholas II of Russia. Son of Alexander III and Marie of Denmark, sister of Queen Alexandra.

Nightingale, Florence 1820-1910. Studied at Kaiserswerth in Germany in 1851. Took volunteer nurses to the Crimean war in 1854. On return did much work to reform nursing services in the second half of the 19th century.

Nona Kerr. From 1897 lady-in-waiting to Victoria Battenberg.

O'Connor, Sir Nicholas. British Ambassador in St. Petersburg 1897-98.

Obolensky, Princess A. Lily (born Countess Apraskine). Lady-in-waiting and close friend of the Imperial family, especially Nicholas's sister Xenia.

Olga. Grand Duchess of Russia. Eldest child of Nicholas and Alexandra.

Orbeliani, Princess Sonia. Lady-in-waiting to Tsarina Alexandra.

Orchard, Mrs (Orchie). A member of the Grand Duke of Hesse's household. She was appointed in Princess Alice's time in 1866 and remained with Princess Alix when she became Tsarina.

Pagenstecher, Dr Herman b. 1844. Eye specialist. Ran a famous eye clinic at Wiesbaden.

Paléologue, Maurice. French Ambassador in St Petersburg 1914-1917.

Parratt, Walter (later Sir Walter). Organist of St George's Chapel, Windsor.

Perponcher, Deta. Gräfin Margarethe von Perponcher. Lady-in-waiting to Empress Vicky and great friend of Emily's in the Prussian court.

Phipps, Harriet. Maid-of-honour to Queen Victoria. Became Queen Victoria's personal secretary.

Ponsonby, Sir Henry 1825-1895. Private Secretary to the Queen from 1870-1895; for seventeen of these years also Keeper of the Privy Purse.

Poore, Tommy. 1899-1967. Son of Margie.

Prince Michael of Greece. Grandson of Grand Duchess Olga, sister of Nicholas II.

Princess Christian. Princess Helena. See Queen Victoria's children.

Reid, Dr Sir James 1849-1923. Resident Physician and Physician- in-Ordinary to Queen Victoria i.e. her personal physician.

Riedesel. Baron Riedesel zu Eisenbach. A member of the Grand Duke of Hesse's household.

Roberts, Field Marshal Lord Frederick Sleigh.1832-1914. Commander-in-Chief of forces in India 1885-1893. Commanded British forces in South Africa from December 1899 to December 1900. Died St Omer 1914.

Russell. A member of the British Embassy in St Petersburg.

Sandro. Prince Alexander of Battenberg. See Battenbergs.

Schneider, Frau. A member of Princess Alix's household. She instructed Alix in Russian. She remained with the Tsarina until 1918 and was shot by the Bolsheviks.

Schröder, Baron. Neighbour of the Lochs in Englefield Green. Part of the banking family with relations in Hamburg.

Severns. Husband (John) and wife, who looked after his cousin John Ruskin in the last years of the artist's life.

Seymour, Dorothy. Daughter of Lord William Frederick Ernest Seymour, aunt of David Loch. VAD in Russia in 1917. Helped Princess Christian at various times. Worked in a Red Cross Hospital in St Petersburg as a VAD in 1916-17. Witnessed the Revolution and kept an illustrated diary of the events. Married General Sir Henry Cholmondeley Jackson.

Sharratt. Coachman who lived in the grounds of The Cottage, Englefield Green. His wife looked after the laundry in the early years. Had come with the Loch family when they left Tittensor, the house they had sometimes lived in on the Stafford Estates in the 1870s.

Shem. See Skinner.

Skinner, Shem. Violinist. Married Fred Liddell in 1887. Mother of David, Cecil and Guy. Died in childbirth 1901.

Susan Baring. See Baring.

Tatiana. Grand Duchess of Russia. See children of Nicholas II and Alexandra.

Taylor, Sir William. A member of Princess Christian's household in the 1900s. Accompanied her to South Africa.

Thora, Princess. See children of Princess Helena and Christian of Schleswig Holstein.

Uncle Jo. Joseph Joachim

Vicky. Empress Vicky. Princess Victoria. See Queen Victoria's children

Victoria Helena, Princess (Thora, Tora). See children of Princess Helena and Christian of Schleswig-Holstein.

Victoria, Princess. Princess Louis of Battenberg. See children of Princess Alice and Louis IV.

Victoria, Princess of Prussia. See children of Empress Vicky and Friedrich III.

Vladimirs, Grand Duke Alexandrovich 1847-1909. Uncle of Nicholas II. Married to Grand Duchess Maria Pavlovna from Mecklenburg in Germany. Their palace was close to the Winter Palace on the bank of the Neva.

von Grancy, Fräulein. Member of the household of the Grand Duke of Hesse-Darmstadt. Her family had been associated with the Grand Dukes throughout the 19th century. The one Emily knew was Wilhelmine, who remained with the Hesse children after their mother's death.

Wassilitchikoff, Mlle. A member of the Tsarina's household. Sometimes referred to by Emily as K. Wass and Katousch.

Watson. The resident clergyman at the 'English Church' in St Petersburg.

Westerweller, Baron. Major-General Chamberlain to the Grand Duke of Hesse.

Xenia, Grand Duchess. Sister of Nicholas II.

Yorke, Hon A. Had been a member of the Prince Leopold's household, the son of Queen Victoria who suffered from haemophilia. After Leopold's death, remained attached to the royal households and became a good friend of Emily.

Bibliography

Abbreviations: RA Royal Archives. QV Queen Victoria. PRO Public Record Office, Melbourne

Alexander, Hélène, *A Garden of Fans*, The Fan Museum, Greenwich, London, 2004

Ash, Russell, *Alma-Tadema*, Pavilion Books Limited, London, 1973

Baedeker, *London and its Environs 1900*, Facsimile Old House Books, The Old Police Station, Moretonhampstead, Newton Abbot, Devon, UK

Baedeker, *Russia 1914*, reprinted 1971

Bainbridge, Henry Charles, *Peter Carl Fabergé, Goldsmith and Jeweller to the Russian Imperial Court*, Spring Books, 1971 (originally Batsford),

Barbican Art Gallery, *Russian Style 1700-1920, Court and Country Dresses from the Hermitage*, Catalogue, Russian Style Exhibition, Barbican Art Gallery, Barbican Centre, London, 1987, ISBN 1 870163-001

Bater, James H, *St Petersburg, Industrialisation and Change*, Edward Arnold, London 1976, ISBN 0 7131 5846 8

Belyakova, Zoia, *The Romanovs: the way it was*, Ego Publishers, St, Petersburg, 2000

Bennett, Daphne, *Vicky, Princess Royal of England and German Empress*, Constable, London, 1983, ISBN 009 465330 5

Blue Guide, Mawdsley, Evan, *Moscow and Leningrad*, A&C Black, London, 1991
ISBN 0-393-30773-5

Booth, John, *The Art of Fabergé*, Bloomsbury Publications Ltd, London, ISBN 0-7475-0602-7

Buchanan, Meriel, *The Dissolution of an Empire*, London, 1932,

Buxhoeveden, Sophie, *The Life and Tragedy of Alexandra Feodorovna, Empress of Russia*, Longmans, Green and Co, London, New York, Toronto, 1930

Cecil, David, *Lord M*, Constable, London, 1954

Chirol, Valentine, *Fifty Years in a Changing World*, Jonathan Cape, London, 1927

Chomet, S, *Helena, a Princess Reclaimed*, Begell House, New York, 1999, ISBN 1-56700-145-9

Christian, H H Princess, *Alice, Grand Duchess of Hesse*, John Murray, London, 1885

Churchill, Winston, S, *My Early Life*, Oldhams Press Ltd, London, 1947

Connell, Brian, *A Manifest Destiny*, Cassel and Co., London, 1953

Cowles, Virginia, *Edward VII and His Circle*, Hamish Hamilton, London, 1956

Dormandy, Thomas, *The White Death, a History of Tuberculosis*, Hambledon Press, London, 1999, ISBN 1 85285 169 4

Duff, David, *The Shy Princess,* Frederick Muller Ltd, London, 1974, ISBN 0 58410264

Everyman's Encyclopedia, J M Dent and Sons, London and Toronto, 1931-32

Ferro, Marc, *Nicholas II, The Last of the Tsars*, Viking, London, 1990, ISBN 0-670-83880-2

Figes, Orlando, *Natasha's Dance*, Allen Lane, The Penguin Press, London, 2002, ISBN 0-71399517-3

Fletcher, Sheila, *Victorian Girls, Lord Lyttleton's Daughters*, Hambledon Press, London 1997, ISBN 1 85285 150 3

Frazer, Eugenie, *The House on the Dvina, A Russian Childhood*, Corgi Books/Mainstream, Edinburgh, 1984

Frowde, Henry, Ed, *Catherine Grace Loch, A Memoir*, London, 1905

Fulford, Roger Ed., *Darling Child: letters between Queen Victoria and the Princess Royal 1871-1878*, Evens Brothers Ltd, 1976

Galitzine, Katya, *The Romanov Legacy* (photocopy of part)

Geissler, Uwe, *Painting Porcelain*, Schiffer Publishing Ltd, 1995, ISBN 0-88740-899-0

Gelardi, Julia, *Born to Rule*, Headline, 2005, ISBN 0 7553 1391 7

Gilliard, Pierre, *Le Tragique Destin de Nicolas II et de sa famille*, Payot & Cie, Paris, 1921

Hapgood, Isabel Florence, *Service Book of the Holy Orthodox-Catholic, Apostolic Church*, 6th Edn, Antiochian Orthodox Christian Archdiocese of North America, Englewood, New Jersey 07631, 1983

Hedley, Olwen, *Round and About Windsor*, Oxley and Sons, Windsor, 1948

Hibbert, Christopher, *Queen Victoria, a Personal History*, Harper Collins, London, 2000, ISBN 000638843 4

Hough, Richard, *Louis and Victoria, The First Mountbattens*, Hutchinson, London, 1974, ISBN 0 09 121160 3

Hough, Richard, *Queen Victoria: Advice to a Grand-Daughter*, London, 1975

Hudson, Helen, *Cumberland Lodge*, Phillimore and Co. Ltd, Chichester, 1989, ISBN 0 85 033 688 0

Hughes, Kathryn, *The Victorian Governess*, Hambledon Press, London 1993, ISBN 185285 002 7

Humphreys, Rob and Richardson, Dan, *St Petersburg*, 1995 ISBN 1-85828-133-4, The Rough Guides 1995

Keen, Edith, *Seven Years at the Prussian Court*, Everleigh Nash Company Ltd, London, 1916, Re-printed in *Royalty Digest*, 1997, ISBN 1-905159-28-5

Kelly, Laurence, *St Petersburg, a Traveller's Companion*, Constable, London, 1981, ISBN 0 09 463980 9

Kennet, Victor and Audrey, *The Palaces of Leningrad*, Thames and Hudson, London, 1973, reprinted 1984

Komelova, Galina and Vasilyev, Vladimir, *Masterpieces of Russian Culture and Art*, The Hermitage, Leningrad, 1981, Sovetsky Khodozhnik, Moscow 1987

Kuhn, William M, *Henry and Mary Ponsonby*, Duckbacks, 2003, ISBN 0 7156 3230 2

Levi, Peter, *Beaumont 1861-1961*, Andre Deutsch, London, 1961

Loch, Catherine Grace, *The Adventures of Miss Brown, Miss Jones and Miss Robinson at Biarritz and in the Pyrenees*, privately printed by S A Cowells, Anastatic Press, Ipswich (undated, c. 1876)

Loch, Gordon, *The Family of Loch*, privately printed Edinburgh, 1934

Longford, Elizabeth, *Victoria RI*, Weidenfeld and Nicolson, London, 1964

Longford, Elizabeth, *Darling Loosy, Letters to Princess Louise 1856-1939*, Weidenfeld and Nicolson, London, 1991, ISBN 0 297 81179 7

Longford, Elizabeth, *Louisa Lady in waiting*, Jonathan Cape, London, 1979 ISBN 0-224-01712

Lyons, Marvin, *Russia in Original Photographs, 1860-1920*, Routledge and Kegan Paul, London and Henley, 1977, ISBN 0 7100 8653 9

Mahaffy, J P, *Principles in the Art of Conversation*, London 1887

Marie Louise, H H Princess, *My memories of Six Reigns*, Evans Brothers, London, 1956

Massie, Robert K, *Nicholas and Alexandra*, Victor Gollanz, London, 1968

Maylunas, Andrei & Mironenko,Sergei, *A Lifelong Passion, Nicholas and Alexandra Their Own Story*, Weidenfeld and Nicholson, London, 1996, ISBN 0 297 81520 2

McLees, Nun Nectaria, *A Radiance Gathered, The Life of Alexandra Romanov, Russia's Last Empress*, Valaam Society of America, Chico, California, 1992, ISBN 0-938635-90-5

Mikhailovich, Sergei and Prokudin-Gorski (photographer), *Photographs for the Tsar*, Robert H Allhouse Ed, Sidgwick and Jackson, London, 1980

Millar, Delia *Queen Victoria's Life in the Scottish Highlands Depicted by her Watercolour Artists*, Philip Wilson, London, 1985, ISBN 0 85667 194 0

National Museums of Scotland, *Nicholas & Alexandra – The last Tsar and Tsarina*, NMSE Publishing, a division of NMS Enterprises Ltd, National Museums of Scotland, Chamber St, Ednburgh EH1 1JF, 2005, ISBN 1 901 663 99x.

Newby, Eric, *The Big Red Train*, Weidenfeld and Nicolson, London, 1978, ISBN 0 297 775542 1

Nicolson, Harold, *Lord Carnock*, Constable & Co Ltd, London, 1930

Packard, Jerrold M, *Victoria's Daughters*, Sutton Publishing Company Ltd, Stroud Glos, 1999, ISBN 0 7509 2358 X

Pakula, Hannah, *An Uncommon Woman*, The Empress Frederick, Phoenix Giant Paperback, London 1997 ISBN 1 85799 853 7

Pakula, Hannah, *A biography of Queen Marie of Roumania, The Last Romantic*, Phoenix Giant Paperback, London 1998 ISBN 1 85799 816 2

Paléologue, M, *An Ambassador's Memoirs, July 1914-May 1917*, (Translated F A Holt), Published 1924, Reprinted by Octagon Books, New York, 1972 ISBN 0-375-96185-9

Pares, Bernard, *Letters of the Tsaritsa to the Tsar 1914-1916*, Duckworth, London,1923

Parlett, David in *Oxford Dictionary of Card Games*, OUP 1992 ISBN 0-19-869173-4

Physch, John, *The Victorian and Albert Museum, history of its building*, Victoria and Albert Publications,1982

Piotrovsky, Boris, *The Hermitage*, Aurora Art Publishers, Leningrad 1987

Pitcher, Harvey, *Muir and Merilees*, Swallow Books, Cromer, 1994. ISBN 0-905265-03-3

Pope-Hennessy, James, *Queen Mary 1867-1953*, Allen and Unwin, London, 1959

Prince Michael of Greece, *Nicholas and Alexandra, The Family Albums*, Tauris Parke Books, London, 1992, ISBN 1-85043 494-8

PRO 5853/P/0000 000003V2 (Letter book NGV)
PRO 5863/P/0000 000003V2 (Letter book NGV)
PRO 04363/P/0000 000015

QV Queen Victoria's Journal May 20, 1876

RA Z 48/11 Empress Frederick of Germany to Queen Victoria
RA ADD A18/HV Princess Helena Victoria to Queen Victoria Oct 30, Nov 5, Nov 16, Nov 17, Dec 15, Dec 18 1897, Jan 11, Jan 19 1898
RA S13/104 Emily Loch to Queen Victoria May 4, 1886
RA L11/8 Emily Loch to Sir Henry Ponsonby Feb 14, 1886
RA Z83/29 Princess Helena Victoria to Queen Victoria July 19, 1888
RA GV 0589/1 Emily Loch to Lord Stamfordham Nov 1, 1912
RA GV 0589/2 Lord Stamfordham to Emily Loch
RA Add A18/MV Emily Loch to Princess Thora

Reid, Michaela, *Ask Sir James*, originally Hodder and Stoughton, London 1987, Reprinted in Large Print by The Ulverscroft Foundation, 1989

Roberts, Jane (Ed) *Unfolding Pictures*, Royal Collection Enterprises Ltd, London, 2005

St George, Andrew, *The Descent of Manners*, Chatto and Windus, London. 1993

Scholes, Percy A, *The Oxford Companion to Music*, Oxford University Press, London New York and Toronto, 1942

Snowman, A Kenneth, *Fabergé, Catalogue of exhibition June 23-September 25 1977*

Stevens, William Barnes, *Petrograd: Past and Present*, Grant Richards, London, 1915

Seaman, W A L and Sewell, J R *Russian Journal of Lady Londonderrry 1836-37*, History Book Club, 1973

Strachey, Lytton, *Queen Victoria*, Chatto and Windus, London, 1921

Summers A and Mangold T, *The file on the Tsar*, Fontana Collins , London, 1977

Talbot, Frederick A, *Railway Wonders of the World*, Cassell and Company, Limited, London, New York, Toronto and Melbourne, undated

Trevelyan, G M, *British History in the Nineteenth Century (1782-1901)*, Longmans, Green and Co Ltd, London, 1928

Troyat, Henri, *Daily Life in Russia under the last Tsar,* George Allen and Unwin, London, 1961

Turner, E S, *Taking the Cure*, Michael Joseph, London, 1967

Wechsberg, Joseph, *The Lost world of the Great Spas*, Wiedenfeld and Nicolson, London, 1979, ISBN 0 229777680-0

Van der Kiste, John, *Childhood at Court 1819-1914*, Sutton Publishing, Stroud, 2003, ISBN 0 7509 3437 9

Vickers, Hugo, *Alice, Princess Andrew of Greece,* Penguin Books, London, 2001,

Warner, Marina, *Queen Victoria's Sketch Book*, Macmillan, London, 1979, ISBN 0 333271 327

Warren, Herbert T, *Christian Victor: the Story of a Young Soldier*, John Murray, London, 1903

Weintraub, Stanley, *The importance of being EDWARD, King in waiting*, John Murray, London, 2000 ISBN 0-7195-5767 4

Wilson, A N, *The Victorians*, Arrow Books, Random House, London, 2003, ISBN 0 09 945186 7

Wilson, A N, *After the Victorians 1901-1953*, Hutchinson, London, 2005 ISBN 0 09 179484

Winchester, Clarence Ed. *Shipping Wonders of the World*, Amalgamated Press Ltd, London, undated c 1938

Windsor Local History Publications Group, *Windsor: a Thousand Years, 2001,* ISBN 0 9505 567 50

York, Duchess of with Benita Stoney, *Victoria and Albert: A Family Life at Osborne House*, Prentice Hall Press, New York, 1991, ISBN 0 13 950882 1

Yorke-Davies, Nathaniel, *Health and Condition in the Active and Sedentary*, Low, Marston and Company, London, 1894

Youssoupoff, *Prince Felix, Lost Splendour*, Jonathan Cape, London, 1953

Zeepvat, Charlotte, *Prince Leopold* , Sutton Publishing Limited, Stroud, 1998, ISBN 0-7509-1308-8

About the Author

I now live in the Highlands of Scotland with my husband and dog leading a quiet out-door life. We lived in Cyprus and Malaya when our two boys were growing up, and teaching the young of all ages about the fascination of the natural world kept me in touch with youth and nature, and I made use of my degree in Zoology. We returned to England and for twenty-five years we lived near Oxford but with annual visits to Scotland. I continued to teach adults at the Women's Institute College near Abingdon and widened my education listening to the many other lecturers and the experiences of the 'students' in the College. An interest in history began to take over, especially in the Victorians who had never suffered from me being taught about them at school, and this has become an increasing joy in the years we have lived in Inverness-shire.

Entries in italic denote illustrations/photographs.

L

Q

R

S

T